KIANGSI PROVINCE

FUKIEN

PROVINCE

HINGNING

MEIHSIEN
(KAYINGCHOW)

Tung (East) River

Han River

CHAOCHOW

Swatow

WAICHOW

South China Sea

ONG

ONG

miles

| 0 | 25 | 50 | 75 | 100 |

| 0 | 50 | 100 | 150 |

kilometers

Hsien boundaries are approximate.

Bier

Sojourners and Settlers

CHINESE MIGRANTS
IN HAWAII

Sojourners and Settlers

CHINESE MIGRANTS
IN HAWAII

Clarence E. Glick

HAWAII CHINESE HISTORY CENTER
AND
THE UNIVERSITY PRESS OF HAWAII
Honolulu

Library of Congress Cataloging in Publication Data

Glick, Clarence Elmer, 1906–
  Sojourners and settlers: Chinese migrants in
  Hawaii.

  Includes bibliographical references and index.
  1. Chinese Americans—Hawaii—History.   2.   Hawaii
—Foreign population.   I.   Title.
DU624.7.C5C46   996.9′004951   80–13799
ISBN 0–8248–0707–3

The jacket photo of a Honolulu Chinese family, circa 1912, is
reproduced courtesy of Helen Kam Fong and the Hawaii Multi-
Cultural Center.

Contents

Tables

Maps

Preface

AMONG the many groups of Chinese who have emigrated from their ancestral homeland and settled overseas, none has been more remarkable or created more interest than the Chinese in Hawaii. Typical of this interest is an inquiry I received from an ethnologist in Leningrad who wrote to ask what accounted for the way Chinese in Hawaii have fitted in so well with the Hawaiian-American society of the Islands. This book does not pretend to answer that question completely, but it does present evidence that the Chinese migrants who came to Hawaii, especially those who stayed and established families in the Islands, laid the foundations for the incorporation of Hawaii-born Chinese into the economic, political, cultural, and social life of Hawaii's multiethnic community. Coming from South China, largely as laborers for sugar plantations and Chinese rice plantations, but also as independent merchants and craftsmen, the migrants found themselves in a land of open opportunity. In making the most of this opportunity, the migrants not only contributed to the Islands' economic development, but many were themselves transformed from villagers bound by ancestral clan and tradition into participants in a mobile, largely Westernized social order.

The study on which this book is based was originally concerned with the organizations established in Hawaii by the migrants during the second half of the nineteenth century and the early part of the twentieth. Chinese societies in the Islands were of particular interest because they had not been characterized by the open and sometimes violent conflict which had brought so much attention to "tongs" in San Francisco, New York, and other large cities in various parts of the world where there were colonies of overseas Chinese. To understand the diverse character and functions of the over two hundred organizations founded by Chinese migrants in Hawaii, it was necessary to consider the migrants' background in China, the circumstances under which they came to the Islands, the economic, cultural, and social adjustments they made, and the factors that led so many of them who had come as sojourners, intent on "making their fortune" and returning to China, to become settlers in Hawaii.

The original study dealt primarily with the estimated 46,000 migrants who came to the Islands before Hawaii was annexed to the United States in 1898. All but a hundred or so had arrived during the last half of the nineteenth century, all but some 2,500 between 1875 and 1898. About 95 percent were males, mostly young adults, and during the early 1880s they made up more than half of all the adult males in Hawaii. It was not until the decades of 1890–1910 that any considerable number of Chinese women came to the Islands and the Hawaii-born Chinese population began to multiply. At the time the original study was completed in 1938, about 3,500 of the migrant men who had come to Hawaii before Annexation were still living in the Islands; many heads of families were still actively engaged in their businesses or other occupations, others had retired, and some, comparatively few, were single, older, indigent men dependent on more prosperous Chinese or on public welfare. Most of the societies organized by the migrants were still led by members of the migrant generation.

In the present work I have followed the migrants on through the 1940s up to 1950. By that time only a tiny fraction of the pre-Annexation migrants were still alive, and the organizations they had founded that were still in existence were being led by Hawaii-born Chinese and some of the thousand or so Chinese who had entered Hawaii after 1900. Hawaii-born Chinese made up nearly 90 percent of the Islands' Chinese population in 1950 and controlled almost all the Chinese businesses. Occupational data from the 1950 census demonstrated the favorable economic position migrants had made possible for their Hawaii-born children and grandchildren, a position that 1970 census data confirmed.

By 1950 the People's Republic of China controlled Kwangtung province, and the land and buildings in which migrants had invested in their home villages and districts were being absorbed into communes. The last few migrants who had clung to their dream of retiring in their home villages now concluded that this plan was no longer feasible. Most of the pre-Annexation migrants remaining in Hawaii after 1930 had become permanent settlers; even those who kept in touch with their kinfolk in China were more interested in the future of their American children, grandchildren, and great-grandchildren, most of whom were in Hawaii, than in the villages of their childhood.

The first section of this book deals with the several streams of migration from China, beginning with the pioneer merchants and entrepreneurs who came during the first half of the nineteenth century and helped initiate the economic development that was eventually to attract thousands of migrants during the second half of that century. It is commonly assumed that the present-day Hawaii-born Chinese are descendants of sugar plantation workers, but that assumption is far from accurate. Several thousand migrants did work on the sugar plantations as contract or as "free" day laborers. Other thousands, however, came to work as free day laborers in Chinese-controlled agricultural enterprises, especially rice plantations. Hundreds of other migrants, especially those who came to work in firms owned by relatives and other Chinese, never had any plantation experience. It might have been expected that since most of the migrants came from a rural background in China they would have remained concentrated in agriculture, especially since that was the main source of income in the Island economy during the period of the migrants' occupational careers. Nevertheless, large numbers of them moved from agricultural work into urban occupations. Occupational mobility among the migrants in Hawaii was far greater than among the Chinese in the continental United States or in many overseas Chinese colonies.

Later chapters discuss the movement of the migrants and their children into the economic mainstream of Hawaii, their concentration in Honolulu, the evolution of Chinatown as the nucleus of the urban Chinese community, the opposition the migrants encountered from other groups, and the complex of organizations they developed in coping with this opposition and other problems that arose as they made their adjustment to the migrant situation. As a collection of people with a great many differences stemming from their old-world origins, and at the same time treated categorically as a single group by others, the Chinese community was a product of both differentiation and integration among the migrants. The last chapters deal with the changing relationships between the migrants and their homeland and examine how the shift from sojourner attitudes to settler attitudes influenced the personal and group orientation of the migrants and their Hawaii-born children.

It still remains for someone to make a study concentrating on the Islands' Hawaii-born Chinese, who are now mostly third, fourth, and even fifth-generation descendants of early migrants. In addition to an account of the economic prosperity of the Hawaii Chinese community as a whole and the political and cultural achievements of many of its members, there should be an analysis of the survival of over fifty of the societies the migrants organized between 1880 and 1930, as well as of the scores of organizations formed by second- and third-generation Chinese. Attention should be paid to the membership of Hawaii-born Chinese in the whole gamut of multiethnic and nonethnic organizations in the Islands. The increasingly high rate of outmarriage among Hawaii-born Chinese men and women, now above 60 percent according to official reports, should be examined. It would be important to describe the renewal of interest in Chinese culture and in their migrant forebears' experience among Hawaii Chinese, but no one could responsibly say of the Hawaii Chinese, as a recent sociologist said of Chinese in the mainland United States, that they "provide a living museum of nineteenth-century Cathay" or that they "live much of their lives out of touch with the host society." If there is a "host society" in Hawaii, the Hawaii-born Chinese are part of it.

Changes in the United States immigration laws since 1950, especially those made in 1965, have resulted in a new influx of several thousand Chinese immigrants, mainly from Hong Kong and Taiwan and mainly into Honolulu rather than the rural areas or the other islands of Hawaii. They now make up about 10 percent of the Islands' Chinese population. The experiences of these new migrants are very different from those of the earlier migrants discussed in this book. Some theses have already focused on these new migrants; but more research, especially into their relations with Hawaii-born Chinese, would be enlightening.

My original study was conducted during the years 1929–1932 and 1935–1937 while I held combined teaching and research appointments in the Department of Sociology at the University of Hawaii. I learned to speak a few words of Chung Shan Cantonese and Hakka, the two main languages spoken by Hawaii's Chinese migrants, but by that time many of the migrant leaders in Honolulu, especially those who had come as youths, could be interviewed in English. Chinese students and friends served as interpreters with those who could not speak English or preferred to speak Chinese. I learned to read enough Chinese characters to identify the subjects of documents and articles written in Chinese pertaining to the migrants, and Chinese university students employed through the National Youth Administration made translations and collected data from Chinese society records. Two China-born friends, Young Hing Cham and Wing-Iu Leung, with whom I had lived for some months in Honolulu, were my guides when I spent the summer of 1932 in China, with my headquarters in Choy Hung village in Chung Shan district. I traveled through much of that district and into the See Yup districts as far as Toi Shan city, talking to returned migrants and observing the impact of the *wah kiu* ("overseas Chinese") on their home villages and districts.

The Transcription of Chinese

The reader will find inconsistencies in the romanization of Chinese words. In the text an attempt has generally been made to romanize Chinese words as closely as possible to their pronunciation by Chinese migrants in Hawaii, primarily following the Chung Shan Cantonese spoken in the Islands. The same words in See Yup or Sam Yup Cantonese may be spelled slightly differently, still more differently in Hakka. No attempt has been made to include Mandarin equivalents; for readers familiar with Chinese dialects or speech groups other than those used by the migrants in Hawaii, a glossary has been included. The spellings of Chinese words included in quotations add to the inconsistencies but have been maintained as found in the original sources. Most Chinese proper names—of individuals, organizations, places, and the like—are not in italics; Chinese terms and phrases have generally been italicized and translated in the text when first used.

Acknowledgments

MANY people have helped in many ways—supplying information, making translations, offering personal insights, giving professional assistance, and providing financial support for the project.

When my original study was underway in the 1930s, several faculty members and students were most helpful, especially Romanzo Adams, Andrew W. Lind, Tin-Yuke Char, and Bung Chong Lee. Chinese students in my classes added much to my understanding of the changing Chinese community. Members of Chinese societies whom I interviewed were cooperative and generous with their time. Hawaiian government offices and private agencies gave access to their files. Throughout the course of the work, librarians at the University of Hawaii and the Archives of Hawaii have been exceptionally patient and helpful.

Leaders of the Hawaii Chinese History Center encouraged me to extend the original study and prepare it for publication. Among them, Irma Tam Soong, executive director emeritus, Puanani Kini, president, Tin-Yuke and Wai-Jane Char, Wing-Tek Lum, and Larry F. C. Ching have been particularly helpful.

I am indebted to Irma Tam Soong for preparation of the Chinese glossary. Norma A. Lum and Karen A. Motosue, director of the Hawaii Multi-Cultural Center, aided in selection of the pictures; Wayne Warashina, also of the Center, did repographic work for several pictures; Gene Kassebaum assisted in producing the index; Freda R. Hellinger typed the manuscript.

Most of all I am indebted to my wife, Dr. Doris Lorden Glick. Her training in sociology and her experience teaching English and sociology have been applied extensively, imaginatively, and productively to the preparation of the manuscript for publication, most importantly through editorial work. Without her assistance and encouragement the book would never have been completed.

I appreciate greatly the efforts of the Hawaii Chinese History Center in obtaining financial support from the following sponsors:

Larry and Beatrice Ching Foundation
Senator and Mrs. Hiram L. Fong
Mr. and Mrs. Henry Inn
Chinn Ho Foundation
Puanani Kini
Mr. and Mrs. Leong Hop Loui
Louise and Y. T. Lum Foundation
Kee Fook Zane
Hawaii Chinese History Center
United Chinese Society

CHAPTER 1

The Cycle of Migration

CHINESE colonization in the Hawaiian Islands falls entirely within the period of European developments in the Pacific Basin—the two centuries since the Western world first learned of the existence of the Hawaiian archipelago and its Polynesian inhabitants. During the first third of this period only a few Chinese, probably less than a hundred, migrated to the Islands; for the most part Chinese colonization in Hawaii was a phase of the era of Chinese migration overseas that began near the middle of the nineteenth century. This era was characterized by a vast expansion of the area of the globe to which Chinese emigrated, by the impetus given to emigration by the contract labor system, and by an enormous increase in the numbers of Chinese overseas. Chinese migration to Hawaii was largely a consequence of the development of plantation agriculture in the Islands, a development which led to the assisted immigration of laborers from Asia and other parts of the world. An account of the whole cycle of Chinese migration to Hawaii, however, requires some attention to the few Chinese pioneers who came to the Islands before the middle of the nineteenth century.

The Pioneers

Shortly after the Western world came to know of the Hawaiian Islands through Captain Cook's discovery in 1778, Hawaii became important to ships trading between South China and the northwest coast of America. The Islands provided welcome ports for securing fresh water and provisions as well as harbors in which to spend the winter months. Not surprisingly, Hawaii soon became known in China; Chinese began to appear on ships calling in the Islands,[1] and one Chinese was reported to be living there even as early as 1794.[2] It is more remarkable that by 1828 between thirty and forty Chinese were among the four hundred foreigners estimated to be living in Honolulu,[3] because this was still during the period of a Chinese imperial edict forbidding Chinese subjects to leave China.

During the first half of the nineteenth century a few more Chinese adventurers defied the edict in order to come to Tan Heung Shan ("Sandalwood Mountains"), as Hawaii was called by the Chinese. The name had its origin in the sandalwood trade between Hawaii and China through which Hawaii made its first strong impression upon the Chinese. As early as 1792 foreign traders were bargaining with Hawaiian chiefs for sandalwood to take to China,[4] and before the forests were depleted, about forty years later, several million dollars worth of this fragrant wood had been sold in the Canton market. Even though this trade ended before most of the Chinese migrants came to Hawaii, Tan Heung Shan remained a Chinese name for Hawaii.

The activities of the early Chinese pioneers foreshadowed the settlement patterns which developed among later Chinese migrants. Some of them attempted to make their fortunes in agriculture, especially sugar production, but by far the larger number were businessmen and artisans who found economic opportunities in the principal island ports.

Commercial sugar production in Hawaii, although eventually taken over entirely by American and European companies and management, was first undertaken by Chinese entrepreneurs. It was, at the same time, the first occupation specifically known to have been followed by a Chinese in Hawaii. Hawaiians enjoyed the juice of sugarcane flourishing in the Islands but did not know about making sugar. Several Westerners speculated about the commercial possibilities of a sugar industry, and word of this reached South China where sugar had been made for centuries. According to an account published in 1852, the first Chinese sugar maker, Wong Tze-Chun, arrived in 1802 with a village-type sugar mill and boiling pans on a ship engaged in the sandalwood trade. Unfortunately Wong chose to start his enterprise on Lanai, a dry island not well suited to sugar. A year later he gave up his unprofitable venture and returned to China.[5]

In spite of this unpromising beginning, by the 1830s sugar production was undertaken with somewhat greater success by Chinese-owned companies which had established businesses in Hawaii and which provided both capital and Chinese personnel skilled in sugar making. One such firm, Samsing & Co., although based in Honolulu, was manufacturing sugar at one time or another at Waimea, Kohala, and Hilo on the island of Hawaii and at Lahaina on Maui, with *tong see* ("sugar masters") brought from China.[6] In the 1840s and 1850s at least half a dozen Chinese sugar masters were producing sugar on the island of Hawaii. These men, who were engaged in enterprises with the Hawaiian governor of the island, became citizens and landowners, married Hawaiian women, some of them of very high rank, and settled on that island.[7] Even after traditional Chinese methods of making sugar could no longer compete with new processes using steam-powered machinery imported by Caucasian planters, Chinese entrepreneurs on various islands continued for some time to raise sugarcane and sell it to Caucasian-owned mills.

The most famous of the early entrepreneurs was Chun Fong from Chung Shan district in Kwangtung province, whose career in the Islands extended from the 1840s to 1890. Afong, as he was known locally, had many business interests in Honolulu where he married a Hawaiian woman of noble lineage by whom he had twelve daughters and four sons. He became the largest shareholder in Peepeekeo Plantation near Hilo. In 1888, with 326 laborers and about 1,200 acres in sugar, this plantation ranked twelfth among seventy-nine plantations and mills in "number of hands." Afong is reported to have received $600,000 for his share in the firm when he retired to China in 1890.[8]

Sugar production was only one of many economic opportunities open to the early Chinese. A report by the marshal of the Hawaiian kingdom in 1852 stated that thirty-seven Chinese were in business in the vicinity of Honolulu.[9] Samsing & Co., with several partners, operated a general merchandise store, a bakery, and other enterprises. The Tyhune Store, apart from handling Western and Chinese dry goods and similar merchandise, had a wholesale business in wines and spirits as well as owning vessels and boats. In the 1840s Tyhune (Wong Tai-Hoon) had started a branch store in Koloa, Kauai, and in 1852 he applied for a retail store license in Lahaina, Maui.[10]

Chinese business pioneers in the Islands not only formed companies among themselves, but some of them joined other foreigners in commercial enterprises. Atai, one of the two founding partners of Hungtai Co., was in business with William French, a New Englander who first came to Hawaii in connection with the sandalwood trade. Atai and French owned the Canton Hotel in Honolulu during the 1830s, and Atai also assisted French in the latter's unsuccessful attempt to establish a sugar plantation at Waimea, Kauai, with Chinese sugar-making equipment and Chinese employees brought by Atai from China in 1835. In the 1830s Tyhune, even while engaged in his own business, was a part-time employee of an American firm, Ladd & Co., which with a few other Chinese employees brought from China was establishing a sugar plantation at Koloa, Kauai.[11]

Early Chinese businessmen in Hawaii recruited other Chinese from China to join them as partners in their business and also as employees. Some were relatives who became part of the original firm or who started related businesses in other parts of the Islands. Ahung, Atai's partner in the firm of Hungtai Co., had three relatives who worked at one time or another in the firm's Honolulu store. One of them later went into business in Lahaina, Maui. Tyhune turned over all his businesses in 1853 to a brother, Achun, who had himself been in business in Lahaina at least as early as 1833. Other Chinese, such as the sugar masters, were recruited as employees because of their special skills. One document mentions a Chinese employed by Hungtai Co. as a bookkeeper; Chinese were brought in to open French's tannery at Waimea, Hawaii; Chinese carpenters were employed in 1829 on a building for French in Honolulu; and Chinese cooks and waiters were brought in for the Canton Hotel.[12] This recruitment of Chinese workers by Chinese businessmen in the 1830s and 1840s established a pattern that was followed by the Caucasian members of the Royal Hawaiian Agricultural Society who in 1852 began recruiting laborers from South China for their sugar plantations.

Plantation Expansion and a New Era of Colonization

It is one of the odd twists of history that even though Chinese were pioneers in Hawaii's sugar industry, Caucasian planters, rather than Chinese, were responsible for recruiting and employing the largest number of Chinese brought in to work the Islands' sugar plantations. This is readily understandable when one considers the circumstances under which the Hawaiian sugar plantations developed. As a profit-making venture, large-scale agriculture for the world market requires a combination of resources: long-term control of land suitable for the desired crop; large amounts of capital; entrepreneurial and technical skills; an adequate, stable labor force; and access to markets where the crop is in demand at prices high enough to provide a return on investment. The failure of many early Western-owned sugar ventures, as well as the short lives of most of those undertaken by Chinese, shows how risky it was to try to meet all these requirements. Beginning in the 1840s, however, a series of events on the American mainland and the growing influence of Westerners, especially Americans, in the Hawaiian kingdom produced a situation favorable to American and European capital investment but of less advantage to Chinese in the sugar industry. Demand for sugar on the American mainland, particularly California, though fluctuating wildly for several years, finally created an American market for Hawaiian sugar. In the 1840s Hawaiian rulers under American influence were persuaded to abandon the traditional control of land by kings and chiefs for the Western system of landownership. The Great Mahele (land division) with its enabling legislation permitted foreigners to own or lease land with more security than under the old system, lessening the risk of long-term investment in the sugar plantations. Although Chinese, like other foreigners, were permitted to buy land, the American and European businessmen were able to get control of larger tracts and more capital for plantation development.

The stage was almost set, then, for Caucasion-controlled sugar firms to play a major role in Hawaii's new economy. Very early, however, the planters faced the problem of securing an adequate, stable labor supply which for a long time remained one of their most worrisome concerns. Hawaiian sugar planters were not alone in this predicament—sugar, copra, coffee, tea, and rubber planters in Fiji, Ceylon, Malaysia, Indonesia, and other tropical areas during the postslavery era were having to cope with the same problem. They had to find laborers willing to do the heavy, dirty, and monotonous work of premechanized field labor at wages low enough to enable the plantations to return a profit to their investors.

In Hawaii, as elsewhere, planters first turned to the indigenous population for labor, but they soon concluded that a more satisfactory body of workers should be imported. There were the familiar assertions of the "natives' natural indolence" and their "inconstancy," "caprices," "licentious and indolent habits."[13] While it has been common to cite these charges, often summarized as the "Hawaiians' laziness," as the sole cause for the Hawaiians' inadequacy as a plantation labor supply, the situation was not that simple. Hawaiians were not unaccustomed to hard work. In their traditional economy Hawaiian commoners had probably worked as hard for their chiefs as they were required to work in the cane fields, but on the plantations they were not working under the traditional system for people to whom they owed loyal service. Hawaiians also had other opportunities— some of them could remain on their kuleanas (small properties they had received in the Great Mahele), they could find work in the port towns and in California, or they could go to sea. Nevertheless, Hawaiians were the largest element in the plantation labor force until the late 1870s. In 1873 nearly four-fifths of the laborers on thirty-five plantations were Hawaiian. About half of all Hawaiian men were working on plantations, but even if every able-bodied adult Hawaiian male had done so there would still not have been enough of them after the mid-1870s to meet the planters' needs.[14] The Hawaiian population had been terribly diminished by disease and continued to decrease while the plantations were expanding and requiring more and more workers.

Recognizing the limitations of the Hawaiian labor supply, sugar planters in Hawaii followed the common pattern of looking for workers in those areas of the non-Western world which were not yet becoming industrialized, where there was a plentiful supply of low-skilled, manual labor, and where the wages offered by the plantations were attractive in contrast to what the workers could get in their native lands. Among various possible sources of labor, China seemed most promising to Hawaii's planters. There were favorable reports on Chinese contract laborers from Amoy, Fukien province, who had been imported by sugar planters on Reunion Island in 1845 and into Cuba in 1847. After China was defeated in the Opium Wars of 1839 and 1858 the Chinese government tolerated the recruiting of Chinese as contract laborers; widespread poverty and the turmoil in South China caused by the Taiping Rebellion (1850–1864) contributed to the willingness of Chinese to seek their livelihood overseas.

Plans by Caucasian planters in Hawaii to import labor from China crystallized in 1850. The Royal Hawaiian Agricultural Society, organized that year, regarded this as its most important and pressing task. However, the Society's first attempt to carry out such a plan was a fiasco. In September 1850 a shipowner who agreed to bring in a boatload of Chinese laborers was given a sum reported to be about $10,000; he sailed off toward China and was never heard of again.[15]

The second try was more successful. Captain John Cass, out of London on the 460-ton bark *Thetis*, put in at Honolulu in April 1851 while en route to San Francisco from Hong Kong with Chinese passengers attracted to California by the Gold Rush. The following August he signed a contract in Honolulu with the Society to recruit and bring to Hawaii 200 laborers. He returned on 3 January 1852 with 175 men to be employed as field laborers and 20 who were to work as "houseboys." Each of these men, when recruited in Amoy, had been advanced six dollars to be refunded later out of their wages. The contracts field workers had signed stipulated that they were to work for a period of five years at wages of three dollars per month in addition to their passage, quarters, food, and clothes. The laborers were sent in groups of about twenty-five to sugar plantations on three islands.

Captain Cass apparently had found his contract with the Society profitable. He remained in Honolulu for nearly six weeks, during which time he placed advertisements in Honolulu papers inviting orders for laborers whom he would recruit in China. He did not receive orders for as many men as before, but he left for China on 12 February and returned on 1 August 1852, bringing back ninety-eight men, presumably again recruited in Amoy.[16]

These first imported Chinese laborers were received with general favor and encouragement. The first newspaper account of their arrival expressed the hopes and cautious optimism with which this "experiment" was being tried:

> The subject of cheap labor is one which has for a considerable period engaged the attention of the planters here, as an indispensable requisite to successful competition with Manila and China, in the production of sugar and coffee. The scarcity of native laborers . . . induced those engaged in agriculture to make the experiment of introducing from overflowing China a class of laborers which, it was believed, would combine a good service with economy. . . .
>
> The experiment to be thus tried is one of considerable moment to the islands, and we are glad to see it tested. . . . The result will be watched with great attention by all interested in the success of agriculture here. Should it prove successful, still larger numbers will doubtless be brought from that populous empire, where a mere existence, under a grinding despotism, renders such an escape to a more favorable land a boon readily seized by these industrious people. . . . We sincerely hope that their introduction here may prove, not only serviceable to

the islands, but also to themselves; and that they have exchanged want and oppressions for a comfortable home and the protection of a government and people actuated by Christian principles.[17]

The planters themselves praised the men as well as the scheme of using imported labor on the plantations:

> The Chinese brought here in the Thetis have proved themselves quiet, able and willing men, and I have little doubt, judging from our short experience, that we shall find coolie labor to be far more certain, systematic, and economical than that of the natives. They are prompt at the call of the bell, steady in their work, quick to learn, and when well-fed will accomplish more, and in a better manner, than any other class of operatives we have. The cost of importing coolies is fifty dollars per man, and it has been estimated by those who employ them that their wages and support amount to a trifle under seven dollars per month. . . . To all those planters who can afford it, I would say procure as many coolies as you can, and work them by themselves, as far as possible separate them from the natives, and you will find that, if well managed, their example will have a stimulating effect on the Hawaiian, who is naturally jealous of the coolie and ambitious to outdo him.[18]

A few months later, after some difficulties with the newly imported Chinese, a speaker addressing the Royal Hawaiian Agricultural Society pleaded for "patience," "good sense," and a "parental attitude" in dealing with them:

> The introduction of Cooly labor is as yet an experiment, but a very important one. It promises well, and its success depends on the judicious management, and comfortable treatment they may receive. It is an entire change—in language, manners, dress, modes of living, and doing: and your own good sense will teach you to forbear, and while it requires patience on your part, it can be no less trying to them, untaught as they are. You must have sympathy with honest labor. It is not enough that you fulfill the contract to the letter, but the relation to them should be parental—mind always governs—and where there is a drop of Anglo-Saxon blood it is sure to rule. This Chinese race next to our own are destined to figure in the drama of the Pacific; and I regret that the authorities of California should undertake to make any discrimination between them and other foreigners. They are industrious, economical, and careful, filling a space for which our people are not adapted. That they can be made useful on the continent and here, there can be no doubt, and to accomplish this the only sure way is, so far as compatible, to exercise a parental control over them. They

should not be left to the care of indiscreet agents. They will obey one master cheerfully, more they dislike; not differing in this particular from all the rest of the world. It is an interesting combination of the ancient nation, with the new.[19]

It was not long, however, before there were complaints about the laborers. Prince Liholiho referred to "their faults and a considerable disposition to hang themselves" but nevertheless maintained that "they have been found very useful. . . . Some of our largest sugar and coffee plantations are now chiefly dependent on them."[20] A planter claimed that "among themselves, they are quarrelsome and passionate and have many dangerous fights." Although the men had been indentured for five-year periods, there were complaints in 1854, two years after the first importations, that they were leaving the plantations and becoming vagrants in Honolulu. At the same time some of the planters were undoubtedly glad to be relieved of their obligation to pay the wages and other expenses of men who left their plantations—sugar in this decade was not as profitable for the Island producers as had been anticipated. Neither the Society nor the government undertook to import more laborers until 1864.

Little is known of what happened to these men brought from Amoy. As soon as they arrived it became clear that the Chinese dialect they spoke was unintelligible to the Chinese from Kwangtung province already living in the Islands. An article in the *Polynesian* included a list of words in the Fukienese dialect (in romanized spelling with English equivalents) that would be useful in giving directions to these workers.[21] An American who had been a missionary in Canton and who visited Chinese "camps" on Maui in 1856 wrote that the Cantonese Chinese storekeepers and the Fukienese laborers found it easiest to communicate with each other in the Hawaiian language.[22]

Very few people in Hawaii, even or perhaps especially those of Chinese ancestry, realize that there was a time when Fukienese-speaking Chinese in the Islands outnumbered those speaking a Cantonese dialect. Since almost all later Chinese migrants were from just a few coastal districts of Kwangtung and spoke one or another Cantonese dialect or Hakka, the early role of the Fukienese in the Chinese colonization of Hawaii has been little known. No Fukienese societies, such as those formed among the Cantonese and Hakka migrants in Hawaii, were ever organized. Although the majority of the Fukienese laborers probably returned to China, a few Fukienese, presumably from among those who were imported in 1852, did settle down in Honolulu.[23] So far as is known, no more contract laborers were brought to the Islands from Fukien.

During the dozen years before aided importation of Chinese laborers for Caucasian-owned plantations was resumed, some Chinese migrants came to the Islands in connection with various Chinese enterprises. Between 1853 and 1864 officials reported the arrival of 411 Chinese, an average of only 34 per year.[24] Some of these came to Hawaii from California and other parts of the West Coast.

The situation changed when the Civil War in America brought new prosperity to Hawaiian sugar planters. Sugar, which had brought seven cents a pound in 1860, had advanced by 1864 to seventeen cents. In response to renewed clamor for imported laborers, the government took steps to facilitate further immigration, but under greater control.[25] A Board of Immigration was organized early in 1865 and the Commissioner of Immigration, Dr. Wilhelm Hillebrand, himself was sent to Hong Kong (not to Amoy) to arrange for recruiting about 500 "strong and healthy" Chinese, 20 to 25 percent to be married women.[26] During 1864 only 9 Chinese had arrived; 615 landed in 1865. Of these, 522, including 52 women and 3 children, came on two boats chartered for the Board. Chinese entrepreneurs probably brought the other Chinese laborers who arrived during this year. Some 117 Chinese reached Hawaii in 1866, some 210 in 1867. Sugar exports jumped from less than 750 tons in 1860 to over 9,000 tons in 1868, but ups and downs in business conditions in the United States in the late 1860s and early 1870s, together with the duty collected on sugar in American ports, slowed plantation expansion and reduced the need for imported laborers. In 1870, however, the government, responding to renewed demands from planters, did assist in bringing in 188 Chinese, only 2 of whom were women.

Successful negotiation of a Reciprocity Treaty with the United States, permitting Hawaiian sugar to enter American ports free of duty, brought new prosperity to the sugar industry. By 1896 Hawaii was exporting seventeen times as much sugar as in 1876. Even more important in its effects on Chinese immigration, the Reciprocity Treaty also exempted Hawaii-produced rice from duty. Exports of rice from Hawaii, almost all to the Western United States, quadrupled within six years.[27] During this period and for the next two decades rice was grown in Hawaii almost entirely under Chinese management by Chinese labor.

The simultaneous expansion of sugar and rice cultivation during the late 1870s and 1880s created an unprecedented demand for laborers. Importation was greatly accelerated with government support or acquiescence—primarily of Chinese and Portuguese but also of several hundred Norwegians, Germans, and South Sea Islanders. From 1874 to 1877 the Board of Immigration gave active and financial assistance to a few Chinese entrepreneurs who especially wanted Chinese laborers for their plantations. In 1876, for the first time, the number of Chinese migrants arriving in Hawaii exceeded one thousand. At least a thousand of the 1,283 Chinese arrivals during that year came through the enterprise of three Chinese firms in Honolulu with a certain amount of financial aid from the Board of Immigration.

From this date onward the Hawaiian government's concern was not to stimulate and subsidize Chinese labor migration but to regulate it. The great acceleration of Chinese immigration is evident in Table 1 showing the yearly number of Chinese arrivals from 1852 to 1899.[28] During the decade preceding 1876 an annual average of only 130 Chinese had landed in Hawaii, but the decade from 1876 to 1885 had an average of 2,596 Chinese arrivals per year. To understand the fluctuations during this latter decade—as well as the reduced migration between 1885 and 1895 and the surge of Chinese arrivals just prior to annexation—we must turn to other forces operating in the Hawaiian kingdom.

Agitation against Chinese Immigration

Anti-Chinese feeling, especially as expressed by the relatively small Caucasian population, paralleled the stream of Chinese migration—developing slowly at first, rising to its greatest intensity during the late 1870s and the 1880s, and then diminishing. (See population data in the Appendix.) Early contacts between Caucasians and Chinese in the Islands were generally quite superficial, and the Caucasians were more likely to have a sense of superiority toward the Chinese than a feeling of antagonism. Visitors to the Islands, writing about their impressions of the Chinese they saw there, usually focused on what they considered the bizarre appearance of "this most peculiar people."[29] Francis Olmsted, a Yale science professor who stopped briefly in Honolulu in 1841, wrote:

> Among the foreigners resident in Honolulu, are several Chinese, the singularity of whose costume cannot fail of attracting one's attention. It consists of a large frock with ample sleeves, reaching down about mid-

Table 1
Arrivals of Chinese in Hawaii: 1852–1899

Year	Number of Arrivals	Year	Number of Arrivals
1852	293	1876	1,283
1853	64	1877	557
1854	12	1878	2,464
1855	61	1879	3,812
1856	23	1880	2,505
1857	14	1881	3,924
1858	13	1882	1,362
1859	171	1883	4,243
1860	21	1884	2,708
1861	2	1885	3,108
1862	13	1886	1,766
1863	8	1887	1,546
1864	9	1888	1,526
1865	615	1889	439
1866	117	1890	654
1867	210	1891	1,386
1868	51	1892	1,802
1869	78	1893	981
1870	305	1894	1,459
1871	223	1895	2,734
1872	61	1896	5,280
1873	48	1897	4,481
1874	62	1898	3,100
1875	151	1899	975
		Total	56,720

Note: Data for 1852–1878 are taken from the *Report of the President of the Bureau of Immigration,* 1886, pp. 266–271. Data for 1879–1899 were compiled by the writer primarily from the *Annual Report of the Collector-General of Customs* (Honolulu, 1880–1900). Slight differences appear in the annual reports of different branches of the Hawaiian government with regard to the number of Chinese arrivals. Several thousand duplications are included in the number of arrivals due to the reentry of migrants who had temporarily left the Islands.

way between the waist and the knee. For the lower dress, they wear a pair of pantaloons made very full, and these together with peaked shoes having thick, wooden soles, complete their costumes. Their black hair is braided in a tail, a yard long, which usually hangs down the back and vibrates from side to side, like a pendulum, as they walk through the streets; a loss of these tails, which many of them coil up around their heads, would be regarded as a great disgrace.[30]

Diaries and journals of Caucasian residents of Hawaii during the first half of the nineteenth century—the trading, preplantation period— show that although Caucasians tolerated, patronized, and made use of Chinese traders and artisans, there were few social relationships between the two groups. An 1842 entry in the journal of a New Englander who was one of the few Caucasians on intimate terms with the Chinese in Honolulu shows that other Caucasians frowned on social contacts with the Chinese: "A Ball was contemplated by Mr. Marshall and others at the Chinamen's Hall, BUT, some of the nobility, Yankee Women, could not think of going to the Chinamen's Hall to dance!!! O mores—Temporum!!!"[31] In contrast, many Chinese had quite close social relationships with Hawaiians. Most Chinese residents during this early period learned enough of the Hawaiian language to be able to communicate in it and many had Hawaiian wives and families. Whatever anti-Chinese feeling did appear later among Hawaiians was as likely to be a reflection of, if not actually instigated by, Caucasian agitation as the result of any grievance toward the Chinese.[32]

Through most of the latter half of the nineteenth century Caucasians who were influential in Island affairs were divided on questions concerning Chinese immigration. Some who were concerned about the continuing depletion of the indigenous population contended that Chinese were a "cognate race" of the Hawaiians who would "revitalize" and "rebuild" that group. This, in fact, was one of the early arguments in favor of subsidizing Chinese labor importation. The offspring of early Chinese immigrants and Hawaiian women were generally regarded very favorably. Chinese with Hawaiian wives were commonly said to "make good husbands and fathers."[33]

From the 1860s onward, however, some Caucasians who were inclined against the Chinese contended that the predominantly male Chinese group coming to the Islands to work on both the sugar and rice plantations was "a corrupting influence on the native female population" and was promoting the "demoralization of the natives." The Hawaiians were "victims of coolie debauchery"; "few marry native women, a much larger number take them without marriage." One clergyman asserted that the "wifeless Chinese" had a "pernicious" effect upon the social life of the natives and that "there is no doubt but that many native households in all parts of the country are maintained in comparative affluence by the intimacy of Chinese with their females." He felt, however, that this "corrupting" influence was "not more than the presence of a similar number of unmarried whites would be." Another less moderate view was that the Hawaiian "should be protected from this pig-tailed invasion which threatens him with nothing less than destruction and extinction." The spread of smallpox among Hawaiians from ships bringing new Chinese immigrants in the early 1880s added support to opponents of Chinese immigration. One editor referred to the Chinese as "these beasts in human form" who brought "their unmentionable diseases, opium pipes, and the accursed leprosy."[34]

Antislavery sentiment in America intensified the concerns of those who had doubted the wisdom of using contract labor in Hawaii. When the Hawaiian government, under pressure from planters, recruited over five hundred Chinese in 1865, voices were raised against the "coolie trade," calling it a "slave trade" promoted by a "pro-slavery ring" and proclaiming that "coolieism" was "more damnable than any southern slavery ever was."[35] In 1868, not long after the U.S. Congress in a resolution condemned contract labor importation, the Hawaiian government did moderate the terms of the Masters and Servants Act by assuring contract workers additional rights and prohibiting flogging, but legal and penal sanctions for enforcing the contracts were retained. Despite the critics' opposition to the system, the government recruited 188 additional Chinese contract laborers in 1870.

During the 1870s and early 1880s another theme in the opposition to Chinese immigration was the undesirability of admitting migrants who were predominantly adult males, especially after the 1872 census report showed that Chinese males outnumbered Caucasian males. Expression of opposition was somewhat subdued, however, by the realization that if the anticipated Reciprocity Treaty brought a boom in sugar production, additional laborers would be needed. Planters continued to favor importing Chinese male workers, willing to come without wives and children, as the cheapest source of labor. Nevertheless, the opposition was sufficient to lead the government, with the planters' acquiescence, to begin, in 1877, a much more costly importation of Portuguese families for plantation labor. During the period this importation continued (1877–1888) only about 30 percent of the eleven thousand Portuguese immigrants were adult males. In 1877 the government also stopped paying subsidies for Chinese male importations, but it continued for a while to subsidize immigration of Chinese women in the interest of balancing the Chinese population, though without much success.[36]

Chinese male immigration increased even without government subsidy. By the late 1870s enough Chinese from South China villages had been successful enough in the Islands to convince thousands of relatives and neighbors in their home districts of the desirability of migrating to Hawaii. Money remitted by Chinese already in the Islands bought passages for new migrants. Perhaps even more important was the growth of a group of wealthy Chinese entrepreneurs in Hawaii who saw the profits that could be made by advancing money at high interest rates to penniless kinsmen and former fellow villagers who wanted to emigrate[37] and by employing some of these newcomers at low wages, especially in their own agricultural enterprises.

The situation was already growing tense when an unprecedented wave of Chinese migrants struck the Islands. In 1878, some 2,464 Chinese, nearly all men, arrived. This was almost twice the number of Chinese who had reached the Islands in any previous year. An additional 3,812—98 percent of them male—landed in 1879, then 2,505 in 1880, then 3,924 in 1881. That the circumstances of this migration were questionable is indicated by this excerpt from an ordinance issued by King Kalakaua on 24 December 1880: "Evils have arisen from the conduct of unauthorized and irresponsible persons acting as brokers, runners or shipping-masters between immigrants arriving in the Kingdom, but who are not under contract for service, and persons desiring to employ them. . . ."[38]

The year 1883 brought another wave, the greatest yet, of Chinese migrants. In a three-month period over 3,600 Chinese men were added to an adult male population of about 35,000. Of the 15,846 Chinese arrivals during the five years 1879–1883, over 98 percent were males. The census of 1884 reported 17,068 Chinese foreign-born males as compared with only 871 females. The same census enumerated only 12,412 Hawaiian males between the ages of fifteen and fifty; Chinese adult males made up nearly half the entire adult male population.[39] Anti-Chinese feelings burst out more bitterly than before. Newspapers, letters, pamphlets, sermons, reports, and other documents which appeared during the rest of the 1880s record the intensity of the antipathy and the nature of the accusations against the Chinese male immigrant. It was charged that he "is not a genuine immigrant"; he "does not settle down to make a home"; "his sole object is to save himself enough money to get back to China"; "every spare dollar that a Chinaman saves goes to China"; he "is clannish, and insists on living in communities of other Chinamen"; he "despises our customs and manners and maintains his own."[40]

It was along economic lines, however, that anti-Chinese agitation was most effective. Occupational changes among the Chinese migrants created tensions that were related to conflicts between dif-

ferent segments of the Caucasian population. The Islands' basic
source of income during these decades was plantation agriculture,
and everyone was fairly well agreed that this enterprise depended on
laborers with a low plane of living and willing to work cheaply. Chinese on the plantations did work which Caucasians did not want;
they were no threat, therefore, to the security of Caucasians who
were entrenched in the preferred positions in the plantation system
or in the towns. It was the nonagricultural Chinese workers, men
seeking positions above those of domestic service and manual labor
in the towns, who were likely to compete directly with Caucasian artisans and tradesmen and to be regarded as a threat to the latter's occupational security. What irritated their Caucasian competitors was
that the Chinese who worked cheaply on the plantations were still
willing to work cheaply in other occupations. It was fair enough for
Chinese to do this on menial jobs; it was "unfair competition" when
Chinese accepted lower pay for work Caucasians and others wanted
for themselves.

Even as early as the late 1860s the increasing visibility of Chinese doing the work of artisans in the towns brought protests. One
newspaper was so successful in arousing the skilled-labor class of
Caucasians and Hawaiians against the government's encouraging
Chinese labor importation that interests friendly to the planters and
the government's policy took over the paper as a defense move. In
the early 1880s there were more forceful protests against Chinese
who were not working in agricultural jobs and were moving by the
hundreds into artisan and commercial occupations. In 1882, during a
period when hundreds of the Chinese immigrants were not signing
contracts with sugar plantations, the minister of a leading Honolulu
church saw the Hawaiian and "white mechanic" (Caucasian skilled-
worker) losing out to the "Chinese bachelor":

> Everywhere the Chinaman is quietly, peaceably, smilingly but persis-
> tently displacing the Hawaiian. Nothing is more absolutely sure, which
> is not already an accomplished fact, than this: That as a laborer, small
> farmer, shopkeeper, and tradesman the Chinaman will crowd the na-
> tive Hawaiian to the wall, and will take his place. . . .
>
> The Chinaman is a bachelor. More than that, he will herd like a
> beast, with his fellows, to save rent, and live on rice and refuse from
> the butcher's stall. If necessity compels he can exist, and work, on 25
> cents a day. We cannot afford to bring our white mechanics and small
> tradesmen into competition with Chinese bachelor wages. We cannot

afford to so reduce the earnings of this class of our white men that they can no longer afford to marry, or, being married, cannot properly support their families and educate their children. Here is a phase of this Chinese question, which is already being felt in Hawaii, and is certain to be increasingly felt in the future. In it there is the promise of a conflict. And in that conflict, my sympathies are with the white mechanic, and his family, as against the Chinese bachelor.[41]

The minister continued:

If you will ride slowly through the Chinese quarter with your eyes open, you will go to your home with food for thought. You will find watchmakers' and jewelers' shops, tinshops, shoe shops, tailor shops, saddle and harness shops, furniture shops, cabinet shops and bakeries all run by Chinamen with Chinese workmen. You will find anything from a stove, or a shawl down through drugs, groceries, notions and whatnot.[42]

Three years later the editor of *The Friend* warned:

Five years residence on the Pacific Coast taught us this fact: *No nation can afford to have its white mechanics and working-men brought into competition with the Chinese.*

Such is the case in Hawaii, and she is paying the penalty: her white small-tradesmen, mechanics and working-men are steadily, remorselessly being driven out of the kingdom. It is only a question of time when of these classes all who remain will be a few master-mechanics. . . .

We cannot afford to have our white mechanics live as the Chinese do. Civilization and religion both forbid it. Brought into competition with cheap Chinese labor, marriage, and a home, and a family is an impossibility to the mechanic and working-man. Such a state of things means immorality and utter demoralization. . . .[43]

The writer's reference to five years on the Pacific Coast indicates that some of the opposition was a carry-over to Hawaii of the anti-Chinese views so widespread among Caucasians in California during this period. It is also likely that the Workingman's Union, an anti-Chinese political group formed in 1883, was patterned after the vehemently anti-Chinese Workingmen's Party organized in California in 1877. The Workingman's Union carried on vigorous propaganda through open meetings and pamphleteering.[44] Sometime after this group disappeared it was succeeded by the Mechanic's and Workingman's Political Protective Union. After the "Reform Constitution" of 1887 took away the franchise from naturalized Chinese migrants, there was an election in which the major political parties appealed to Caucasian and Hawaiian voters with anti-Chinese proposals.

Through the 1880s and 1890s government policy was probably most influenced by a change in the Caucasian planters' attitudes toward the Chinese. They were coming to realize that they were not going to enjoy the benefit of plentiful, cheap Chinese labor which might have been expected from the great influx of migrants from China during the late 1870s and early 1880s. Nearly 14,000 Chinese men had entered the Hawaiian Islands during the five years ending with 1882, but only 5,037 Chinese were working on the sugar plantations in 1882.[45] Chinese who had been brought earlier by the Hawaiian government could hardly evade signing contracts with the planters. However, the influx of the early eighties was largely unstimulated, unfinanced, and relatively uncontrolled by the government. It was manipulated largely by none-too-scrupulous captains of tramp steamers and by Chinese entrepreneurs, thoroughly familiar with the local situation, who maneuvered to get the men into the country without being forced to sign contracts of indenture to the sugar plantations. This strategy soon brought from the planters such protests as the following:

> We are the party to dictate the terms. . . . A Chinaman once at large in the country is a different man to deal with than when he is seeking admittance.
>
> We desire Chinese to come here in suitable numbers, bringing their wives, and submitting to the restrictions of enlightened government. But we do not wish unlimited numbers of males, unregulated, and defying our laws.
>
> Chinamen are cunning, and quick to perceive their advantages, and to avail themselves of all the protection which civilized law affords, but they are able to evade the restraints of the laws as no other people can. Their clannishness and secret organizations give them a power which is difficult to meet. They are good servants but undesirable masters.[46]

Prompted by complaints about the Chinese, the government turned to Japan for contract laborers. By 1896, only ten years or so after Japanese immigration began,[47] Japanese males outnumbered Chinese males and had become, indeed, the most numerous group of men in the Islands. A larger number of Japanese men arrived in the single year of 1899 than the entire population of Chinese men in Hawaii after a century of immigration. Hundreds of these Japanese left the plantations, as the Chinese had done, and forged their way into semiskilled, skilled, and commercial occupations. "Unfair Chinese competition" became "unfair Japanese competition" or "unfair Asiatic competition"; now the Japanese were the main object of hostility. The following example is from a U.S. government report on labor in Hawaii in 1905:

> A prominent builder and official of an employers' organization in Honolulu said: "White men have left the country by hundreds on account of the competition of Asiatics." . . . Many large employers are decidedly opposed to having a Japanese on their force for the very reason that they realize that they are training up future competitors in their business. "I won't teach men to cut my throat," was a typical expression from a large employer. . . . Many small merchants are now feeling the effects . . . of encroaching Asiatic competition and are doggedly carrying on a struggle which they believe to be hopeless, but still unable to bring themselves to the point of sacrificing their stock and withdrawing from business.[48]

With Annexation Chinese labor immigration ended but Japanese laborers, as well as Korean laborers, were allowed to come in for several more years. As the Chinese migrant group declined both in actual and relative numbers, expressions of anti-Chinese feeling also diminished.

From Regulation to Exclusion

After anti-Chinese agitation in the West led to America's Chinese Exclusion Act of 1882, some Chinese migrated from the West Coast to the Islands, and others who had been on the way to the West Coast came to Hawaii instead. One reason they chose to come to Hawaii was that most migrants already in the Islands came from the same districts of Kwangtung province as most of those migrating to the United States. Many of the 3,600 Chinese who arrived in Hawaii in the early months of 1883 had undoubtedly been recruited by Chinese entrepreneurs in those districts for migration to the United States; when hundreds of these men, unexpected and unsent for by the Hawaiian government, refused to sign plantation labor contracts, the government ordered that departures of Chinese from Hong Kong

for Hawaii be stopped. Later in 1883 the government permitted limited immigration of Chinese laborers because of renewed demands
from the Caucasian sugar planters and Chinese rice planters.

The regulations concerning entry of Chinese male laborers were
changed many times during the succeeding decade. For the most part
no restrictions were imposed on the entry of Chinese women and
bona fide children—this in response to protests against the predominantly adult male composition of the Chinese group in the Islands.
Once importation of Japanese plantation laborers was well under
way, the government's policy became essentially that of restricting
Chinese immigration so that Chinese arrivals would not exceed Chinese departures. The effectiveness of this policy is indicated by Custom House statistics which show that during the nine years between
1886 and 1895 the departures of Chinese men actually exceeded the
number of arrivals by 1,988—and probably as many as half of those
arriving during this period were men who entered on return permits
or permits for nonlaborers. The total number of Chinese foreign-
born males in Hawaii dropped from 17,068 to 14,522 in the six years
between the censuses of 1884 and 1890.

By 1894, Japanese laborers outnumbered Chinese on the sugar
plantations by 21,294 to 2,734.[49] In fact, scarcely ten years after Japanese labor importations were started the labor force had become so
predominantly Japanese that planters wanted to restrict the "inunda-
tion" of the Islands by Japanese migrants.[50] A committee of the
Planter's Labour and Supply Company complained of the dangers
faced by planters when they hired a labor force preponderantly Japanese; the committee claimed that the best policy was to have a labor
force made up of workers of different nationalities. Some planters
asked that Chinese labor importation be renewed. Legislation in the
early nineties had allowed limited immigration of Chinese laborers
provided that they engaged only in agricultural or domestic service.

The Republic of Hawaii, which replaced the Hawaiian monarchy overthrown in 1893, was more plantation-oriented than the
monarchy had been and responded willingly to the planters' demands for imported Chinese labor. During 1895, some 1,087 Chinese "agriculturalists" were admitted under contract, most of them
going to sugar plantations and a few to the Chinese rice plantations.
Early in 1896 the government announced its policy requiring plantation agents who applied for laborers to ask for twice as many Chinese as Japanese: "This was an effort on the part of the Executive to

more evenly balance the immigration of plantation laborers."[51] Anticipating that annexation to the United States might stop Chinese immigration, 6,277 additional Chinese contract laborers were brought in during 1896 and 1897. At the same time, the incipient annexation stimulated immigration of other classes of Chinese. More nonindentured Chinese males arrived in 1898 than in any year since 1885, more Chinese children than since 1891, and almost twice as many Chinese women as had entered during any year of the half century of Chinese immigration.

Custom House data show that between 1852 and 1899 Chinese arrivals totaled more than 56,000 (Table 1). These figures, however, include the returning entries of Chinese residents who had made trips to China and other parts of the world. The actual number of individual Chinese migrants who came before Annexation can only be estimated. The estimate offered here, 46,000, is one that other analysts have also used.[52] Annexation formally took place on 12 August 1898; on 24 November an American official took over the duty of controlling Chinese immigration. With the application to Hawaii of the Chinese Exclusion Act, the pioneer era of Chinese migration to Hawaii drew to a close. The experience of the pre-Annexation migrants, as individuals and as members of formal and informal groups, is the primary concern of this study.

Migrants who remained in the Islands as residents became involved in establishing a community which was to become part of Hawaii's multiethnic society. Chinese who entered from the mid-1880s onward in one or another exempt category played a disproportionate role in this process. They included merchants, bankers, newspaper editors, Chinese-language-school teachers, physicians, Christian ministers and priests, priests of Buddhist and Taoist sects, professors, artists. Merchants were the most numerous of the men in these categories; there were probably no more than a few hundred in all the other categories combined. Men in these categories could bring their wives, even after Annexation, and their children born in Hawaii qualified for American citizenship under the principle of jus soli. These families helped to reduce the preponderance of males in the Hawaii Chinese population and to provide a broader basis for the perpetuation and ultimate growth of a Chinese ethnic group in Hawaii.

After Annexation various attempts, all unsuccessful, were made to renew importation of Chinese laborers, especially by sugar planters and Chinese rice planters, before Congress passed the Immigration Act of 1924. This act, which came at the height of anti-Japanese agitation on the West Coast, effectively limited immigration from Asian countries such as Japan, Korea, and India to 105 a year, apart from those who could qualify for entry under one of the exempt categories. Early in 1944, after repeal of the Chinese Exclusion Act in 1943, China was given the same quota of 105 per year in addition to those in exempt categories, and Chinese migrants were granted the right of naturalization. After World War II immigration from China was further opened up by such congressional legislation as the War Brides Act of 1946, the Walter-McCarran Act of 1948, the Immigration and Nationality Act of 1952, the Refugee Relief Act of 1953, the Refugee Escape Act of 1957, and, most important, the amended Immigration and Nationality Act of 1965. One effect of these laws has been the arrival in Hawaii, since World War II, of a very different group of about five thousand Chinese migrants concentrated in Honolulu.

CHAPTER 2

On the Sugar Plantations

OF the estimated 46,000 Chinese migrants who came to Hawaii before Annexation, probably two-thirds to three-fourths began as laborers on sugar or rice plantations, with the larger number working initially on sugar plantations. Hawaiian sugar plantations during this period, though having some unusual features, shared the basic characteristics of the plantation system as it was developing in many parts of the nonindustrialized world.

In the premechanized era, sugar plantations needed not only a large supply of laborers willing to work at wages low enough to return a profit to investors, but also a stable force of workers remaining on the plantation long enough to pay for the costs of recruiting and importing them and to carry through from one crop to the next. To keep imported laborers on the plantation for at least a minimum period, sugar planters in Hawaii during the latter half of the nineteenth century availed themselves of two legal measures that were generally integral parts of the plantation system: first, a form of indenture or contract binding the laborer to the plantation for a stated period under stipulated conditions; second, legal sanctions with judicial machinery to enforce the contract.[1] The indenture system lessened the risks incurred by entrepreneurs who undertook plantation agriculture on economic peripheries by assuring them labor over a given period. The legal basis for this arrangement in Hawaii was the Masters and Servants Act which had been enacted two years before the first Chinese laborers were imported to Hawaii in 1852. It applied not only to plantation labor but also to other types of employment such as domestic service. In fact, the original intent of the act was to protect Hawaiians who were going to sea on whalers. It had its greatest significance, however, in the development of the sugar plantations.

The Contract Labor System

From a purely utilitarian point of view the Chinese imported workers had characteristics which made them one of the most satisfactory labor groups in the early phases of plantation development. Their industriousness, perseverance, and adaptability became proverbial. The willingness of Chinese workers to endure hardships, undergo the physical risks of penetrating and opening up undeveloped areas, and put up with the minimum essentials of living accommodations became well known. Employing them was profitable not only because they were willing to work for low wages but also because the cost of their maintenance was minimal since they rarely brought families with them. Even during the height of the anti-Chinese agitation in the 1880s the vital role played by Chinese laborers in plantation development was recognized:

> That the Chinese are in most respects undesirable is a fact of which the present Government is and has always been convinced. But that they were necessary in the beginning, to give an impetus to agriculture, to supply labor not obtainable elsewhere cannot be denied.
>
> Relying upon their work, at cheap rates, planters were enabled to purchase machinery, erect buildings, irrigate and drain on a large scale, all of which they would not have been able to do, nay would not have dared to attempt, had they not been able to count upon steady labor, at moderate rates, and for a stated term.[2]

The characteristics that made the Chinese so attractive to plantation management must be understood in the context of the situation from which the migrants came. It was this situation which produced both their qualities as workers and their willingness to sign contracts to work as laborers overseas. Some excerpts from the autobiography of one of the less fortunate Chinese who came to Hawaii illustrate how meager was the life of many villagers in South China and how desperately hard they had to struggle for a bare subsistence:

> In a small crowded village, a few miles from Hong Kong, fifty-four years ago I was born [1882]. There were four in our family, my mother, my father, my sister, and me. We lived in a two room house. One was our sleeping room and the other served as parlor, kitchen, and dining room. We were not rich enough to keep pigs or fowls; otherwise, our small house would have been more crowded than ever.
>
> How can we live on six baskets of rice which were paid twice a year for my father's duty as a night watchman? Sometimes the pea-

sants have a poor crop; then we go hungry. During the day my father would do other small jobs for the peasants or carpenters. My mother worked hard too for she went every day to the forest to gather wood for our stove. . . .

Sometimes we went hungry for days. My mother and me would go over the harvested rice fields of the peasants to pick the grains they dropped. Once in a while my mother would go near a big pile of grain and take a handful. She would then sit on them until the working men went home. As soon as they go we ran home. She clean and cook the rice for us two. We had only salt and water to eat with rice. . . .[3]

While it is generally true that poverty at home and the hope of economic betterment abroad were basic in bringing thousands of Chinese to the plantations, many different circumstances and motivations led individual Chinese to migrate. The following cases show how the context varied:

Mr. Lum, born in 1869, was the only son and oldest child in a family of seven children. His early life was one of poverty and hardship. His father used the larger, middle room of their three room house for a store, selling foodstuffs and a few necessities. The people in the village, however, were poor and bought the goods "on account." Often these bills remained unpaid. Money became scarce, and debts were incurred. Suddenly the father died, leaving debts and the support of the family to his wife and thirteen year old son. An uncle who returned to the village about this time from the Hawaiian Islands, where he was a partner in a sugar plantation, finally persuaded the widowed mother to let her young son go with him to Hawaii. The boy made a contract with his uncle whereby he was to work on his uncle's sugar plantation on the island of Hawaii for ten years at ten dollars a month. His passage was to be paid by the uncle, but upon reaching the Islands an amount of his monthly pay was to be taken until the passage expenses were refunded. With his [clothing] in a small bamboo valise, he left his native land, in 1882, for Hawaii.[4]

Wong Wai was born in 1871 in a village in Duck Doo, Chung Shan district. He comes from a family of four children, being the second son and child. His parents were rice farmers and were of the poorest class of laborers. Although it is customary for a boy to marry early, he could not afford this because of extreme poverty. He did not go to school. . . . Wong heard stories of the better conditions [in Hawaii], told by returning laborers. Seizing the opportunity in 1894, he signed up with the Hawaiian Sugar Planters' Association as an immigrant laborer to work on the sugar plantations and was brought to Honolulu, to be immediately assigned to the ——— Sugar Company on Maui. . . .[5]

A weak government and local instability in South China during the latter half of the nineteenth century added to the conditions which led some Chinese to sign contracts for plantation work in Hawaii:

> We came as contract laborers through lack of steamer fare. . . . You see, although we belonged to a family of wealth we were impoverished by feud. Our family owned 40 to 50 *mou* . . . and dozens of workmen were hired during the harvesting season. We had two steady watchers of the fields the year-around. . . . In a bloody feud between the Chang family and Oo Shak village we lost our two steady workmen. Eighteen villagers were hired by Oo Shak to fight against the huge Chang family, and in the battle two men lost their lives protecting our pine forests. Our village, Wong Jook Long, had a few resident Changs. After the bloodshed, we were called for our men's lives, and the greedy, impoverished villagers grabbed fields, forest, food and everything, including newborn pigs, for payment. We were left with nothing, and in disillusion we went to Hong Kong to sell ourselves as contract laborers. We were very young then. I was 22, and my brother was four years younger.[6]

Most of the Chinese migrants came from villages in delta regions south and east of Canton or from the central coastal districts of Kwangtung province. In order to reach the ports from which the emigrant ships sailed—chiefly Canton, Whampoa, Hong Kong, and Macao—the men usually started out in groups, walked to the inland ports, and traveled by small vessels, along canals or rivers, through districts which were unfamiliar and sometimes unsafe. Chinese migration to Hawaii was not characterized by the atrocious and harrowing experiences of kidnapping and shanghaiing, imprisonment behind barracoons in the port cities of South China, maltreatment on shipboard, or inhuman dealing in "coolie flesh" which have blackened accounts of the "coolie trade" to many other areas. Hawaii was renowned for the generally humane way it imported Chinese labor. Dr. Hillebrand, the commissioner of immigration who was sent to China in 1865 when importation of Chinese labor was reopened, was a respected Honolulu physician who supervised the negotiations and shipment of the men. Advertisement for workers was directed by a German missionary; within a few weeks more than enough men had applied. Each man who embarked was to be given a free passage to the Hawaiian Islands, a present of eight dollars, two suits of clothing, a winter jacket, a pair of shoes, a bamboo hat, a mat, a pillow, and bed covering. The vessels were prepared for a 56-day passage and fitted out with berths, water, firewood, cooking utensils, Chinese provisions, medicines, and a "hospital" on deck; an interpreter and a Chinese doctor were to be provided on each vessel; twenty of the passengers were to act as cooks for the five hundred immigrants, six as overseers and two as stewards, each to receive payment in advance for such services. And a rail partition was to be erected on the vessels to separate the "male and female passengers on board."[7] Contracts signed in 1870, like the one quoted later, had similar stipulations.

Even with such provisions, the passage, some four thousand miles by the most direct route, was long, tedious, and often trying. Before 1880 most of the migrants came on sailing vessels which sometimes took as long as seventy days for the trip. Conditions on the ships were crowded and uncomfortable; there was much uneasiness, even near panic when contagions broke out. One Chinese migrant recalled the discomfort and uncertainties of his passage to Hawaii and his arrival in the Islands:

> Like most immigrants, Mr. Lum had the idea that from the moment he caught the boat there would be comfort and happiness. But all seemed the opposite. As he was going on board, he had to struggle his way through a huge crowd. Everyone was afraid that he would be left behind, so as soon as the way was opened everyone just rushed to get on board and when he was finally aboard he was all out of breath. The next disappointment came soon after. Mr. Lum expected to find a room with a bed like the ones which he had seen in the Hongkong hotels but which he had never lain on; at home he had always slept on a hard, board bed; in Hongkong he had slept many a night on the hard, cold, stone sidewalks. On the boat he found himself standing in one room crowded with hundreds of other Chinese laborers, and when night arrived he found himself sleeping on a mat which was placed on the deck. Then too when supper was served he had the same things that he ate at home and at Hongkong with the exception that on board he had melon and cabbage in addition to rice and salt fish.
>
> To add to all this disappointment he was seasick. He found the room to be very stuffy with so many people that the steamer smell made him sick. As the voyage continued he wished more and more that he had stayed at home.

One day a person who slept next to him was sick with smallpox. This fact frightened him very much, but his fright was dismissed for this man was taken to another part of the ship so as to be away from the rest of the crowd. Mr. Lum was then confident that it would not be so easy for him to get the disease. It was very fortunate for them all that this man was quickly removed for no one else caught the disease. . . .

On their arrival in Honolulu several white men came on board and eyed them. They spoke to his uncle in a language that Mr. Lum didn't understand. . . . At last the door opened and he stepped on the solid ground of the Hawaiian Islands. . . . His uncle told him that they were taking another boat to a nearby island within two hours. Mr. Lum was disappointed for he thought he had reached his destination. He was not keen about this idea for he detested sea life. However, he did not say anything in objection for he knew that he should obey his uncle. . . .[8]

Precautions by immigration authorities to minimize the danger of introducing contagious diseases proved as obnoxious to the Chinese as such efforts have been to steerage immigrants elsewhere. After several epidemics in the early 1880s had caused many deaths, chiefly among the already diminishing Hawaiian people, quarantine facilities were set up on an island near the mouth of Honolulu harbor, where Chinese immigrants were landed and kept under the observation of physicians for a few days. Chinese residents and others protested this procedure and some even compared the quarantine to the barracoons of Macao. True enough, landing on the quarantine island instead of disembarking in Honolulu prevented men who had promised to ship to the plantations from evading contracts. At the same time it facilitated the indenturing of many free immigrants. An 1881 ordinance required free immigrants who did not "make engagements for their services" to furnish "satisfactory evidence that they will not become vagrants or a charge on the community for their support." Being held in quarantine hindered the newcomers from arranging with Chinese residents to meet the demands of the ordinance instead of signing with plantations.

Even though the government tried to avoid the worst abuses of laborer recruitment, some migrants were disillusioned after reaching Hawaii. Men who had agreed to ship to the plantations often came to feel that they had been exploited and deceived by government officials or by Chinese who assisted the plantations in securing contract laborers. One Chinese recruiter narrowly escaped being killed by an angry mob of some two hundred Chinese who charged that he had deceived them when they signed their labor contracts.[9] On one plantation it was revealed (in 1897) that Chinese recruiters soliciting laborers in villages of South China had received so many more applicants than could be assured passage to Hawaii that they had charged the men twelve dollars—about one full month's wages—for the chance to be selected.[10] And it may be added that the Chinese agents licensed by the government to assist in indenturing Chinese at the quarantine station in Honolulu were cordially disliked by the newcomers.

The contracts under which the Chinese migrants entered the plantation system varied in details from period to period but the following example shows their general features. The monthly wage was gradually increased, the length of the contract was reduced to three years, and contracts signed in the 1890s did not permit the migrant to remain in the Islands except in agricultural work or domestic service.

LABOR CONTRACT[11]

Honolulu, Hawaiian Islands

_____1870

I _____ Party of the first part, a native of China, a free and voluntary Passenger to the Sandwich Islands, do bind myself to labor on any of the said Islands, at any work that may be assigned me, by the Party of the Second part, or their agents, upon the terms and in the manner within specified, for the term of Five Years from this date.

_____ Party of the second part, do agree and bind themselves, or agents, to conform fully to the within Agreement,

Signed_____

Witness_____

Signed_____

MEMORANDUM OF AGREEMENT by the Agent of the Hawaiian Government.

No Contract can be made in Hongkong.

All Emigrants must go as Free Passengers.

Each Emigrant shall be given him, 1 heavy Jacket, 1 light Jacket, 1 Water-proof Jacket, 2 pair Pants, 1 pair Shoes, 1 pair Stockings, 1 Hat, 1 Mat, 1 Pillow, 1 Blanket.

A present of Ten Dollars to be paid the day before the ship sails.

In no instance will any deduction from wages be made for Clothes or Money advanced in Hongkong.

A free passage to Sandwich Islands, with food, water, and Medical care, given each Emigrant.

The Master to pay all Government personal Taxes.

All Children to be taught in the Public Schools, free of any expense to the Parents.

Each Man to receive $6 for each month labor performed of 26 days.

Each Woman to receive $5 for each month labor performed of 26 days.

The wages to be paid in Silver, upon the first Saturday after the end of the month.

No labor shall be exacted upon the Sabbath, only in case of emergency, when it shall be paid for extra.

All emigrants who are employed as House Servants, when their duties compel them to labor Sundays and evenings, shall receive for men, 7 dollars per month, for women 6 dollars per month.

Three days Holiday shall be given each Emigrant at Chinese New Year and a present of $2.

These three days time to be counted the same as if employed.

In all cases, the Master to provide good and sufficient food and comfortable House Room.

In case of Sickness, Medical attendance and care free.

No wages during illness.

Each Emigrant to find his own Bed clothing.

Each Emigrant, upon arrival in the Sandwich Islands, to sign a contract (to work for such Master as may be chosen for him by the Government Agent) for the term of Five Years from the time of entering upon his duties, to work faithfully and cheerfully according to the laws of the Country, which compel both Master and Servant to fulfill their Contracts.

Families shall not be separated; the Government particularly desire that men will take their wives.

Every Emigrant shall have all the rights and protection under the law that are given to any Citizen of the Country.

At the expiration of the five years each Emigrant has a right to remain in the Country, or to leave it.

> SAML. G. WILDER.
> H.H.M. Commissioner of
> Immigration.

Hongkong, April 18, 1870.

Although the provisions of the contract might seem to imply that the men were assigned more or less arbitrarily, with no regard to personal relations among the laborers themselves, this was not always the case. Planters requested laborers in large lots. A group of young Chinese relatives, villagers, or shipboard friends could almost certainly be assured of being sent to the same plantation by obtaining contracts numbered serially one after another. Once contract migration was well established, workers already on the plantations sent back letters telling incoming clansmen and fellow villagers which plantations to avoid and which were the best to ship to.[12] Moreover, immigration authorities helped make it possible for Chinese who had become Christians in China to concentrate in certain plantation communities.

The Plantation Experience

Caring for and handling Chinese contract laborers, once they arrived on the plantations, posed several problems which were complicated by the differences in race and culture between planters and workers. One of the first problems had to do with food. In the early decades of Chinese importation the contracts required the planters to furnish food for the laborers. At that time most workers already on the plantations were Hawaiians whose diet consisted primarily of such locally available foods as poi (made from taro), fish, and sweet potatoes—a diet quite different from that of the South Chinese for whom the staple food was rice. Until locally produced rice became plentiful and cheap, stinting on the amount of rice provided Chinese workers was a source of complaint. The position taken by one planter is suggested by a notice posted in 1866:

> The owner of the Waihee Plantation wishes to inform his Chinese laborers that he intends strictly to fulfill his part of the contract and expects his laborers to perform theirs. He will provide comfortable lodging and sufficient food—i.e., as much as his laborers can consume without waste—but he will not nor has he agreed to give as much of any one kind of food as his laborers choose to consume. Hitherto he has indulged their choice on the rice question till most of his laborers have learned to eat other kinds of food grown in this country. He now intends to allow each man and woman for the present year at least 1 pound of rice each day [and] the customary allowance of meat or fish

and kalo [taro] and sweet potatoes without stint except to prevent wanton waste. He also gives a piece of ground to his laborers and has provided them with vegetable garden seeds—and a separate cooking place for the preparation of such food as they may wish outside of that prepared by the plantation cook.

The people of this country are not ignorant of the manners and customs of the people in China—and it is well known yams which are somewhat similar to our kalo and sweet potatoes are articles of food in China.[13]

The housing furnished by the plantations, though simple, seems to have caused few problems. Men were usually housed in long, unpainted, frame buildings. The Chinese were accustomed to sleeping on a mat thrown over a wooden platform, and plantation houses usually had wooden ledges, two or three feet from the ground and about three feet wide, where the men could place their mats and, if they wanted to, hang mosquito nets. From six to forty men would be assigned to a single room.[14]

Since the Chinese were brought to the plantations primarily for unskilled manual work in the fields and around the mills, no complicated or extensive communication between them and their employers was expected. Even the simplest tasks called for some directions, however. A pioneer planter and his secretary, interviewed in 1930, were asked how the first workers were told what to do. The secretary answered, "By the toe of the foot. They could point and use the boot to the seat of the pants." The crude brutality implied in this remark was not common, though, and in fact much more useful ways of giving directions quickly developed. Chinese workers who became familiar with Hawaiian or pidgin English commonly acted as interpreters. The planter said that "it didn't take long for some of the Chinese to pick up Hawaiian. Hawaiian was the first language they learned here. Some people are naturally gifted in picking up languages. There was one of our men—Tai Fu. He picked up Hawaiian in no time. We made him one of our interpreters." Later the migrants contributed Chinese words and syntax to the pidgin English that spread throughout the Island plantations.

On a large plantation the contract laborer actually had little direct contact with the Caucasian owner or manager. On the job he was supervised by, and at the orders of, a luna (overseer) who was generally of a different ethnic group—in the early days a Hawaiian or part-Hawaiian, later on perhaps a Portuguese, Norwegian, or German imported migrant—someone who did not know his language, his cultural background, or even the extent of his agricultural knowledge and skills. Probably the greatest single source of trouble on plantations was friction between field workers and lunas, certainly not unusual in worker-supervisor situations but exacerbated here by cultural differences.

Apart from field work under the direct supervision of a non-Chinese luna, two other systems of sugar cane production developed that gave Chinese workers more discretion and independence: the *ukupau* (Hawaiian for "job done") and the "contract." Under the *ukupau* system a certain quantity of work was set by the plantation as a day's job. The laborer could work as rapidly or as slowly as he pleased and could quit when the stipulated work was completed. The planter quoted above said that in his long experience the *ukupau* system had proved to be the best to use with Chinese labor. Under the contract arrangement a group of Chinese laborers worked under a Chinese who contracted with the plantation to carry out a given undertaking at a stipulated sum per acre, per ton, or per job. At one time more than three hundred Chinese laborers were under the control of two Chinese contractors on one of the larger plantations on Maui. It was expected that Chinese laborers would be more content to work under this system than under the more impersonal control of non-Chinese lunas; they could work under arrangements which took account of the demands and values of their cultural background. Sometimes the contractor, with plantation approval, recruited his laborers from among his own clansmen or fellow villagers in the expectation that they would compose a more stable group because of their traditional ties and would work harder because of their personal obligations to the contractor. The system also lent itself to cooperative arrangements by which the laborers could share in the profits with the contractor.

Another type of cooperative scheme worked out among the laborers themselves was described by the same planter:

> The Chinese usually made one of their gang the cook. He would fix their breakfast, and then cook their dinner and bring it hot to the field. They had to have hot dinner and hot tea to drink. The man who was made the cook usually shared just the same as the rest of the men. They would divide up what they made, so that all got the same. . . . Another thing was the dope. Y—— Fat was the one I learned this from:

He told me that when he went to the field to work, and the cook brought his meals to him, he found that in the top of the bucket was a little paper or envelope with the dope in it. All the men, he said, took their dope that way with their dinner. The cook would have to see about getting the stuff and fixing it up the same as the rest of the meal.

On some Hawaiian plantations the daily life of the workers was closely regimented in the interest of maintaining an efficient work force. The nature of this regimentation was implicit in the rules that plantations usually drew up and posted. In 1866 Waihee Plantation established the following rules, which were probably stricter than those that became customary later:

1. Laborers are expected to be industrious and docile and obedient to their overseers.

2. Any cause of complaint against the overseers, of injustice or ill treatment, shall be heard by the manager through the interpreter, but in no case shall any laborer be permitted to raise his hand or any weapon in an aggressive manner or cabal with his associates or incite them to acts of insubordination.

3. The working hours shall be ten each day, or more, if by mutual consent, in which case they shall have extra pay, but when work is not pressing, laborers will be allowed to stop on Saturdays at 4 o'clock.

4. When laborers desire to have a stint for the day's work, the overseer shall be the judge of the amount required, then laborers shall have their choice, to accept [the stint] or to work their usual 10 hours; on this subject there shall be no appeal.

5. Laborers are expected to be regular and cleanly in their personal habits, to retire to rest and rise at the appointed hours, to keep their persons, beds, clothing, rooms, enclosures, and offices clean, and are strictly forbidden to enter that part of the cook house set apart for plantation cooking arrangements. A fire place will be provided for the latter purpose and permission given to cut indigo for firewood.

6. Rooms will be set apart for married laborers, and a separate bed will be provided for each male unmarried laborer, which they are expected to occupy except in case of continued illness—no two men shall be permitted to occupy the same bed.

7. No fires will be allowed after 6½ p.m. and no lights after 8½ p.m.; every laborer is required to be in bed at 8½ p.m. and to rise at 5 a.m., the hours before breakfast being devoted to habits of cleanliness and order about their persons and premises. During the hours appointed for rest no talking permitted or any noise calculated to disturb those wishing to sleep.

8. A separate lodging house will be provided for those whose sickness or inability to labor shall last over 24 hours and all persons on the sick or disabled list are required to submit to such treatment and obey such directions as are given by the medical attendant and manager.

9. It is required that laborers sick or unable to work shall immediately report themselves through the interpreter to their overseer or to the manager as any person absent from work without permission shall be considered and punished as a deserter.

10. Each laborer shall be held responsible for any sickness or inability to work which shall result from breaking the laws of this land or the sanitary rules of this plantation.

11. Gambling, fast riding, and leaving the plantation without permission are strictly forbidden.

Working and living conditions varied widely during the decades when the largest numbers of Chinese were in the plantation work force. Some plantations, such as Grove Farm on Kauai, are remembered as having considerate management with concern for the workers' welfare and respect for their customs.[15] On others where management was more impersonal there was less regard for the workers as human beings. The prevalence in Hawaii of resident planters managing their own plantations contributed to more paternalism than in most other plantation areas where absentee ownership was common. Although the time came when this paternalism was resented, it at least ameliorated the harsher aspects of plantation life and work.

The Masters and Servants Act had provisions not only for enforcement of contracts on behalf of the employer but also for recourse to officials by laborers who felt themselves abused or unjustly treated. Although whipping was prohibited by the act, complaints were occasionally filed with the government. Wray Taylor, secretary of the Board of Immigration in 1897, reported to the board on visits he had made to several plantations on the islands of Kauai, Maui, and Hawaii to investigate complaints and recommend action to resolve them. After inquiries about mistreatment of Chinese laborers at Lihue Plantation he recommended that the head luna be discharged and that the manager "be reprimanded and held to strict account for the better treatment of laborers in the future. This was done and since then no further complaints have come from Lihue." At the same time, fifteen of the Chinese laborers who were considered ringleaders in the riot on Lihue Plantation that had led to the investigation were "by order of the Court, returned to China."[16]

Workers felt, with some cause, that the laws were more readily enforced for the employers than for themselves. There is some evidence to support complaints about collusion between the planters and the legal authorities to the disadvantage of the laborers. A sheriff on the island of Hawaii, writing in 1897 about Chinese plantation workers who resisted the efforts of police to serve warrants of arrest sworn out by the plantation manager, reported to the marshal of the Hawaiian government:

> The P—— [Plantation] Chinese were vigorously prosecuted for their riotous conduct in resisting the Police. Their two most prominent leaders were sentenced to one year each at hard labor. Eight of the next worst were given six months each. Ten of the next worst were given four months each. Twenty-three of the next worst were given three months each, and the balance were prosecuted for deserting contract service and sentenced to pay costs and ordered to return to work, which they have done, and are now working better than they have ever done before since they came to the Plantation.
>
> I got the Manager to give me the names of the men who had made the most trouble on the Plantation, and then asked the Judge to grade their sentences so that they would be coming back little by little the worst ones coming back after the others, so as to have the Plantation work going on smoothly. I trust that this action will work well for I am convinced that Mr. M——, the Manager, has been too lenient with his Chinese. . . .[17]

In a report on labor in Hawaii in 1899, Wray Taylor gave "a general view of the real state of affairs" on the plantations:

> Every labor camp is a busy hive. Work is going on, and work is paid for and is what the men come here for.
>
> Now, what are the hardships? The main one is compulsory work under a master. Here the law compels. At home, need held the whip. They expected to work when they came; but the comparison with free men makes compulsion seem a hardship. Generally they are contented. The sewing machine is common in every camp. The tailoress plies her trade. The petty shopkeeper, with his room nearly filled with goods, drives his bargains with his countrymen. . . . There is food enough and a place to eat and sleep and live in, equal in comfort to that they have left behind. . . . Sunday is a day for rest in most cases. The barber is in demand. Clean clothes are donned, and pipe and cigarette lend solace. No one would dream of hardship to look in their faces. . . .

But let some real or fancied grievance break the monotony, and the scene changes. A tin pan is beaten noisily to alarm and summon the camp. The motley crowd gathers, generally at night. The leaders harangue their followers, and the mob, most of them ignorant of the real cause, rush off to demand redress or punish the offender.

The grievance is generally an assault by the overseer upon some laborer, a fine considered unjust, a compulsion used to obtain unwilling work, or a privilege withdrawn. The grievance is to the individual, and the crowd make it their own. It is not generally felt very deeply, and in most cases a little tact smooths out everything, and the even flow of events is again attained. . . .

It may be gathered that, as a rule, plantations furnish all that the law demands, but are not carried on primarily for the purpose of elevating the laborer to the standard of western civilization and morals any more than other corporations. . . .[18]

Most contracts in the nineteenth century stipulated twenty-six working days of ten hours. Work started early, and even though men worked overtime during busy seasons there was a good deal of free time in the late afternoons and evenings and on Sundays and holidays. Until about 1910 most of these men were young—of 6,894 Chinese entering contracts in 1895–1897 almost half were under twenty-five years old, three-fourths under thirty, and nine-tenths under thirty-five.[19] As Taylor implies, the plantations provided little for these men to do when they were not working. Most plantations, during the years most Chinese were employed on them, were quite isolated and the laborers under contract seldom got into town. Since there were few Chinese women and families, and on some plantations none, there was little semblance of the stabilizing family and clan life these young men had left behind.[20] There were no clan or village elders to exert control. Usually the plantation did house Chinese workers separately from those of other ethnic groups in what was generally called "the Chinese camp," with an older Chinese, who had several years' experience on the plantation, as "headman" or manager. Sometimes he was responsible for order in the camp, collected rents from the day laborers living in the camp, assisted in paying wages, and served as interpreter, labor contractor, labor recruiter. Commonly the headman operated a store selling the men Chinese and other goods. This store was a common meeting place for workers with nothing else to do. Sometimes the headman had his wife and family with him; if so, they helped tend the store and often made and mended clothes for the bachelor laborers.

One spare-time activity was gardening. Most of the workers had been farmers at home, and on the plantation they cultivated plots where they grew the vegetables favored in Chinese cooking. Growing bananas and raising pigs, ducks, and chickens were other ways laborers could supply themselves with the kinds of food they liked to eat and at the same time reduce their food costs. This arrangement became more prevalent when contracts no longer required planters to supply food to the laborers and also when Chinese remained on the plantations as day laborers.

Nevertheless, the young men who lived in the camps were often bored with the monotonous plantation life. It is little wonder that vices spread as they usually do in frontier communities with an abnormal preponderance of males. Opium smoking was widespread. An elderly Chinese addict explained to a social worker in the 1930s that "there was very little to do when work was over, and the other fellows who were having a good time smoking asked me to join them, so to be a good sport I took up opium smoking, not realizing that I would probably have to die with it."[21] During the year 1873, with less than two thousand Chinese men in the Islands, the Custom House reported the arrival of more than 2,700 pounds of opium and 900 "pills"; it was asserted that three-fourths of the Chinese at that time were addicts.[22] Opium smoking seems to have gone on fairly undisturbed on many plantations, especially during the three decades preceding Annexation, even though rules against the practice were commonly posted. The cook who included "dope" in the field workers' lunches, for example, was apparently not stopped from doing so. In the 1930s several Chinese migrants, too old or too incapacitated for work and seeking help from social welfare agencies, were victims of the opium habit they had acquired as young men on the sugar or rice plantations.

Gambling flourished on the plantations. In 1882 Frank Damon, a missionary working among the Chinese in Hawaii, commented on this widespread practice as he observed it while visiting plantation camps:

> Here we found quite a company of Chinamen. As we came into the main room of their house I was led to feel that to some at least we were not very welcome guests. There had arrived before us, one of those gambling "tramps," who earn an infamous livelihood by going around from plantation to plantation, leading the laborers to waste their hard earned wages in gambling. This vice seems to have a tre-

mendous power over the Chinese. It is especially prevalent on the sugar plantations—where the men are left to do pretty much as they list, after they have left the field and mill. . . . We had the pleasure at Hanamaulu of breaking up an evening's sport. The men themselves seemed kind and received us pleasantly—while the disappointed "Gambler," left us the field. . . .[23]

According to Chinese informants, lotteries—*chee fa*—were widely patronized by Chinese both on and off the plantations, and an elaborate system facilitated the betting. Runners would visit a district and collect money for placing bets. The money would be passed to agents higher up in the business until it finally reached Honolulu, where it would be placed in Honolulu-based lotteries. Notices of winnings would be relayed in the reverse order and commissions taken by each middleman involved.

During most of the decades that Chinese migrants entered Hawaii as contract laborers, the plantation work force also included a large number of Hawaiians, both men and women. As indicated in the previous chapter, some Caucasians encouraged liaisons between Chinese men and Hawaiian women as a way of "rebuilding the native race"; others concluded that such relations were "demoralizing the natives." In any case, numerous migrants did associate freely with Hawaiian women, some casually, others establishing permanent family ties. The migrants' relations with Hawaiian women were a factor in some of the anti-Chinese feelings among Hawaiian men.

Getting Off the Plantation

Although several hundred Chinese workers brought to the plantations as contract laborers remained on them throughout their working life in Hawaii (as day laborers after they were no longer on contracts), by far the greater number left the plantations when their contracts expired. In spite of the arrival of over 14,000 Chinese during the six years prior to 1882, only 5,007 of the plantations' 10,253 workers in 1882 were Chinese. During periods when importation of Chinese contract laborers was restricted—roughly from 1886 to 1895 and from 1898 on—the number of Chinese plantation employees diminished rapidly. Less than half as many were on the plantations in 1892 as in 1888, and of the 8,114 Chinese working on sugar plantations on 31 December 1897 over half had left by 1902.

Some of the reasons for this exodus were related to the reasons why laborers had to be brought in under indenture. Other reasons are apparent in the causes of dissatisfaction with plantation life, including the regimentation and subordination to non-Chinese lunas who offended or at times actually mistreated the workers. Taylor singled out "compulsory work under a master" as the main hardship felt by the workers. The problem of workers leaving the plantation at the end of their contracts, if not before, was a matter of constant concern to management. As early as 1869 one planter in Hawaii said of his Chinese contract laborers: "I find them good servants. . . . One objection I have to this class of labor is that although offered double their present wages to renew their contracts they refuse to do so."

This problem was not peculiar to sugar plantations in Hawaii; it has been characteristic of the contract labor situation everywhere. In some other parts of the world planters and governments collaborated to keep imported laborers on the plantation by deporting those who refused to renew their contracts. No such measure was used in Hawaii, although in the 1890s the Republic of Hawaii adopted regulations under which Chinese who left agricultural work were to be returned to China. This was a fairly elastic provision since there were many other types of agriculture developing in Hawaii which Chinese could and did go into.

One important reason for leaving the plantation was the feeling that there was little opportunity for promotion in the plantation hierarchy.[24] The ratio of supervisory and skilled jobs to unskilled on the plantation in the premechanized era was very low, so even if they had been given their share of such jobs few Chinese could have moved into them. Moreover, many Chinese felt that they were not given an equal opportunity with part-Hawaiians and Portuguese who were promoted to lower management and skilled jobs. Census returns from eighty-four plantations in 1882, more than a generation after the first Chinese labor importations, showed that only 3 of the 5,007 Chinese male employees held preferred positions—as sugar boilers—the others being listed as "laborers."[25] Seventeen years later, in 1899, only 94 of the 5,969 Chinese workers were among the 2,019 plantation employees in skilled positions; of these 94, there were 6 sugar boilers, 4 bookkeepers and clerks, 16 engineers and firemen, 31 carpenters, 2 blacksmiths, and 1 painter. If Chinese skilled employees had made up the same proportion of the total skilled employees that the Chinese composed of the total on the sugar plantations' payrolls, they would have held almost four times the number of preferred positions actually reported for them.[26]

Connected with this inability to secure the better-paying preferred positions was discontent with wages. Although plantation labor in Hawaii at any given date has been better paid than labor on sugar plantations almost anywhere else in the world, and although wages down into the 1940s were much higher than payment for similar types of work in South China, the Chinese laborers generally came to feel that plantation wages were too low. The wages stipulated in contracts ranged from the $3 a month plus board offered in 1852 to $15 a month without board in the late 1890s—with deductions for those who did not work the standard month of twenty-six working days. Actually, most Chinese laborers on the plantations after 1888, except for the years 1896–1899, did not work under indenture but as "free" or "day" laborers. Nevertheless, their wages did not average much above those of the contract laborers. During the 1870s day laborers received about $10 a month; in 1886 Chinese plantation workers averaged $13.56 a month.[27] The average monthly wages for Chinese day laborers in 1892 were reported to be $17.62 while the average for all day laborers was $18.83 a month.[28] Chinese "skilled hands" were reported to receive an average daily wage of $1.22 in 1902 and $1.11 in 1915.[29]

Added to dissatisfaction with plantation life and work was the discovery of more appealing opportunities in the Islands. Wages offered to the plantation recruits might have seemed very high before they left China, but before long many of them became convinced that they could earn more money, under more satisfying conditions, off the plantation. Plantation development itself, of course, stimulated other enterprises which multiplied job opportunities. Between 1882 and 1930, while the total number of gainfully employed persons in Hawaii rose from 39,531 to 154,270, sugar plantation employees increased only from 10,243 to 49,532. Off-plantation workers, therefore, had multiplied from nearly 30,000 to over 100,000 in this period. Chinese leaving the sugar plantations moved into these rapidly expanding occupational opportunities as laborers. Eventually many of them became entrepreneurs who themselves employed migrant laborers.

The Plantation as Haven

Even with the general movement of Chinese workers off the plantations, several hundred Chinese did remain there for many years, continuously or intermittently, and some of them never left. Ten years after the final Chinese importations in 1897 there were still more than 3,000 Chinese sugar plantation workers, and twenty years afterward more than 2,000.[30] As late as 1930 some 570 alien Chinese remained on sugar plantation payrolls. A survey in March 1936 of the Chinese clients of the Old Age Department of a Honolulu social agency showed that 78 of the 490 men on relief reported that they had been employed on sugar plantations for twenty years or more. Several plantations continued to care for their old Chinese laborers who were no longer able to work after having spent most of their adult years in the fields or sugar mills.

Aside from the tiny minority who worked into preferred positions on the plantations, many of those who remained were the more improvident, less capable, less ambitious migrants who found in the paternalistic plantation system a degree of security and protection they could not find elsewhere in the competitive Island community. In 1930 George N. Wilcox told the writer about an old Chinese retainer on his plantation:

> I don't know just when Ahee came to Hawaii, but he came here from California. I remember that he was with us in 1880; when I came back from the legislature that year I was going about the various camps on the plantation, and as I came along one of the water ditches, there was Ahee lying on the ground, kicking his feet up in the air like some baby. He has been with me ever since. He must be nearly eighty years old now.
>
> He has lived up at P—— camp for the last fifty years and in all that time, up till four years ago, he had never been down to Lihue, some four miles away. Four years ago some of the men took him down to Lihue to show him how the town had changed since 1880. He's still a "water luna" up in that section of the plantation.

An elderly Chinese, living in a Chinese society building in one of the sugar-growing areas of Hawaii in 1935, admitted to being an opium smoker. He told about his life in Hawaii through an interpreter:

> Chan says that he is about sixty years old and that he has not had any work for over a year now. He wishes he could get work to do. He receives about six dollars a month from the relief funds, through the Chinese woman at the Fook Yum Tong.
>
> Chan came to Hawaii in 1897 from Hoi Ping district as a contract laborer on the sugar plantations. He worked on the sugar plantations for over thirty-five years but never saved any money. Chan thought

the work on the plantation was not too hard for the pay he got. The money, however, was always spent in having a good time, and now he is old, has no money, cannot go back to his village in China, has nothing to live on here except what he gets from relief funds.

Chan has never been to Honolulu since he came to Hawaii thirty-eight years ago. He hears that it is now a big city. Of course, he has never made a visit back to China. Nor has he received any letters from the home village for several years. He has not written any letters to relatives either, for they expect him to send them money when he writes. He does not know whether his father and mother are still living or not; he was a younger son in the family and never married. His life, he says, has been wasted. "Take the advice of an old man and don't do the same thing."[31]

Another improvident plantation worker gave his life history to a Hawaii-born Chinese social worker in 1936:

Lum Tai was born in Lung Doo, Chung Shan district, in the year 1873. He was the second child in a family of six children. Early in childhood he had been taught to till the soil. The family was too poor to send any of the children to school. . . . His father urged him to come to the Hawaiian Islands to work so that money could be sent home to provide better care for the younger children. The family had heard through returning laborers that living conditions were better with good pay and shorter hours. It was Lum's intention to return some time to his native village and buy himself a wife and settle down to the life of a Chinese farmer. Taking all the money the family could get together, which meant much sacrifice on the part of his father, he paid his passage on a steamer from Hongkong to Honolulu. He had forty-two dollars in American money upon his arrival.

Soon after landing in the Islands he received a letter from his father stating that he had been married by proxy. He knew who the woman was, but as was the Chinese custom, the matchmaking was done by friends of both families. The woman died a few months after the marriage ceremony.

After spending a few weeks in Honolulu, he went to the sugar planters' employment agency and was immediately given work at W—— plantation, where he signed a three-year contract. He worked in the fields and received nineteen dollars[?] a month, plus a "turnout" bonus. Just about this time large groups of Chinese laborers were drifting to the —————— Sugar Co. because the arrangement of the camps was better and because of the laxity of the camp police in matters of gambling and opium smoking. He followed suit and got a job at that plantation, remaining there, off and on, for the past thirty years. Lum applied at the plantation for a pension but was refused because his work record is poor. He has done only an average of twelve days of work per month for the past five years. He was described as not dependable and oftentimes more independent than the management liked. The plantation social worker stated that she knew the man and considered him as being of the vagrant type. He will try and get by with what he can as long as he can. . . .

Lum claims that he has no insurance, does not belong to any Chinese society, has no other resources. He is without relatives in the Territory or in China. Arrangements were made to transfer the man to the agency's boarding home for aged Chinese men in Honolulu.[32]

New Opportunities

At the end of his contract period the ambitious Chinese who came to Hawaii as a contract laborer to make his fortune was a free man in a land of opportunity. The next chapters consider the occupational adjustments, patterns of economic enterprise, forms of settlement, and occupational movements of the migrants who left the sugar plantation labor force, as well as those who were never a part of it.

CHAPTER 3
On the Rural Frontier

SINCE Hawaii's primary attraction for the nineteenth-century Chinese migrants was the chance it offered them to improve their personal and family fortunes, thousands of them were alert to the opportunities offered by Hawaii's open resources. They undertook a large number and variety of enterprises and in doing so expanded the frontier economy beyond the limits of its development by the politically and economically more influential Caucasians.

Chinese Rice Plantations

As the first plantation labor group to be imported into Hawaii, the early Chinese lived and worked under conditions that would not be tolerated by Hawaii's workers today. Yet they had one significant advantage: arriving at a time when the Hawaiians were rapidly declining in numbers and there were relatively few other foreigners to compete with them, Chinese had the chance to enter, almost unhindered, a number of occupations for which their experience and skills fitted them. The most important of these occupations for several decades was rice production.

Rice growing was the basic agricultural activity in the delta regions of Kwangtung province from which nearly all the migrants came, and most of them were familiar with the age-old methods of rice production. Climatic and other agricultural conditions were even more favorable for rice production in Hawaii than in the immigrants' home districts. Land easily convertible into rice fields was readily available, since along with the depopulation of Hawaiian districts had gone a decline in the cultivation of taro, a crop the Hawaiians raised by wet-farming methods in low-lying or terraced patches. Rice growing had been started in 1858 by H. Holstein, horticulturist of the Royal Hawaiian Agricultural Society, and Caucasian rice planters were able in 1862 to export about three hundred tons of cleaned rice. Chinese moved into the industry and developed it rapidly. They were responsible for making rice production the second most important source of income in Hawaii's economy through most of the rest of the nineteenth century.[1]

As migrants intent upon accumulating wealth, Chinese would not have grown rice in Hawaii for mere subsistence as in China; they grew it for a market. The rapid growth of the Chinese immigrant population on the Pacific Coast of North America (United States, Canada, and Mexico) created a demand which Hawaii could supply more profitably than could any other rice-growing area of the time. Increasing numbers of Asian immigrant groups in Hawaii also brought about a large local demand. During the 1860s Chinese growers introduced the Chinese varieties of rice in greatest demand on the Pacific Coast and, for nearly half a century, virtually monopolized rice production in Hawaii.[2]

Within a few years after Chinese entered the industry, those parts of the Islands suitable for the crop were in rice production. Abandoned taro lands were taken over, swamps and marshes were reclaimed, tiny terraces were built far up ravines. By 1875 about 1,000 acres were in rice, mostly on Oahu. This total area had risen to 7,420 acres by 1890; to 9,130 by 1900; to 9,425 by 1909.[3] Frank Damon, in his account of "Tours among the Chinese" in 1882, described the rice growing he observed on Oahu, Kauai, Maui, and Hawaii and the transformation of the land by the industrious Chinese migrants. On traveling west toward Ewa from Honolulu, he remarks:

> Though there are but twelve or fourteen thousand of this race scattered over our Islands, no very great number, still when you come to consider that they are nearly all strong, healthy working men, in the prime of life, possessed of all the "push" and energy and tireless industry, for which these people are famous you can form some idea of how even this number must make themselves felt in this kingdom. All are at work, in motion on the road, in the field. . . .
>
> A few miles out from town the rice plantations begin, and form a fringe bordering the shore for a long distance. This is the season for planting the rice, and the men are busy in the marshy fields from early morning till evening. The wide expanses lying at the foot of the valleys are just now beginning to be covered with the tender shoots of

the rice, which in a few weeks will grow into a swaying luxuriant mass of verdure. It requires a steady hand and considerable balancing to run along the narrow foot paths separating the fields, for every available inch of ground seems to be utilized. . . .

But for the Chinese, Ewa would be indeed a desolate place. The natives seem to have disappeared from the face of the land. But the former nationality have entered in most emphatically to possess the land and their rice fields stretch in every direction. The large native Church stands sad and solitary on the hill, a mute and eloquent reminder of other days.[4]

Land for rice growing was generally acquired peacefully, although there were occasional fights between Chinese rice planters and Hawaiian taro cultivators, or between different groups of Chinese, over such matters as water rights.[5] Some Hawaiians had an interest in the rice industry because they could rent abandoned taro lands or other unused land to Chinese rice growers—leases might bring as much as thirty-five dollars an acre annually. The large sugar plantations also subleased land that was unsuitable for sugar to rice growers.

As rice production prospered, a plantation system developed which differed from both the rice economy of the Chinese village and the sugar plantation system. Indicative of the sojourner outlook and dominant profit motive was the temporary character of most of the ventures. Little effort was made, at first, to buy the land, even when that was possible: land was usually leased. The general flimsiness of the buildings on the rice plantations showed that at the outset the rice planter did not expect to settle permanently on the land.

Unlike the sugar plantations, rice plantations were usually small and made up of tiny patches. They averaged twenty-five to thirty acres, although a big planter might control a few hundred acres. Chinese methods of rice growing required insignificant amounts of capital for equipment as compared with the huge investments which became necessary on the increasingly mechanized sugar plantations. Cultivation was intensive and called more for painstaking handwork than for machines. Even transportation was customarily handled by the Chinese laborer and his carrying pole rather than by animal or machine. A number of Chinese pooling their small savings could therefore undertake to raise rice.

Moreover, rice plantations did not require highly trained and highly paid managers. Little of the work demanded any more skill or knowledge than the average immigrant had acquired in his own home village. Nevertheless, the rice industry shared with the sugar industry the problem of getting an adequate labor supply. As early as the 1860s Chinese entrepreneurs were importing laborers for both types of agriculture. Some labor for rice cultivation was obtained through government assistance. From 1874 to 1877 Chulan & Co. and other Chinese firms secured financial advances from the government in order to bring in laborers—with the agreement that these firms would try to get the men to pay back the money advanced.

Another source of workers was the sugar plantation labor supply. Some Chinese who came to Hawaii under indenture to sugar plantations bought releases from their contracts with money supplied by Chinese employers. Others deserted during their periods of contract.[6] Planters often suspected that deserters and their subsequent Chinese employers had prearranged to use the sugar plantation indenture system as a device to secure free passage to Hawaii for the laborer. The social distance at the time between Chinese on rice plantations and other ethnic groups in the Islands, except Hawaiians, tended to protect deserters from detection. Most commonly, however, Chinese laborers went into the rice industry after fulfilling their contracts on the sugar plantations.

"Free" migrants, those who did not come in under written contracts, were an important source of laborers for the rice industry. Most of these free migrants were heavily indebted to relatives, to Chinese brokers, or to Chinese employers in Hawaii. Excerpts from documents on Chinese in the 1930s illustrate how this free migration was related to the labor force on rice plantations:

> Probably the oldest survivor of the days of huge rice plantations and mills in Ewa is Ho Yee [born in 1851]. He is seventy-nine years old and is a member of that group of Chinese immigrants who came here in the seventies as independent laborers. Under no obligations of contract, except to pay off the steamer fare, paid for them by village relatives already here, Ho Yee and his brother Ho Leong, when they first arrived here in 1876, plunged into the work they were most prepared for. . . . In Ewa, Ho Yee remained fifty-one years doing rice mill work, first as laborer, then luna, and in later years as manager. His brother remained in the city to do business. It was only six years ago that Ho Yee moved into town for the better opportunities for work and education it had to offer for his children.[7]

> Wong Chiu was born in 1871 near Shekki, Chung Shan district. He was the oldest child and had three sisters and two brothers. The family

owned its own home, but the boys all had to work at herding water buffaloes, and later as laborers in rice fields near the village. Wong had no opportunity to secure any formal education. Wong's father left the family in the village and went to Sydney, Australia, to seek a "fortune." He lived there many years, returning home when he was about seventy. Wong Chiu, after listening to many immigrants who returned to the district, decided that a better living could be made in Hawaii. With money which he secured from his father he came to the Islands in 1895 with a group of immigrants. His passage cost him sixty-three dollars gold. His first employment was on a rice plantation in Manoa Valley, which was managed by a "cousin" of his. He worked on this plantation for three years at thirteen dollars per month plus board and lodging. Then he went to Kauai to help start a rice plantation leased by Wong Sang. . . .[8]

Lum Kwan's native village was in Lung Doo, Chung Shan district. In 1891, at the age of twenty-one, he came to Hawaii, his brother having sent him money for the passage. He went to work for his brother who had a share in a rice plantation at Moanalua, Oahu. At the end of six years, the brother sold his interest in the plantation and they both returned to China. During the year Lum was there, he was married to a girl who was then eighteen years of age. A daughter who was born has now married but has no children. The wife still lives in the village, although Lum has not seen her since 1899. Upon his return to Hawaii, Lum again went to work on a rice plantation.[9]

While the workers' needs may not have been supplied any more amply on the rice plantations than on the sugar plantations, they were undoubtedly handled in a way that was closer to the migrants' customs and expectations. Manager and workers sometimes lived together in a single building; some large plantations had a building where the manager lived with his family along with a few frame structures housing the laborers, a cook house, and the mill. Frank Damon described one rice plantation he visited in Honouliuli, Oahu, in 1882:

A company of fifty or sixty men assembled in the main room of one of the houses. . . . This was one of the largest plantations we visited. Sometimes two or three men only, have a few fields which they cultivate for themselves, and we often came upon houses where there were eight or ten men working their own land. But the larger plantations are owned by merchants in Honolulu, who have a manager acting for them. The houses are destitute of all but the barest necessities of life, except those of some of the more wealthy planters. The woodwork is unpainted. The beds are arranged around the rooms like berths in a ship. Sometimes these are quite prettily ornamented with a border above the netting of Chinese silk, on which graceful sprays of flowers are painted and Chinese characters written. In the center of the room is a large table where the meals are taken in common. They never need lack for rice, and of this most excellent article of diet they seem never to weary. In many of the houses we saw large pictures of their favorite God, with joss-sticks sometimes standing before it. As this was shortly after their "New Year," the vermilion colored visiting cards, received at that season, were arranged in rows on the walls. Over all the doors and windows were pasted slips of the same brilliant paper, on which a variety of propitious wishes for the occupants of the house and their visitors were written. Many of these were in reference to becoming rich, enjoying length of days, etc. One was, I thought, a very pleasant one to have over any door. "Out-going. In-coming. Peace!"[10]

The number of workers on even the larger rice plantations was smaller than on the sugar plantations; all the workers would be Chinese, often relatives, *heung li* ("fellow villagers"), or migrants from the same small district of South China, all speaking the same dialect. Life was not so highly regimented; instead of being controlled by rules and overseers, police and judges, men on the rice plantations were involved in a set of mutual obligations built up from the closeness in which they lived. Desire for gain was shared by rice planters and workers alike, but personal ties tempered any tendencies to put the concerns of efficiency and profit before everything else.

On some rice plantations the workers were hired at stipulated wages with board and shelter—wages which tended to average about the same as those offered for day labor on the sugar plantations. More commonly, however, rice plantation development, like so many other forms of economic enterprise by Chinese immigrants, was carried on by systems in which the workers shared cooperatively in the returns from the crop produced. The two most common systems were known among the Chinese as *fun kung* ("divide work") and *hop pun* ("partnership").[11] The former was a modified "cropper" arrangement between a landlord and an organized group of workers. A man wanting to undertake the job of manager would make an agreement with the landlord and gather together a group of laborers; or a group of men who wanted to undertake the raising of a crop of rice at a given place might select one of their number as a manager who would then work out an arrangement with the landlord. Apart from furnishing the land, which he might himself hold only on a lease, the landlord usually provided all the tools, machinery and draft animals. The agreement was usually concerned first of all with the ratio at which the crop or income was to be divided at the end of the season. For superior rice land the landlord might demand 60 percent of the crop; on less choice land, 50 percent. If fertilizer had to be used, he might furnish 60 percent of it. He agreed to make reasonable advances of money to the men as the season progressed, part of which would be necessary for the men's food and other living expenses, part to be sent to relatives in China. The agreement might also stipulate a minimum price the landlord would guarantee to pay for each bag of paddy produced. In the earlier days of the industry and in the smaller deals, such agreements were only verbal or recorded informally in the Chinese language. Later, after bitter experiences taught some of the Chinese migrants that they could not always trust their countrymen in Hawaii, agreements were drawn up in contracts recognized in the local courts.

The laborers who were partners under this system were usually organized rather loosely under the manager who made decisions after discussion with his partners. Since all were taking a chance on the success or failure of the crop, the manager could not be dictatorial, but he assumed responsibility for assigning partners to jobs such as cooking, gardening, caring for the draft animals, and raising pigs and poultry. Unless there was a bookkeeper he recorded expenses, advances to each man, the days each man failed to work. He hired extra day laborers as needed during planting and harvesting. He might also be responsible for checking the irrigation and drainage of the fields and protecting the grain from birds, as well as supervising the harvest and disposing of the crop.

At the end of the season the group and the landlord made a settlement in accord with their agreement. Joint expenses were deducted from the group's share of the income together with an extra payment to the manager. In larger undertakings with an assistant manager and bookkeeper, these men also received extra payments, smaller than that of the manager. The partners divided the remainder equally among themselves, each man receiving his share after his advances had been deducted.

The *fun kung* system became more common after Annexation when no more laborers could be obtained from China and those in the Islands became less willing to work as day laborers and more insistent upon sharing the profits. In the later years of the rice industry, when there was less trust in an immigrant's word—and also more risk, as the industry declined, that a partner might try to evade his share of losses—it became common to require each man to make a deposit, usually twenty-five dollars, when he joined the partnership. A man who quit lost his deposit.

In the *hop pun* system a few Chinese, usually not more than three or four, would set up an independent rice farm. Each man advanced his share of the money necessary for the undertaking; shares might range from one hundred to several hundred dollars, according to the size of the venture. One man, as spokesman, would arrange for the lease of the land, often through some Chinese agent or rice factor. The men would provide their own food, shelter, the necessary tools and perhaps a draft animal, seed, fertilizer, and so forth, and would perform the labor involved in producing the crop. At the end of the season they would divide the earnings proportionately. These small independent farms, which were likely to lie on marginal rice land, were rather like the small rice farms in South China—more of the work was done by hand than on the larger plantations.

Some Chinese migrants used rice plantation employment as a stepping stone to more profitable occupations; others returned to China after a few years on the rice plantations; others shifted to one type of work after another—leaving the rice fields for the sugar or pineapple plantations, for some other type of agriculture being undertaken by a Chinese migrant, for work in the towns (often, however, returning to rice cultivation). And still others spent a lifetime in Hawaii in the rice industry as laborers or moving up to the status of a rice planter. Ho Yee, whose experience was referred to earlier, spent fifty-one years in the rice industry, rising from ordinary laborer to manager. Other migrants who spent years on rice plantations in Hawaii were less successful, as the following excerpts from three life histories obtained in the 1930s show:

> Yuen Bow's father had been a plantation laborer in Hawaii. In 1888 Yuen Bow left his village near Nam Long and came to Hawaii. For three months he worked on a rice plantation at Heeia, Oahu. Then followed eight years of labor on four different sugar plantations on Oahu and Kauai, where he earned from fifteen to seventeen dollars a month. Several years were spent on a Kauai rice plantation, with occasional work on a nearby sugar plantation during the latter's "grinding season." A little over a year was passed on still another Kauai sugar plantation at eighteen dollars a month. Yuen returned to Honolulu and

finally secured a job in connection with a fish pond which a Chinese operated in Pearl Harbor. Here he received twenty-two dollars per month, board and lodging. He left this position to work for the Hawaiian Pineapple Company at Wahiawa, at $2.50 per day. At the end of two years and two months he quit and loafed for a time in Honolulu. His last work was with another pineapple plantation where he received $1.50 per day. For the past five years Yuen has been a casual laborer in Honolulu.[12]

Chang Wah was born in 1866 in Lung Doo, Chung Shan district. He was the sixth son in a family of fourteen children. Early in childhood he had heard his parents speak of selling the children in the family. . . . As soon as he was old enough, which was ten years, he started working in the neighbors' rice fields. . . . When he heard of the better conditions in Hawaii, in 1890, he . . . approached his parents and other members of the family, suggesting that they pool their resources so that he could be sent here to make more money in order to make life easier for those at home. He was given a hundred dollars which, however, was not obtained until several water buffalo and many of their chickens had been sold. Buying his steamer ticket, he arrived here in 1890. . . .

En route to Hawaii Chang Wah met several other Changs on the boat and through them he heard that a Chang from his village was operating a rice plantation at Mokuleia, Oahu. He started with this man as a laborer at nine dollars a month, plus board and lodging, and he remained with him for ten years. The work was hard but he felt at the time that he was well paid. On this plantation there were no beasts of burden to do the hard work, and he and the other men had to pull the carts themselves and carry the rice from the field to the threshing floor. His relative finally sold out his business and returned to China. Chang Wah then worked for another planter, at Waialua, earning nine dollars a month for the next five years.

Wages on the sugar plantation seemed more attractive, so Chang went to work for the ——— Plantation on Oahu, working as a cane cutter and doing piece contract work for which he averaged about a dollar a day. The work was very hard, but he managed to hold on for ten years, after which, due to his diminishing strength, he was forced to seek lighter work with the rice planters near Waipahu.

By this time he had saved a little money, and entering into a partnership with a Chinese friend, started a rice plantation of their own. As a result of this partnership, which lasted fifteen years, Chang enjoyed considerable financial independence and came to be regarded by the Chinese in the district as a "rich man," since . . . at that time any Chinese was called "rich" who had accumulated a few thousand dollars. The decline in the price of rice, however, forced him out of business and caused him to lose all his money. Chang's chief regret now is that he did not sell out and return to China when he had enough money to have lived comfortably for the rest of his days. He is now unable to make a living . . . and must depend upon relief.[13]

Pang Gum arrived from Lung Doo, Chung Shan district, in 1888, paying his own passage. For a year and a half he worked for a sugar plantation on Oahu for $11.50 a month. For at least twenty-five years Pang worked for a number of rice plantations, among them being Hop Suck Wai, Chu Chong Wai, See Sung Wai, and Hee Hoi. Leaving rice growing, he worked for a pineapple plantation on Oahu for three years, averaging $1.50 a day. Since his last regular employment Pang has been a transient rice laborer in the Koolau district, working about nine months out of the year, spending the other three months in "gambling, drinking, or smoking opium."[14]

Hundreds of men like these three did not establish families in Hawaii. The Chinese who became the eminent rice planters, interested often in other forms of agriculture and in business as well as in rice production, commonly married and reared families. Wong Loy was one of these:

Wong Loy was born in Lung Doo, Chung Shan district, in 1846. A brother who preceded him to Hawaii became a partner in a Chinese firm which was among the most active in the development of the sugar and rice industries, particularly during the sixties, seventies, and eighties. Wong Loy came to Hawaii in 1876 and went immediately into rice cultivation. Rice growing remained his main concern for the next half a century, and before his retirement he had bought considerable rice lands on Oahu and had for many years owned and operated rice plantations and rice mills. Together with two brothers, Wong Loy developed the growing of rice near Kaneohe, on windward Oahu. In 1897, after twenty-two years in Kaneohe, Wong Loy sold out both rice plantations and rice mills and moved to Heeia, Oahu, where he bought rice lands. He did not give up rice farming and rice milling until about 1923.

In 1890, Wong Loy, then well past forty, made a trip to China and on his return to Hawaii brought his bride with him. Mr. and Mrs. Wong have reared ten children, seven boys and three girls. The children received part of their education in Honolulu, although the family continued to live at Heeia. Some of the children were sent to college, at least one of them to a university on the mainland. The oldest son became secretary of a Chinese firm which for three decades, among other things, operated a rice mill in Honolulu and acted as a rice factor. The other sons have become established in other businesses and in the professions.[15]

Chinese agents and factors played a significant part in rice plantation development, much like that of agents and factors in the sugar industry. The export of rice produced in the early days provided opportunities for middlemen who helped the rice planters dispose of their crop. Sing Chong Co. of Honolulu, founded in the 1870s, became one of the most important of these factors. At one time this firm handled the rice production on about four thousand acres, about half the acreage in rice on Oahu, as the agent for planters or managing its own rice plantations. It was also agent for rice growers on other islands, including Leong Pah On, the largest rice grower on Kauai. At the same time it was serving as agent to Chinese sugar planters and, as one of the largest importers of general merchandise, was agent and supplier for many Chinese stores throughout the Islands.[16] Later, when more rice was consumed in the Islands than was exported, rice distribution in Hawaii was handled by both Chinese and Caucasian firms. Large quantities were sold directly to the Caucasian-controlled sugar factors which supplied rice to Caucasian-owned plantations for their Asian laborers. Chinese stores on the plantations and in the villages and towns were the main distributing points for the cleaned rice.

Chinese rice factors made additional profits by processing rice—hulling, cleaning, and polishing. The rice mills and granaries needed for these processes required investments which few planters could, or dared, make. The first rice mills were built during the 1860s, one by a Caucasian, another by Chun Fong. In 1873 Chulan & Co. put up a water-power mill which could turn out two tons of cleaned and polished rice daily.[17] Steam-driven mills which were built later were located more conveniently on Honolulu's waterfront. Chinese-owned City Mill, today one of Honolulu's largest lumber and builders' supply firms, was organized in 1899 to set up a rice mill as one of its major investments. As late as 1929 it was milling 25,000 to 30,000 bags of paddy from independent rice growers on Oahu as well as handling paddy from growers on Kauai.[18] Outside Honolulu many smaller mills were built in the chief rice-growing areas, usually under the control of Chinese rice factors and large rice planters.

The factors controlled several rice plantations directly and many others indirectly. Indirect control was exercised mainly through leases on rice lands and financing of rice growers in return for a lien on the crop. Financing was done directly with the growers or indirectly through credit to stores which made advances of goods and money to the growers.

Two accounts of rice agents and factors illustrate the careers of migrants associated with the development of this industry in Hawaii. First the career of Young Ah In:

> Young Ah In (Y. Ahin) came to Hawaii from Chung Shan district in 1872 at the age of nineteen. For a while he worked as a truck gardener near Honolulu. Rice cultivation appeared to be more profitable, however, so he started the Tung Sun Wai Plantation at Palama with a number of relatives who had come from the same village. Young is said to have imported the first pair of water buffaloes from China to use as draft animals in the rice fields, being financed in his venture by a Haole [Caucasian] whose Hawaiian princess-wife owned the land which Young leased for rice.
>
> From this beginning his interests in rice growing increased until he controlled several hundred acres of rice, including about seven hundred acres at Waikiki and Pawaa alone. Rice plantations which he controlled or for which he was agent were located on Oahu at Palama, Waikiki, Moanalua, Halawa, Waipio, Kalauao, Waipaau, and Kawai-hapai; and on Kauai, at Hanalei. Two rice mills were established, one in Palama and the other at Ewa. During the eighties Young organized Chin Wo Co. in the Chinatown of Honolulu, a firm through which the rice was exported or distributed to stores throughout the Hawaiian Islands. This firm was one of the chief Chinese stores in Honolulu for several decades and did an immense importing business, especially of Chinese provisions and merchandise. Young also owned several smaller stores in the vicinity of his rice plantations as well as one in Hilo, Hawaii.
>
> Young's wealth was increased by real estate activities, the building and renting of stores and homes, located in districts in Honolulu into which the Chinese were moving. At one time these rentals were said to amount to about two thousand dollars per month. In his later years Young held interests in many other businesses and enterprises and was once reputed to be among the wealthiest of the Chinese in Hawaii.[19]

Another leading Chinese figure in the rice industry was Ching Shai:

Ching was a native of On Ting village, Chung Shan district, where he was born in 1869. Several years before his birth an uncle, Wong Kwai, came to Hawaii where with several Chings he formed a partnership which became the eminent firm of Chulan & Co. Starting as a merchandising establishment this company developed an immense importing and exporting, wholesaling and retailing business. In addition it developed considerable interests in sugar plantations and became one of the largest rice factors in the Islands.

Ching Shai came to Hawaii in 1882 and went to work as a field laborer at ten dollars a month on a sugar plantation in Kohala, Hawaii, which at that time was being operated by Chulan Kee. Two years later he was made a field foreman, with a raise in pay to twelve dollars per month. His uncle found him a promising youth and gave him hopes of rapid promotion in the firm. In order to prepare for this possibility, he attended a night school conducted by missionary workers in Kohala. His immediate interest in the school was to learn English, since the Chulan Company's plantation sold all its sugarcane to a nearby mill owned by Americans.

Two years later he was taken into the office as a bookkeeper and arrangements were made so that he could attend day school and do his work in the office at night. Much of the money he earned during those early years was sent back to the village to help his widowed mother and two sisters.

Late in 1890 Ching became a naturalized citizen of the Hawaiian kingdom and shortly afterward he married a Chinese-Hawaiian girl, the daughter of one of the assistant managers of the Chulan plantation.

After ten years in Hawaii, Ching visited China to see his mother, who was ill, and to transact business for his uncle's firm. During his stay, marriages were arranged for his two sisters. A marriage was also arranged for Ching. Upon his return to Hawaii in 1894, his Chinese wife was left in the village with his mother.

Ching found that during his absence the plantation had been sold to the American firm which owned the mill, and his uncle was heavily engaged in the rice industry on Oahu. Wong, who was getting along in years and wanted to retire, asked Ching to take over the management of his rice plantations and rice mill at Punaluu, Oahu. The industry was prosperous and in addition to sending money to his mother and wife in China, Ching was able to put aside considerable savings. He opened a small grocery store in the Palama district, carrying mainly Chinese goods which were sold to the large settlement of Chinese farmers there. A trusted elderly Chinese man was put in charge of the store. Some years later another store was opened in the Kakaako section of Honolulu. Provisions and merchandise for the stores were im-

ported directly from China together with similar goods which were ordered for the Chulan Company's rice plantations, some of which were
located on Oahu, others on Kauai.

Ching's largest and most successful undertaking was the establishment of the Oahu Rice Mill, in Honolulu's Chinatown, in 1908. Four
relatives were the other partners in the company. Starting on a moderate scale, the firm rapidly grew until it became one of the controlling
rice factors in the whole industry. In an effort to deal more effectively
with problems facing the rice industry in Hawaii, Ching became one of
the founders and most tireless workers in the Anglo-Chinese Rice Merchants' Association. In 1915 he made a trip at his own expense to
Washington, D.C., to plead for a change in the immigration laws enabling the entrance of Chinese who would work on the rice plantations.
During World War I, he served as a member of the rice-distributing
commission. His death occurred in 1919 while on a trip to China with
his family.[20]

A government official who surveyed the rice industry in 1890
estimated that during the busy seasons one Chinese was employed
for each two acres of rice, concluding that 3,710 men were employed on the approximately 7,420 acres in rice cultivation. Shortly
after the turn of the century 5,643 Chinese were reported to be engaged in rice production.[21] This was at or near the peak of Chinese
employment in this industry. After 1909 rice cultivation in Hawaii
declined rapidly; from 9,424 acres in rice in 1909, there were only
5,801 in 1919.[22] In the 1916 petition of the United Chinese Society to
the U.S. Congress to allow 30,000 Chinese laborers to enter Hawaii,
it was said that 7,098 acres of rice land had been abandoned for lack
of labor.[23] Even if Congress had acceded to the request, however,
competition from rice agribusiness in California would ultimately
have forced the additional laborers to go into other occupations or
return to China. By 1933 over 45,000 tons of rice were imported
from mainland United States—almost thirty times the Hawaiian rice
crop that year, and about twice the size of the largest amount Hawaii
had ever produced in one year.

By the late 1930s rice growing in Hawaii, so far as the Chinese
were concerned, was mainly a thing of the past. A few old Chinese
men, here and there, could still be seen planting, cultivating, harvesting, even flailing rice in the ancient way. A few believed that the old
days when Chinese made so much money in rice would return. In
1936 one elderly Chinese rice planter said that he had learned at a

Chinese temple that by 1939 rice would again be profitable; incense burned daily before the shrine in his house. In the meantime, he was trying his luck at raising taro.

Even before competition from California rice had made rice growing in Hawaii unprofitable, Chinese rice planters had been subleasing or selling their land to Japanese rice growers. A 1932 survey showed that 62 percent of the Hawaii-grown rice was being cultivated by Japanese. At first the Japanese sold their paddy to Chinese-owned rice mills; then, gradually, they took over the mills too. Rice land that Chinese had leased from sugar plantations went mostly into sugar production. Some rice land was used for taro growing and truck gardening.[24] Chinese who had been fortunate or foresighted enough to buy land for their rice fields or mills and to hold on to it eventually found it profitable to put the land to nonagricultural uses—especially land in the Waikiki, Manoa, Palama, and Kakaako sections of Honolulu and areas bordering on Pearl Harbor.

Other Forms of Rural Enterprise

No other agricultural activity was so lucrative for the Chinese as the rice industry, which in prosperous years produced a crop valued at more than $3 million. Nevertheless, hundreds of Chinese immigrants engaged in many other agricultural enterprises throughout the Islands. Near the towns, along the shore, in the lowlands, up in the valleys, far up on the cooler, more temperate-climate slopes of the mountains, the "ubiquitous bands" of Chinese farmers sought to wrest from the land the wealth which had lured so many of them to Hawaii.

Plantation systems with agents and factors were developed in connection with some of these activities, much as in the rice industry but on a smaller scale. Some enterprises producing export commodities were brief episodes in the general economic expansion, exploited temporarily and abandoned when the resources or market failed. In 1847 Chinese farmers produced twenty thousand barrels of Irish potatoes on leased land at Kula, on the cool slopes of Haleakala, for export to California; but by the mid-1850s the potato boom had faded.[25] In the 1850s other Chinese who had found an edible mushroom growing on dead tree branches in rainy mountain areas began exporting this delicacy to Chinese buyers in California and later to China. This enterprise lasted until the late 1880s; at its peak in 1864 nearly 180 tons, valued at about $35,000, were exported.[26] About the same period Chinese were also involved in a brisk trade in *pulu*, a fibrous material secured from the tree fern and certain other ferns and used especially in mattresses until it was replaced by cotton.

A few other export commodities lasted longer and played a larger part in the fortunes of the Chinese. Two of these were coffee and bananas. Throughout the nineteenth century most attempts to grow coffee commercially in Hawaii, nearly all failures, were made by Caucasians using Hawaiian, Chinese, and Japanese labor. Gangs of Chinese laborers contracted to clear land for coffee planting. An 1898 report states that "the prevailing labor is Japanese, though natives, Chinamen, and Portuguese are employed. . . . I found the planters preferred the Chinese to the Japanese, because they are more tractable and work better without overseeing."[27]

By 1910 most coffee production had become concentrated in the Kona section of the island of Hawaii; independent farmers, mostly Japanese migrants and their families, were handling from five to fifteen acres of coffee on leased land. Most of the storekeepers in Kona at this time were Chinese and a mutual arrangement developed in which the farmers, low on capital, got their goods on credit from the storekeepers, paying off their debts at the time of harvest.[28] Into this setup came the Hawaii Coffee Mill, established about 1906 by Chinese partners in the Wing Hing Company, an import-export firm in Honolulu's Chinatown. One of Wing Hing Company's main businesses became that of roasting, packaging, and marketing coffee; in 1934 the firm was renamed Wing Coffee Company "to give the cosmopolitan buyers an easier time with the name."[29] A branch of the firm was opened in Hong Kong to assist in the import-export business. Hawaii Coffee Mill, with its parent firm in Honolulu, was an important link in the chain of business arrangements. Like other coffee mills of Kona it also supplied goods on credit to stores in Kona dealing directly with coffee farmers—with the lien on the crop bringing the green coffee to the mill and in turn to the coffee roasting and marketing firm. Hawaii Coffee Mill, which was only one of several competing mills, went out of business in the early 1970s, although coffee is still packed and sold under the Wing label.

Like coffee, bananas were at one time grown in Hawaii for export as well as for local consumption, and for several years Chinese were active in producing, exporting, and distributing this fruit locally. Chinese migrants, familiar with banana growing in their home villages,[30] were employed as laborers on banana plantations established in the 1880s and 1890s by Caucasian planters who were taking advantage of the demand for bananas by California's growing urban population. Nearly 20,000 bunches were exported in 1880; this output increased to more than 120,000 bunches in 1896 and 280,000 in 1915.[31] Competition from Central American producers brought a decline in Hawaii's banana exports, but this was more than made up for by the local demand as Hawaii itself was rapidly growing in population. Chinese were employed by Caucasian export firms as well as by Caucasian-owned banana plantations. Lum Hoon, who worked for one of the most successful of the banana exporters, E. L. Marshall, selected and marked the banana bunches in the fields on Oahu to be exported, saw that they were delivered to the warehouse in Honolulu in time to be loaded on ships for San Francisco, and supervised the work at the warehouse.[32] Most Chinese in the banana industry, however, simply leased plots of a few acres to grow bananas to be peddled from house to house or sold to local stores. By the 1920s banana production and marketing were being taken over largely by Japanese migrants and their families.

During the twentieth century pineapples have been Hawaii's second most important agricultural export and the pineapple industry the second largest employer of agricultural laborers. This industry developed after Annexation had cut off immigration of laborers from China, but a few hundred Chinese workers who had come in during the 1880s and 1890s did move from sugar to pineapple plantations during the early decades of this century. The boom in pineapple production which came with the development of mechanized canning procedures expanded the market of Chinese farmers who had been selling fresh fruit to local consumers, for now they could readily sell much larger quantities to Caucasian-owned canneries. Perhaps the most successful of these farmers was Au Young (also known as On Young), who came from Toi Shan district to Hawaii in 1897. By the 1920s, besides operating a general merchandise store at Wahiawa on Oahu, he was producing pineapples on several hundred acres in that area. He ultimately sold his pineapple holdings to California Packing Company for a reported $350,000, as this firm moved toward controlling enough plantation acreage to supply its pineapple cannery with all the fruit it could process.[33] The pineapple boom also resulted in one of the greatest business reverses experienced by Chinese migrants. A *wui (hui)* of Chinatown businessmen decided in

1919 to get a share in the pineapple boom by buying a cannery, obtaining control of several hundred acres of land, and growing pineapples for their cannery. These ventures failed and one man alone lost several hundred thousand dollars.[34]

Supplying the Local Market

As the Islands' population grew, Chinese migrants took over or developed other agricultural enterprises to meet local demands. One product in increasing demand was poi made from taro. The basic food in the Hawaiians' diet, it became popular among residents of other ethnic backgrounds. Almost as soon as poi became a marketable commodity, Chinese where active in cultivating taro, converting it into poi, and distributing it to the stores.

Small partnerships of Chinese, mostly working under the *fun kung* and *hop pun* systems, secured hundreds of acres of taro land which had been cultivated for centuries by Hawaiians and prepared new paddies on low land that had previously been of little value. Chinese taro raisers and poi manufacturers were on all the main islands, but most numerous on Oahu where the largest urban Hawaiian population lived.

Few data are available concerning the total production and value of this commodity. For the years immediately preceding World War I the annual output of taro was estimated at a value of from $400,000 to $500,000. In 1930, some 775 acres were in taro, with an output valued at $500,000 or more.

The following biographical sketch of a Chinese who rose from the position of a taro cultivator to "Taro King" illustrates the development of the taro industry by the Chinese and its relation to other enterprises undertaken by Chinese in Hawaii:

> Lum Yip Kee first came to Hawaii in 1884, at the age of nineteen, from Koon Fah village in Duck Doo, Chung Shan district. For three and a half years he worked as a taro planter in Manoa and Palolo valleys, sections of the Honolulu district which did not develop as residential areas of the city until many years later. Lum then returned to China in 1887 and shortly afterward was married. A few years were spent in Saigon, in connection with a Chinese firm there.
>
> At the age of twenty-seven, Lum returned to Hawaii and engaged again in the taro and poi business. During the next seven years he became the operator of two taro plantations, one in Manoa Valley on the

present site of the University of Hawaii, the other nearer the sea, in Moiliili district. Relatives and fellow villagers came from China and worked on his plantations. A "poi factory" was set up on the Moiliili taro plantation. An importing and general merchandise firm, Wing Tuck Chong, was also established with the main store in the Chinatown of Honolulu and with two outside branches. During the Chinatown fire following the 1899 plague, the main warehouse of the firm was destroyed at a loss of $30,000, only some $10,000 of which was returned by the government during the settlement of damage claims. About this time Lum made his second trip to China, in order to transact business with firms from whom he secured Chinese merchandise and to visit his wife and family. The latter finally came to Hawaii in 1902.

A new store was established in the Aala section of the old Chinatown. Being the only store in Honolulu run by a person from Koon Fah village, it became a popular gathering place for Chinese from this and the neighboring villages of Duck Doo district. Mrs. Lum was also of the Chang clan, which was the most powerful clan of the district, and many of the clan members had come to Hawaii. Later this store was moved into the heart of old Chinatown, on Maunakea Street, where in 1925 it was destroyed by fire.

In 1905, together with a Chinese who became one of the leading figures in the poi industry, Lum established the Oahu Poi Factory, by the 1930s the largest in the Territory. With other Honolulu Chinese, he also set up the Honolulu Poi Factory in 1913, and in 1915 founded the See Wo Poi Factory, which at one time was the largest in the Islands. Through these three large poi factories, Lum and his associates attained virtual control of the Honolulu poi market. Several hundred acres of taro land at one time were under his control, either directly or indirectly through financial advances to Chinese taro growers in return for a promise of their crop at harvest time. The taro lands which he controlled were located mainly in Manoa Valley, Palolo Valley, Moiliili—all in the Honolulu district—and at Kahaluu on windward Oahu.

Lum's interests were not limited, however, to the taro and poi business and to his stores. He acquired large interests in the rice industry. From 1913 to 1918 the Lung Doo Wai, which had large rice plantations and which acted also as a rice factor, was managed by Lum and Yee Yap, who after several years as a rice planter had become a prosperous merchant in Honolulu. Some seven hundred acres of rice land in the Waikiki area of Honolulu were under the control of the Lung Doo Wai, as well as other rice lands on Oahu. Lum became one of the organizers and directors of the Chinese American Bank in 1916; in 1922 he was the chief organizer of the Liberty Bank and served as its president for eight years. He was one of the founders and for years treasurer and director of the Aala Market, Ltd., where stalls were rented to Chinese and Japanese butchers, fish dealers, grocers, and fruit and vegetable dealers. Capital in this market was held by both Chinese and Japanese. Lum at one time was also treasurer of the Hawaii Suisan Kaisha, a Japanese fishing organization started in 1922, two years after the founding of the Aala Market. Other businesses in which Lum became especially interested included the Hawaii Sales Company (musical instruments), L. Koon Chan Building Co., Wai Yip Building Co., Toon Fat Building Co., Kauluwela Cottage Co., United Chinese Trust Co., and Lum Yip Kee, Ltd., the latter a real estate, investment, and holding corporation. Many acres of the land acquired for taro and rice farming within Honolulu later became extremely valuable in the family realty business as residential and commercial Honolulu extended into these areas.[35]

By the 1930s taro growing had been taken over largely by Japanese and Korean migrants, but Chinese continued to receive income from taro by leasing land to these new growers. During the thirties Chinese still controlled most of the poi factories and the marketing of poi; the poi factories, however, were subsequently taken over by others, mainly Japanese.

During the late 1800s and early 1900s Chinese throughout the Islands largely controlled the production and sale of fruits and vegetables which were marketed locally. Their truck farms, like the banana farms, were usually on small plots of land in various locations suited to the growing requirements of different plants. Many fruits and vegetables which Westerners desired could only be grown in cooler climates such as those of Kula, Maui and Waimea, Hawaii; others could be grown successfully in the warmer and wetter areas of the lowlands. In the latter districts Chinese farmers could also grow the vegetables and some of the fruits they had grown in their home villages, the demand for which increased as the Chinese population grew. In time, other Asians and ultimately residents of all ethnic identities in Hawaii incorporated many of these vegetables into their diets. Much the same sequence applied to the fruits which came into the market, such as litchis, longans, pomelos, white limes, kumquats, loquats, and Chinese varieties of mangoes and persimmons. Several flowers introduced from China were also grown and marketed commercially for lei-makers and florists—the Chinese jasmine (pikake), Chinese violet (pakalana), narcissus, lotus (and lotus root), and Chinese varieties of chrysanthemum and gardenia.[36]

These commodities were not usually marketed through Chinese factors or agents, since they required small capital and little credit; they did not have to be processed before marketing and were often sold by peddlers, frequently the farmers themselves, going from door to door. Nevertheless, storekeepers near truck-farming areas located far from consumer centers (which might be on other islands) commonly served as middlemen, giving credit as in the coffee industry.

Outside the towns Chinese found several other ways to try to make their fortune. Most widespread, on all the islands, was the raising and marketing of pigs, chickens, and ducks and the sale of chicken and duck eggs. A few with the necessary capital and initiative acquired ranch land on which they raised horses and mules for sale and produced beef cattle for the meat markets; still others prospered by operating dairies. Several hundred who came from coastal villages and had experience as fishermen went into this occupation, catching and peddling fish, eels, crabs, and lobsters. The more enterprising migrants eventually operated stalls in the fish markets, sometimes employing other migrants to do the fishing. Some, having more capital, bought or leased the fish ponds that had been built along the shores hundreds of years earlier by the Hawaiians and had fallen into disuse. These ponds were generally stocked with mullet—highly prized by Chinese and in demand in the Chinese restaurants.

In still other ways migrants tried to wrest a good living, if not a hoped-for fortune, from the resources of rural Hawaii: the agricultural lands, the mountains, the sea. Many of them failed; some succeeded for a while until the natural resources were exhausted or the markets disappeared; others got their start in these ventures and moved on to more lucrative and longer-lasting enterprises. The variety is quite impressive—it includes growing tobacco or cotton; making honey; producing *awa*, the narcotic drink used by Hawaiians and others; making firewood for sale to townspeople; digging wells; boring for artesian water; catching whales off the Kona coast; catching sharks off Oahu. One very successful enterprise developed when a Chinese businessman, who had acquired a ranch of several thousand acres for raising beef cattle, found an ohia forest on the property and made a large amount of money from logging operations.[37]

Table 2 gives some indication of the extent to which the Chinese worked at nonurban pursuits during the forty to fifty years when Chinese migrants were most involved in them.[38] These data do not differentiate between the migrant and Hawaii-born generations

Table 2
Chinese Men Engaged in Rural Occupations in Hawaii: 1884–1930

Year	Number of Chinese Male Agriculturists and Rural Laborers[a]	Number of Chinese Males Reporting Occupations	Percentage	Number of Chinese Employees on Sugar Plantations[b]
1884	13,200	—	—	5,600
1890	10,400	13,067	80	4,000
1896	13,300	16,610	80	6,000
1910	7,216	13,742	53	2,800
1920	5,026	11,110	45	2,300
1930	2,143	8,571	25	800

Note: Unless otherwise specified, data for this and subsequent tables are based on government census reports for the Hawaiian kingdom (prior to 1896), the Republic of Hawaii (1896), and the United States (from 1900 onwards). Classification of occupational data reported in tables prior to 1940 was compiled by the writer and Dr. Doris L. Glick. Since comparability of totals from census period to census period is at best approximate, percentages should be regarded as suggesting general trends only.

[a] Data are allocated in terms of the treatment in the text. Allocations are made as consistently as possible from census to census.

[b] Data are approximated from nearest dates available to correspond with the month each census was taken.

of Chinese, but during the first three census periods, at least, almost all of those enumerated were migrants; moreover, migrants still constituted a large proportion of those in nonurban agricultural and other rural occupations in the later census periods. Table 2 shows that in 1884 some 13,200 Chinese were in rural occupations, and during the 1890s four-fifths of the employed Chinese males were engaged in developing Hawaii's rural resources. But at these same times less than half the rural Chinese workers were on sugar plantations. Following Annexation, with the subsequent decrease of the Chinese migrant group and the increase of the Hawaii-born Chinese group, the total number and also the proportion of Chinese in these nonurban occupations showed a steady decline. By 1930 they made up only about a fourth of the total Chinese males employed.

A typical pattern of these rural enterprises was a growth in the number of Chinese engaged in them, achievement of dominance in the market, and then a decline in the number of Chinese participants as other ethnic groups succeeded them, especially in production of the commodity. Some migrants spent a whole lifetime at these pursuits; in some cases the children of migrants continued the nonurban occupations in which their fathers had been successful. But data in the table indicate that by 1920 the majority of the Chinese in the Islands had turned to other occupations. It becomes appropriate, therefore, to consider the urban occupations which replaced those followed by so many of the migrants in the rural areas of the Islands.

CHAPTER 4

On the Urban Frontier

CHINESE who migrated to Hawaii before Annexation could not have imagined the variety of occupations the Island economy would offer them. Nor indeed was it possible for most of those on the Hawaiian frontier in the nineteenth century to foresee the complex occupational structure that would develop with the expansion of Hawaii's economy, its eventual incorporation into the economic and political system of the United States, and its integration into a world economy.

Compared with more developed industrial areas, the occupational structure on the Hawaiian frontier was simple. Fully four-fifths of its workers during the 1880s were employed in unskilled or semiskilled jobs, mostly in rural areas. Above them in the economic hierarchy was a small stratum of better-paid craftsmen and proprietors of small businesses; at the top was a still smaller number of relatively high-income entrepreneurs and professional people. Even though most Chinese migrants who came before Annexation entered at the bottom of the economic order as unskilled workers, their work contributed to the expansion of Hawaii's economy and to the resulting increases in the number and types of occupations opening up. The occupations becoming available had a preference scale based primarily on their relative remuneration, especially during the earlier decades of the migrant period. In Hawaii, where traditionally there have been no rigid racial or ethnic barriers to occupational movement, Chinese migrants could move upward readily on this scale.

While they were moving into new positions in Hawaii's expanding division of labor, most of the migrants were still outsiders in the emerging Hawaiian society. Generally, the occupations they were moving into were of the kinds that met the needs of other ethnic groups but required very little in the way of personal contacts. Moreover, many if not most of these jobs were not wanted by the Hawaiians or the relatively small number of Caucasians in the Islands. This sort of situation, in which members of different ethnic or racial groups play different roles in a division of labor without becoming integrated into a common society, has been labeled "symbiotic" by sociologists who borrowed the term from the natural sciences. Just as different species living in the same environment can form a mutually beneficial ecological pattern, different ethnic groups living in the same geographical area may perform roles that supplement one another. In this sense, many of the Chinese migrants entered symbiotic occupations in which they carried out tasks that were beneficial to the other groups in the society while still leading personal lives largely within their own group.[1]

Trade and Opportunity

From the beginning of their experience in Hawaii Chinese tended to gravitate into trade, as they have commonly done wherever they have gone as migrants. Trade, as sociologists and anthropologists well know, is almost universally the main, and sometimes the only, basis upon which persons of different ethnic groups make contact with one another. As Louis Wirth said in discussing the Jews as traders in the Gentile world, "trade relationships are possible when no other form of contact between two peoples can take place."[2] Utterly different in language, religion, customs, and historical background from either the indigenous Hawaiians or the Western foreigners, Chinese traders played an important part in the new economic and social order that was developing in the Islands. In the relatively impersonal role of the trader the Chinese migrant could carry on a successful business, even become a wealthy man, without acquiring more than a small part of the culture of the people among whom he was living and with whom he was trading.

Chinese pioneers such as those in Samsing & Co. and Hungtai Co. who came to Hawaii in the first half of the nineteenth century had quickly found opportunities as traders. Of the 8 Chinese among the 315 foreigners in Honolulu whose occupations were listed in an 1847 register, 5 were proprietors of stores. Only seven years later 73 commercial licenses were issued to Chinese, including 3 for wholesaling businesses, 3 for retail firms, 32 for "hawking and peddling," 2 for "plantations," 2 for "horses used for hire," and 1 for a boat. Since many of these licenses were issued to firms with two or more partners, the number is striking. The total Chinese population, all males, could not have been much more than 375 at the time, and this number would have included the 275 to 290 laborers and "houseboys" who had been brought to Hawaii in 1852 under five-year contracts. Apparently most of the noncontract Chinese in Hawaii were engaged in trade.

A common beginning for the Chinese trader, especially one who came to Hawaii without capital or family connections to Chinese already established in business, was that of rural peddler or urban "hawker." Several Chinese contract laborers made their first move off the plantation by becoming peddlers in rural areas. Probably some of them began peddling their own garden produce or fish they had caught themselves even while still working on the plantation. As in many areas with a scattered rural population, poor roads, and no ready access to stores, peddlers in Hawaii met a real need, and for several reasons the Chinese migrants were well suited to this role. In the 1930s a young Hawaii-born Chinese described how Chinese migrants made the transition from agriculturist to trader and storekeeper:

> Even though the Chinese emigrant has been a farmer, or a worker around the village, nearly every one of them has had some experience at bargaining. I know, for instance, that my folks used to go into Macao about once a week to peddle their produce. Peddling has been taken up as a sort of secondary occupation. Many of the families have little or no land; there may not be enough land to keep the whole family busy. Some of the individual members will try selling something in order to make some money. When they go overseas, many of them soon get into peddling and hawking. . . . The peddler gets a little money and buys a box of fruit, some peanuts, and then carries them around selling them. When he has been at it a while, and has saved some money, he gets a cart and increases his stock. Eventually he may set up a small shop.[3]

The experience of bartering in the markets of South China was useful to many migrants in nineteenth-century Hawaii when much of the rural trade with Hawaiians was on a barter rather than a cash basis. Moreover, Chinese in the rural districts were outsiders who could strike bargains without having to take into account the personal claims to which Hawaiians were subject when trading among themselves. Another of the Chinese peddler's advantages was that he knew or could make contact with Chinese merchants in the larger towns of the Islands and could exchange products collected in the rural districts for goods as well as for cash.

George N. Wilcox, the retired manager of Grove Farm on Kauai, recalled in 1930 the role of the Chinese peddlers on Kauai in the 1860s when he had the only store in the Lihue district:

> I kept that store for a while. . . . People had to go a long way to get things if they came there. . . . That was when the Chinese went about Kauai as peddlers. Since there was but the one store, they would get what they could carry, or take some little cart, and peddle their goods from place to place. When night came, they would put up at the best place they could find. You know the Hawaiians are very hospitable. The Chinaman would pick out the biggest house he could find and simply go there and put up for the night. . . . It was the peddlers who later started other stores on the island on sites leased from Hawaiians.[4]

Carrying his small stock of goods into remote Hawaiian villages, the peddler was the middleman in an arrangement that was mutually advantageous to the three main ethnic groups in the economy—the Chinese themselves, the Hawaiians, and the Caucasians. Through these small trading activities many Chinese were able to accumulate the money they sought either to return to their home villages in China or to establish themselves in more permanent businesses in the Islands. The Hawaiians could exchange their produce for the foreign goods they were learning to enjoy, while the Hawaiian government received added revenues through license fees and taxes on the peddlers. The Caucasian businessmen, especially the wholesalers, profited from the spread of a commercial order throughout the Islands as indigenous Hawaiians were more and more drawn into the new money economy.

Even in the larger towns, such as Honolulu and Hilo, the Chinese peddler with his carrying pole remained a familiar sight well into the twentieth century. Before the proliferation of neighborhood grocery stores, housewives in the growing residential areas bought most of their fresh food from peddlers. A writer in 1893 mentioned the advantage to the householder of having peddlers bringing produce to the house "instead of having to trudge off in the early morning to the market for their breakfast supply. . . . [Now] he will be greeted by plodding John Chinaman, borne down with the weight of a pair of baskets laden with a supply of all the Hawaiian and half the foreign catalogue of green groceries, with something in the fruit line, additional, half the time."[5]

One outstandingly successful Chinese migrant who moved from the plantation into peddling and then into increasingly successful businesses was Chun Hoon. In 1961 the Chun-Hoon family was featured as an "Island success story" in a publication of the Chinese Chamber of Commerce of Hawaii:

> The father came here seventy-four years ago [1887] to work as a sugar plantation laborer. Today his fifteen children are business and professional people, all well educated, all prominent in community affairs. Chun Hoon did not stay on the plantation long—only the three years necessary to fulfill his contract. Making use of the English he had learned during his short time in Hawaii, Chun Hoon went into business for himself. He was a peddler in those early days, a familiar sight to housewives in the Nuuanu, Makiki, and Manoa valleys. For he called from door-to-door, selling the wares he carried in baskets that swung from the ends of a bamboo pole.
>
> Chun Hoon was an honest, friendly young merchant whose business expanded enough to warrant a small shop at the corner of Union and Hotel St. Aided by his wife, Lee Oi, whom he married in 1895, Chun Hoon grew from a small retailer to an exporter of pineapples and bananas. At the time of his death in 1935, he was the sole supplier of fruits and vegetables to the U.S. Army in Hawaii. Chun Hoon not only sold fruits and vegetables, but he owned the fields from which his produce came. The family's retail outlets also grew during the years and today include Chun Hoon and Everybody's Super Markets, Chun Hoon Pharmacy, a drive-in, and Chun Hoon Dress Shop.[6]

Not all the Chinese retailers started out as peddlers, of course; there were several other avenues by which they went into business. Some of them worked first for firms owned by Caucasians or Chinese; some started as partners with fellow clan members or other *heung li*; some saved up money while working at other occupations and then invested it in small stores which they and their family operated. However it came about, the number of retail businesses owned and operated by Chinese migrants grew steadily in the latter part of the nineteenth century.

In the twelve-year period 1872–1884, the number of retail licenses issued to Chinese quadrupled from 103 to 412. Over half the stores licensed in 1872, 1878, and 1884 were outside of Honolulu, unlike the Caucasian-owned stores which were heavily concentrated in that city. The Chinese stores were scattered here and there in rural settlements, villages, and plantation towns throughout the Islands. On the island of Kauai, for example, the seventeen Chinese stores in 1878 were in eight different communities; the forty-two on the island of Hawaii were in at least twenty-six communities. Often the Chinese store was the only one in a large district and typically it was a general store. One "Kimo (Pake)" advertised in 1884 that he was a "Dealer in Groceries, Provisions, Dry Goods, Clothing, Crockery, Glassware, Cutlery, Harness, Saddles, and every description of General Merchandise" at Hawi, Kohala, Hawaii.[7] Store proprietors often provided other services besides selling merchandise, as can be seen in this 1897 advertisement by a Chinese storekeeper whose surname was Tom but who did business as "Awana":[8]

Awana,
Dry Goods, Groceries, Hats, Shoes,
General Merchandise

	Beef	
Pork	Meats	Mutton
	Poultry	

Island Produce.
Blacksmith Shop.
Best Horse Shoeing in Maui.
Restaurant—Excellent Meals Served on
    Short Notice.

Makawao, Maui, H.I.

For several decades the Chinese steadily increased their share of the retail business of the Islands. During the 1866–1889 period, while the total number of retail licenses issued in Hawaii more than tripled (196 to 626), the number issued to Chinese increased more than seven times (54 to 393), with the Chinese retailers' share of the licenses growing from 28 to 63 percent.

Many Chinese retail ventures relied on the partnership system to bring together capital and personnel. The same attitudes that had given rise to small cooperative enterprises in agriculture carried over into commercial ventures. In addition to those who started the business, partners often included employees who acquired shares after working for the firm for some time. The regular income of an individual partner in such a business might not have been much above that of a laborer or agriculturist. According to two Chinese migrants writing in 1900, "a high-class merchant drew a salary of $40 a month; a middle-class merchant, $30; and a low-class merchant, $20."[9] However, a partner leaving a firm after many years might receive several hundred dollars, or even several thousand, for his share.

By about 1910 the number of Chinese retail dealers reached a peak (1,067) and declined slowly during the next twenty years to 996. After constituting a majority of the retail dealers for over a quarter of a century, their proportion declined to less than one-third by 1930. Many Chinese had risen in the occupational scale through the medium of trade; so did later immigrant groups who also had been brought in at the bottom of the economic order as unskilled workers on plantations. Japanese immigrants, the next large group brought into the Islands, moved into the retail field just as the Chinese had done. Even though the actual number of Chinese retailers had not greatly decreased by 1930, their percentage among all retail dealers had declined steadily since 1890. This decline was particularly marked in the rural areas, villages, and small towns of the Islands where Chinese migrants had done most of the retail business for several decades. By 1910 they made up only 39 percent of the retailers outside of Honolulu, only 30 percent in 1920, and only 20 percent in 1930. This reduction was concurrent with the decrease in the numbers of Hawaiians and Chinese in the nonurban districts and the great increase there of immigrants and immigrant families of other ethnic groups, such as the Japanese, Koreans and Filipinos. Members of these groups who left plantation work during these decades were following the same course as the earlier Chinese: going into peddling and establishing small stores. The converse of this pattern was the concentration of Chinese businesses in Honolulu, where 53 percent of all Chinese retailers were located in 1910, 63 percent in 1920, and 70 percent in 1930.

Even though the Chinese share of the total retail business in the Islands declined after 1890, retailing occupied a steadily increasing proportion of the Chinese employed male population. By 1930 there were four and a half times as many Chinese retailers as would have been statistically expected if the occupational distribution among Chinese males had been exactly like that of the employed male population of Hawaii as a whole. The number of Chinese salesmen and clerks in stores also grew steadily during the forty years from 1890 to 1930 (164 to 809). From 1896 to 1930 Chinese males were increasingly overrepresented in these occupations; by 1930 their occupational index[10] had reached a high of three and a third times statistical parity. Nevertheless, their proportion of the total number of persons in these occupations began to decline in the decade between 1920 and 1930, when Hawaii-born members of other ethnic groups—especially Japanese—began coming to maturity and entering the retail field in larger numbers than the Chinese.

Other Symbiotic Occupations

Many of the other occupations entered by the migrants fulfilled the needs of other groups who did not want such work, while not demanding of the Chinese much knowledge of the other groups' cultures. Among these occupations were those of laundrymen; tailors, dressmakers, and shoemakers; restaurant and café proprietors, cooks, waiters, and bakers; house servants, gardeners, and "hostlers" (stablemen). As on other frontiers with a scarcity of women, many tasks traditionally carried out by women were performed by men—and by men of a different cultural group with a lower standard of living than those who wanted the services. Dressmaking, laundering, and domestic service, for example, were not typically male occupations in either Chinese or Western societies, but many migrants decided that such jobs were preferable to agricultural or other manual labor. During the migrant period most such occupations called for painstaking handwork but little capital or equipment so they could be undertaken by migrants who did not have the means to start other businesses.

Laundrymen

The demand for laundry workers rose with the growth of an urban population in the Islands.[11] By the 1870s, it seems, commercial laundering was done almost entirely by Chinese. By 1880 public concern about the way Chinese laundries were operated led to the passage of an act placing "all laundries and wash houses" under the control of the Board of Health and requiring that laundering "for hire" be done in buildings erected by the government and supervised by health authorities.[12] The census of 1884 enumerated 325 Chinese "washermen" in Honolulu, 76 in the rest of the Hawaiian kingdom, and no laundry workers of any other ethnic identity. The business directory of the Islands in 1896 listed 40 laundries in Honolulu, 4 in Hilo, and 5 on Maui; all, except one in Honolulu, were operated by Chinese.

For many migrants laundry work was only a convenient temporary base providing shelter, income, and contacts while they looked for better opportunities. Lee Chau, who came to Hawaii from a See Yup district shortly before Annexation, was one such migrant. Through other migrants he got a job in a laundry in Hilo. The work was hard and distasteful, the hours were long, and he soon saw he was getting nowhere. After about six months he left the laundry to become a cook for the partners and employees in a nearby Chinese business. His experience in this shop eventually enabled him to open his own store in Hilo. From retailing Lee branched out into wholesaling and by the 1920s his firm, Kwong See Wo, was one of the largest Chinese businesses on the island of Hawaii, grossing about $250,000 a year. When he was interviewed in 1936 he said that many of his customers were Caucasians and other non-Chinese.

The number of Chinese working as laundrymen steadily decreased after 1910. Nevertheless, they continued to be overrepresented in this type of work for some time, with six times statistical parity in the Islands as a whole and more than four times in Honolulu in 1920. By 1930 women were taking over many of the laundry jobs. By 1950 most laundry work in the Islands was done by women, few of whom were Chinese; only 2 percent of the workers in this occupation were Chinese males. With the passage of the migrant generation, there was no longer any basis in the Islands for the old stereotype of the Chinese as laundryman.

Domestic Servants

Another occupation in which Chinese migrant men once had a large role was domestic service. Two of the eight Chinese in Honolulu in 1847 were servants. Twenty of the first boatload of 195 Chinese imported in 1852 signed contracts to work as "houseboys" for five years at two dollars a month. In succeeding years other Chinese house servants were obtained under the contract labor system; 17 of a boatload of 188 Chinese imported under the auspices of the Board of Immigration in 1870 signed contracts to work at seven dollars per month as house servants, most of them for Caucasians. By far the greater portion of the Chinese men who worked as servants, however, entered the occupation as free employees after having worked, especially as cooks, on the plantations or in Chinese camps in rural Hawaii. A Chinese who migrated to Hawaii in 1884 indicates that some came as free immigrants with the intention of securing household employment at the start: "My oldest brother went to Tan Heung Shan [Hawaii] in 1879 because my cousin was there. Two years later my second brother went. They wrote home telling my parents that they were working for a white devil as cooks and as housekeepers. They wanted me to go too because it was a good place to make money and learn *fan wah* ["the foreigners' language"]."[13] The census of 1884 included a special tabulation of Chinese, Hawaiians, and "other nationalities" in Honolulu in occupations "other than agriculturalists and contract laborers." For the category of "servants," the census listed 100 Chinese, 46 Hawaiians, and 23 of other nationalities. In the same order, the figures for cooks were 151, 9, and 72, for gardeners, 27, 26, and 81. Over one-fifth of the 1,283 Chinese in the occupational tabulations were in domestic service categories.

In their large number of immigrant men and the exceptionally small number of immigrant women in domestic service, Chinese differed radically from other immigrant groups. Until the aging Chinese migrant servants retired, occupational indices show increasing overrepresentation of Chinese men in this occupation. The index for 1930 is the highest for any of the occupations dealt with in this chapter except for laundrymen in 1920. However, their share of the total number of jobs in domestic service decreased as later immigrant groups brought more women and established families more quickly than had the Chinese—especially, at first, the Portuguese and Japanese. While non-Chinese families who employed cooks, housekeepers, gardeners, and other servants during the latter part of the nineteenth century probably depended largely upon Chinese migrant men, by 1910 only one-fifth of the 5,317 servants (male and female) were Chinese men. By 1930 they were only 12 percent of the total and by 1940 only 1 percent—86 men in a total of 8,520. Obviously, as the migrant Chinese servants retired, they were not replaced by Hawaii-born Chinese males.

The tendency for Chinese men to remain in service to one family for many years was seen by their employers as evidence of loyalty, devotion, and concern for the welfare of the employer and his family. It was commonly said of a Chinese servant that he had become "a part of the family." Not infrequently such servants received rewards beyond their regular wages. Some of the earliest Chinese wives to come to the Islands were brought at the expense of employers of Chinese servants; the servants' children were often well educated, even in universities and graduate schools in the continental United States, or secured preferred, well-paid positions through their parent's employer.[14] Unmarried servants were sometimes pensioned and returned to their native villages after years of service.[15] Nevertheless, the life histories of many of those who remained unmarried, or who could not bring their families to Hawaii, are rather pathetic. These are stories of hopeful migration, subsequent addiction to gambling or opium, improvident manhood and loss of ambition, substitution of the employers' families for their own, and increasing dependence upon the benevolence of permissive employers. Such histories are similar to those of the migrants who never left the plantations and depended upon plantation paternalism for security in their declining years. A Chinese servant whose life followed this pattern was described to the writer in 1936 by his former employer:

"Cooky" was with us for ten years. He was an excellent cook. He was a crackerjack—if anything went wrong about the house, Cooky could fix it, was mechanically inclined, had a good brain up here. We paid him forty dollars a month for doing *everything*—all the cooking, housework, laundry, yard work, and the like.

One thing we could not do, though, was give him all his pay—if we did, the next day it would be all gone and he would soon be around asking for more: "Pay ahead; next time, cut," he would say. We got so we would only give him two or three dollars at a time. I have the habit, after finishing my lunch, of lying down on the lounge for a while. Cooky would come in: "You give me t'ree dolla, huh?" If I gave him some money he would go back to the kitchen, clean things up a little faster than usual, and pretty soon he would disappear. We wouldn't see any more of him for several hours. We supposed that he went down to Chinatown and gambled all his money away. We never suspected that he smoked opium. He always stayed in the little house out in the back yard and we never went in there.

As the time went on and on and he was always broke, we got quite concerned about what would happen to him when he got too old to work. Finally we told him that it was clear he couldn't work many years longer and that he would have to begin saving money. To make sure that he did so, we thereafter laid some of his wages aside and we paid him a good interest on the money saved. He said he wanted to go back to China whenever he quit work. [Cooky hadn't been back for forty years; meantime his wife and two daughters had died. He had no close relatives left, but he wanted to go back.]

Finally Cooky got sick. We took him to our doctor who said that some of the arteries leading into the heart were enormously enlarged, that Cooky might live a long while, again he might suddenly drop dead.

Cooky told us one of his friends had told him about a firm in China which promised big returns on investment, and wanted us to turn the money over to him so he could invest it. We were afraid of that, however, and finally convinced him that it would be best for us to send his money to our relative in Canton, which was not far from his village, and that A—— would be glad to be his banker. After buying his ticket and giving him some spending money for along the way, we sent the rest to A—— and instructed him to give out the money in small amounts at a time.

So Cooky went. He had saved, or rather we had saved for him, about $180. It seemed a shame, too—for ten years he had been making $480 a year, and from presents, tips from our friends, and the like he got around $500 a year, in addition to room, board, and lots of cast-off clothes—he never had to buy clothes. He could have saved quite a large part of that $5,000 if he had planned better—let alone all the money he made before he came to work for us. Opium had taken most of it. We heard that he bought the second-grade stuff—the scrapings from opium that had already been smoked.

Cooky came to A—— in Canton several times to get money. Sometimes he arrived like a "big" man, in a sedan chair, with two coolies carrying him. Once he asked for $100 to buy himself a wife: "Not a Number One wife, Number Two kind all right." Another time he wanted money to buy a house in the village. It seems the house had been passed down to a cousin of his who was willing to sell it. . . . A—— visited him in his village once. He found Cooky smoking opium. The villagers didn't like it—they had been trying to prevent opium smoking in the village, but there he was, hard at it.

Barbers

In China barbering was a despised occupation. Sons of barbers, no matter how talented, were not allowed to compete in the imperial examinations.[16] Although 22 of the 34 barbers in Honolulu reported in the 1884 census were Chinese, the migrants did not try to fill the many positions for barbers that opened up with the increasing urbanization of Hawaii's population. Of the 76 barbers listed in the 1896 directory only 21 were Chinese; in 1910 there were only 43 Chinese among the 393 "barbers, hairdressers, and manicurists"; in 1920, 23 out of 537; in 1930, only 13, including for the first time a Chinese woman, of a total of 883. In 1950 the number of Chinese women had increased to 49, in a total of 1,103, but only 2 Chinese males were in this category. In all census periods from 1910 to 1950 the Chinese were very much underrepresented.

Food Service Workers and Owners

In the nineteenth and early twentieth centuries, public eating places were in great demand by the large number of familyless men among the Caucasian and other resident and transient foreigners in Hawaii. Few Caucasians or Hawaiians operated restaurants during that period, although most of the saloon keepers were Caucasians. It was mainly the Chinese who met the demand for food service, especially in the port towns. Chinese migrants who had cooked for fellow workers on sugar and rice plantations and in Chinese-owned stores, laundries, and other businesses found they could turn this experience to more profitable use. Tam Fong was one of these migrants:

> Tam Fong was born in Wong Leong Doo, Chung Shan district, in 1876. There were four children in the family—two sons and two daughters, Ah Fong being the oldest. His grandfather had been a teacher and had given the children considerable training. Ah Fong attended school for ten years, until he was about nineteen. His parents arranged to get a wife for him, but before the wedding date the girl died. This was considered a very unlucky omen, and Ah Fong decided to come to the Hawaiian Islands. He arrived with a group of over one hundred laborers in 1898.
>
> Upon arrival, he and about ten others signed a contract for three years to work for the W—— Plantation on Oahu at $12.50 per month. During part of these three years he was a cook in the Chinese camp. When the contract expired, he decided to quit the plantation and to work in a restaurant as a cook. Ah Fong accordingly went to Honolulu, where he worked in a "coffee shop" owned by a relative on King Street at the edge of the downtown district. He had free lodging and meals at the shop and received at the start four dollars per week.
>
> He liked the work as cook, but at the end of five years he decided to work for himself and succeeded in securing a position in a prominent Haole home in Nuuanu Valley; beginning at nine dollars per week, his wages were raised to twelve and later to fifteen dollars a

week. He stayed with this family three years. He then worked in a Haole home at Waikiki for many years.

In the early 1930s Ah Fong served as second cook in one of the Honolulu schools, earning thirteen dollars per week. Being laid off—he was an opium smoker—he secured jobs as cook in various downtown restaurants, shifting from one to another. Finally his health became such that he was unable to obtain any more work.[17]

Between the 1850s and the turn of the century, the majority of the "victualling" licenses were issued to Chinese. In 1866 Chinese had 58 percent of these licenses and 85 percent in 1889.[18] They operated all of the 19 "coffee saloons," 42 of the 48 restaurants, and 10 of the 18 bakeries in Honolulu listed in the 1896 directory, as well as 32 of the 39 "coffee saloons," 19 of the 23 restaurants, and 7 of the 8 bakeries in the rest of the Islands. In 1910, although they were no longer so dominant in the food business, 59 percent of the male restaurant, café, and lunchroom keepers were still Chinese. By that time Japanese migrants leaving agricultural work had begun to cut into Chinese control of this field. Twenty years later Chinese men made up only 31 percent of the male proprietors in food service and by 1950 their proportion had declined to 22 percent.[19] Throughout this period, however, Chinese men continued to be statistically overrepresented in this field as shown by the occupational indexes—3.9 in 1910, 4.9 in 1930, and still above 3 in 1950.

Two well-known Chinese restaurants started in Honolulu by Chinese migrants are illustrative—one in the Chinatown section, the other in the Waikiki tourist area. Wo Fat Chop Suey, Ltd., at the corner of Hotel and Maunakea Streets, claims to be "the oldest chop sui house in Hawaii." In 1885 six migrants from Chung Shan district joined to start the Chinese restaurant and pastry shop which since the 1930s has been known as "Wo Fat." After the original founders died, several of their sons continued to operate the restaurant along with their other business interests. In 1937 two prominent Chinese, Chang Nee Sun, son-in law of one of the founders, and Henry Awa Wong (for years known locally as "Mayor of Chinatown"), joined Leong Han and Charles Tim Lee, each a son of one of the founders, and with new capital they constructed a three-story building which was expanded in the 1950s to increase seating capacity to a thousand persons. Wo Fat is a popular location for banquets of Chinese organizations and for wedding receptions within the Chinese community, and it is patronized by both Chinese and non-Chinese who like Cantonese cooking.[20]

The most colorful, though ultimately not the most successful, of the Chinese immigrant chefs and restaurant proprietors was Chong Pang Yat, who portrayed himself as "Me P. Y. Chong" in pidgin English advertisements. Born in the 1890s in Shekki, Chung Shan district, he was brought to Hawaii by his father, Chong Park Shun, who during the early decades of this century in Honolulu was a teacher and principal in Chinese-language schools as well as editor of a Chinese-language newspaper.

Starting as chef and manager of a small Chinese restaurant in Honolulu, Chong Pang Yat soon gained a reputation as a chef possessing unusual culinary skills. With a flair for publicity and self-promotion, he attracted financial backing from both Chinese and non-Chinese supporters. This backing enabled him to establish and to expand "Lau Yee Chai," which became the most publicized and popular Chinese restaurant in the Waikiki area in the 1930s, 1940s, and 1950s. It was the first Chinese restaurant in Honolulu to use elaborate Chinese architecture, interior design, and decor to attract customers looking for Chinese atmosphere as well as Chinese food. His overly optimistic and expansive plans led him into bankruptcy, however, and his restaurant was closed.[21]

Chinese in the restaurant business actually more than doubled in number between 1930 and 1950 and the trend has continued. With the popularity of Chinese food among Hawaii's residents of all ethnic groups, as well as among the increasing number of tourists, Chinese restaurants have multiplied. Most of today's Chinese restaurants are owned and managed by American citizens of Chinese ancestry, although a substantial proportion of the cooks are Chinese aliens who have migrated to Hawaii since 1950. One change in the Chinese restaurant picture that has occurred since World War II is the greater availability of Chinese cuisines other than Cantonese, reflecting the difference between the older Chinese migration, almost entirely from Kwangtung, and the later migration from other regions of China.

Employment of Chinese as waiters has fluctuated with changes in the restaurant business in Hawaii. In the latter part of the nineteenth century most waiters were Chinese migrants; as late as 1910, some 61 percent of the male waiters were still Chinese, but their proportion declined as the Chinese share of the restaurant business in the

Islands decreased. At the same time the proportion of women in this occupation increased. In 1910 women filled only about one-fourth of the positions and less than half in 1920. This share rose to 61 percent in 1930 and more than 90 percent in 1950. For several decades, however, relatively few of the women working as waitresses were Chinese—none in 1910, less than 4 percent of the total in 1920, only 9 percent in 1930. In recent years Chinese women have outnumbered Chinese men waiters in Chinese restaurants, and they also work in other restaurants and fast food places.[22]

A Transition Phase

The decreasing proportion of Chinese men in most types of employment discussed so far in this chapter strongly suggests that overrepresentation in symbiotic occupations was only a transition phase in the experience of the Chinese in Hawaii. They were the occupations in which newcomers could find economic rewards while unprepared to participate fully in Hawaiian society at large. It was not until other immigrant groups followed the Chinese off the plantations that the Chinese faced competition in these fields. However, Chinese migrants who had become familiar with the Western values and practices gaining ground in Hawaii, especially the migrants who had Hawaii-born and Western-educated children, tended increasingly to move from these occupations into others that were higher on the economic scale, socially more acceptable in the status order emerging in Hawaii, and more involved in the Islands' multicultural social system.

The opportunities for occupational mobility on the Hawaiian frontier presented a great contrast to the occupational continuity of the migrants' home villages, where kinsmen carried on the same occupations generation after generation. Labor for individual wages was uncommon in the villages, and money (as distinct from land, buildings, and other tangible property) had only a small part in family and clan life. In Hawaii, instead of continuity and submission to custom there was mobility and personal decision. Staying on the same job or with the same employer indefinitely suggested lack of ambition and want of foresight. Most migrants had their first experience with money of their own after arriving in the Islands; from the beginning they worked for wages or calculated anticipated earnings in dollars. In the early decades a migrant's status was judged primarily on how much money he had accumulated, no matter how, but as the migrants remained in the Islands they came to recognize the relative social status, as well as the relative remuneration, of different occupations within the Western economic structure and value system. Skilled jobs, clerical and sales positions, and proprietary occupations —the white-collar jobs—were seen as not only better paid than unskilled and semiskilled jobs but also as more prestigious. A hierarchy of occupations in China was, of course, well known among the migrants.[23] What they learned in Hawaii was that an individual could improve his economic position and personal social status by his own efforts, without regard to his ancestral or kinship identity.

Moving into the Mainstream

Fortunately for most Chinese migrants leaving agricultural work, their occupational careers coincided with a great increase in the number of jobs above the unskilled and semiskilled levels; moreover, unlike Chinese who migrated to the mainland United States, they did not face overwhelming competition from Caucasian workers ready to fill these better jobs and claiming prior right to them. The 1890 census in Hawaii, the first to attempt a tabulation of all employed persons by major occupational categories and by "nationality," makes it possible to estimate that of the 38,930 employed males in the Islands, only about 6,000 were in skilled, clerical and sales, proprietary, and professional occupations.[24] By the time of the 1930 census nearly 50,000 of the 136,460 employed males were in these four occupational classes—a tremendous increase in the proportion of these preferred types of employment as well as a large increase in the total number of jobs. In 1890 only 2,547 of the nearly 39,000 employed males were reported as of American, British, French, German, and Norwegian nationalities; in 1930 only 24,943 of the 136,460 employed males were Caucasians of North European ancestry. Even if all these men had been employed in these four occupational classes they would not have filled half the positions in 1890 and only half in 1930.

A little over 13,000 Chinese males were employed at the time of the 1890 census; about 1,700 of them, 13 percent, were employed in one or another of these four classes of occupations. Most of these 1,700 were among the "stayers," one might say, from the 25,000 to 30,000 migrants who had come to Hawaii during the previous twenty-five years (Table 1). The number and percentage of Chinese employed in these preferred occupations increased steadily from 1896 onward, reaching 3,161 in 1910, about one-fourth of all employed Chinese males. Comparable numbers and percentages for succeeding census periods were: 3,691 (33 percent) in 1920; 4,403 (51 percent) in 1930; 4,785 (61 percent) in 1940; 5,958 (74 percent) in 1950; 7,409 (75 percent) in 1960; 9,773 (73 percent) in 1970.

Census employment data do not differentiate between foreign-born and native-born individuals of ethnic groups, but age data show that less than 2 percent of the employed Chinese males in 1910 could have been Hawaii-born. By 1910, then, at least a fifth of the migrant males then employed had established themselves in occupations above the unskilled and semiskilled levels. The entry of Hawaii-born males into the work force after 1910 makes it impossible to determine the full extent to which migrants penetrated the preferred occupational classes. Migrants still made up nearly 90 percent of the employed Chinese males in 1920, but by 1930 this proportion had declined to about 60 percent. By 1950 nearly 90 percent of the employed Chinese males were Hawaii-born.

Migrants in Skilled Occupations

Census reports, business directories, newspapers, and other publications of the 1880s and 1890s show Chinese migrants in each of the following categories of skilled workers:

Baker	Furniture maker and repairer
Barber	Gasfitter
Basket and chair maker	Goldsmith, silversmith
Blacksmith, horseshoer	Gunsmith
Boot maker, shoemaker	Harness and saddle maker
Bricklayer and stonemason	Hatter
Butcher	Jeweler
Cabinetmaker	Locksmith
Carriage maker	Machinist
Carver, seal maker	Musical instrument maker
Cigar maker	Painter
Coffin maker	Plumber
Dressmaker	Printer, typesetter
Engraver	Rice miller

Sail maker	Upholsterer
Sign painter	Watchmaker
Sugar boiler	Well driller
Tailor, cutter	Woodturner
Tinsmith	

Nearly all these crafts were common to a preindustrial and pre-mechanized order. Some of the skills required were brought to Hawaii by migrants who had learned them in China and continued to use them in the traditional way in the Hawaiian Chinese community. Other migrants adapted these skills to meet the demands of non-Chinese customers and the Chinese in Hawaii who had become acculturated to Western ways. Some of these trades were unknown in the home villages of the migrants who learned them after emigrating.

Among the crafts transplanted to Hawaii to serve the Chinese community in the Islands were those of the goldsmith, silversmith, and jeweler. Demand for Chinese-style jewelry increased with the growing numbers of Chinese families in Hawaii, especially in Honolulu. The 1884 census reported nine Chinese jewelers in Hawaii. One early jewelry manufacturing firm, Sun Wo Company, was established in Honolulu in 1888. In 1913 its manager, Chun Jew Kwong, had as a partner Fong You, reputed to be "an expert and artistic designer," who worked as head of the manufacturing department. Chun Jew Kwong had two sons in the firm, one working with his father in the business end, the other "acquiring practical experience by working at the bench."[25] A similar firm, established in 1907, was the Bo Wo Company, headed by Nip Chan Poo who had been born in Sun Wui, Kwangtung, about 1868 and had come to Honolulu in 1891 "to engage in business." Nip Chan Poo and his partner Lum King apparently had learned their craft in China.[26] For a while most of the jewelry makers and watchmakers in Hawaii were Chinese; in 1930 they still had almost three times statistical parity in these trades.[27]

Other crafts that could have been learned in China were those of the baker, barber, cabinetmaker, carpenter, coffin maker, furniture maker, shoemaker, sign painter, and tailor. These crafts could be carried on in Hawaii in traditional ways for Chinese customers or adapted to meet the tastes and needs of other groups or Westernized Chinese. One craftsman who seems to have done both was Quong

Fung Hin. Born in 1850 in Shekki, the largest town in Chung Shan district, he came to Hawaii as an independent laborer. He soon got a job as a carpenter, having learned that craft in Shekki, and later opened his own carpenter shop in Honolulu under the name Tuck Leong Cheong. Chinese carving, painting, and lacquer work in Chinese temples and restaurants were among his specialties, and he was said to be "an artist with bamboo and paper."[28] Another migrant, Lee Chu, learned carpentry in Quong's shop in the 1880s and later became the proprietor of the first Chinese firm in the lumber business in Hawaii. A native of Chung Shan district, where he was born in 1869, he was brought to Honolulu in 1883 by his father who had a Chinese store there. Lee attended school for four years before going to work in Quong's shop. After four years there he went on his own in carpentry and contracting work; five years later, with support from a number of Chinese businessmen, he started the Oahu Lumber and Building Co. of which he became president and manager.[29]

The largest number of Chinese skilled workmen during the 1880s and 1890s were in the building and woodworking trades, especially as carpenters and painters. Some of these were employed on the plantations, since these were the years when plantations were expanding rapidly and needed construction workers as well as field hands. Probably some of those working for the plantations had learned carpentry, masonry, and cabinet work in China; others learned the skills on the plantations. Other migrants, like Quong and Lee, entered these trades without going through a period of contract labor on plantations. One of these was Hee Kau Kee, whose career was described in a 1913 publication on the Hawaii Chinese:

> Characteristic of the patient industry with which the Chinese who have come to Hawaii have built up competences from small beginnings is the history of Mr. Hee Kau Kee, one of the best-known painters and decorators of Honolulu. . . . Just twenty-two years ago, when he was a boy of eighteen . . . young Hee Kau Kee left his home in China to come to Hawaii which he had heard of as the golden land of opportunity for young men who were not afraid of work and had no means with which to start in business for themselves.
>
> On his arrival in Honolulu, casting around for something to do, he was offered the chance to operate a fish pond, and knowing something about fish he took it. He continued in this business for one year and then went to Hawaii to cook for the rice plantation laborers. At the end of three years he tired of cooking and decided to learn a more

profitable trade, so he returned to Honolulu and started to acquire a knowledge of house painting. He found this trade entirely to his taste and after he had been painting and decorating houses for eleven years, he decided he knew enough to go into business for himself and he did so.

He opened [a] store on Nuuanu Street . . . with the savings of his years of work for others. . . . He has worked on many of the larger office buildings and residences of the city and his services are in demand.[30]

This sketch of Hee Kau Kee's career does not reveal who taught him the painter's trade, but it might very well have been some Caucasian housepainter with whom he started as a helper.

Fifteen of the 264 carpenters reported in the 1884 census were Chinese, as were 10 of the 83 painters. The 1910 census, the next one reporting relevant data, showed that Chinese carpenters had increased to 205, one-tenth of the total, and the 80 Chinese painters, glaziers, and varnishers constituted one-fifth of all workers in these occupations. Nearly all of them would have been of the migrant generation.

Like Chinese craftsmen in the building trades, some Chinese tailors and shoemakers were migrants who had learned their skills in China; others became apprentices in tailoring and shoemaking firms in Hawaii. Chinese clothing businesses prospered in Hawaii. According to the 1896 directory, 42 of the 69 Honolulu firms of dressmakers, tailors, and "merchant tailors" were owned by Chinese, as well as 27 of the 40 such firms in other districts of the Islands. Chinese tailors supplied the market with work clothing of all varieties, and by the 1890s Chinese tailoring firms competed with Caucasian-owned clothing stores for customers buying Western styles of men's suits and haberdashery. During the 1880s, 1890s, and 1900s Chinese men also worked as ladies' dressmakers.[31] In 1910 there were 373 Chinese tailors, 58 percent of the men in this occupation in the Islands. By 1930, however, there were only 115 (22 percent of the total) and by 1950 only 32 (12 percent). In this field, as in others, Chinese migrants were being replaced by members of other ethnic groups rather than by Hawaii-born Chinese.

Shoemaking, like tailoring, was an occupation in which migrants found opportunities in the Islands. As early as 1869 a Honolulu business directory listed 5 shoemakers among the 69 Chinese included. Later directories show increasing numbers, and by 1910 some 64 percent of the 170 shoemakers in the Islands were Chinese. While this proportion had declined to 28 percent by 1930, the last census period for which such data were reported, Chinese were still very much overrepresented in this occupation—in fact, they had four and a half times statistical parity.

The careers of two Chinese migrants, Chun Kim Chow and Ng Nam, reveal a striking contrast in occupational mobility in the shoe repair trade. Chun Kim Chow came to Hawaii in 1898 at the age of twenty-nine after working as a steamship stoker. He worked first as a maker of Chinese printing seals, but when the demand for such seals fell off he went to work for a cobbler, learned the trade, and in 1904 opened his own shoe repair shop in the central business district of Honolulu. Four years later he added a retail shoe department and then expanded the business until, before he died in 1957, he and his family owned and operated a chain of shoe stores in downtown Honolulu with branches in other districts of the city and on three other islands. Three publications devoted to prominent Hawaii Chinese give Chun Kim Chow's biography, but only one of them mentions "Ng Nam, 'dean' of the shoe repairmen in Honolulu," an employee of the Kim Chow Shoe Store who "takes pride in his work, the same as he has for more than 30 years."[32]

Getting Established in Business

Even though the number of Chinese craftsmen in Hawaii attracted attention and even antagonism from Caucasian and part-Hawaiian competitors during one period, there actually were more Chinese migrants in clerical, sales, and proprietary occupations than in the skilled trades. During the 1890–1930 period, when it was comparatively easy for migrants to improve their economic position, they took advantage of opportunities to establish themselves in a wide variety of businesses. Publications on the Chinese in Hawaii are replete with success stories of migrants who made their way up in the business world. Some of the businesses in which they engaged declined or became obsolete even during the migrants' lifetimes; others changed; many were expanded and carried on by the migrants' Hawaii-born descendants. Accounts of migrants who established themselves as agents, managers, partners, or owners of business firms show that by 1930 they had been involved at one time or another in the following enterprises. This list cannot be regarded as complete:

Agency for Chinese rice plan-
    tations, sugar plantations,
    pineapple growers
Auto repair shop
Bakery
Cigar factory
Coffee roasting and
    distribution
Cold storage
Commission agency
Construction firm
Cracker factory
Dairy
Dressmaking shop
Drugstore, herb store
Finance company
Fishing company
Fish market
Fruit processing
Furniture factory
Hack stand
Hotel
Ice cream factory
Import-export firm
Investment company

Jewelry factory and store
Labor recruiting
Land company
Livery stable
Lumber company
Lumber mill
Machine shop
Noodle factory
Paint contracting
Photography studio
Poi factory
Printing company
Publishing firm
Realty company
Restaurant, café, lunch-
    room, coffee shop
Retail clothing store
Retail general store
Retail grocery store
Rice mill
Soda water company
Tailoring firm
Theater
Trust company
Wholesale firm

Many of these migrant businessmen shifted from one field to another before finally becoming established in a successful enterprise. Often they were active in several businesses simultaneously: as investor, agent, director, partner, manager, owner, or in some other capacity. By the 1930s, when most migrants still in the Islands were ending their working careers, those who had made the most money had done so in the rice, poi, and coffee industries, the export-import trade, wholesaling operations, large retail stores, investment, and real estate development.

Involvement in the Island business community required migrant firms to deal with Caucasians and Hawaiians, especially those owning or controlling leased land, purchasers of crops raised by Chinese, representatives of shipping lines and warehouses, bankers, government officials, attorneys, and tax experts. These contacts were generally fairly impersonal, requiring of the migrant only a limited command of English or Hawaiian. Social relationships were usually restricted to the occasional Chinese banquet or civic affair. Migrants often turned over such contacts to Chinese associates who were more familiar with Western culture than they themselves were. Where this was possible the less acculturated businessman could confine most of his personal contacts to the Chinese community.

There seems to have been a sequence of three phases in the occupational accommodation of Chinese migrant businessmen, a sequence corresponding roughly with three stages in the economic development of Hawaii over the last two hundred years. During the first phase they were barterers and traders, associated with Caucasian businessmen bringing the Islands into the Western commercial order, and selling goods which came mostly from the North Atlantic region. In the second phase, while still carrying on the earlier activities, Chinese migrants served as "ethnic" businessmen, supplying goods and services desired by a growing Chinese immigrant population and doing business mainly with other Chinese. In the third phase, some migrants, especially in their later years, became part of the Islands' cosmopolitan business community which developed as Hawaii approached economic maturity—no longer a frontier but an integral part of national and international commerce.

Business in the Islands lost much of the ethnic character of the second phase after the importation of foreign agricultural workers virtually ended in the early 1930s; by then the population was becoming increasingly made up of people born in Hawaii and Caucasians from mainland United States. As immigrants became more and more acculturated to Hawaii's increasingly Westernized society, and as their Hawaii-born and American-educated offspring outnumbered them, linguistic, sentimental, and nationalistic ties diminished as advantages in business transactions between people of the same ethnic origin. Products from the migrants' homelands were now in less demand than those advertised to the American consumer in newspapers and magazines and on radio and television. In these circumstances few businessmen of Chinese ancestry depend solely or even mainly upon members of the Chinese community as customers; nor do they act in the old symbiotic or middleman role of the "Chinaman" trader. They function as part of the general business community—selling canned food, textiles, automobiles, and other commodities from all parts of the world to customers of all ancestries, and themselves buying these products from dealers of other ethnic origins.

True enough, more than a few migrant businessmen had trouble adjusting to the third phase. Many Chinese retailers who kept their stores going after others had given up fared poorly. During the 1920s and 1930s the traditional business practices followed by Chinese storekeepers were frequently criticized by younger, Hawaii-born Chinese. The criticisms ranged from the appearance of the stores to their accounting and financial practices. From the Chinese-American point of view, many of the stores were not kept clean, the goods were not arranged attractively, the window displays and advertising were ineffective, and not enough attention was paid to how the customers were served. Stock inventory practices were considered inadequate to determine turnover and consumer preferences: too much capital was tied up in goods not in regular demand (such as those bought only for certain festivals), and excessive stocks of other goods were carried. Credit was overextended to customers, tying up capital and increasing risk of losses. Accounting practices were regarded as inadequate: assets were undervalued, injuring the store's credit standing; profit was not regularly calculated; division of profits among partners and shareholders at the end of the year often left the firms with inadequate reserves. Small shops with limited capital were seen as losing out to larger firms with a wider choice of goods at lower prices. A basic criticism was that the traditional partnerships and family business arrangements, as compared with an incorporated joint-stock company, were poorly adapted to the organization and operation of a modern store.[33]

The need for Chinese proprietors to become nonethnic businessmen was generally referred to as the "need to modernize." Migrant Chinese who succeeded in doing so were likely to have had Western-educated associates who could reorganize the business and manage it under the new system. One Chinese migrant who had operated a general merchandise store for years in a plantation community turned over his capital to his Hawaii-born, American-educated sons, who made him president of the chain of grocery stores they opened in Honolulu. The management of another Chinese-owned neighborhood grocery store was turned over to an experienced Caucasian who expanded it into a chain of modern supermarkets. Such supermarkets in Hawaii stock "ethnic foods" for Chinese as well as other customers, but most of the stores in Honolulu's Chinatown which used to cater primarily to Chinese customers and sold mainly Chinese goods have gone out of business. This happened not only with Chinese grocery stores but others as well. Kum Pui Lai, writing in 1935, noted that Chinese jewelry stores which had been prosperous during the 1900–1920 period had already begun to lose business as second- and third-generation Hawaii Chinese turned from the traditional jewelry favored by their parents to Western patterns and designs. Chinese jewelers did not offer the new patterns the younger Chinese wanted.[34]

The migrant businessmen's adjustment to circumstances in the third phase was affected not only by their own way of doing business but also by certain elements of the Islands' financial community. For many decades the only banks in Hawaii were owned by Haoles (Hawaiian word commonly used to refer to Caucasians), and Chinese businessmen felt that the banks were unduly restrictive in making loans to non-Haole clients. This was one reason why two Honolulu banks were organized by Chinese—the Chinese American Bank in 1916 and the Liberty Bank in 1922. Both banks had trouble getting on a sound footing. Unlike the Sumitomo Bank and the Yokohama Specie Bank which were established in Honolulu as branches of banks in Japan with capital from their parent banks, the Chinese-organized banks were entirely local and had to compete at first for the limited capital and deposits of the Chinese in Hawaii. The Chinese American Bank, along with many other banks in the United States, was closed in 1932. In the Chinese community it was widely believed that this bank need not have closed if it had been helped by the two big "Haole banks" in the way a Haole-owned trust company, allegedly in worse condition than the Chinese bank, was saved by a bank loan. The Chinese American Bank reopened in 1936 as the American Security Bank and it and the Liberty Bank are still thriving institutions. In the earlier years of these banks there was strong rivalry among Chinese for the top positions, probably not only for prestige but also because such positions carried influence in allocating loans to Chinese clients. Now, however, a multiethnic staff of officials and employees in their central and branch banks competes for business among persons of all ethnic origins.

The Intermediary Roles

As the Chinese community grew and prospered, Caucasian business firms—banks, insurance companies, shipping agencies, wholesalers,

and others—became increasingly interested in the Chinese as customers and clients. In the period from the 1890s to the 1930s especially, these Caucasian firms employed several Chinese migrants who
could act as intermediaries between the firms and the Chinese business community. Migrants who could read and write Chinese as well
as speak it, who were respected by their fellow countrymen and
trusted by their Caucasian employers, who could help the Caucasians
understand the Chinese and vice versa, were employed as clerks and
salesmen and sometimes in higher positions. Some migrants who
secured such employment had learned English in night school after
coming to Hawaii as adults. More commonly they had been brought
to the Islands as children or youths and, like Ho Fon, had been educated in mission schools:

> Ho Fon's uncle who lived in Hawaii had become a labor agent in the
> 1870s, receiving a bonus of twenty-five dollars from the Hawaiian
> government for each Chinese brought in for plantation labor. In 1876,
> when fifteen years old, Ho Fon was brought from his village in Chung
> Shan district to Hawaii on an American sailing vessel chartered to
> bring in Chinese laborers recruited by his uncle.
>
> After arriving in Honolulu, Ho attended the Fort Street Mission
> School (later known as Iolani School), from which he graduated.
> Among his schoolmates were several persons who later became impor-
> tant figures in Hawaii, including George R. Carter who became gover-
> nor of Hawaii (1903 to 1907), A. G. M. Robertson, later a judge, An-
> tonio Perry, later chief justice, and W. M. McInerny, later a senator.
> During part of the 1880s he lived with a Caucasian who was influential
> in Honolulu at the time, a Mr. Crabbe who was married to a Hawaiian.
> In this home Ho perfected both his English and Hawaiian.
>
> In 1883 Ho joined the *Tan Shan Sun Bo* (Hawaii News), the first
> Chinese newspaper in Honolulu, as manager and translator. Several
> Chinese merchants turned to him to handle letters written in English or
> Hawaiian.
>
> He became a "faithful church member" at the Fort Street Chinese
> Church which in its early years was helped by a number of Caucasians,
> including members of a prominent missionary family, the Damons. A
> member of this family recommended Ho for a position as teller in the
> Bishop Bank, shortly after several Chinese customers had transferred
> their business to another Haole-owned bank. According to one ac-
> count Ho's first task was to win back the Chinese to Bishop Bank,
> which he did.
>
> Ho spent most of his thirty-two years of service with this bank in
> charge of the Chinese department, taking care of financial matters that

concerned Chinese, particularly those who had little or no command of English. He was empowered to make loans to Chinese merchants up to $600 without security. At the time of his retirement, in 1929, George S. Waterhouse, vice-president, and J. O. Carter, assistant cashier, characterized Ho Fon as "a man of sterling worth, whose honesty and integrity are of the highest quality."[35]

The usefulness to the migrant of this intermediary role is demonstrated by the career of Chung K. Ai, who became well known in Hawaii as C. K. Ai. For him, as for other Chinese, employment by a Caucasian was a start toward becoming an independent entrepreneur:

> In 1879, when he was fourteen years old, C. K. Ai was brought from Sai San village in Chung Shan district to Kailua, Kona, where his father, Ako, had a store. After a short stay there he was sent to Honolulu where he attended Fort Street Mission School for two years. Leaving school before graduation and still not very proficient in reading and speaking English, he spent two years assisting in his father's business ventures on the island of Hawaii. At eighteen he came back to Honolulu to try his own luck in business with some financial aid from his father. A partnership tailoring business in Chinatown failed. To improve his English he attended evening classes at Reverend Frank Damon's school. His interest in Christianity, which had begun at Fort Street School, led to his joining Fort Street Chinese Church; he remained a member of this congregation for the rest of his life, becoming one of its most influential leaders and largest contributors. One result of this was that he became well known and respected by influential Caucasians who served on the board of the church until it became independent of the Hawaiian Board of Missions in 1919.
>
> Through his father, Ai came into contact in the 1880s with James I. Dowsett by whom he was employed as clerk-bookkeeper from 1887 until Dowsett's death in 1898. After proving his competence and reliability, Ai was allowed by Dowsett to supplement his wages by undertaking a variety of ventures in his spare time: he imported goods from China, including matting, silks, peanut oil, tea, cigars, shoe leather, and nails, using Dowsett's warehouse for storage until the goods were sold; he contracted to have firewood made on property near Nanakuli and stored at the warehouse until sold to Honolulu residents, especially to Chinese; he imported pineapples from Kona for sale in the Honolulu market; with Chinese partners he contracted to dig wells; he started a coffee shop in Chinatown to be operated by another migrant; he had a building put up for a fish market near the waterfront. There were other ventures; some were profitable, some failed.

In 1898 Ai was the main promoter of City Mill Company, a rice mill and lumber business in which several Chinese bought shares. Before the company could start business the buildings were destroyed by the Chinatown fire of 1900. Losses amounting to tens of thousands of dollars were finally repaid through Ai's determination. City Mill was rebuilt, with Ai as president, and today it is a large, successful business managed by one of Ai's sons, with a cosmopolitan body of sales clerks and customers.[36]

Migrants in intermediary roles were greatly outnumbered by Hawaii-born Chinese. For members of the "early second generation," beginning with a few born in the 1860s and 1870s, as well as for migrants, employment by Caucasians provided an entrée into the Honolulu business community. The careers of these earlier Hawaii-born Chinese, such as William Kwai Fong Yap, are very much like those of the migrant intermediaries:

William Kwai Fong Yap was born in Honolulu in 1873, the son of Hakka Chinese immigrants who had become Christians in China. He was educated at the Fort Street Mission School. At the age of thirteen he started his apprenticeship in a tailor shop and worked at this trade for eight years. During the last two years of this time he also served as a clerk and interpreter in the law office of Charles L. Carter. From 1894 to 1899 he was a clerk in the government postal service of the Republic of Hawaii. For the next twenty-eight years he was associated with the Bank of Hawaii, first as a collector and finally as an assistant cashier in charge of the Chinese department. In his later years, with some of his eight sons, he developed real estate, investment, and insurance businesses.[37]

Chinese employees of Haole companies had a variety of jobs. Some of them sold life insurance, fire insurance, and automobile insurance to Chinese clients; Chinese salesmen in Haole automobile agencies competed with each other for "the Chinese business"; clerks who read and spoke both Chinese and English handled transactions with Chinese immigrant storekeepers for Haole wholesale firms and commission merchants; Chinese-speaking salesmen in Haole retail stores attended to Chinese-migrant customers; clerks helped Haole lawyers and tax experts deal with their Chinese immigrant clients; Chinese-speaking reporters for English-language newspapers covered events among the Chinese in Hawaii and to some extent in China; they were interpreters and assistants for investment companies, building-and-loan associations, collection agencies, real estate firms, and a number of other businesses dealing with Chinese migrants.

Although positions in Haole firms had some advantages for Chinese who were qualified to provide liaison with the Chinese community, those who took such positions often found their advancement within the firms limited. Some were content to remain in subordinate positions, but others came to resent what they felt to be discrimination. In any case, with their practical experience in Western business methods, many of them went into business for themselves —not into ventures that were typically carried on by migrants in the second phase, but into enterprises like the Haole-owned firms in which they had been employed. These former intermediaries made up the vanguard of the Hawaii-born Chinese businessmen of the third phase.

A Place in the Professions

Between the 1880s and 1920s a very few Chinese migrants held positions in the learned or professional occupations. Publications of this period mentioned Chinese migrants as government interpreters and translators, newspaper editors, teachers, school principals, doctors, temple priests, Christian clergymen, and religious workers, but in some of these categories there were only two or three individuals at a time. The total was very small. With few exceptions the migrants who held these positions worked with their fellow Chinese. Their roles were largely within transplanted Chinese institutions or institutions that had developed in Hawaii to meet the needs of the Chinese immigrants and their families. None of the migrant Chinese professionals competed directly with Caucasians in the same professions. In fact, except for the few Western-trained physicians and professors they were not prepared to participate in the Western professional world. At the same time, they did hold positions requiring proficiency in written Chinese, a qualification shared by few others in Hawaii, even among the Chinese migrants. Unlike most of the migrants, those who came as professional workers were not likely to have been attracted to Hawaii by the hope of becoming rich; as a group, they were quite poorly paid.

Interpreters and Translators

With the migration of thousands of Chinese to the Islands, government offices needed literate Chinese who could serve as interpreters and translators in administering laws and regulations and who could deal with legal offenders among those Chinese who neither spoke nor understood Hawaiian or English. The Board of Immigration, for instance, needed interpreters and translators in regulating Chinese immigration and dealing with immigrants; health authorities, quarantine officials, immigration inspectors, revenue and customs officers could hardly have functioned without interpreters and translators. The police and the courts relied on a Chinese staff who could speak not only Hawaiian or English or both but also several Chinese dialects—as well as being able to read and translate written Chinese.

In the early days those who could qualify for such positions were mainly migrants who had been educated both in China and Hawaii. Ho Fon, mentioned earlier, had such a dual education and occasionally served as a court interpreter. Another such migrant was Chuck Hoy, an interpreter with the U.S. Immigration Service in Honolulu from 1908 to 1920. He had received some Chinese education in his native Chung Shan district and some English education at the Fort Street Mission School in Honolulu.[38] Most of these positions, however, came to be filled by Hawaii-born Chinese, some of whom had been sent back to their fathers' villages for their early education and who later completed their schooling in Hawaii. Later, other Hawaii-born Chinese qualified for these positions by being educated in Chinese-language schools, as well as English-language schools, in Hawaii or by learning Chinese at home. William Kwai Fong Yap's service in the office of a Caucasian attorney in the 1890s illustrates how Hawaii-born Chinese served as interpreters and translators.

Religious Workers

Another professional role for Chinese migrants rose in the 1850s and 1860s from the concerns of Caucasian Christian missionaries and teachers who had been working among the Hawaiians since the 1820s. As the number of Chinese migrants multiplied, they attracted the attention of Caucasian Christians in Hawaii who, for several reasons, insisted that something be done to Christianize this new group. There was fear that the "heathen Chinese" would have a bad influence on converted Hawaiians; there was interest in continuing work among Chinese migrants who had been converted to Christianity before leaving China; and there was a desire to convert migrants and especially children of migrants who were not Christians. Although a few Caucasian religious workers in Hawaii had been missionaries in

China and knew some of the dialects spoken by the migrants, it was felt that Chinese Christians were needed to work among their fellow countrymen in the Islands. The first Chinese engaged by Caucasians to evangelize the migrants was Samuel P. Aheong, "an educated and talented Chinese" who had come to the Islands in 1854 as a laborer:

> On his arrival at the islands he . . . was employed by Mr. Torbert at Makawao [Maui]. While in the Rev. Mr. Green's school, and under the teaching of his daughter, Mary, this young Chinaman learned to speak and read the English language with great ease and fluency. So much were his services valued by the Hawaiian Board [of Missions] that during the last year of his evangelistic labors he received a salary of $1,200. He relinquished his store at Lahaina [in 1868] to engage in preaching the gospel to his countrymen, who ever listened to his addresses with delight, for he could speak in several of the dialects of China. . . . In May 1870 . . . he left with his Hawaiian wife for China, where he died.[39]

In 1875 the YMCA in Honolulu engaged a Chinese colporteur, Sit Moon, to come from San Francisco to work among the Chinese in the Islands. In 1878 the Hawaiian Board of Missions again undertook work among the Chinese and the next year helped some Chinese Christians establish the Fort Street Chinese Church in Honolulu. A Chinese evangelist, Kong Tet Yin, who had gone to Australia to work among the Chinese there after being trained by the Basel Mission in Kwangtung, was brought to the Kohala Sugar Company's plantation on the island of Hawaii in 1878 to work among the Chinese Christians there.[40] During the last quarter of the nineteenth century and the first few decades of the twentieth, Chinese Christian clergymen were brought from China and from overseas Chinese communities to serve the Chinese congregations of several churches founded by the Hawaiian Board of Missions (Congregational) and by Anglican missionaries.

After Annexation a few Chinese Christian ministers and their families entered the Islands under the exempt-categories provisions of the Chinese Exclusion Act. The 1910 census reported eleven Chinese clergymen; thirteen were reported in 1920 and nine in 1930. Probably most, if not all, of these were migrants, although subsequently most of the Christian ministers of Chinese ancestry have been second- or third-generation Chinese born in Hawaii or on the U.S. mainland. The early Chinese religious workers were among the best-educated migrants in the Islands, even though their salaries were small compared with the incomes of some of the Chinese rice planters and merchants in their congregations. With their literacy in Chinese and usually in English, their ability to speak both languages, and their identification with influential Caucasian Christians, they were important links between the Chinese and Haole communities. Most of them came with wives or married Chinese women in Hawaii, and many of their descendants have been prominent in Hawaii's religious and educational institutions.[41]

Teachers

When Chinese Christian churches were organized, beginning in the late 1870s, classes in English were commonly held at the church building with Caucasian volunteer teachers. Most of the students in such classes were youthful migrants, some of whom, like Ho Fon and C. K. Ai, had come to join fathers or older relatives in the Islands. Some migrants who had established their families in Hawaii, however, wanted their children to learn to read and write Chinese, a concern that grew stronger as these children increased in number. Chinese Christian ministers were among the first Chinese-language teachers in Hawaii, taking on this responsibility as unpaid volunteers. A few literate migrants who had clerical jobs such as those of bookkeepers in Chinese stores gave private tuition to Chinese children. The 1884 census included data for teachers but no Chinese were reported in this occupation. Census data on teachers were next issued in 1910 when forty-seven Chinese males and twenty-one females were reported in this profession. A few of these would have been migrants holding positions as Chinese-language teachers, but most of them would have been Hawaii-born Chinese who by that time were teaching in the English-medium government and mission schools for children of all ancestries, including in 1910 more than three thousand children of Chinese ancestry.

One of the first migrants who came to Hawaii specifically to teach Chinese was Chong Park Shun. Educated in Chinese classics, he came to Hawaii in 1900 and became teacher and principal of the Honolulu Anglo-Chinese Academy. In 1909 he was employed to teach Chinese at Mills School, a Congregational-sponsored school near Honolulu's Chinatown, in which Chinese boys made up most of the students. Later he taught in Wah Mun School, one of two Chinese-language schools opened in 1911, and by 1913 he had become its principal. Two other teachers in that school were brought from Yokohama, Japan, where they had been teaching in a Chinese school. Another migrant, Young Kum Hoy, was brought from Chung Shan district in 1916, when he was sixty years old, to teach in Wah Mun School. He had earned the degree of *sau choy* at the age of seventeen through examinations in Peking.[42]

Because of their low salaries, teachers in the Chinese-language schools generally took on other jobs calling for Chinese literacy, such as those of editors and writers for Honolulu Chinese newspapers and clerical work in Chinese businesses. More educated than most Chinese migrants, this small group played an important part in the developing Chinese community. Several became leaders and influential members of the many Chinese societies organized by the migrants.

College Professors

The establishment of an arts and science college at the University of Hawaii brought about the appointment, in 1920, of the first China-born member of the faculty—Dr. Tien Mu Wang—to teach Chinese. A few other China-born and China-educated faculty members were added in the 1920s and 1930s to develop the Chinese language courses and to lecture on Chinese history and civilization, Chinese art, literature, philosophy, and religion. Most influential of these was Shao Chang Lee, who had received part of his university education at Canton Christian College and Tsing Hua (Peking) and part at Yale and Columbia universities. These intellectuals were highly regarded by the Hawaii Chinese community and became another link between the Chinese and other groups in the Islands, especially the Caucasian intelligentsia, even though most of them eventually returned to China or, like Professor Lee, went on to U.S. mainland colleges and universities.[43]

Newspaper Editors

Chinese-language and Chinese-English newspapers published in Honolulu by local Chinese created positions for a few editors and writers who were part of the small professional group among the migrants. The 1884 census reported that two Chinese in Honolulu were editors; the next census giving such information, that of 1920, listed only two Chinese in the Islands (both in Honolulu) under the category of "authors, editors, and reporters"; only five were similarly listed in the 1930 census, three of them in Honolulu. There is no way of knowing whether or not those reported by the census in this category had other occupations such as that of Chinese-language teachers. At least two migrants, Chong Park Shun and Hee Jack Sun, combined their careers as Chinese-language teachers with newspaper editing. At different times they were editors of the *Lung Kee Sun Bo*. Hee was also editor of the *Sun Wan Yat Bo* in Hilo and later of the *Sun Chung Kwock Bo* in Honolulu.[44] Some migrants who were competent in written Chinese took time from other careers to write articles for Honolulu Chinese papers, but they probably would not have been enumerated as authors or reporters in the census.

Physicians

The 1884 census listed thirteen Chinese as "druggists," none as "physicians and surgeons." The 1896 census reported fifteen Chinese as "doctors" and did not specify the occupation of druggist. In the U.S. censuses of 1910 and 1920 only four Chinese were reported as physicians and surgeons. Thirteen of the "doctors" in 1896 were probably migrants who called themselves such because of their knowledge of Chinese herbs and drugs which they prescribed and dispensed from their drugstores, as the thirteen "druggists" of 1884 probably also would have done. The other two reported in the 1896 census may have been Dr. and Mrs. Khai Fai Li. Dr. Li and his wife (Kong Tai Heong) came to Hawaii in that year after medical training with European physicians at Canton Medical College and practicing briefly in Hong Kong. They opened an office in Honolulu's Chinatown and for some time their practice was almost entirely among Chinese; later on they had patients from the many ethnic groups in Honolulu, where they practiced throughout the rest of their medical careers.[45]

It is apparent, then, that by the 1930s the Chinese migrants who remained in Hawaii had found places in a wide range of occupations, skilled trades, businesses, and professions, and that even though many of them were still culturally isolated from the mainstream of Hawaii's Westernized, multiethnic society, they were an integral part of the Island economy. The next chapter discusses the shifts in attitudes and economic behavior of the migrants as they changed from sojourners into settlers.

CHAPTER 5

Settlement, Investment, Entrenchment

"WHEN I landed, all I wanted was a thousand dollars in Chinese money," a well-to-do migrant reminisced to a friend many years later. Another prosperous migrant who had come to Hawaii in 1877, when he was twenty years old, told a Honolulu reporter fifty-six years later, "I had always planned on returning to China," but he never did.[1] Like these two, almost all the migrants came to the Islands as sojourners thinking their stay would be a temporary phase of their lives, an interlude during which they could make enough money to provide a better life for themselves and their families in China. Over half of them did, in fact, return to live there permanently; but many others became settlers, having come to think of Hawaii as their permanent home and the future home of their descendants. This was particularly true of those who became established in trades, businesses, and professions and who were reluctant to give up the advantages they had gained in the Hawaiian economy. Others remained because they had gradually lost their close ties with village and kin in China and no longer felt the pull of earlier claims upon them.

Investment and the Sojourner

As long as migrants regarded themselves as sojourners in the Islands, they tended to be more interested in long-term investment in China than in Hawaii. Unmarried migrants and migrants whose wives and children remained in the home villages sent much of their earnings back to their families. If a migrant prospered, increases in his remittances might make possible a better home in the village and expanded landholdings for his family. Even when he had his wife and children with him in Hawaii, as long as he thought of himself as a *wah kiu* ("overseas Chinese") he continued to send substantial sums of money back to kinsmen in his village. Little is known about the amounts of migrants' remittances. One figure reported by the Chinese consulate was $3,930,000 remitted from Hawaii in 1930;[2] in that year there had been only about 5,300 employed Chinese foreign-born males in the Islands. While the amounts remitted by the Hawaii *wah kiu* in earlier years are not known, they must have been considerable between 1880 and 1930. Even though most migrants were earning only a few hundred dollars a year, thousands of them were employed and sending money home.

Besides sending money to kinsmen, some of the wealthier migrants who retained the sojourner outlook sent large sums of money for investment in trading firms, industries, and other enterprises in China or in the foreign-controlled areas along the China coast. Some of them, especially importers and wholesalers of Chinese goods, invested in businesses in China in order to reduce commissions to middlemen. During the 1920s Lee Ong, whose home district was Toi Shan, managed a retail and wholesale firm in Honolulu, Yuen Chong Co., dealing mainly in Chinese groceries. Apart from his branch store in Pahala on the island of Hawaii, Lee was also involved in establishing a firm in Hong Kong, Tai Yuen Chong Co., which exported Chinese goods. Another migrant, Leong Han, divided his time in the 1920s between his three firms: Wing Sing Wo Co., Ltd., a large retail and wholesale business in Honolulu, Wing Sing Fat Co., an export firm in Hong Kong, and Wing Sing Yuen, a bank in Shekki, Chung Shan district.[3] Other migrant entrepreneurs appeared to be interested in building up businesses in China through which they could have secure sources of income when they returned to live there permanently. Several prominent Hawaii Chinese businessmen, for example, pooled capital in the mid-1920s to establish a department store, Tai Tung Co., Ltd., in Shanghai.[4]

Savings in Hawaii

When migrants began to change from sojourners into settlers and became more acculturated to a money economy with all its business and financial institutions, they kept more and more of their savings in Hawaii. The village-reared migrant with little experience in handling money had not been familiar with financial institutions like banks, savings and loan associations, investment companies, and building and loan companies. Some migrants kept their savings in cash, on their person or in some hiding place. Even as late as 1931, for instance, when a 54-year-old migrant living in a Chinese society building in Tin Can Alley, Honolulu, was arrested for possession of opium, he was found to have considerable cash hidden there. Narcotics agents "found a tin of opium, two pipes, scales, a loaded revolver of Spanish make, and currency amounting to more than $1,400. Silver coins and paper money in envelopes were hidden in crevices in the attic and were claimed by Lum. In a false-bottom box they also found $400 in paper money which the Chinese said was also his."[5] Other migrants entrusted their money to kinsmen, friends, or business associates, sometimes to their regret.

Immigrant Loan Associations

Migrants who were still suspicious of Western savings institutions could get interest on their savings through the *wui*—a traditional Chinese credit or loan association they had transplanted to Hawaii. In the South China villages the *wui*, also referred to in Hawaii as the *hui*, was commonly an arrangement among families well known and trusted by one another, rather than between individuals.[6] A family without adequate funds to meet a financial obligation, such as paying for the wedding of one of its members or the education of a promising scholar, might invite ten or fifteen families to organize a *wui*. Each family would put up a like sum large enough to total the amount desired. This pool was to be made up periodically as many times as there were members. The initiating family took the first pool and hence was bound to pay its share each succeeding time. At the end of a predetermined period, perhaps at the end of a harvest, the families involved would meet and bid for the second pool—all except the one which had already received it. The family willing to accept the pool with the largest deductions—willing to accept perhaps 9.50 yuan from each family in a 10 yuan per family pool—received it. Deductions were made only by those who had not yet taken one of the pools. Drawings continued periodically until each family in the *wui* had received a pool.

The last family to receive a pool had been able to pay the reduced amounts more often than any other and received the full amount at the last meeting since no other family had a right to bid for it. This family, therefore, put in the least and got out the maximum amount. (The first family, of course, had also received the full amount but paid the most in.) A family with no urgent need for money found it profitable to delay receiving the money until the end. In the village society the *wui* was more a method of mutual aid in crises than a business concern; relations between participating families characteristically remained friendly; profit making was subordinate to personal obligations. The initiating family was especially grateful to the others for their willing and sympathetic assistance.

In Hawaii the *wui* was typically used by individual migrants or by partnerships—often to secure money for opening a new business or expanding an old one, as well as for other less directly economic purposes. The participants in the earlier *wui*s were almost invariably relatives or friends among whom there was mutual trust. Those who had received the pool had to be relied on to continue paying their shares until the final drawing. This responsibility was a moral obligation enforced by desire to maintain status among friends, not a contractual relation enforced by law and the courts. The *wui* was ordinarily organized by immigrants who did not have sufficient economic standing in the business community at large to secure a commercial loan or did not know enough about financial institutions to apply for such a loan.

The wage and money economy of the Islands, and the increased ability of Chinese immigrants to accumulate money, changed the *wui*. In the 1920s some *wui*s would be for as much as five thousand dollars, though most ranged from a few hundred dollars to a thousand. The bids for the pool at the drawings permitted a much higher rate of interest than could be made in many other investments; a *wui* member might make a profit of 5 percent or more per month. Migrants whose attentions were focused largely upon making money came to look upon the *wui* more as a profit-making opportunity than as a system of mutual self-help among friends. The more businesslike the *wui* became, the faster the friendly relationships tended to recede into the background. Desire for profit drew men into *wui*s composed of casual acquaintances who all too frequently failed to continue the payments or even exploited the practice to their own advantage. Instead of postponing receipt of the pool in order to profit by the high returns, some would secure the pool in the early drawings and then leave the Islands or otherwise avoid the subsequent payments expected of them.

Efforts to change the *wui* from a system depending on personal relations, moral obligations, and honesty into a formal and contractual arrangement, one involving promissory notes and pledges of securities, destroyed the close personal relationships of the earlier organization. Such efforts did not eliminate the risks, however, since it was difficult to enforce the contracts legally. Eventually, because of these changes, it became easier, safer, and cheaper for the migrant with good securities to borrow money through a financial institution. The risks involved in the *wui*, longer residence in Hawaii, increased acculturation to Western ways and institutions—all tended to change the Chinese immigrant into a savings bank depositor.[7]

Savings Deposits

Data concerning savings bank deposits by ethnic groups are available only for the period 1910–1936, but this was the period when more and more Chinese migrants were becoming settlers. In 1910, when 14,094 Chinese men and women were gainfully employed in Hawaii, Chinese held only 881 savings bank deposit accounts in Hawaii, totaling only about $290,000. These accounts increased rapidly after World War I—4,788 in 1920; 13,124 in 1925; 16,641 in 1930—even though the number of Chinese gainfully employed had decreased to 9,779 by 1930. The large number of Chinese deposit accounts in 1930 is partly explained by the practice among Chinese parents in the 1920s of opening a savings account for each child, often at the time of the one-month-old baby celebrations when gifts of money from relatives and friends of the parents were received. This practice seems to have been more characteristic of families settling down in Hawaii than of those accumulating funds in the father's name to be taken back to China. Part-time working students and wage-earning women, married and unmarried, also made up a large number of the Chinese depositors. By 1925 the per capita savings deposits for Chinese exceeded those for all other groups in Hawaii except Caucasians, and continued to do so at least until 1936. Up to that year the peak amount of money in these accounts—more than $5.3 million—came in 1929, amounting to a per capita savings deposit of about $200. The depression and money exchange speculation probably accounted for the decline of per capita deposits to less than $150 in 1936.[8]

Investment in Real Estate

Several migrants made fortunes in the real estate business, especially in Honolulu. One early migrant who took this route to wealth was

Y. Anin (Young Anin). A sketch of his life, published in 1913, notes that he had come from Chung Shan about 1873, worked for a while as a rice planter, and then opened a restaurant:

> After four years, Mr. Anin realized that with the constant coming of immigrants to Hawaii, real estate would prove profitable not only as an investment but as a business, and disposing of his restaurant he entered this field. He remained in this business for several years and acquired large property interests in Honolulu and about the islands which he still retains.
>
> About ten years ago Mr. Anin with several other influential and wealthy Chinese decided that the city of Honolulu stood in dire need of a clean sanitary fish market where the products of the sea could be kept fresh and displayed for sale in tempting style, and through Mr. Anin the Oahu Fish Market Company, the largest institution of its kind in the Islands, came into existence. This market covers half a block and contains a number of stalls where not only fish but other fresh meats and vegetables are retailed. . . .
>
> His residence, once that of a prince of the royal family of Hawaii, is beautifully furnished. . . .[9]

By the 1930s, besides two Chinese banks, there were Chinese-owned investment and trust companies as well as building and loan organizations; these, along with similar Caucasian-owned financial and investment firms, were providing loans to Chinese builders and mortgages for Chinese homes and real estate ventures. By 1930 Chinese had two times statistical parity as bankers, two and a half times parity as real estate agents and officials, one and a half times as builders and contractors, and two and a half times as insurance agents, managers, and officials (see Table 6).[10]

Data concerning Chinese investment in real estate cover the first three decades of this century, the decades in which the shift from sojourner to settler attitudes among migrant Chinese was most marked. In 1901 the real estate taxes of Chinese in Hawaii amounted to only about $8,000, although approximately 18,000 Chinese men were gainfully employed in the Islands at that time. In 1911, with 13,000 men still employed, only 507 Chinese were paying taxes on real estate assessed at less than a million dollars. In 1920 the number of Chinese on the real estate tax rolls had more than doubled and their taxes had risen to more than eleven times the taxes paid in 1901. By 1930 taxes on property assessed at $15.5 million were paid by 3,070 Chinese, even though the number of Chinese employed men had dropped to 8,085. Like the assessed value of real property, the per capita assessed value had increased markedly from 1911 to 1930. A comparison of the Chinese with other groups in Hawaii for this period shows that while Caucasian, Hawaiian and part-Hawaiian, and Portuguese groups each exceeded the Chinese in per capita assessed value of real property in 1911, by 1930 the Chinese were surpassed only by the Caucasians.[11]

Instead of farmland, which sojourner migrants usually bought in China, most of the property in Hawaii in which migrants first invested was in the business districts of Honolulu and towns on the other islands. They bought lots and buildings where they themselves or other migrants operated stores and small factories, garages and service stations, taxi stands and quick-food counters, restaurants, dance halls, poolrooms, and theaters. They invested in business blocks with offices for realtors, notary publics, lawyers, dentists, and physicians. Later they sensed the growing desire of Chinese migrant families to move out of the business districts and built housing for them in residential districts. Gross income returns for 1934 showed that on the island of Oahu 279 Chinese individuals, 25 partnerships, and 19 Chinese corporations secured rental licenses and reported a total gross income from rentals of $811,042.[12] Chinese individuals and corporations took out more licenses for rentals in 1934 than for any other kind of business, and partnerships for this purpose were outnumbered only by those concerned with "general merchandise, groceries and meats." A larger and larger transient population attracted to Honolulu and a growing number of city residents seeking houses to rent demonstrated to the Chinese, as well as to other investors, the economic advantages of rental property. By the 1930s Chinese landlords had units in nearly every part of Honolulu rented to people of all ethnic origins. Tourists from the U.S. mainland looking for apartments near Waikiki Beach or househunting military families in Makiki or Kaimuki were likely to find that many of the places offered to them were owned by Chinese. Many Hawaii-born Chinese doctors and dentists, schoolteachers and enterprising housewives, as well as Chinese migrant businessmen, became landlords of tenements, apartment houses, duplexes, and bungalows.[13] A rent control survey in the early 1950s reported that 25.4 percent of all rental units in Honolulu were controlled by Chinese.

Success in this field was not guaranteed. Some Chinese who invested in rental property during the booming 1920s found themselves in financial straits or bankruptcy when real estate values in Hawaii dropped during the depression of the 1930s. A second-generation Hawaii Chinese student writes of the impact this crash had on her family:

> We were living quite comfortably until 1929 when the real estate boom came along. We invested all our money in real estate and when the crash came, we were quite hard up. We all worked after school to help the family in educating us. There were people who were glad we were broke. They certainly thought mother was going to give me away for marriage to someone to help our family budget. Mother and Dad felt bad but they never showed their feelings in front of us. They knew we felt bad too.

Nevertheless, Chinese in Hawaii continued to regard land as one of the best investments. In the 1960s, when real estate values in Hawaii had risen to heights undreamed of in the 1920s, a successful second-generation Hawaii Chinese businessman cited his father's counsel to "buy land—it's the one thing that doesn't disappear" as a reason to buy property even at the new high prices.

Entrenchment by Hawaii-born Chinese Males

Estimates presented in Table 3 indicate that nearly all employed Chinese males reported in the censuses of 1890, 1896, and 1910 were migrants; about 90 percent in 1920 and 60 percent in 1930 were still of the immigrant group. But by 1940 about 80 percent of the employed Chinese males were Hawaii-born; by 1950, about 90 percent. Economic entrenchment during these latter decades, therefore, was increasingly achieved by Hawaii-born Chinese. The money that migrants spent on the education of their Hawaii-born children, as well as other help they gave toward advancing their children's careers, turned out in the end to be the best investment the migrant generation made.

The attainment of a remarkably favorable position within Hawaii's occupational structure by the children of Chinese migrants can be demonstrated in two ways: first, with census data showing the percentage distribution of employed Chinese in a hierarchy of occupational classes over the period of years for which such data are available (Table 3); second, by means of occupational indices, showing the extent to which Chinese were statistically overrepresented or

Table 3

Percentage Distribution of Chinese Men Employed in Hawaii by Occupational Class: 1890–1970

Occupational Class	1890	1896	1910	1920	1930	1940	1950	1960[a]	1970[a]
Preferred classes	11.6	9.9	22.9	32.7	50.1	59.3	72.7	74.2	73.0
Professional	0.1	0.2	0.6	1.6	4.7	5.7	10.7	16.6	21.6
Proprietary	5.9	4.9	9.7	10.4	14.2	14.7	17.3	15.6	14.0
Clerical, sales	1.3	1.8	5.4	11.5	20.7	28.7	26.2	21.3	17.9
Skilled	4.3	3.0	7.2	9.2	10.5	10.2	18.5	20.7	19.5
All other classes	88.4	90.1	77.1	67.3	49.9	40.7	25.5	22.3	27.0
Farmer	11.6	12.7	9.2	4.4	4.3	1.6	1.0	0.9	0.4
Semiskilled	1.6	2.5	5.6	5.6	5.9	12.0	11.4	10.0	9.2
Domestic, service	8.1	9.1	12.1	12.6	13.1	12.3	7.8	7.1	11.4
Unskilled	67.1	65.8	50.2	44.7	26.6	14.8	5.3	4.3	6.0
Total	100.0	100.0	100.0	100.0	100.0	100.0	98.2[b]	96.5[b]	100.0
No. males employed	13,067	16,610	13,742	11,110	8,571	7,853	8,085	9,866	13,401
No. migrant males employed[c]	13,042	16,550	13,502	9,885	5,271	1,600	900	N.A.	1,650
No. Hawaii-born males employed[c]	25	60	240	1,225	3,300	6,253	7,185	N.A.	11,750

Note: Terms used in this and later tables regarding occupational classes are abbreviated to facilitate presentation. "Occupational class" is referred to in recent censuses as "major occupation group." "Professional" comprises "professional, technical, and kindred workers"; "proprietary" comprises "managers, officials, and proprietors, except farm"; "clerical, sales" combines "clerical and kindred workers" and "sales workers"; "skilled" comprises "craftsmen, foremen, and kindred workers"; "farmer" comprises "farmers and farm managers"; "semiskilled" comprises "operatives and kindred workers"; "domestic, service" combines "domestic workers" and "service workers, except domestic"; "unskilled" combines "farm laborers (wage workers) and farm foremen" and "laborers, except farm."

a Data for 1960 are based on a 25 percent sample; for 1970 on a 20 percent sample; both samples included men in armed forces.

b Occupations not specified in 1950 amounted to 1.8 percent, in 1960, to 3.5 percent.

c Estimates for migrant and Hawaii-born males are based on census tables of age composition of all Chinese males and of Chinese employed males.

underrepresented from decade to decade in these same occupational classes (Table 4).

The most important indicator of the economic progress of the Hawaii-born Chinese is found in data regarding Chinese males in professional occupations. The proportion of professional men among the Chinese migrants in 1890 was extremely small—only about one-tenth of 1 percent (Table 3). Over the eighty years covered in this table the professional class showed an enormous proportional increase as Hawaii-born Chinese made up a growing part of the Chinese male employed group. By 1950 the 865 Chinese males in the professions—nearly all Hawaii-born—made up almost 11 percent of all employed Chinese males, and Table 4 shows that they were over-represented in this occupational class about one and a half times. They included accountants and auditors, architects, artists, chemists, Christian clergymen, dentists, draftsmen, engineers, lawyers and judges, newspaper editors and reporters, optometrists, professional musicians, pharmacists, photographers, physicians and surgeons, religious and social welfare workers, schoolteachers and college professors, and surveyors.

Most of these professions required years of Western, university-level education, and for a majority of them it was necessary to secure enough financial backing to go to the continental United States for training. These requirements signify that the Chinese who entered the professions were among those most acculturated to Western thought and values. In a very real sense their economic adjustment may be seen as growing out of their acculturation, whereas the economic adjustment of the immigrant generation and the Hawaii-born with little or no Western education represented only an accommodation to Western culture and economy. Hawaii-born men who estab-

Table 4
Occupational Indices of Chinese Men Employed in Hawaii by Occupational Class: 1910–1970

Occupational Class	1910	1920	1930	1940	1950	1970
Professional	0.4	0.5	1.0	1.2	1.5	1.4
Proprietary	2.8	3.1	3.0	2.0	1.8	1.6
Clerical, sales	1.4	2.1	3.5	2.9	2.1	0.7
Skilled	0.8	0.6	0.5	0.8	0.9	1.3
Farmer	1.4	0.8	0.9	0.6	0.3	0.7
Semiskilled	0.7	0.7	0.9	1.1	0.7	0.8
Domestic, service	2.6	2.8	4.1	1.9	1.0	0.7
Unskilled	0.8	0.8	0.5	0.3	0.2	0.8

lished themselves in the professions came to represent to the Chinese the peak of the occupational hierarchy: they enjoyed the highest social prestige not only among the Chinese but in the wider community as well.[14] This recognition is a marked departure from the aspirations and attitudes of most migrants, who attached higher prestige to the proprietary class than to the professional. They respected wealth, and migrants in traditional Chinese professions had low incomes in comparison with successful migrant businessmen. At the same time, the migrants' knowledge of Western culture was generally too limited to allow them to enter most of the remunerative Western-type professional positions opening up in Hawaii.

The economic entrenchment of the Hawaii Chinese, both immigrant and Hawaii-born, is evident in the steadily increasing proportion of those in the other three classes of preferred occupations as well as in the professions. While only about 5 percent of the Chinese men employed in 1896 were in "managerial, official, and proprietary" occupations, the percentage had risen to 14 in 1930 and to 17 in 1950. In clerical and sales occupations the percentage increased from about 2 in 1896 to 26 in 1950, in skilled occupations from 3 to 18.

Migrants had almost three times their statistical share of the managerial, official, and proprietary positions in Hawaii in 1910 and about one and a half times their share of clerical and sales jobs. Chinese continued to be overrepresented in these classes even though the numbers of employed immigrants went down rapidly each decade from 1910 to 1950. In 1930 Chinese males still had three times statistical parity in the former class and three and a half times parity in the latter. By 1950, when all but about 10 percent of the employed Chinese males were Hawaii-born, Chinese still had about two times statistical parity in both occupational classes. These data support the view that a disproportionately large number of the migrants who established families in the Islands were in business and able to get preference for their sons in managerial, proprietary, clerical, and sales occupations. Another factor in Chinese overrepresentation in these classes after 1910 was the concentration of Hawaii-born Chinese in the cities and towns where managerial and clerical positions in government (federal, territorial, and county) were also concentrated.

Migrants in skilled jobs had increased from 565 in 1896 to 982 in 1910, more than doubling the percentage of Chinese males in this class of occupations. Chinese in these occupations increased most

Migrants on board ship arriving from China; in the background, migrants returning to Hawaii after a visit to China. 1901. Hawaii State Archives.

Workers cutting sugarcane under the direction of a luna. 1896. Hawaii State Archives.

Planting rice in lower Makiki, Honolulu (an area at present changing from residential to commercial use). About 1900. Hawaii State Archives.

Bringing taro to town; on the left, a typical Chinese store of the period. About 1910. Hawaii State Archives.

Chinese carrying food and tea to field workers, 1912. Peddlers used just such carrying poles. Hawaii State Archives.

A produce store in Honolulu's Chinatown, about 1910. Hawaii State Archives.

The Honolulu store of a Hawaii Chinese wholesale-retail firm with related businesses in Hong Kong, Shekki, Maui, and San Francisco. Flowering narcissus plants indicate the Chinese New Year season. 1920s. Courtesy of Irene Chang Letoto.

News center on Beretania Street in Honolulu's Chinatown. Before 1900. G. Bertram Collection, Hawaii State Archives.

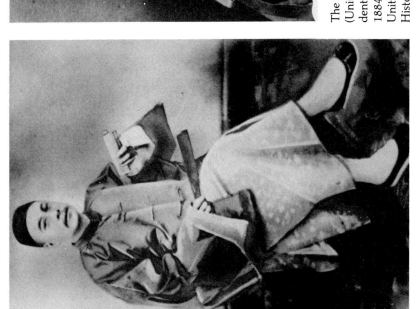

The first two leaders of the Chung Wah Wui Goon (United Chinese Society). *Left*, C(hing) Alee, President 1884–1892; *right*, Goo Kim, Vice-president 1884–1892, President 1892–1900. Courtesy of the United Chinese Society and the Hawaii Chinese History Center.

Residents fleeing the 1900 Chinatown fire, moving across town to Kawaiahao Church grounds under the direction of guards. Hawaii State Archives.

Dragon dance passing Goon Yum (Kuan Yin) Temple, corner of River and Kukui streets in Chinatown. About 1905. G. Bertram Collection, Hawaii State Archives.

The first Chinese Consulate in Hawaii, 1933. The building, the former home of a Honolulu Chinese businessman and organization leader, was purchased with funds raised by Hawaii Chinese. Photo from *Report on the Purchase of the Premises for the Chinese Consulate in Honolulu.*

Wo Hing Wui Goon, Lahaina, Maui. The clubhouse of one of the more than thirty Hoong Moon societies in the Islands. About 1908. Hawaii State Archives.

Lung Doo Chung Sin Tong, Honolulu. The first clubhouse of this district association. 1910. Courtesy of the Lung Doo Society.

Main hall used jointly by the United Chinese Society and the Honolulu Chinese Chamber of Commerce. 1929. Courtesy of Leigh-Wai Doo and the Hawaii Multi-Cultural Center.

A few of the Hawaii and West-Coast members of the revolutionary society Tung Ming Wui meeting in San Francisco with Dr. Sun Yat-sen (first person from left in second row). About 1910. Courtesy of Au Siu Hen (Edward S. H. Au).

A funeral procession in downtown Honolulu on its way to the Manoa Chinese Cemetery. 1932. Collection of the author.

Ching Ming (spring festival) at Lin Yee Chung (Manoa Chinese Cemetery). April 1977. Courtesy of Norma A. Lum and the Hawaii Multi-Cultural Center.

A Honolulu Chinese family, about 1915. Courtesy of Larry F. C. Ching.

A Honolulu Chinese family, about 1909. Courtesy of (Mrs.) Git Lee Chow and the Hawaii Multi-Cultural Center.

Sixty-first anniversary portrait of a Honolulu merchant and organization leader, with sons, daughters-in-law, and grandson. About 1921. On Char Collection, Bishop Museum.

Second generation wedding party at the clubhouse of See Dai Doo Society, Honolulu. 1933. Courtesy of David W. L. Au and the Hawaii Multi-Cultural Center.

rapidly between 1940 and 1950, with nearly a fifth of all Chinese employed males in skilled jobs in 1950, when the number stood at 1,496. Employment of additional workers of Chinese ancestry by the Navy and War Departments after the attack on Pearl Harbor was the greatest single cause of this increase. According to one report, 52 percent of the workers promoted at the Pearl Harbor Navy Yard in 1943 were Chinese.[15] During this period, few if any persons of Japanese ancestry were employed in the Pearl Harbor military installations. Skilled occupations in which Chinese males were statistically overrepresented in 1950 included airplane mechanics and repairmen, electricians, machinists, radio repairmen, plumbers, tinsmiths, coppersmiths, and sheet-metal workers. In skilled occupations as a whole, however, neither migrants nor the Hawaii-born reached statistical parity during the period 1896–1950.

The proportion of Chinese who were farmers (owners and managers as distinct from farm laborers) declined steadily after the turn of the century to only 1 percent by 1950. In actual numbers the decrease is remarkable; more than 2,100 Chinese farmers were reported in 1896 but less than 100 in 1950. From almost one and a half times statistical parity in 1910, they had less than one-third in 1950. Most Hawaii-born males, even though descended from migrants who had mainly been farmers or farm laborers in their ancestral villages, left or avoided agriculture in favor of urban occupations.

The proportion of Chinese employed in less skilled occupations also decreased as more of the migrants became settlers and an acculturated group of Hawaii-born Chinese grew up. Whereas about two-thirds of all Chinese workers in the 1890s were doing unskilled work, only about one-twentieth of Chinese men in 1950 were in unskilled jobs. Only about one-fifth as many Chinese men were doing unskilled work in 1950 as might have been expected from their proportion of the employed male population. In domestic and other service work the percentage of Chinese workers so employed increased between 1896 and 1930 but decreased during the next two decades. The actual number peaked in 1910 with 1,622 and thereafter dropped to only 631 in 1950.

The 1940 census differentiated clearly between domestic workers in private households and other service workers; most Hawaii-born Chinese males in service jobs would have been among the 880 Chinese "service workers other than domestic" rather than among the 86 in domestic service. The Hawaii-born were probably concentrated in such service jobs as those of firemen, policemen, cooks, waiters, bartenders, hospital orderlies, janitors, and porters. These were the jobs that many Hawaii-born males reared in rural Hawaii would qualify for, especially those whose families had wanted their children to begin earning money rather than continue their education. The one occupational index at the lower levels of employment that showed overrepresentation for Chinese as late as 1940 was for the service category. The rise in this index from 2.5 to more than 4 in 1930, in spite of decreasing numbers of migrants in the labor force, resulted from the fact that the proportion of all employed males in this category decreased more rapidly than the proportion of Chinese in it.

The percentage of Chinese males working in semiskilled jobs rose through the 1890 to 1940 period. From 1890 to 1920 this increase was largely because of migrants moving from unskilled to semiskilled work. With the proportion of migrants among Chinese workers declining after 1920, the increasing percentage of semiskilled workers from 1920 to 1940 indicates that it was the Hawaii-born Chinese without much education who were working into these occupations. Not until 1940 did Chinese representation in these occupations come down to statistical parity.

Grouping together the upper four classes of occupations (Table 3) and comparing them decade by decade with the lower four highlights the increasing entrenchment of Chinese men in the preferred occupational classes. In contrast with the sojourner migrant period when only about one-tenth were employed in occupations at the upper levels, in 1950 nearly three-fourths were concentrated in these occupations.

This phenomenal improvement must be seen in the context of the extensive economic changes occurring in Hawaii during this period. Migrants in the 1890s had to try to improve their position in an economy in which four fifths of the available jobs were unskilled. By 1950 Hawaii's economy had become much more urban, and military-related expenditures and tourism were replacing the sugar and pineapple industries as the leading sources of income. Occupational data for all male employees in 1950 show that only 23 percent of them were in unskilled jobs; at the higher levels the percentages were: professional, 7.3; proprietary, 9.5; clerical and sales, 12.5; skilled, 21.0—a total of 50.3 percent for the upper four classes of occupations. In that year, however, nearly three-fourths of the Chinese men were in these upper four classes. The contrast was even greater for the first three classes—54 percent of the Chinese, 29 percent for all males.

The success of Hawaii-born Chinese in consolidating the gains of the immigrant generation and in reaching into other preferred positions is strikingly demonstrated by the wide range of occupations in which Chinese males had been able to achieve statistical parity or even overrepresentation by 1950 (Table 5). Especially impressive is the fact that all but four of the forty-seven occupations were in the upper levels or preferred classes of occupations. Moreover, fourteen of these forty-three were professional occupations, few of which migrant men could have qualified for. Another thirteen were in the managerial, official, and proprietary class—the one in which migrant men had attained their greatest success—but the 1950 group included some occupations, such as federal, territorial, and county administration, which few migrants could have entered.

Another way of documenting the occupational success of the Chinese in Hawaii is provided by data available for 1930, when about three-fifths of the employed Chinese males were still of the migrant generation. Table 6 lists occupations in which Chinese in Hawaii and the continental United States had statistical parity or were overrepresented. Note the striking differences between the two groups of Chinese, most of whom originated from the same districts of Kwangtung province. Hawaii's greater openness to occupational movement is revealed in the wider range of business and professional activities among Island Chinese in 1930 as compared with Chinese on the U.S. mainland. In the continental United States, where Chinese had been seriously restricted in their occupational choices for several decades, they were heavily concentrated in five or six occupations. In these occupations they were highly overrepresented, with twelve times statistical parity as restaurant keepers and seventy-four times as laundry operatives. Under the conditions of greater freedom in Hawaii the Chinese had entered many occupations of higher income and prestige in numbers that were equal to statistical parity or above it. Of the fifteen professional occupations listed in the 1930 census, for example, the Chinese in Hawaii were overrepresented in eight, in contrast to none on the mainland. Of the fifty-five preferred occupations listed, Chinese were overrepresented in thirty-five in Hawaii and only seven on the mainland. Moreover, the wide range of occupations in which the Chinese in Hawaii had achieved statisti-

Table 5

Occupational Indices of 1.0 or Over for Chinese Men Employed in Hawaii: 1950

Occupation	Occupational Index	Occupation	Occupational Index
Professional		*Clerical*	
Accountants, auditors	2.7	Bookkeepers	3.3
Architects	1.0	Stenographers, typists, secretaries	1.7
Artists, art teachers	1.3		
Chemists	1.7	*Sales*	
Dentists	3.3	Hucksters, peddlers	1.6
Designers, draftsmen	2.8	Insurance agents, brokers	1.9
Engineers (civil)	2.5	Real estate agents, brokers	2.9
Lawyers, judges	1.0	Salesmen in wholesale trade	1.2
Pharmacists	2.5	Salesmen in retail trade	1.9
Photographers	1.5		
Physicians, surgeons	2.8	*Skilled, craftsmen, foremen*	
Social, welfare, recreation workers	1.4	Bakers	1.2
Surveyors	1.3	Electricians	1.4
Teachers[a]	1.2	Linesmen, servicemen (power)	1.1
		Machinists, job setters	1.6
Managerial, official, proprietary		Mechanics, repairmen (airplane)	2.3
Officials, inspectors (federal)	1.4	Mechanics, repairmen (radio, TV)	1.7
Officials, inspectors (territorial, local)	1.5	Plumbers, pipe fitters	1.2
Other specified managers and officials	1.8	Tailors, furriers	1.8
Managers, officials (proprietary—salaried)	1.5	Tinsmiths, coppersmiths, sheetmetal	3.6
Wholesale trade	1.5		
Retail trade	2.4	*Semiskilled*	
Finance, insurance, real estate	1.5	Meat cutters (except slaughterhouse)	4.5
Managers, officials (proprietary—self-employed)	2.4	Operatives, public administration	1.6
Construction	1.0		
Manufacturing	1.5	*Service workers*	
Wholesale trade	2.5	Cooks (except private household)	3.1
Food and dairy products stores	3.8	Waiters, bartenders, counter workers	1.7
Eating and drinking places	3.2		

Source: Andrew W. Lind, "Mounting the Occupational Ladder in Hawaii," Romanzo Adams Social Research Laboratory Report, no. 24, January 1957 (mimeographed): Hawaiian Collection, Hamilton Library, University of Hawaii at Manoa.

a Not elsewhere counted.

Table 6

Occupational Indices of 1.0 or Over for Chinese Men Employed in Hawaii and the Continential
United States: 1930

	Occupational Index	
Occupationa	Chinese Males in Hawaii	Chinese Males in Continental U.S.
Professional		
Dentists	4.0	—
Draftsmen	1.9	—
Photographers	1.8	—
Accountants, auditors	1.7	—
Civil engineers, surveyors	1.6	—
Chemists	1.4	—
Physicians, surgeons	1.3	—
Schoolteachers	1.0	—
Proprietary		
Restaurant, café, lunchroom keepers	5.0	12.7
Retail dealers	4.9	2.0
Insurance agents, managers, officials	2.6	—
Real estate agents, officials	2.5	—
Manufacturers	2.3	—
Bankers, bank officials	2.0	—
Managers, officials in manufacturing	1.8	—
Wholesale dealers, importers, exporters	1.6	3.5
Garage owners, managers, officials	1.3	—
Builders, building contractors	1.3	—
Hotel keepers, managers	—	1.0
Clerical, sales		
Office boys	4.5	—
Clerks in stores	4.5	3.7
Bookkeepers, cashiers	4.4	—
Clerks (except in stores)	3.4	—
Stenographers, typists	3.4	—
Salesmen	3.2	1.2
Agents, collectors, credit men	1.9	—
Commercial travelers	1.5	—
Skilled		
Bakers	4.5	—
Shoemakers, cobblers (not in factory)	4.3	—
Tailors	3.4	—
Mail carriers	3.2	—
Jewelers, watchmakers, goldsmiths, silversmiths	3.0	1.0
Compositors, linotypers, typesetters	1.3	—
Machinists	1.0	—
Mechanics	1.0	—
Painters, glaziers, varnishers (building)	1.0	—
Farm		
Farm managers, foremen	—	1.2
Farmers (owners, tenants)	1.1	—

Table 6 (Continued)

	Occupational Index	
	Chinese Males in Hawaii	Chinese Males in Continental U.S.
Occupation[a]		
Semiskilled		
Sailors, deckhands	—	6.7
Fishermen, oystermen	—	2.4
Deliverymen (bakeries, stores)	1.8	—
Chauffeurs, truck and tractor drivers	1.1	—
Guards, watchmen, doorkeepers	1.1	—
Operatives in iron and steel, machinery, vehicle industries	1.0	—
Domestic, service		
Servants	5.4	21.9
Laundry operatives	5.2	74.1
Waiters	5.1	22.8
Unskilled		
Janitors, sextons	2.6	—
Laborers, porters, helpers in stores	1.8	—
Garage laborers	1.1	—
Laborers (domestic and personal service)	1.0	1.6

a The numbers of specified occupations for which comparable data were available, by classes of occupations, are as follows: professional, 15; proprietary, 11; clerical, 8; skilled, 21; semiskilled, 14; farm, 2; domestic, 4; unskilled, 13.

cal parity or better suggests that the Island group was much more secure occupationally than the mainland group—less dependent, that is, upon a few symbiotic occupations.

Chinese Women in Employment

The entry of Chinese women into paid employment has been another remarkable phase of the economic adjustment of Island Chinese. Throughout the period of Chinese immigration, and in fact through the first two decades after American exclusion laws were applied, a distinctive feature of the Chinese group was the small number of gainfully employed women. Even when Chinese women migrants increased, especially during the 1880s and 1890s,[16] relatively few worked regularly in paid jobs, in sharp contrast to women of other immigrant groups. In the more numerous Punti group, husbands who brought wives to the Islands were usually prosperous enough not to require, or desire, their wives to work outside the home. Moreover, footbinding of Punti women effectually prevented wives from becoming wage earners.[17] The ninety-eight Chinese employed women reported in the 1890 census constituted only about one-seventh of the Chinese females fifteen years of age or older. Some of them would have been Hawaii-born. Eighty-five who were listed as laborers or as farmers would have been mostly Hakka women who did not practice footbinding; women in many of the Hakka families, which had started coming to Hawaii as early as the 1860s, worked in sugarcane fields, in rice paddies, and on truck farms, especially in districts where Hakka Christian farming families were concentrated.

The 1896 census reported 1,419 foreign-born Chinese women living in Hawaii, in addition to 48 Hawaii-born Chinese females fifteen years old or older, but only 100 Chinese employed women. In 1910, only 352 of the 2,300 Chinese women were reported as employed; probably more than half of them were Island-born. Ten years later, Chinese employed females still numbered less than 500, although there were nearly 1,500 foreign-born Chinese women twenty-one years of age and older and about 600 Hawaii-born Chinese females fifteen years of age and over.

The small proportion of Chinese women working outside their homes was in accord with Chinese village customs and attitudes. Except for families in dire poverty, women would rarely have been allowed to leave home to work for money; those who did so were a class apart. Because of this attitude, most early immigrant parents were unwilling to have their daughters get the kind of education that would prepare them for paid work. Chinese Christian families and other Chinese families influenced by Western attitudes in Hawaii, however, were less likely to object to education for their daughters, and most of the employed Chinese women in 1910 and 1920 probably came from such families. The readiness with which Chinese women could find paying jobs during the early part of the twentieth century and their substantial contribution to family incomes help to explain why the old attitudes faded away even among the more conservative Chinese:[18] between 1920 and 1930 the number of gainfully employed Chinese women increased 145 percent, from 493 to 1,208. By the 1920s and 1930s most immigrant parents had lived in the Islands twenty or thirty years or longer, and they came to tolerate and even encourage their daughters' going out to work. The percentage of Chinese women reported by the census as employed rose from 14 in 1920 to 26 in 1930, 32 in 1940, 35 in 1950, 43 in 1960, and 52 in 1970.

Along with the increase in numbers of employed Chinese

women there was a remarkable improvement in their occupational distribution (Table 7). Sixty-four of the 98 employed in 1890 were reported as unskilled laborers, 21 as farmers. Most of the other thirteen were probably in some kind of service work. This distribution indicates the sort of employment that could be found at that time by foreign-born and Hawaii-born women, mostly unschooled or poorly educated, living in rural areas.[19] In contrast, nearly 70 percent of the women employed in 1930 were in professional, proprietary, and clerical and sales occupations; very few were reported as farmers and unskilled laborers. It is especially remarkable that 37 percent had professional positions, since these required advanced schooling, indicating the great change in Chinese immigrants' attitudes toward their daughters' education. In fact, so many daughters and granddaughters of Chinese immigrants had become schoolteachers that by 1930 they represented 14 percent of all women schoolteachers in the Islands and constituted one-third of all Chinese employed women.[20] Because of the high proportion of teachers, Chinese employed women had nearly eight times as high a percentage in the professional category as employed Chinese men in 1930. The census reported 442 Chinese women in professional occupations and only 259 men. More Chi-

Table 7
Percentage Distribution of Chinese Women Employed in Hawaii by Occupational Class: 1890–1970

Occupational Class	1890	1910	1930	1940	1950	1960[a]	1970[a]
Preferred classes	3.0	31.6	70.8	61.6	77.2	73.6	72.5
Professional	2.0	7.5	36.6	23.5	20.9	21.4	19.0
Proprietary	1.0	4.8	7.4	6.8	7.5	6.3	5.4
Clerical and sales	—	12.5	23.1	29.7	47.5	44.9	46.2
Skilled	—	6.8	3.7	1.6	1.3	1.0	1.9
All other classes	97.0	68.4	29.2	38.4	22.8	26.4	27.5
Farmer	21.4	—	2.6	0.4	—	0.4	0.1
Semiskilled	—	0.3	6.4	16.3	8.6	9.5	7.9
Domestic, service	—	14.9	16.0	16.5	12.6	11.5	17.9
Unskilled laborer	65.4	53.2	4.2	5.2	1.2	0.8	1.6
Occupation not specified	10.2	—	—	—	0.4	4.2	—
Total	100.0	100.0	100.0	100.0	100.0	100.0	100.0
Number women employed	98	352	1,208	2,835	3,803	5,775	9,819

a Data for Chinese women for 1960 are based on a 25 percent sample; those for 1970 are based on a 20 percent sample.

nese men (56) were in teaching than in any other profession, but proportionately more men than women were in professions requiring
university and postgraduate education, such as medicine, dentistry,
law, and engineering. In 1930 primary and secondary school teaching in Hawaii required only five years beyond elementary school,
although many teachers had college degrees.

The high proportion of Chinese women in the preferred occupations continued through other census periods covered in Tables 7
and 8. The actual number in the professions continued to grow even
though the occupational index for Chinese women professionals decreased after 1930. The percentage decline in the professional class
was offset by the increasing number and percentage of Chinese
women in clerical and sales occupations. The changing proportions
of Chinese women in these two classes of occupations reflect changing employment opportunities in the Islands, especially in Honolulu,
as well as changes in the relative position of Chinese women when
second- and third-generation women of other immigrant groups became qualified for jobs at the upper occupational levels. For one
thing, competition for teaching positions increased. Young Chinese
women became unwilling to teach on the neighbor islands where
very few Chinese lived any longer, so schools on those islands were
increasingly staffed by teachers of other ethnic groups, especially
Japanese. At the same time, Chinese women were more attracted to
clerical jobs and their rising pay scales in government and private industry in Honolulu.

By 1930 Chinese employed women were in a much better posi-

Table 8
Number and Occupational Indices of Chinese Women Employed in Hawaii by Occupational Class:
1930–1970

Occupational Class	Number Employed				Occupational Index			
	1930	1940	1950	1970	1930	1940	1950	1970
Professional	442	665	795	1,866	1.6	1.5	1.3	1.1
Proprietary	89	193	285	534	1.7	1.2	1.1	1.1
Clerical and Sales	279	841	1,807	4,532	1.7	1.6	1.3	1.1
Skilled	45	46	50	190	0.7	1.2	0.9	1.1
Farmer	31	12	—[a]	9	1.5	0.3	—[a]	0.2
Semiskilled	77	462	327	778	0.8	1.2	0.7	1.0
Domestic, service	194	468	479	1,757	1.9	0.6	0.6	0.8
Unskilled laborer	51	148	46	153	0.4	0.4	0.3	0.7

[a] Data for farmers were included in the proprietary class in 1950.

tion than were employed women in the Islands as a group (Table 8). They were markedly overrepresented in professional, proprietary, and clerical and sales occupations and were below statistical parity in skilled, semiskilled, and unskilled jobs. The overrepresentation of the parent generation in proprietary occupations was, to be sure, a great advantage to Chinese women who went into proprietary and clerical and sales occupations themselves. Chinese women were overrepresented as farmers, even though few in number, probably because widows of Chinese immigrant farmers continued to own and operate their husbands' farms.

Table 9 specifies the occupations in which Chinese women were statistically overrepresented (occupational indices above 1.0) in 1930 and 1950. In 1930 there were five types of jobs (other than farm

Table 9
Occupational Indices of 1.0 or Over for Chinese Women Employed in Hawaii: 1930 and 1950

Occupation	Occupational Index	
	1930	1950
Professional		
Teachers	2.0	1.7
Accountants, auditors	—	1.7
Social, welfare, recreation workers	—	1.2
Librarians	—	1.2
Proprietary, officials, managers		
Retail dealers, store managers	2.1	—
Managers, officials, proprietors (self-employed)	—	1.7
Restaurant, café, lunchroom keepers	1.2	—
Clerical, sales		
Saleswomen, clerks in stores	2.8	1.1
Bookkeepers, cashiers	2.4	1.4
Clerks (except in stores)	1.4	—
Stenographers, typists, secretaries	—	1.3
Telephone operators	—	1.1
Farmers		
Farm owners and tenants	1.5	—
Semiskilled		
Tailoresses	1.9	—
Operatives (clothing industries)	1.6	—
Operatives (canning industries)	1.5	—
Service workers		
Waitresses	1.4	—
Unskilled laborers (canning industries)	1.7	—

owners and tenants) below the skilled level in which their indices were above parity; in 1950 there were none. Chinese women in 1950 were overrepresented in nine occupations in the clerical and sales, proprietary, official, and managerial, and professional categories, but, surprisingly, they were below parity as retail dealers and store managers in which they had had twice their statistical share in 1930. The wider distribution of Chinese women through the professional occupations is shown by the fact that whereas they were overrepresented in only the teaching profession in 1930, they were overrepresented in four professions in 1950.

Employment and Income

The occupational data have demonstrated the movement of Chinese up the occupational ladder during the period when most of the employed Chinese men were migrants and during the later decades when the employed Chinese group was increasingly Hawaii-born. Data that would make it possible to correlate improvements in occupational status with income are not available, but miscellaneous information points to the general trend. Starting with the contract laborers—the earliest migrants who came in considerable numbers— it will be recalled that the first group, who came in 1852, received $3 a month and board; contracts in 1870 called for $6 a month and board; in the late 1890s, $15 a month (if twenty-six days were worked) without board. Most Chinese who stayed on sugar plantations after their contracts ended worked as day laborers instead of signing another contract. During the 1870s these day laborers were paid about $10 a month; in the mid-1880s, about $13.50 a month; in the 1890s, about $15 to $18 a month; in the 1900s and 1910s, still less than $1 a day with a work year of 312 days. The few Chinese who were employed as "skilled hands" on the sugar plantations in 1915 were paid an average of $1.11 a day.[21]

On the basis of data in Table 3 it can be estimated, therefore, that about 80 percent of the 13,000 to 18,000 employed Chinese men during the 1890s were receiving no more than $250 to $300 per year in cash wages, and more than 60 percent of the 13,742 employed in 1910 were receiving no more than $300 or $400 per year, although some of these men undoubtedly added to their income by after-work activities such as gardening, fishing, and peddling.

Information about the incomes of migrants at levels above those of unskilled labor and domestic service is even scarcer. The 1913, 1929, and 1936 publications on the Chinese in Hawaii are silent on this subject, but they do contain success stories of a few hundred migrants who became comfortably well off, some of them even quite wealthy. Chun Fong, the migrant businessman who received about $600,000 for his share in a sugar plantation before returning to China in 1890, is a well-known example of the migrants who "made their fortune" in Hawaii. In the early 1930s Chinese friends assured the writer that at least five migrants in Honolulu at that time were millionaires. Emphasis on success stories undoubtedly gives a distorted impression of the general situation among migrants of the 1890s and early decades of this century. Migrants in sales and clerical jobs in that period probably received little more in cash wages than ordinary laborers, although they usually received meals and lodging in addition and had some prospect of becoming a partner in the business.

Much later, in 1939, a survey of white-collar male workers in Hawaii reported that the Chinese included in the survey received an average monthly pay of $124 (about $1,500 a year); Caucasians received an average of $139 a month, Japanese $98 a month.[22] How near the $1,500 a year was to the median income of Chinese males is unknown, but about 40 percent of the Chinese males at that time were in semiskilled, service, and unskilled occupations with lower average incomes than those of white-collar workers, while about 20 percent were in the proprietary and professional occupations with higher average incomes.

The favorable position of Chinese in Hawaii's economy was documented for the first time in census reports when the 1950 census included income data for 1949. Median income for Chinese males receiving income, $2,964, was 27 percent higher than the median of $2,340 for all males—and highest of all ethnic groups for which results were reported. Caucasian males came second with a median income of $2,856, followed by Japanese ($2,427), Hawaiians and part-Hawaiians ($2,369), and Filipinos ($1,995). Comparable data for females in 1949 showed the median for "all races" to be $1,247; Chinese females had the highest median income of any ethnic group reported ($1,887), followed by Caucasians ($1,551), Japanese ($1,207), Hawaiians and part-Hawaiians ($999), and Filipinos ($548).

The 1970 census report on incomes in 1969 showed that the median income of all males with incomes had more than doubled since 1949, as had the median for the four ethnic groups on which such data were published. Again, Chinese males had the highest median income ($8,000)—20 percent above the median of $6,529 for all males. Japanese males came second with $7,839, followed by Caucasians ($6,173) and Filipinos ($5,252). The median for Chinese females ($3,594) was above that for "all races" ($3,222) but below that of Japanese females, who had the highest median income ($3,623).

Data on family incomes for 1969 show a similar high position for the Chinese with a median income of $14,179—23 percent above the median for all family incomes ($11,554). Japanese families had a median income of $13,542; Caucasians $10,508, Filipinos $9,289. Similarly a higher proportion of the Chinese males were receiving incomes of $15,000 or more—14 percent compared with 12 percent of the Caucasian males, 10 percent of the Japanese males, and 2 percent of the Filipino males.[23] If the census had reported individual incomes of $50,000 or higher, the data would undoubtedly have shown a higher proportion of Caucasian men receiving such incomes than Chinese or men of other ethnic groups. In any case, data given for 1949 and 1969 indicate that Chinese as a group were not only well entrenched financially but in a superior economic position in comparison with other groups in the Islands.

The success of the Hawaii-born Chinese in establishing themselves in preferred occupations and in favorable financial circumstances has created a problem that is becoming apparent among the younger generation. Since most Chinese parents in the Islands can give their children opportunities for superior educational and occupational training, the young anticipate employment at upper occupational levels. But young Chinese are coming into the job market at a time when openings on these upper levels are not increasing as rapidly as in their parents' youth, nor as rapidly as young people of all ethnic groups are prepared to fill them.[24] In some preferred occupations the supply of qualified applicants already exceeds the demand —the outstanding current example is that of several hundred more college graduates with teaching credentials than the school system is employing. Competition from persons of other ethnic groups seeking to rise on the occupational scale also means the loss of the initial advantages enjoyed by Chinese migrants and the early group of educated Hawaii-born Chinese.

CHAPTER 6

Urbanization

EVEN though most of the Chinese migrants to Hawaii came from rural villages and found their first opportunities in agricultural areas of the Islands, they and their Hawaii-born descendants have been constantly attracted to the urban areas of the chief ports: Honolulu on Oahu, Lahaina and Wailuku on Maui, and Hilo on the island of Hawaii. The very earliest Chinese immigrants, as resident traders and domestic servants, were largely concentrated in these ports, but in the plantation frontier period of the 1850s to 1890s the Chinese population in the rural districts grew more rapidly. The geographical redistribution of the Chinese and their eventual concentration on the island of Oahu, especially in Honolulu, resulted from a complex of economic, cultural, and social changes. Urbanization in Hawaii was not peculiar to the Chinese, of course, nor was Hawaii different in this respect from the continental United States, but the particular circumstances in which the Chinese in Hawaii became concentrated in urban areas were related to other changes taking place among the Chinese migrants and their families. Among these circumstances were the business and employment opportunities opening up in the towns, the growth of Chinese families with the bringing in of more Chinese women, the location of women and families in the urban areas, and the gradual movement of rural families into the towns and into Honolulu.

The urbanization of the Chinese was not as conspicuous while new migrants were arriving from China, especially during the 1880s and 1890s, as it was later on. Chinese migrants in the rural areas outnumbered those in the towns for several decades, but with the restriction of Chinese labor immigration and the return of many sojourner laborers to China both the numbers and the proportion of Chinese in nonurban areas fell rapidly. On every island except Oahu the Chinese population decreased steadily, even though the total population of each island was increasing. At the same time, Chinese who remained on those islands were increasingly concentrated in the towns rather than remaining distributed through the rural areas. On the island of Hawaii the Chinese population, mostly migrant men in rural areas, reached a peak of 4,934 in 1884—20 percent of the island's total population of 24,991 and over a fourth of all the Chinese in the Islands. By 1910 the number of Chinese had gone down to 2,995, only 5 percent of the island's population, but 15 percent of these Chinese were in Hilo, the main town and port of the island. By 1950, when the total population of the island had grown to more than 68,000, the Chinese had declined to 1,360, with 61 percent of them concentrated in Hilo. The majority of the Chinese remaining on Maui in 1950 were clustered in the towns of Wailuku, Kahului, and Lahaina; those on Kauai, in Lihue and Kapaa.

Oahu, like the other main islands, had large sugar and rice plantations employing Chinese workers, and there was a rural Chinese population of independent farmers, especially after Honolulu's growing population provided an expanding market for fresh produce which was difficult to bring in from the other islands. More Chinese went into truck farming on Oahu than on any other island. In 1884, a time of heavy immigration of Chinese agricultural laborers, 42 percent of all Chinese in the Islands were already on the island of Oahu in rural and urban districts. By 1900 this proportion had risen to 54 percent. During the early decades of this century the buildup of the naval base at Pearl Harbor and other military installations on Oahu, outside of Honolulu, provided civilian jobs that attracted many Chinese. But it was the growth of the Chinese population in Honolulu which largely accounted for the fact that 72 percent of Hawaii's Chinese were on Oahu by 1920 and 91 percent by 1950.

Concentration in Honolulu

Every census from 1853 to 1970, except for 1890, has shown an increase in the number of Chinese residents in Honolulu (Table 10). During the fifty years after Annexation the number of Chinese in Honolulu nearly tripled—in spite of the return to China of thousands of sojourner migrants and the deaths of others. In 1930 Chinese in Honolulu outnumbered those in San Francisco, which that year had the largest Chinese population of any city in the continental United

Table 10
Chinese in Honolulu and the Hawaiian Islands: 1853–1970

Year	Number of Chinese in Hawaiian Islands	Number of Chinese in Honolulu	Per- centage	Total Honolulu Popu- lation	Percentage of Total Island Population in Honolulu	Percentage of Chinese in Total Honolulu Population
1853	364	124	34	11,455	16	1
1866	1,206	370	31	13,521	22	3
1872	1,938	632	31	14,852	27	4
1878	5,916	1,299	22	14,114	24	9
1884	17,939	5,225	29	20,487	25	26
1890	15,301	4,407	29	22,907	26	19
1896	21,616	7,693	36	29,920	27	26
1900	25,767	9,061	35	39,306	26	23
1910	21,674	9,574	44	52,183	27	19
1920	23,507	13,383	57	83,327	33	16
1930	27,179	19,334	71	137,582	37	14
1940	28,774	22,445	78	179,326	47	13
1950	32,376	26,724	83	248,007	50	11
1960	38,119	30,078	79	294,194	47	10
1970	52,583[a]	48,897	93	442,397	58	11

Note: Chinese data for 1853–1890 are for foreign-born only. The area defined as "Honolulu" was not constant in all censuses.

a U.S. census tabulation procedures have resulted in the inclusion of certain part-Chinese in the category
Chinese, and the exclusion of other part-Chinese. It is estimated that "unmixed" Chinese in 1950 totaled
about 29,500, in 1970, about 30,000. See Clarence E. Glick, "Interracial Marriage and Admixture in
Hawaii," Social Biology 17(1970):278–291.

States. From 1884 onward a higher proportion of the Hawaii Chinese
than of the total Hawaii population was concentrated in Honolulu,
and in the 1880s and 1890s one-fourth of Honolulu's population was
Chinese.

The urban occupations opening up in Honolulu were the main
objectives of Chinese moving from the other islands and from the
rural areas of Oahu. Less than a fifth of Hawaii's employed Chinese
men had urban jobs in the Honolulu district in 1884 (Table 11); by
1930 this proportion had risen to more than three-fifths and by 1950
to more than five-sixths. After Hawaii-born Chinese women entered
the labor force, they were concentrated in Honolulu even more
heavily than the men.

It is impossible to say how much of the growth of Honolulu's
Chinese community resulted from the movement of migrants from
rural areas and small towns, but by 1930 this movement had clearly
become less important than the cityward movement of Hawaii-born
Chinese. By that time migrants who had come to Hawaii before Annexation had spent over thirty years in the Islands. Most of those

Table 11

Chinese Employed in Honolulu and in the Hawaiian Islands Exclusive of Honolulu: 1884–1970

	Males			Females		
Year	Employed in Honolulu	Employed in Hawaiian Islands Exclusive of Honolulu	Percent-age of Total Employed in Honolulu	Employed in Honolulu	Employed in Hawaiian Islands Exclusive of Honolulu	Percent-age of Total Employed in Honolulu
1884	2,918[a]	13,600[b]	18[b]	N.A.	N.A.	—
1910	5,004	8,736	36	169	183	48
1920	5,143	5,967	46	310	183	70
1930	5,287	3,284	62	882	326	73
1940	6,028	1,825	77	2,239	596	79
1950	6,829	1,332	84	3,504	328	91
1960	9,281	585	94	5,775	366	94
1970[c]	12,364	951	93	9,174	587	94

a Not included are 1,206 men reported as agriculturists, pig and poultry raisers, and fishermen.

b Estimated.

c Data are for the Honolulu Standard Metropolitan Area, which in the 1970 census included the entire island of Oahu.

who had been interested in moving into the city had probably done so early in their careers, and as the years passed fewer and fewer of the rural migrants sought employment in Honolulu. Only 40 percent of the Chinese men fifty-five years old and over, most of them migrants, were in Honolulu in 1930, while 75 percent of the men under that age (fifteen to fifty-four) were in the city. In the mid-1930s several hundred of the Chinese husbands and unmarried Chinese men in Honolulu were persons who had been born and reared in other Island communities. These men commonly belonged to families which moved from the country member-by-member, as described in this account written by a Honolulu Chinese student in 1937:

> About forty years ago my maternal grandfather and grandmother emigrated from China to Oahu. They settled in a section of the island known as W—— and became rice planters. . . . Later two boys and four girls were born to them.
>
> My mother was the eldest child in this family. The children all grew up and went to school in W——. My mother was married to my dad in 1912. My dad had come to Oahu from China with his parents when he was about four years old. After dad's and mother's marriage, they moved to Honolulu to set up housekeeping. In the long space of fifteen years, four children were born to them.
>
> In the meantime my elder Uncle Wah came to live with us in

town when he was about fifteen. Uncle Kwock followed him to live in our home a few years later. Many years passed and after becoming successful in business, Uncle Wah married and established his own home in ———, then the most select section of [Honolulu] [according to the Chinese]. Then, after Uncle Wah became fully settled in his new home, my grandparents and two younger aunts moved to town to live in his home. My other Aunt Mei had married a Chinese of W——, and they operated a little store where groceries and general merchandise were sold.

Uncle Kwock went to live with Uncle Wah in due time. The house, it seems, was purposely built large enough to accommodate my grandparents, aunts, uncle, and Uncle Wah's own family.[1]

Some immigrant parents who had settled in rural districts or small towns did move into Honolulu late in life, long after their grown-up children had gone to the city. Retired or unable to continue working, they went to live in their children's homes in Honolulu. Tyau Fook was one of these parents:

Mr. Tyau Fook was born in Sun On district, Kwangtung, China. Coming to Hawaii at an early age he became a merchant at Kula, Maui. To Mr. and Mrs. Tyau were born seven sons and three daughters. The older sons moved to Honolulu and secured work there. One became a plumber, another an employee for a lumber company, another a clerk in a Chinese-owned furniture store. One of the daughters married a Chinese living in Honolulu. After operating his store for almost forty years at Kula, Mr. Tyau finally sold out and he and Mrs. Tyau and the younger children moved into Honolulu to live with the older married sons in a large house in the Palama section of town. At the time of Mr. Tyau's death in 1937, there were, in addition to his wife and ten children, five daughters-in-law, nine grandsons, fourteen granddaughters, and two great-grandchildren, all living in Honolulu.[2]

Latecomers into the city included a number of aging familyless migrants. Many of these were men who after a lifetime in agricultural labor had failed to provide for their old age. They turned to the city hoping for help from more successful relatives, from *heung li*, from some Chinese organization, or as a last resort from a public welfare agency.

The phenomenal concentration of the Chinese in a single city in a region dominated by plantation agriculture until World War II cannot be explained entirely by the movement from the rural districts and small towns. Two other factors were important: direct migration to Honolulu from China and the disproportionate establishment of Chinese migrant families in Honolulu rather than in other parts of the Islands.

Hundreds of youths and men, usually kinsmen of migrants already living in Honolulu, came directly to jobs in Honolulu without following the usual pattern of going first into rural work. This was particularly true during the 1880s and 1890s, with smaller numbers coming in after 1900. Admission of these migrants as members of categories exempted from exclusion was facilitated by the growth of the Chinese merchant class in Honolulu.

Probably most important of all was the fact that from the 1870s onward a higher proportion of the families established in Hawaii by migrants were in Honolulu than elsewhere in the Islands. Census data for 1884 and 1890 show that while only about one-fourth of the Chinese men in Hawaii were in Honolulu, they had about three-fifths of the foreign-born Chinese wives. Immigration permits issued to Chinese women between May 1893 and November 1898 show that 74 percent of the women expected to live in Honolulu, even though only about a third of the migrant men were located there.[3] Chinese families continued to be concentrated in Honolulu: about half of them in 1896, two-thirds by 1920, three-fourths by 1930, five-sixths by 1950.[4] In 1896 half the Chinese children in the Islands were in Honolulu though only a third of the total Chinese population lived there. In 1910, when over half (56 percent) of the Chinese still lived in other parts of the Islands, three-fifths of the Hawaii-born Chinese lived in Honolulu.

Chinatown: The Nucleus

As in other cities with sizable Chinese migrant populations, one district in Honolulu came to be known as Chinatown or the "Chinese quarter," even though there was never a time when this section was exclusively Chinese or when all Chinese in Honolulu lived there.[5] Honolulu's Chinatown could be more accurately described as the nucleus of the Chinese community—a place where the Chinese first concentrated and which continued to be the center of Chinese business and social life even after Chinese residences were dispersed throughout the city.

Concentration of the Chinese in this area began in the 1850s; in 1866 over half the 370 "Chinese foreigners" in Honolulu lived in the downtown section, which included the low-lying land immediately northwest of the present central business district, the area that came to be called Chinatown. Forty-one other Chinese lived directly south of that section, nearer the mouth of Honolulu harbor, in an area which was then part of the waterfront and trading district. One hundred others, most of the remaining Chinese residents, were reported as living in the sections of Honolulu that were the chief residential areas of the Caucasians; most of these Chinese were undoubtedly domestic servants. A few Chinese in the Honolulu district but on the outskirts of the town were engaged in farming or trading with the Hawaiians who were the main residents of these outlying sections.

The 1869 business directory of Honolulu gave the addresses of sixty-nine Chinese businesses, nearly all in the Chinatown section.[6] During the 1870s Chinese business activities continued to be centralized in this one section of downtown Honolulu. In 1872 the stores of 96 percent of the Chinese who had retail merchandise licenses were in this area, and in 1878 about 83 percent. All the Chinese wholesale firms were located there in 1872 and 1878.[7] In 1884, some 79 percent of the retail licenses obtained by Honolulu Chinese were for firms located in what the census report of that year called "the old Chinese quarter," as were 82 percent of the "victualling" licenses and all but one of the wholesale licenses. The common practice among Chinese during that period of living on their business premises explains the 1884 census report that more than 70 percent of the Chinese males and three-fourths of the approximately 350 Chinese migrant families in the Honolulu district lived in that same area.

A news item on 8 January 1886 noted that "new buildings go up at a fabulous rate of speed on the Chinese end of King Street." Later that year, in what the newspapers called "the Chinatown fire," over thirty acres of buildings in the "congested Chinese quarter" burned down. Although government authorities attempted to enforce regulations requiring that new buildings in the burned out area be fireproof, a larger and even more disastrous fire occurred there in 1900. A few years later it was reported that "Chinatown has again been largely built up of wood, and is getting more and more congested; a building is added here, a cook-house there, a shed in another place (for this is the way Chinatown grows)."[8]

Like many Chinatowns in other parts of the world, the one in Honolulu was located on the least desirable ground near the center of the city. Part of the land was low and pestilence-ridden. An editorial written in 1899, about six months before bubonic plague broke out in Chinatown, recognized the health hazards of the area:

> Some three or four acres in the section called Aala, west of the mouth of Nuuanu stream and above King Street, were set aside by the last legislature for a park, with a view of becoming a place of recreation, especially for the poorer classes of the city who are largely congregated in the low grounds adjacent as well as in Chinatown. The land, flooded at high tide, has already been partially filled up by the harbor dredger. . . . The periodical flooding of these low grounds will always be a menace to the public health. It would be ultimate economy to cart one hundred thousand loads from Aala Park to fill up those sections, even if the use of the park were thereby delayed five years. The poor people would suffer less by the continued lack of a park than by living on low and pestilential ground.[9]

This area of Honolulu had actually been known among Caucasians as the "native quarter" before it acquired the designation of Chinatown, and for decades more Hawaiians lived in it than Chinese. In 1884, at the peak of anti-Chinese agitation, over 4,200 of the 10,700 persons in the Honolulu wards most closely corresponding with the "Chinese quarter" were Hawaiians; only 3,780 were Chinese; over 2,700 were of "other races," mostly Portuguese and other Caucasians. The 3,780 Chinese in this district constituted only 73 percent of the 5,225 Chinese reported by the census in Honolulu; the other 1,445 were distributed through all the other ten wards, composing from 5 to 26 percent of the population of these other wards.

The presence of so many Hawaiians in the Chinese quarter was a matter for comment by some Caucasian observers. In 1882, in a sermon warning against "unfair competition" from Chinese, a Honolulu minister nevertheless observed that "while the Chinese are steadily, surely, displacing the Hawaiians, yet among all our many races thrown together in this little kingdom, no two so completely fraternize as do the Chinese and the Hawaiians. They buy and sell with each other, work together, live together, and intermarry as no other races among us."[10] A writer for an 1896 Honolulu directory noted that "the Chinese quarter of town, which is also largely inhabited and frequented by natives, occupies a considerable portion of the center of town. The two races mingle a great deal together."[11]

This intermingling of different ethnic groups in Chinatown continued, but with constant change in the origins, numbers, and proportions of groups in the area. In 1930, although 3,000 more Chinese were living in Honolulu than in San Francisco, Honolulu's Chinatown was much less predominantly Chinese than that of San Francisco. In that year only 47 percent of the people living in the Chinatown area were Chinese and less than 5 percent of the 19,334 Chinese in Honolulu lived there, the others being widely dispersed throughout the city. Thirty-seven percent of the other people in Chinatown were Japanese, 9 percent were Hawaiians or part-Hawaiians, 2 to 3 percent (each) were Filipinos, Koreans, and Caucasians.[12] Interspersed among the Chinese stores and clubhouses were businesses operated by Japanese, Koreans, Hawaiians, Filipinos, and Caucasians; living quarters above the business premises were occupied by tenants from every group in Honolulu's multiethnic population, as they still are today. Nevertheless, even though Chinatown's population has never been exclusively Chinese and even though each succeeding decade has seen a smaller proportion of Honolulu's Chinese living in the area, the district has continued to be the focal point of the commercial, cultural, and social life of Honolulu's Chinese.

The impress of early Chinese residents, businessmen, and city officials on the old Chinatown area and nearby districts remained for many years in the Chinese and Hawaiianized Chinese names of lanes and paths: Chun Hoon Lane, Afong Lane, Achi Lane, Tai Ping Lane, Young Kee Lane. Though most of these have disappeared in the redevelopment of central Honolulu, the forty or so acres bounded by the Honolulu waterfront, Nuuanu River, Beretania Street, and Nuuanu Avenue are still thought of by older Honolulu residents as Chinatown. For decades the center of activity for Chinese migrants, their children, and their grandchildren all over the Hawaiian Islands, Chinatown was to them *wah fau:* "Chinese port."

CHAPTER 7

The Migrants' Chinatown

HONOLULU'S Chinatown did not come into being by statutory segregation of the Chinese from other ethnic groups or even because of extralegal restrictions upon the area in which they could live. The concentration of migrants there was essentially the product of those qualities of human nature that lead people in a strange environment to seek out and associate with others who speak their language and share their particular needs and desires, attitudes and habits, beliefs and practices. In fact, Chinatown in Honolulu was not so much a district as a way of life. The migrants, reared in a cultural milieu which stamped them as markedly different from other ethnic groups in Honolulu, could have more satisfying contacts there than they could have with non-Chinese. Chinatown, in this sense, was a form of accommodation to the experiences and problems of life in a new and strange social world. It was a place where the migrant could relax from the strain of life in a foreign land, continue contacts with the homeland, and find help in times of crisis.

Chinatown, like each individual migrant, has had a life history marked by changing phases. The Chinatown way of life constantly underwent modification and reorganization until it became only a remnant of what it was during the years when the Chinese community was primarily a community of sojourner migrants. Concurrently, the degree to which individual migrants felt themselves identified with the Chinatown social milieu varied from phase to phase in their own life cycles. Any characterization of life in Chinatown during the decades it was dominated by the migrant generation must be a generalized account of what a changing Chinatown meant to a number of individuals who themselves were adjusting to the immigrant experience. Without doubt, the greatest changes in Chinatown occurred when the basic mode of life among the Chinese was shifting from that of sojourner immigrant men living alone or in groups to that of more conventional and stable families. In 1884 more than 4,500 of the 5,225 Chinese in Honolulu were immigrant men; there were only about 350 families.[1] By 1950, in contrast, there were more than 6,000 Chinese families and less than 6 percent of Honolulu's 26,724 Chinese were foreign-born males. Over the years the growing number of families, spread throughout Honolulu, tended to eliminate or moderate some of the more demoralizing features of the early Chinatown, diminish the importance of some of the older Chinatown activities and institutions, change others, and build up new ones.

In the 1880s and 1890s Chinatown life was dominated by activities and organizations meeting the needs and wishes of sojourner immigrant men. Their conception of themselves as being in Hawaii temporarily to take advantage of any opportunities they could find predisposed them to cultural isolation. Beyond the necessary and sometimes unpleasant economic relations with non-Chinese, caution about the law enforcement agencies of the "foreign" Hawaiian government, and somewhat indifferent curiosity about the bizarre behavior and beliefs of other foreigners, the *wah kiu* was generally little concerned about the life going on outside his own small social world.

Many of the migrants who congregated in Chinatown, especially in the evenings and on Sundays, lived in other parts of Honolulu or in rural Oahu, but Chinatown was where they could find a welcome from kinsmen, *heung li*, or friends with whom they could enjoy relief from the strain of impersonal contacts and exasperating encounters with the *fan kwai*. In Chinatown the migrant was not ridiculed for wearing a queue or stared at curiously because of his long fingernails or the half-dozen long hairs growing from a mole on his face. He could hear the familiar sounds of his own dialect and did not have to strain to make himself understood in a foreign language.

To Caucasian observers the Honolulu Chinatown of the 1880s or 1890s doubtless resembled the picture Dr. A. W. Palmer, a minister of the main Congregational Church in Honolulu, recalled as his childhood impression of San Francisco Chinatown:

> It was dirty, overcrowded, rat-infested and often diseased. It was poorly built with narrow alleys and underground cellars . . . more like a

warren of burrowing animals than a human city. It seemed uncanny because inhabited by a strange yellow race who wore "pigtails," talked an outlandish lingo in high falsetto voices, were reputed to eat sharks' fins and even rats, and to make medicine out of toads and spiders, and who sprinkled garments for ironing by sucking their mouths full of water and then squirting it out over the clothes. And Chinatown was accounted vicious because it was the haunt of gambling, opium smoking and lotteries. . . .[2]

A Chinese observer in the late 1920s, on the other hand, points to the emotional significance of Chinatown to the Chinese immigrants themselves.

> Most of us can live a warmer, freer, and a more human life among our relatives and friends than among strangers. . . . Chinese relations with the population outside Chinatown are likely to be cold, formal, and commercial. It is only in Chinatown that a Chinese immigrant has society, friends and relatives who share his dreams and hopes, his hardships and adventures. Here he can tell a joke and make everybody laugh with him; here he may hear folk tales told and retold which create the illusion that Chinatown is really China.[3]

Maintaining the Home Ties

One of the most important ways in which Chinatown at first met the needs of the sojourner migrant was by providing means for keeping contact with his parents, his wife if he had one, and others in his home village. No matter whether he was a laborer on one of Oahu's sugar plantations, a worker in the rice paddies, taro patches, or banana fields, an employee in a Honolulu laundry, tailor shop, or noodle factory, or a servant in some Haole house, Chinatown was his link to the home he had left in China.

Few migrants could read or write the Chinese language. If a migrant wished to send a letter to his relatives at home, the chances were that he would have to find someone who could write his letter for him, and when he received a message from home he needed someone to read it to him. Men who could do this were most readily found in Chinatown. This was one reason why Chinatown was busiest on Sundays when laborers came there from rural Oahu and other sections of the city of Honolulu. The problem of maintaining contacts with home was complicated by the lack of adequate postal and banking systems in China. If a relative or fellow villager happened to be making a trip to the native village or returning for good, the migrant might send his letter and some money with him, but such opportunities came too seldom. Thus the Chinatown store became an invaluable institution for the migrants. A Honolulu Chinese described how the stores in Honolulu's Chinatown at that time were still performing these services in the early 1930s:

Take Wing Sing Wo store on Hotel Street, for example. You go in there any day and you will find a great many letters stuck into a wire rack which stands in the back of the store. These letters are for Chinese who communicate with their folks at home through this store. Suppose a man in Honolulu wishes to send some money to his mother in Ngai How village in See Dai Doo [Chung Shan district]. He will be likely to go to Wing Sing Wo rather than to some other firm because it has a sub-branch store in Hachak Hee, the market town in See Dai Doo nearest the village of Ngai How. If he was from another district he would go to some store in Chinatown run by people from that district. The Ngai How man goes to Wing Sing Wo and says he wants them to write a letter for him. He tells the writer of the letter what he wants said. Perhaps he can only send a little money this time: he has been out of work; times are hard; he wishes he were able to send more money. Sometimes the letter is written as the man dictates; sometimes the writer listens and then writes it later. These writers know what the proper things are to say and what this man's folks will like to hear.

Most of the men who could write Chinese, especially in the old days, were the bookkeepers in the stores. In the old days, one used to get twenty-five to fifty cents for writing one of these letters, and many Chinese used to make pretty good money at it, for there were many Chinese who could not write a letter or who did not want to do it themselves. The professional writer uses more high-sounding phrases, so that the letter is more impressive upon the people at home who read it. I have heard some of the old men complain that they can't make easy money anymore by writing letters. At the present time there is such a surplus of Chinese in Hawaii well-educated enough in Chinese to write letters, be bookkeepers, clerks, schoolteachers, etc., and so much competition for the business of remitting money that the stores doing this business now keep several bookkeepers and offer to write the letters free of charge. Every day that a boat is sailing for China, there are many Chinese in Wing Sing Wo's store to get letters off and the bookkeepers are surely kept busy then. On Sundays, Chinese come into Honolulu from out in the country districts partly for this purpose.

Through Wing Sing Wo's connections in Hachak Hee, the letter is delivered and an acknowledgment, perhaps an answering letter, returned through the same system, addressed to the man in care of Wing Sing Wo. A few days after a boat arrives from China, the stores usually put in the paper a list of the names of people for whom letters are waiting at their store. It is more or less a standing joke in the Chinese community to ask a person if he isn't expecting a letter at such and such a store, implying that he has been prosperous enough to be sending money to his relatives in his home village.[4]

The difficulty and expense of maintaining these contacts with home help to explain why most of the men wrote only when they were sending money—perhaps only once or twice a year, such as before Chinese New Year or some other festival period. This association between mail and money became so firmly established that migrants who were not able to send money home stopped writing altogether.

Chinatown as Social Center

The Chinatown store was also a social center where the migrant could enjoy intimate and personal contacts. The newcomer especially felt the need for such association and soon learned the location of stores operated by people from his own or a nearby village. Here the *heung li* exchanged news from home, talked over old times, or reviewed local gossip and scandal. The merchant himself was usually the best-informed person about his home village. He heard read, or read himself, the letters his *heung li* received. He especially welcomed visits by villagers who had only recently come from China.

The appearance at the store of an immigrant who had been home to China for a visit was as important as a personal letter. He also brought news and family tidings from the village to the immigrants in Honolulu. He could relate events with a personal touch and could give his views on village gossip. Sometimes he brought small bags of herbs, beans, yam flour, or sweets from the wives, parents, mother-in-laws, or godparents to the immigrants. The returned immigrant also helped to refresh memories of the village as shown by the following conversation heard in a store:

Immigrant: "E-hee!" (as he enters the store and sees the returned immigrant) "So soon come back? You went how long?"

Returned Immigrant: "I used up the few bits (money); have to come back. Went home for thirteen months."

Immigrant: "Have son born?"

Returned Immigrant: "Picked a daughter."

Immigrant: "Also good. Have pregnancy when you come?"

Returned Immigrant: "Don't know. Your family everyone peaceful. Ah Wah (the immigrant's son) very nice. Studies at the village school. Your wife asked you send a little more home—not enough to spend."

Immigrant: "I make not enough! For a time, no work. Village peaceful?"

Returned Immigrant: "Very peaceful—but some small burglaries. Last month Ah Sai Pak lost a coop of seven chickens. Somebody said Ah —— stole them. Don't know. Now in the village many young men have nothing to do. Very bad. They do whatever bad. Much gambling and eating opium."[5]

Another dimension of the Chinatown store's significance as social center for the village migrant is suggested by Bung Chong Lee:

The store was a club where the immigrant had status. His words found meaning; he could be understood and his conversation appreciated. He could talk at length and be listened to. He could boast of his catching the largest cricket on a certain hill and of seeing the largest snake in a certain rice field in China. He talked of his achievements; he shared his sentiments, his experiences, his memories with his fellow villagers. Every little nook, hill, and lane, the temple, the goddesses, and the many village legends were reviewed in intimate detail. Through gossip in the stores, the village mores were reenforced, and the immigrant's life was organized.[6]

The Chinatown store had frontier and village characteristics rather than those of the usual urban business establishment. The merchant's Chinese customers were mostly other *wah kiu* who were bound to him in one way or another. He did business with them personally and informally. A customer might stay to chat for an hour. The store usually had quarters where those in the business cooked, ate, and slept, and a villager coming into Honolulu from rural Oahu or from another island might be given a meal or two at the store or find lodging there overnight without paying. A *heung li* just arriving from China might put up at the store for several days until he found work and accommodations elsewhere; the storekeeper was a helpful source of information about jobs available on Oahu. A Chinese political exile could usually find some store in Honolulu's Chinatown that would provide him temporary lodging and security, as well as a place where he could carry on propaganda freely among sympathetic listeners. Villagers' clubs usually had their informal beginnings at some Chinatown store, and officers of other Chinese immigrant societies which had no headquarters of their own commonly held their meetings on Sundays at the store of one of the members.

Hotels and commercial lodging houses for Chinese migrants were rare in spite of the large number of familyless Chinese men in the Islands. Migrants staying in Honolulu temporarily would seek lodging with friends or relatives, and familyless men employed in Honolulu expected to live at their place of work or another provided by the firm. As Chinese immigrant societies prospered and built their own clubhouses, members and occasionally nonmembers would be put up free or at small cost. The clubhouses became centers for informal friendly gatherings, games and gossip, and eating and drinking for members who did not live in them—especially on weekends. Many members who married and established family homes continued to use their society clubhouses as social centers, much like the Elks Club.

Another informal social center in the old Chinatown was the Sunday marketplace. In South China markets were usually held at the market towns six times each lunar month, but in Hawaii most Chinese had to adjust their work schedules to fit the Westerners' organization of life around a weekly cycle. Sunday had been established as the Sabbath in Hawaii under the influence of the missionaries and according to Western practice, but it was not a day for religious observance and rest for most Chinese migrants. Sunday was Chinatown's busiest day. Early in the morning Chinese farmers, gardeners, poultry raisers, pigraisers, and others left their homes in rural Oahu and brought their produce to Chinatown's Sunday morning market. Chinese living in Honolulu looked forward to Sunday morning as the time when they could buy the choicest vegetables and meats and the freshest eggs. But buying and selling seemed almost secondary to the opportunities the market offered for meeting friends, discussing crops, gossiping about acquaintances, exchanging jokes, and other convivial activities of a people for whom market days in their homeland had been among their most exciting times.

The Sunday market was not a complete replica of the marketplace at home. Many of the commodities sold in the South China market were missing, as well as many of its personalities. The traveling herbalist with his trick performances and facile sales talk; the traveling merchant; the transient craftsman who journeyed from one market town to the next—all were absent. The drugs of the herbalist and the wares of the traveling merchant were supplied by the permanent stores of Chinatown, where craftsmen were also located. In the Chinatown market produce and other goods were sold for cash; unlike village markets, barter was rare. For years, these cash sales involved haggling over the price; only gradually did *but yee ga* ("no two price") become common. The presence of customers of other ethnic groups, especially Hawaiians, also made the Chinatown market different from those in the migrants' home districts.

Sunday was the day for other Chinatown activities too. With the formation of Chinese societies in Chinatown, Sunday noon, at the close of a busy morning, was commonly the time for the organizations' business meetings or social functions. Sunday afternoons became the customary time for funerals of prominent Chinese, as it was the most convenient time of the week for the busiest people in the Chinese community.

There was little demand at first for restaurants catering to Chinese cash customers, but later several eating places for Chinese were established in Chinatown, and combination bakeries and teahouses became popular during the 1920s and 1930s. These eating places and teahouses, like the stores, became favorite gathering places for Chinese, more for the relatively sophisticated residents or workers in Chinatown than for rural (and frugal) migrants who felt more at home sitting in a dimly lighted fellow villager's store. In the twenties and thirties the most popular teahouse was Sun Yun Wo,[7] in the center of the Chinatown district, where this writer often went with Chinese friends. Day after day Chinese businessmen and intellectuals filled the large room on the second floor of this establishment for *dim sum*—second breakfast or early lunch. The tables were bare, their crosspieces well worn by the feet that had been propped up on them. Chinese bamboo stools still lined the walls for use at banquets, but common chairs had replaced them at the tables laid with chopsticks and Chinese crockery. Each guest prepared his own tea by pouring boiling-hot water into a bowl containing tea leaves; there were no teapots. Over the plates of such foods as *siu mai, kau tse, ma tai shu, dau sa bau* and over the bowls of tea, groups of Chinese conversed on many subjects. In one corner a group might be discussing the increase of freight rates on goods from China or the troubles of dealing with customs officials. In another corner a group of young newspapermen might be discussing the recent turns in the political affairs of China or an editorial in the last issue of the *Sun Chung Kwock Bo*. At one table a group of Chinese-language-school teachers might be lamenting the lack of interest shown by their students in mastering Chinese. At another table an elderly, poorly clad Chinese man might be listening intently while a young man read to him and explained a letter from China, or translated a letter written in English by a son attending college on the U.S. mainland. Here was laughter and heated argument, and above the bustle and talk the waiters could be heard singing their orders down the dumbwaiter to the kitchen below. In earlier years no women would have been seen in such a place of eating and leisurely conversation, but by the thirties one occasionally saw a local-born Chinese girl there, perhaps bringing some Caucasian friends seeking atmosphere of the old Chinatown. In restaurants like this Chinese societies would hold their annual banquets; the *wuis* would have dinners at which monthly bids were opened; the sixty-first birthdays of prominent Chinese would be celebrated; visiting friends would be entertained and famous Chinese passing through Honolulu would be honored.

Commercialized Vice

In Chinatown the sojourner migrant was exposed, often for the first time, to commercialized vice. The ordinary young man in the village of the type from which most Chinese migrants came during the 1870s, 1880s, and 1890s was closely supervised by older members of a dominating family or kinship group. Any individual liberty he enjoyed was the freedom to act within boundaries prescribed and approved by family mores. He had no money to spend as he wanted. For most of these young men opium smoking, illicit relations with women, and serious gambling were out of the question. Villagers knew that such practices were prevalent in the cities but they did not approve of them within the family. It was not merely that such habits were considered bad for the individual; anyone who indulged in them brought disrepute to the whole family clan. Wayward behavior soon became a subject of village gossip.

Most of the Chinese migrants came to Hawaii from districts located only a few miles from Hong Kong, Canton, or Macao, and some villagers who went to those cities to seek their fortunes indulged in the pleasures they found there. C. K. Ai reports that a granduncle who had made and lost a fortune in Canton returned to live in the village where "like so many of his generation" he was a confirmed opium smoker. Macao, the Portuguese colony which was "within four hours' walk" of Ai's home village, had by the nineteenth century become notorious for opium, gambling, and prostitution. Ai said that although "friendly gambling" was customary among relatives at lunar New Year in his home village, excessive gambling, presumably in Macao, brought disgrace to his nephew and the nephew's wife.[8]

Conditions in Hawaii were, on the whole, not favorable to maintaining village standards of morality. Here the young migrant, even if he had kinsmen in the Islands, was not under the daily surveillance of family members. If he went to the sugar plantations he entered a contract as an individual and was treated as one rather than as a member of a family group. Wherever he worked, he received money which he alone could decide how to spend. His personal behavior was restricted only by plantation rules, employers' demands, and laws of the Hawaiian government—all of them "foreign" agencies toward which he felt no personal or traditional obligations. Instead of living in a stable community with strong mores, the migrant was in a world of transitory relationships and conflicting standards of conduct. The extremely abnormal age-sex ratio of the society in which the migrants lived in the 1880s, 1890s, and early 1900s contributed to the spread of habits which family control would have restricted in the village.

It was easy for the migrant to start gambling and smoking opium in Chinatown. Whiling away the time at a friendly game at a Chinese store or society clubhouse not infrequently led to more serious gambling. In the lodging quarters of a store or a Chinese society's clubhouse the newcomer or visitor could be invited to join others in smoking opium. Store proprietors and older members of the society might disapprove, but they were not usually in a position to interfere as kinsmen in the village might have done.

As gambling and opium smoking spread, there were migrants who saw the profits to be made by exploiting these habits, and the subsequent commercialization made Chinatown the center of a network of gambling operators, opium importers, and opium sellers which spread throughout the Islands. The "banks" or headquarters for lotteries—*chee fa* and *bark gup biu* ("white pigeon ticket")—were located in Chinatown;[9] certain stores and runners in Chinatown and on all the islands received commissions for handling tickets and bets. At first the major operators and participants were Chinese, but it was not long before Hawaiians, Caucasians, Japanese, and others were taking part. In fact, at one time lotteries were so popular with the Hawaiians that some *chee fa* tickets were made up of Hawaiian words.[10] By the 1930s the number of unattached Chinese men had diminished and this form of gambling was not so prevalent among the settled Chinese family men; most of the lottery ticket buyers were reported to be Hawaiians and part-Hawaiians, Japanese, and Filipinos.[11]

The popular table games in the "gambling dens" of Chinatown were *fan tan, pai kau,* and *sup chai.* The "dens" were usually barricaded rooms on an upper floor; when watchers warned that the place was about to be raided, operators tried to get rid of evidence of a game before the police could break in. If the operators succeeded, the police might find the men just sitting on stools around the walls of the room, talking idly among themselves.

Some Caucasians in Honolulu protested against the gambling that was known to go on in Chinatown, but their objections were generally ineffective. English-language newspapers carried stories about lotteries, gambling dens, and arrests and convictions, and occasionally editorials condemned the flagrant disregard of antigambling laws in Chinatown.[12] Antilottery laws were passed and from time to time the banks were raided and operators arrested, but most banks were soon back in business. Officers who were supposed to enforce the laws were themselves suspected of taking money from the gamblers. In fact, from the 1880s into the 1920s most Caucasian residents, along with lower-rank government officials who were mostly Hawaiians, were probably indifferent toward the way Chinese migrants spent their spare time as long as they kept to themselves. Even as late as the 1930s police appeared to have been quite tolerant toward gambling among the Chinese. When this writer went with two China-born students to Manoa Chinese Cemetery to observe Ching Ming ceremonies in April 1931, dozens of Chinese, mostly elderly men, were playing *fan tan* and *pai kau* even while the ceremonies were being performed. Some twenty tables were set up on the edge of the cemetery—less than fifty feet away from a part-Hawaiian policeman who directed traffic but ignored the gambling that went on for several hours. The students pointed out a detective of Chinese ancestry who seemed to be enjoying the whole affair.[13]

As with gambling, Chinatown was the center of the opium business which extended throughout the Islands. Some storekeepers, heads of Chinese camps, Chinese labor contractors, and others were unscrupulous about the business—in fact, it has been charged that some Chinese employers of the early days forced their Chinese laborers to accept opium as part of their wages. It is more likely that Chinese employers complacently accepted their laborers' use of opium, obtained it for them, dispensed it to them, and deducted the price from wages. In Chinatown itself there were many places where opium could be bought and smoked. Tyhune, in business in Honolulu from 1833 to 1853, was said to have provided rooms for "his countrymen addicted to the use of opium."[14] Some of the Chinese imported from Amoy in 1852 were reported to be habitual opium users and some of them who came to Honolulu after leaving the plantations became involved in stealing and peddling opium from Caucasian-owned drugstores.[15]

Almost from the beginning, the government's main concern was not use of the drug by Chinese but the danger that their "pernicious habit" might be "acquired by His Majesty's native born subjects," as indicated in the preamble of an 1856 act prohibiting the importation and sale of opium except when prescribed by licensed physicians. From 1860 to 1874 the government attempted to confine the use of opium, except for medicinal purposes, to the Chinese by issuing licenses to Chinese to import and sell opium only to Chinese. Annual auctions of these licenses proved to be a lucrative source of government revenue. The extent of the trade and its profitability were demonstrated when a Chinese bid nearly $47,000 for the one license auctioned in 1874. By this time scores of Chinese migrants, in addition to the import-license holder, were profiting in one way or another from the habit among their countrymen.

The legislature of 1874 returned to the policy of prohibiting the importing and selling of opium except for medical treatment. From 1876 to 1892 almost every legislature was pressured to reenact an opium licensing bill. The Chinese business community was embarrassed in 1880 when certain Chinese merchants in Honolulu were reported to have been involved in bribery concerning an opium licensing bill. (King Kalakaua had vetoed one passed in 1878.) A more notorious case was exposed in 1887. Late in 1886 the legislature had passed a bill providing for an opium monopoly license to be sold for $30,000. The license was awarded to a Chinese who was later reported to have paid $80,000 to King Kalakaua through an intermediary. The scandal was intensified when it was learned that another Chinese merchant and rice planter connected with one of the largest Chinese firms in Honolulu had given the king "presents" amounting to $71,000 with the understanding that he would receive the license. The legislature repealed the opium act and reenacted previous legislation prohibiting importation, sale, and use of opium.[16]

In spite of the prohibition, opium smuggling and opium use continued. Each year from 1880 to 1900 hundreds of Chinese migrants were arrested and convicted on opium charges. Convicted users who were sent to jail for a few months generally resumed the habit. "Opium joints" were frequently raided, but usually they were so barricaded that evidence could be destroyed or thrown down pipes into cesspools before police could force their way in. And although there was public pressure to stop opium smoking, there were periods when smoking places were protected by arrangements between police and operators. Chinese who wanted opium smuggling stopped and the use of opium reduced were generally cynical about the effectiveness of the police, who were widely believed in the Chinese community to accept bribes.[17]

After Annexation local laws against opium were reinforced by federal statutes and agencies. In spite of the higher risks, *wui*s continued to engage in the traffic, and from time to time local newspapers reported arrests of Chinese and others charged with opium smuggling.[18] By the 1930s, however, the character of the opium traffic and its place in Chinatown had changed. Most of the opium smuggled into Hawaii reportedly was being transshipped to the continental United States or sold to members of other ethnic groups in Hawaii. Chinese opium smokers, mostly aged, unmarried men living in the old Chinese quarter, were still being arrested,[19] but very few Island-born Chinese took up the habit. As the number of first-generation migrants dwindled away, opium smoking among Honolulu Chinese became a thing of the past. Chinese are still occasionally arrested in Honolulu on narcotics smuggling charges, but they are more likely to be from Hong Kong, Singapore, Kuala Lumpur, or Bangkok than from Honolulu, and they are involved in an international traffic which is unrelated to the old opium smoking activities in Honolulu's Chinatown.

Although Chinese migrants in Hawaii were predominantly adult males without families in the Islands, few Chinese women seem to have been brought to Honolulu for commercialized prostitution.[20] During the same period that Chinese tongs in San Francisco were importing women for brothels there, Chinese in Honolulu were not accused of doing so—even during the period of bitterest anti-Chinese agitation. The United Chinese Society of Honolulu, in a petition to the U.S. Congress in 1916 appealing for reopening the importation of Chinese labor, asserted that there were no Chinese women "in the haunts of vice . . . in the whole Territory of Hawaii." The petition called attention to a recent canvass of 107 "unfortunate women" in the segregated district then existing in Honolulu and pointed out that while 82 of the women were of "oriental birth" none was Chinese.[21] The petition did not claim that no Chinese men visited this district. In this same decade Dr. Khai Fai Li opened, in addition to the office he and his wife had in Chinatown, an office in Iwilei on the edge of the red light district because of his concern about the prevalence of venereal disease. His patients, Chinese and non-Chinese alike, came from the plantation areas of rural Oahu as well as from Honolulu.[22]

Cantonese Theater

At about the time of Chinese New Year in 1879 one of Honolulu's newspapers announced a forthcoming event with a mixture of satire and anticipation:

A great attraction will be presented shortly, that will no doubt eclipse all the theatre and circus shows of the Western barbarians. A Chinese dramatic company is about to open and will give a season. It will be extremely interesting, as we learn that one of their plays extends over a period of more than one hundred years. The interludes consist of musical entertainments—principally gongs, cymbals, and firecrackers.[23]

For half a century one of the great delights in Chinatown for members of the Chinese community was "Cantonese opera." A Chinese theater was built in the late 1870s in the heart of Chinatown; the 1884 census reported that eighty-four Chinese men in Honolulu were "theater actors." During that year a Chinese known as Tai On secured "public show" licenses for weekly performances in January —the Chinese New Year season—and for biweekly performances in the remaining months.

Chinese migrants were familiar with theatrical performances by troupes of professional actors who visited their home villages on special occasions—during New Year festivals or at times of ancestral or religious celebrations. At such times performances were given in an improvised open-air theater much as in the days of Elizabethan drama in England. Financial arrangements were made by the clan elders for the entire village. In Honolulu, however, the theater was more like that of the Chinese city than the village. It was a commercial venture undertaken by Chinese promoters, and the theater was part of Chinatown business life. Companies of actors were brought from South China, performances were billed, and tickets were sold to individual playgoers. This is the system with which Westerners are familiar, of course, but to the Chinese migrant it was another change from the clan world of his village. Nevertheless, the opportunity to see familiar drama in a Cantonese dialect was a magnet which drew migrants to Chinatown from other districts of Honolulu and from all over Oahu. Chee Kwon Chun and John Coulter tell about rice planters, as soon as the week's work ended on Saturday afternoon, going on horseback "to town to see Chinese shows, provided by actors from China."[24]

A Chinese student of Chinatowns on the U.S. mainland in the 1920s described Chinese drama of the type that was presented in Honolulu:

An important part of the organization of a Chinese theatre is the orchestra. This is composed of a leader who plays the ox-hide drum, a fiddler, a banjoist, a gong player, and a cymbal player. The orchestra is supposed to accompany the singing, but frequently the noise which the orchestra makes is so loud that even a trained ear can hardly detect the human voice.

A man with little imagination cannot enjoy a Chinese drama. When a Chinese actor prances about, the audience must imagine he is riding a horse. When an actress knocks in the air with her fan, a sympathetic observer must picture in his mind a door that is locked. He must overlook a warrior or a traitor who, after suffering decapitation on the stage, calmly rises and walks away. He must, however, pay no attention to the property man, who comes out again and again to put a label on a bench or chair, transforming it into a bridge, a boat or a pagoda, as the occasion demands. To an uninformed American, all these movements are bewildering, but the Chinese, who have been accustomed to these things from childhood, enjoy them immensely.[25]

It is not surprising that such a theater had little appeal to the non-Chinese in Honolulu in the late nineteenth century. Few of them would have understood (or have been interested in learning) the conventions of Chinese drama, and the music of the theater—particularly the loud beating of gongs—seemed barbarous to the Western ear. A strong puritanical element remained in the missionary community to whom even Western theater had an immoral tinge, and Chinese theater was not only incomprehensible but heathen. Migrants attending the theater expected the performance to continue until midnight or even later, and Cantonese opera required an orchestra. Because some Caucasian residents objected to the "noise" coming from the Chinese theater, the Minister of the Interior included a provision in the public show licenses in 1885 that the orchestra could not play after ten o'clock. A Chinese promoter applying for a license for a forthcoming production, which was to run for twenty-four nights, asked that this restriction "be removed or modified so that the use of gongs, drums and other instruments connected with the orchestra be extended to 11:30 o'clock in the evening, and all plays to cease at 12:00 o'clock in the evening, and the Theatre to be closed at 12:30 A.M." The promoter pointed out "that in order to render effectual any play in the Chinese language, it is necessary to have the use of the gongs and drums." He assured the minister that he would "endeavor to use the gongs and drums in such a manner as to prevent the noise from being considered a nuisance."[26]

Cantonese theatrical productions remained popular from the 1880s until the late 1920s. Professional troupes en route to or from

Chinatowns on the Pacific Coast stopped off in Honolulu where local Chinese businessmen would underwrite their performances in the Chinese Theater and share in the profits. After the Republic of China was established in 1911, women began to appear in these troupes, replacing some of the *tan* actors (males taking female roles). By the late 1920s, however, attendance was dropping off and the sponsors usually lost money. As late as 1930 one could attend an occasional performance of Cantonese opera and see whole families there—grandparents, parents, and young children—but there was not enough patronage to make regular performances profitable. The Chinese productions could no longer draw large audiences of young adult male migrants, and the older first-generation men, especially those who were financially successful, were too busy with commercial affairs, Chinese organizations, and family life to spend long hours watching a Chinese opera. The young Hawaii-born Chinese who had been educated in the American school system were more interested in American movies than in Cantonese theater.

Even though bringing professional troupes to Honolulu was no longer profitable, Chinatown remained for a long time the center of those dramatic and musical events that were most distinctively Chinese. Amateur performances of Cantonese shows were staged by local Chinese dramatic clubs organized by young adult immigrants and some of the Hawaii-born Chinese, especially those who had been sent to China for part of their schooling. Chinese dramas were also put on by students in the Chinese-language schools. When drives were held to raise money for these schools, it was customary for one of the adult dramatic clubs to put on a benefit Cantonese show. With the upsurge of Chinese national consciousness, many of these productions took on a nationalistic flavor. After 1911 a free dramatic performance was usually given at one of the language schools as part of the celebration of Chinese Independence Day ("Double Ten Day").

Chinese movies were brought to Honolulu in the late 1920s and early 1930s, but box-office receipts were too low to pay for showing them daily or even weekly. Silent movies from China were shown occasionally, and the first Chinese talkies made their appearance in a small theater near the old Chinatown district in 1933. The synopsis of one of the silent Chinese movies, *The Loo Yang Bridge,* was printed on the program when it was shown at the Park Theater ("Home of High Class Chinese Movies") on 15 June 1930:

This charming legend relates of the butcher of pigs, who for years had thrown the intestines of the thousands of pigs which he killed into the Loo Yang River. These intestines turn to turtles, snakes, and evil spirits, which cause much damage to those crossing the river. During the passage of a large boat which is nearly upset, a priest hears a voice from the sea, warning to let the boat alone as an exalted person named Tsai is on board. Inquiry brings out the fact that a Mrs. Tsai is on board and the priest informs her that her expected son will become a man of great prominence. Mrs. Tsai makes a promise if this is true she will honour the occasion by building a bridge over this turbulent river for the good of all.

The son is born and in years later is told the promise his mother made; he vows to complete her promise if possible. He passes the Imperial Literature Examinations with highest honours, is selected by the Prime Minister as son-in-law. The marriage takes place and the young couple are much in love with each other. His wife proves herself very capable and through her ability, and under the most extraordinary circumstances, the bridge is finally erected, and still stands as a monument, for the good of the people, erected through the unceasing efforts of a young couple, to whom came all they wished for because of their goodness to others and the unceasing love they bore to each other.

To members of the second and third generations, whose tastes had been formed by American movies, such a plot might have novelty but it was not likely to supplant the Hollywood variety.[27]

Chinatown as Source of Help

In the migrant's personal life, Chinatown was more than a place to relax and keep up contacts with home—it was the place where he could find help in times of crisis. Especially for the pre-Annexation migrant, Chinatown could provide the best substitutes for the physical care and spiritual assistance he would have received at home from family, clan, and village temple.

At home most of the migrant's physical ailments had been treated by the women of his family or other women in his village. It was they who prepared the home remedies and administered the cures according to traditions handed down through generations. Herbs and other drugs were part of the household stock; water bottled on the seventh day of the seventh moon, when it was believed to be especially pure and to have medicinal value, was kept for use in times of illness. Professional or semiprofessional healers would be resorted to only in serious cases which did not yield to home methods. Away from home the migrant had to turn to other sources of care, and the presence of large numbers of familyless men in Honolulu provided a field for many sorts of medical practitioners in Chinatown.

Chinese herb stores took the place of the household supply and offered a much greater variety of remedies than the home would have had. The migrant could buy a bulky package of half a dozen or more ingredients to be brewed into a thick tea for a cold—the package would even contain a piece of sweet preserved fruit for taking away the bitter taste of the tea. All sorts of remedies filled the drawers which lined these stores from floor to ceiling. Some, like the cold preparations, were made up in advance; others, more rare, like the tiny shavings from the horn of a specially killed deer, were made up on the prescription of a Chinese herbalist who owned the store. The herbalists almost invariably had learned their profession from members of the preceding generations in their clan rather than in a professional school; they were generally able to read and write Chinese; occasionally there was one who had taken a degree under the imperial examination system of Manchu days.[28] Such herbalists had not been common in the smaller villages, although they might have been known to the migrants from the larger villages or market towns.

Sufferers from specific ailments could find other practitioners in Chinatown who would undertake to cure them. Chinese barbers were sometimes also masseurs who attempted, by tapping, kneading, or pommeling, to treat such troubles as headaches, insomnia, and nervousness. Others in Chinatown practiced ancient Chinese treatments for rheumatism or aches in various parts of the body. An account given in the 1920s by a Honolulu-born Chinese dentist describes some of the Chinese medical treatments he had known in his youth in Hawaii:

> When a patient appeared with an aching arm, from any cause whatsoever, the "physician" would locate the nerve leading to that part of the body and apply his treatment where it came close to the surface of the body. Treatments were of two kinds, other than massaging.
>
> One was to apply a small amount of powder [moxa] and allow it to burn slowly over the nerve until the patient became insensible to pain at the part affected. The other was by piercing [acupuncture].

Dr. Chang pointed out that persons administering such treatments are not versed in medical science and might cause infections through the use of unsterilized needles or wires. He believes both practices were harmful. Both afford only temporary relief and do not go to the cause of the illness, as is often believed by the patients.[29]

The degree of professionalism among these various practitioners varied from one to the other, and payment was of different sorts. The herbalist usually stipulated prices that were paid in cash, but others might or might not have set fees. Often they were repaid with gifts of food, jewelry, or *li shee* (money wrapped in red paper). This practice, a carry-over from the personal relationships prevailing in the village community, was familiar to the Chinese migrant.

Chinese migrants turned to Western medicine very slowly. When Dr. and Mrs. Khai Fai Li opened an office in Chinatown in 1896, it was many weeks before they had their first Chinese patient; much of their practice was with poor Hawaiians and Portuguese.[30] Today, of course, most of the Hawaii Chinese go to Western-trained physicians and surgeons, but in 1979 there were still four Chinese herb stores doing business in Chinatown. Despite the reluctance of the migrant generation to be treated by Western medical methods, medicine became one of the most prestigious professions among the Hawaii-born Chinese. Although only a few doctors of Chinese ancestry now practice in the old Chinatown area, one of the most successful clinics, owned and staffed by Hawaii-born Chinese physicians and surgeons trained on the U.S. mainland, is close to the original Chinese quarter.

Faith healers, exorcists, and astrologers flourished in the old Chinatown along with druggists, herbalists, and practitioners of physical therapy. The line separating Chinese folk medicine from magic is hard to draw, and to the unschooled Chinese migrant there was little difference between them. Faith healers undertook treatment of fractured bones, epilepsy, and mild forms of psychosis along with the more common run of chronic ailments.

The Chinese temple *(miu)*, transplanted from China though in a form not altogether familiar to the Chinese villager, was another institution of Chinatown to which the migrant could turn for help during times of physical or emotional trouble. The earliest temples were established about the same time as the herb stores and were also private enterprises. The priests, who owned the temples, and the other temple attendants depended for their livelihood on the offerings of those who came to worship and seek the aid of the deities. K. Chimin Wong and Lien-Teh Wu's description of an urban temple in China shows how temples served those who went to them for relief from illness:

> A very common custom is to go to the temples to pray for holy medicine. In this practice, faith is placed in spiritual help more than in medicine, for sometimes none is given. As a rule this is resorted to as a last resource, a fair trial being first given to rational treatment, but often it is prescribed at the very beginning of an illness when the patient's family is very superstitious. Propitious days, commonly the first and fifteenth of the month, are selected for the commencement of the cure. In case of emergency, however, such things are not taken into account. A fasting beforehand, that is, the adoption of certain modes of living in which no meat is allowed, the reciting of prayers, the thorough washing of the body and other minutiae, are supposed to improve one's chance of getting the blessing, for the gods will only listen to the good and clean. After the burning of joss and other offerings, the believer takes a tube from the altar in which is placed a bundle of numbered sticks, passes it over the joss fumes several times, shakes it until one falls to the ground. This is picked up, the number read and a corresponding slip of paper given on which is printed the prescription. . . .[31]

The Chinatown temples were rather different from the village temples in China which ordinarily belonged to the clan or the village and were seldom attended by priests. Rites were performed by the individual worshipers at these village temples or small, open shrines at sacred spots in the village. Urban temples in China had their priests, of course, but in his home village in China the migrant was probably not familiar with them. In Chinatown, where the migrant was much more on his own than in the village, the priests undoubtedly were important in times of stress. Conversely, serving in the Honolulu temples was more lucrative for the priests than serving worshipers in China, as indicated in the story of a young Hawaii-born priest who took over a Chinese temple in Honolulu in 1932 from an elderly migrant priestess:

> Young Siu Hin . . . went to China for a visit. It was there he received his message from the "Fifth Fairy Princess" that he was to become her

interpreter—the means of communication between her and the people. . . . He became the village doctor and healed people, and he told
fortunes. The demands were great, and the returns small, so he returned to Honolulu for a living. Village folk are so poor they gave one
copper or two for his services. In Honolulu he taught [in a Chinese-
language] school and helped in the Goon Yum Mew, the largest temple in Honolulu, until last year. . . . Priest Young has four helpers in
the temple, doing the odd jobs of keeping the light of the gods burning, keeping the altar place clean, and making paper miniatures of offerings required in worship. "He is a saint. He speaks words of truth.
They say he is a protégé of the Fifth Fairy Princess. I had him sing the
staff of my life, and inquired of him the fortunes of my family, and it
was very true." Thus, for the last two months, Young and his helpers
in How Wong Miu have become food for the women's daily talk.[32]

Rites at these temples combined elements of Taoism, Buddhism,
Confucianism, and survivals of ancient nature worship handed down
through innumerable generations of illiterate village folk.[33] Tin-Yuke
Char, discussing religion among Chinese migrants to Hawaii, says
that "the common man . . . is polytheistic in his beliefs and practices.
He embraces folk beliefs of supernatural beings, magic, charms, as-
trology, fortune divinations, and deified warriors, heroes, and sages
taken from legends and fables. In Hawaii, it has been difficult to label
which Chinese temples and shrines are Buddhist and which are
Taoist."[34]

The first temple in Chinatown, in which Goon Yum (Kuan Yin),
Goddess of Mercy, was the principal deity, was built in 1879[35]—the
same year in which other Chinese migrants founded the first Chinese
Christian church a few blocks away. In 1887 Frank Damon, who led
mission work among the Chinese in Hawaii, noted that there were
"in Honolulu three Representative Idol Temples, with an immense
number of shrines in private homes and stores." He described the
three temples in an account which is generally more objective in
tone than that of other Caucasian observers who were condescend-
ing or scornful toward what they regarded as "heathen temples":

> The largest of these temples is specially dedicated to the God How-
> Wong, a deity mainly worshipped by the Chinese coming from the
> district of Heang Shan [Chung Shan], the majority, perhaps, of our
> Chinese people being from this region. This Temple is quite pictur
> esquely situated on the river bank at the foot of Beretania Street. It is

most lavishly ornamented with gilding and most gorgeous colouring. In the main shrine is a carved figure of "How-Wong"; on either side are figures of two other gods, Kwan Tai and the Chinese God of Medicine, to whom petitions are offered in case of sickness.

Another temple, erected since the fire last year, is situated a little off King Street and is dedicated to Kwun Yam, the Goddess of Mercy of Buddhism. She is represented seated on the opened petals of the Lotus and occupies the most prominent position in the temple. Not far away is another temple dedicated specially to Kwan Tai, the God of War. In this temple are also idols representing Tien-How, the "Queen of Heaven," and the "God of Medicine." Kwan Tai is more worshipped on our Islands by the Chinese than any other god. His picture in a shrine is found in many stores, on the rice plantations, and in the houses of the Secret Societies. . . .

The worshipper procures his offering and the services of an assistant from the temple-keeper. This assistant rings the large bell or beats upon the drum to arouse the gods, while the worshipper kneels before the table upon which he has placed his offerings of tea, wine, rice, fruit and fowl. With prostrations and incantations he devotes the essence of this food to the gods, then goes to the shrine upon which the idol reposes and seeks the aid of the divining blocks. These two pieces of wood are thrown down until they fall, one with its oval and one with its flat side to the floor, which is considered a good omen. Then the sacred jar of bamboo splints [chim], each of which is numbered to correspond with the temple-keeper's book of prayers, is shaken until one of the splints falls to the floor. The assistant marks the number with a brush pen. The number is handed to the temple-keeper, who gives the answer according to the number in his book. The paper money is lighted from the incense sticks on the shrine, then carried outside and placed in the brick or metal crematory, and as it burns, the idol receives its essence. Meantime, the assistant gathers together the food, to be taken home for a feast for the friends.[36]

In the mid-1930s there were five temples in Honolulu, apart from the shrines on the upper floor of many of the Chinese societies. None of these temples, all privately owned by priest-caretakers, was located within the old Chinese quarter. Fires in Chinatown had destroyed some of the early temple buildings;[37] those which were rebuilt were located close to, but not in, the old Chinatown. In two of these temples the central deity was How Wong, important to the migrants from Chung Shan who regarded him as their divine patron. Sau Chun Wong, in her study of the temples of this period, says that

How Wong, originally a fisherman's god, was appealed to by "people of any profession or trade . . . for good fortune, protection, business success, and safety in travel to China."[38] Other deities in the temples identified by Wong were Choy Sun, "god of fortune"; Yuk Wong Dai Dei, "king and ruler of heaven and earth"; Hin Tan, "controller of thunder and lightening"; the "Seven Sisters"; Fut Mu, the teacher of Goon Yum (Kuan Yin); and Goon Yum herself.

By this time, most of the worshipers at the temples were no longer migrant men but first-generation women. The ceremonies described in 1937 by Sau Chun Wong, a Hawaii-born Chinese who was herself an active member of a Chinese Christian church, closely resembled those described half a century earlier:

> The ceremonials in all of the temples tend to be . . . of a magical character designed to coerce the gods and spirits to grant the expressed desires of the worshippers [who seek] sons, happiness for departed spirits, family happiness, long life, wealth and health, and security against accident and misfortune.
>
> A worshipper usually brings . . . on special holidays . . . a basket of food composed of some form of animal flesh, as pork, chicken, or fish (or if he is rich, all of the above), wine, tea, and three bowls of cooked rice, and a vegetable dish, as tofu [soybean curd] or "jai" ["monks' food"]. As he enters, he hits a panel and a drum several times to arouse the gods to listen to his supplication and also to chase away the evil spirits that are lurking near. The priest may assist if the worshipper desires. He endeavors to get all the information he can as to the desires of the worshipper. Then he chants . . . while kneeling in front of the shrine. . . . He picks up the pair of kidney-shaped blocks and answers to questions are secured by the throw of the blocks. If both fall with the curved side up, it is a good sign; if one is flat and the other curved, it is also good; but if both fall on the flat side, the future is not propitious and one should take care.[39]

By the 1970s redevelopment of the old Chinatown section and the areas surrounding it, along with the decline in the number of worshipers, has reduced the number of Chinese temples to three. One of these, replacing an older one dedicated to Goon Yum (Kuan Yin), was built on a site donated by a wealthy Honolulu Chinese family. Some of the images from temples that were closed or torn down have been placed in society buildings where worship can be continued before the societies' altars.[40]

In the late 1860s and early 1870s small numbers of migrants sought help in times of crisis at Christian centers in downtown Honolulu like the Reverend S. C. Damon's Bethel Street Mission. These were mostly migrants moving into Honolulu from the enclaves of Chinese Christian laborers in certain plantation and independent farming areas, especially Hakkas who had become Christians before migrating to Hawaii. In 1879 a group of thirty-seven Chinese formed themselves into a Christian congregation which was known for years as the Fort Street Church. Interested Caucasian Christians served on the board and in other ways assisted this congregation until it became independent of the Hawaiian Board of Missions in 1919. By 1881, when the church building near Chinatown was dedicated, there were 248 members.[41]

Problems arose in the Fort Street Church because the immigrant members spoke one or another of two mutually unintelligible dialects: Cantonese and Hakka. There were further differences among them because of the diverse Christian denominations to which some members had belonged before migrating to Hawaii. Some had become Christians through the influence of German and Swiss Lutheran missions; others had become Christians as the result of American Protestant missionary activity in China and the western United States. It was easier for those who had been converted by American missionaries to make the transition to the Congregational services of the Hawaiian Board than it was for those converted by the Lutherans. There was no Lutheran church in Honolulu at that time, but there were Anglicans whose services were somewhat like those of the Lutherans. In 1886 a few members of the Fort Street Church began to meet in a store near Chinatown for services with a newly arrived Anglican minister and his young Hakka interpreter who had been brought to Honolulu at the age of nine and sent to Iolani School. The following year this group, mostly Hakkas, was formed into St. Peter's Mission, later St. Peter's Church, with their church building behind St. Andrew's Cathedral (Anglican), several blocks away from Chinatown.[42]

The first Chinese Episcopal clergyman in Honolulu, Woo Yee Bew, was the son of a Chinese who had been converted to Christianity in South China and had himself been baptized in a Lutheran church near Canton. He had studied theology at an Anglican college in Hong Kong before going to San Francisco and then coming to

Hawaii in 1883. Woo worked in Chinatown with S. C. Damon's son, the Reverend Frank Damon, and was active in the early development of the Fort Street Church before going to Kohala, Hawaii, to conduct services in Chinese for the Christians on the plantation there. After many families from St. Paul's Mission in Kohala had moved to Honolulu, Woo returned and helped organize St. Peter's Church in 1891.[43]

Though the first members of St. Peter's Church were said in one account to be "poor, mostly cooks, yardmen, and storekeepers," the core of this and other early Chinese congregations was made up of families—Chinese Christian families who had migrated together from China or families brought to the Islands as soon as the husband and father could manage it financially. The Chinese Christian churches undoubtedly provided their members a type of personal and moral support which the familyless migrant generally lacked. Chinatown, therefore, played quite a different role in the lives of the Christian migrants who had their families there than it did in the lives of the familyless young men who were working in the city or in other parts of Oahu.

CHAPTER 8
Migrant Families

THE "familyless migrants" referred to so frequently in earlier chapters included two types of Chinese men: those who had not married before emigrating and those who, although married in China, came without their wives or children. The exact proportions of married and unmarried migrants are unknown, but probably more were married than was commonly realized. The census of 1896 reported 13,800 Chinese men as single and 4,027 as married. The same census reported only 1,110 Chinese married women. A few hundred of the men had Hawaiian or part-Hawaiian wives, but it is likely that two-thirds of those reported as married had wives in China and perhaps many who were counted as single also had wives in China. By 1910 the number of Chinese married women in Hawaii had risen to 1,555, but at the same time the number of married Chinese men had increased to 5,674.[1] Many of these men had undoubtedly married on return visits to China; it was common for their families to arrange marriages for them on such visits and for the wives to be left behind to carry out their obligations to their husbands' parents, especially their mothers-in-law. Since, according to Chinese tradition, the wife was expected to produce male heirs for the family, the migrant husband ordinarily did not return to Hawaii until his wife was pregnant or until the first child was born. If this child was a daughter the migrant might stay on until his wife was pregnant again. Generally there were several years of separation before the migrant had saved enough money for another visit home.

The Early Decades

The familyless migrant in Hawaii almost necessarily led a life that was abnormal in comparison with the pattern of his traditional kinship society. Some of the anxieties felt by the wife of one of these *wah kiu* are revealed in excerpts from two letters sent in 1931 to her husband who was working as a waiter in a Chinatown restaurant— letters no doubt composed and written by a professional letter writer:

> A week has passed since I saw you leave. . . . Although my body is far apart from yours, my mind has really always been thinking about you. When I think about how truly and how faithfully you have treated me, when suddenly we two are separated by mountain and ocean . . . —all those things make me feel very sad and regretful. . . . I always pray to God to bless you to enable you to make a good chance [have good luck] so that you can return with your fortune to your home to let me be with you all the time, and to renew the feelings of our hearts. . . . I sincerely hope you . . . not squander your valuable time in the *yin fa chee dee* ["opium and prostitute places"]. . . .

> . . . I wonder when we can ever meet again. . . . But since you have the ambition to seek your fortune abroad I hope you go forward coura- geously so that happiness will be yours. You ought to know time and money are valuable. Whenever they go away they can never return. The place where you can have good times and all those profitless and useless pastimes I sincerely hope, my beloved husband, that you will keep out of them lest they would handicap your future. I know that you are broad-minded so will not reproach me for this outspoken ad- vice. . . . When you have leisure after your work hours, I with ten thousands of strongest longings wish you to write to me to cultivate my stupidness and to relieve my lonesomeness and longing. The weather is getting cold now. You should put on some more clothes and care for yourself in order to relieve my worry. All I would like to say to you is too much and the paper is too short. Wishing you health and prosperity and fortune abroad. . . .[2]

As in most other overseas Chinese colonies, the majority of mi- grants in Hawaii never did establish families in the Islands. Romanzo Adams estimated that 1,200 to 1,500 Chinese before 1900 married or lived with Hawaiian or part-Hawaiian women and established Chinese-Hawaiian families, especially in the rural areas and small towns. Several of the men who had such families also had wives and children in China. Studies of Chinese-Hawaiian families have shown that few children in these families became part of the "Chinese com- munity"; most of them were more closely identified with their mothers' Hawaiian and part-Hawaiian relatives.[3] The Chinese- Hawaiians who were most likely to become identified with the Chinese community in Hawaii were those boys who were taken back to their fathers' villages and reared by the fathers' Chinese wives or other relatives. A middle-aged Chinese-Hawaiian who had been taken to China as a boy was interviewed in 1931; his daughter, who translated her father's Chinese into English, served as interpreter:

> My father said he went back to China when he was eight years old with his father [and] returned when he was nineteen years old. He said he has two mothers. . . . He stayed with this Chinese woman [who] is very nice to him. . . . "China mother very, very good." He said she treated him just like her own son. He said, "Hawaiian mother good too, treat me good, but China mother very, very good." He is more used to her ways. . . . You see he likes Chinese ways and he was brought up in Chinese manner.[4]

Another Chinese-Hawaiian, also reared in China, married there and eventually brought his Chinese wife to the Islands:

> I went to China when I was about seven years old with my father. I stayed there for about twelve years. . . . In China I stayed with my Chinese mother; yeah, my father married a Chinese lady. You know, Chinese style.
>
> I take Chinese mother just like real mother. Yeah, I like her. I still write letter to her. . . . My father died long time, but I write to my mother in Chinese. I stay with my Chinese mother so long, I'm used to her. . . .
>
> I married in China—regular Chinese style. Match-making; I never see wife till that day when I married her. I never bring her with me when I come back to Honolulu. She didn't come till five years after.[5]

Occasionally, as in a few cases known to the writer, a migrant who had a "Chinese family" and a "Hawaiian family" eventually brought his Chinese wife and any children she had to Hawaii and maintained both families in the Islands, sometimes in the same household.[6] The Chinese acceptance of concubinage and the Hawaiian tradition of plural marriages provided a basis for tolerance of such arrangements during the days of the Hawaiian monarchy, in spite of opposition from Christian missionaries. Even after Annexation, lax enforcement of antibigamy laws for two or three decades made it possible for some families of this type to continue without interference from legal authorities.

A few migrants who could afford to do so, especially between 1880 and 1930, accommodated to separation from their wives and children in China by living with Chinese concubines in Hawaii. In some cases the "first wife" and her children never left China. In others the first wife was brought to Hawaii where she and her children were installed along with the concubine and the concubine's children. As one would expect, this arrangement sometimes led to quarrels between wives and between their children, but one daughter of a "second wife," or concubine, wrote in the 1930s about the harmonious family life she had enjoyed in such a household in Hawaii:

> Ours is a large family. Father had eight children; four boys from the first wife and four girls from the second wife. All of us children called the first wife "mother" regardless of whose children we really were. The second wife we call "Jah" which in Chinese means "second mother." This seemingly strange family situation can be explained by the age-old Oriental custom which allows a man to have more than one wife. . . .
>
> Our family is closely integrated, and we all work for the welfare of the home. . . . All earnings by the members of the family were turned over to father. My brothers' pay checks were given directly to father. . . .
>
> All of the boys were educated in private American schools. . . . Father seemed more interested in them than in his daughters. Indeed, it is an accepted fact that in the Orient boys are more highly considered than girls. This is so because they can carry on and perpetuate the family name, thus easing the parent's constant worry of family extinction. . . .
>
> However peculiar may have been the household situation, I can say with sincerity that the happiness I found and the culture I received in my home are equal, if not superior, to the culture that could be got under any other family culture.[7]

That it was not unusual for Chinese migrants in the early decades of emigration to take concubines rather than first wives overseas is shown by Dr. Paul C. F. Siu's study of Chinese families in Chicago in 1933. He found that not one of the dozen or so Chinese women who had come to Chicago before 1900 was a first wife; all were either second wives or concubines.[8] This finding is consistent with Chinese family values that placed great importance on maintaining the ancestral kinship group, of which the sojourner migrant's wife and children were essential parts. Nevertheless, the situation in Hawaii seems to have differed from that in other overseas Chinese communities. It appears that nearly all the married Chinese women who came to the Islands were wives rather than concubines. Personal documents and life histories contain occasional references to Chinese migrants who had both a Chinese wife and one or more concubines, but there is no evidence that the practice was common. Perhaps fewer concubines were brought to Hawaii than to the mainland United States because Hawaiian and part-Hawaiian women were accessible in the Islands whereas non-Chinese women were relatively inaccessible to Chinese migrants on the mainland. There were other differences between Hawaii and the U.S. mainland that appear to have encouraged Chinese migrants to bring their wives (who were usually their only wives) to the Islands: a higher proportion of the migrants in the Islands were financially successful; Hawaii was more similar to South China in climate and physical environment; legal entry was easier before 1924; transportation between Hawaii and China was cheaper and quicker; there was less anti-Chinese agitation and legal discrimination; there were more educational, economic, and social opportunities for Hawaii-born Chinese in the Islands' multiethnic community.

Whatever the reason, the number of married Chinese women in Hawaii—the best clue to the establishment of Chinese families in the Islands—increased steadily over the census periods prior to 1930. There were 559 in 1890; 1,119 in 1896; 1,409 in 1900; 1,555 in 1910; 2,416 in 1920; and 3,212 in 1930. Before 1910 nearly all these women would have been born in China; by 1930 about half of them would have been Hawaii-born. Throughout this period married women born in China, almost without exception, would have had Chinese husbands; and before 1920 this would also have been true of the Hawaii-born Chinese married women. Even though outmarriage of Hawaii-born Chinese women increased during the 1920s, at least five-sixths of those who married in that decade married Chinese men.[9]

It was particularly significant for the development of organized Chinese community life in Honolulu that a high proportion of the Chinese families of Hawaii were in that city—especially by about 1930, when at least half the families were still headed by men of the migrant generation. By 1930 Honolulu had at least three thousand Chinese nuclear families with one or both parents living. The number of Chinese family households in Honolulu was considerably smaller since many families of the migrant generation were of the extended type: one or more families of the married sons living with the sons' parents and unmarried siblings.

Whether the migrant's family was located in Honolulu, in a smaller town, or in a rural area such as a rice-growing district, it was generally recognized that establishing a family in the Islands brought stability into the migrant's life. It also gave his wife a welcome release from the constrictions of living with parents-in-law in the village. In 1936 a Hawaii-born Chinese student explained how setting up a family in Hawaii affected his own mother and father:

> Before my dad got married he was very unsteady. He worked here and there with no concern for the future. During his spare time, like most of his contemporary countrymen, he took to gambling. Sometimes he won but most of the time he lost his money. This kept on until the arrival of my mother. . . . He began to realize his responsibilities to his wife and family. His carefree days were gone and he began to save his money. With what little he had he started his own business. His friends all complimented his industry now. He was a changed man. . . .
>
> My mother got economic security only when she came to Hawaii. While she was in China she had to live with my paternal grandmother. A daughter-in-law has no choice but to be under the domination of a mother-in-law. My mother had to eat what grandmother bought and like it. . . . But as soon as she came to Hawaii and raised a family she was her own boss. Dad gave her money to spend and she was really independent.
>
> In return for her economic security, my mother provided religious security for my father. Mother celebrates the various festivals and holidays, and often goes to the temple to ask blessings for father and his business. In times of illness, mother is the one that prays to the gods for a speedy recovery.[10]

Kinship Ties and Interfamily Relationships

The migrant family in Hawaii could not, of course, be a complete replica of the family pattern within the village and clan in China, but within the migrant Chinese community there developed a network of kinship ties and interfamily relationships which partly grew out of old-world ties and partly replaced them. The tendency of Chinese families in the early days to concentrate in the heart of old Chinatown was an integral part of this process. Since most families of migrant businessmen or craftsmen initially lived behind or above the shops, and since partners and employees in these businesses were commonly kinsmen or *heung li*, the wife from China was likely to find that her neighbors in Chinatown were women she had known at home or knew about through others in her home village. It was in Chinatown, or the districts adjacent to it, that Chinese family life flourished most during the 1890s and the first fifteen years of this century. Here was the greatest concentration of women and children, of family ritual, of communal sharing of crises and celebrations among people whose culture to a large extent isolated them from the community surrounding them. It is not surprising that most of the leaders among the migrant Chinese were men who had families in Hawaii. They were not only among the most stable and responsible —they also had a greater stake in matters affecting the Chinese community than did the familyless migrants.

With the growth of Chinese families in Honolulu, members of the Chinese community were bound together in a way that would hardly have been possible in an aggregation of mobile, familyless adult men. Relationships among such men, each bent on his individual goals, exploiting the resources of a place where they did not intend to settle and even exploiting each other, tended to be touch-and-go—there was less regard for personal claims from the past or for building up permanent ties in the new community. Children, especially within the Chinese tradition, required the migrants to plan for the future. And by a subtle process children brought parents, kinsmen, and fellow villagers into a chain of reciprocal moral obligations that were even stronger than the claims exerted in the business world.

Each event in the family life cycle, from birth to death, was accompanied by ceremonials, rituals, and customs which involved not only the immediate family but also more distant kinsmen, *heung li*, neighbors, the father's business associates, and members of Chinese organizations to which the family, especially the father, belonged. These activities varied from family to family, and even within the same family over the course of time, because folk practices among the migrants were not uniform, even though nearly all of them came from the same small region in China. There were differences between Hakka and Punti, between Cantonese-speaking families of Chung Shan district and those of the See Yup districts, and even between those of different subdistricts of Chung Shan, such as Lung Doo and Kung Seong Doo. Chinese who had become Christians, even though they retained many traditional Chinese cultural practices, observed different rituals than the non-Christian Chinese. In spite of these variations, there was enough similarity to make for mutual understanding and participation by most members of the Chinese community. Interviews with Hawaii Chinese and observations by the writer from 1929 to 1937, life histories, and other personal documents provide descriptions of some of the practices common among first-generation and second-generation Chinese families in the Islands.

Birth of Children

The birth of a child in Chinatown usually initiated a round of solicitous and ceremonial activities. When a child was about to be born the pregnant mother's female relatives and friends who were living nearby gave her help. Some went to the temple or prayed before .family shrines for the safety of mother and unborn child and besought the help and goodwill of the deities. Older women passed on to the young mother the folk wisdom they had brought from China; they warned the mother against doing anything believed to be harmful to her and the child; they advised her on diet and prepared special food for her; they helped her prepare for the delivery.

In the early days of Chinatown, the delivery was usually attended by a midwife who was a relative or family friend rather than a professional and who continued to help the mother through the child's first days. Her services were usually repaid with gifts rather than a fee. On the third day after the child's birth a customary ceremony was to place under the infant's bed an image of the goddess believed to be the protector of infants. The father commonly announced his good fortune in the birth of a child, especially of a son, by sending to relatives and friends trays containing hard-boiled eggs dyed red and pigs' feet pickled in ginger and black vinegar. It was customary for the tray to be returned, uncleaned, with some money wrapped in red paper (*li shee*). During the first month friends and relatives might also send the child such gifts as jade jewelry, gold chains and bracelets, or gold-cloth emblems of Buddha and characters signifying long life, happiness, and wealth to be sewn on the child's bonnet. When a son was born, the father might recognize ties with his kinsmen in China by arranging for a lantern to be placed in the ancestral hall at the time of the Mid-Autumn Festival and entering the son's name in the family register and genealogy. The father would probably send money for a feast to be held by kinsmen on that occasion.

During the first month it was expected that neither the mother nor the child would leave the house. The end of this month was often celebrated by another round of ceremonies. The child in a non-Christian family would probably have his head shaved and would be taken, dressed in red garments, to the temple to be introduced to the gods and receive a name, a prediction of his fortune, and a blessing. Rites would also be carried out before a family shrine to announce the addition of a new family member, especially if the child was a boy who would eventually himself perform rites for deceased ancestors. The "full month" ceremonies often ended with a banquet for dozens or even hundreds of guests, the larger, more elaborate banquets being held for a boy-child who was the firstborn. A rice planter's daughter on Kauai, who had five sisters and four brothers, wrote in 1937 about the rituals carried out when a grandchild was born into her family:

> If the grandchild is one of her sons', grandmother helps to shave the baby's tiny head before the baby is a month old. On this day, she boils a couple of eggs and dyes them red. She places them in a pan of warm water which was prepared for the shaving. She carries the baby gently in her arms over the water, dampens his tiny head, rolls the egg around his head and repeats several lines in Chinese. What these lines mean, I do not know. When this is over, she starts shaving the baby's head with a Chinese shaving razor.
>
> If the child is the first boy, a large dinner is always given on the day he becomes a month old and also when he is a year old. When he is a month old, lots of boiled eggs, dyed red, and roasted pork, pickled ginger, and Chinese sweet breads are wrapped up in packages and given to friends, neighbors, and relatives. Brother is so happy that he offers cigars to everyone of his friends and also to the men in the office where he works. The baby also receives a great many gifts from the family's good wishers.

Two other Hawaii-born Chinese reported, about the same time, the customs their families followed when a child was born:

> The birth of my younger brother was climaxed by a "full month" party, when my brother, a pink little bundle of noise, was displayed to the guests. Father told me he spent more than five hundred dollars for that party and when I [firstborn son] was a month old, he spent nearly a

thousand. I asked him why he didn't save the money for our use when we come to college or start in business. He said, "College education and careers are different things." The celebrations of the births of my sisters were the same, but in a far less intensive degree.

When Sister was a month old, she was dressed in a pink dress. The dress was pink because it was the nearest to red, the lucky color of the Chinese. She also wore some gold trinkets symbolizing good luck and long life. On that day we had a large roasted pig, called a "golden pig." It was put on a stand in the parlor and in front of it were placed candles and other ceremonial articles. Father then bowed and prayed that the gods be generous and that they protect the new-born babe. After that the paper money was burned. Then the pig was cut into slices to distribute to friends and relatives. Preserved ginger, buns, and red-colored eggs were also distributed. These were all symbols of good luck, health, and happiness.

At a full-month banquet guests who had not already given presents to the child were expected to leave money, two dollars or more, conventionally wrapped in red paper. In case the family did not celebrate the occasion by a banquet but delivered the ceremonial foods to the homes of relatives and friends, the *li shee* was given at that time.

Chinese Festivals

Traditional holiday periods such as Chinese New Year and the Moon Festival were occasions for family festivities. Others, such as Ching Ming and the Mid-Autumn Festival, involved ceremonial renewing of ties between living and deceased members of a family. In the traditional observance of such festivals interfamily visiting and obligations were important, and Chinese organizations participated in the Ching Ming and Mid-Autumn Festival ceremonies. Accounts of Chinese New Year written in the 1920s and 1930s by Hawaii-born Chinese students illustrate the intrafamily and interfamily observances of this major annual festival:

Chinese New Year is the greatest holiday of the Chinese people. . . . Months ahead, preparations for its celebration are under way. I recall how my father used to plant narcissus bulbs . . . . I recall how industriously my oldest sister would work at the sewing machine to provide each member of the family with a new suit of clothes. New Year was the time when everybody must look his best, poor as well as rich. There were over ten in our family, so you can imagine how my sister must have stitched till her eyes grew dim . . . in order to finish the clothes in time. . . . I recall how mother would rise up early in the morning to pound rice into flour for the rice pudding and other toothsome delicacies. . . . Then there was the grand house-cleaning day before New Year. . . . The climax of the celebration is just when the clock struck twelve. Firecrackers boomed . . . everywhere could be heard cries of "HAPPY NEW YEAR." Before the altar my father and mother would kaotow and beg divine blessing of the gods for the coming year. Then they would distribute little packages of money to all the children. As early as five o'clock the next morning, guests would be pouring into our house and some more of the tiny red packages would be passed out. Giving away money wrapped in red paper meant good luck, and the more generous a man was, the more prosperous and fortunate his life would be the coming year.

Mother is very particular about what we say on New Year, for it is believed that everything one says on New Year is supposed to come true. So we have to remember not to talk about bad things. . . . Then, too, on New Year's Day we must cleanse our bodies by bathing in water which has pomelo leaves in it. Some of these superstitions seem silly to us, but we have to conform to mother's wishes since she believes in them.

On New Year's Day when one goes to call on people, he must take oranges and tangerines and a piece of pudding. "Li-see" are given to little children for good luck. When a visitor arrives, tea is served. With the tea one must say something congratulating the guest. If the visitor is young one wishes that she will have many more sons. One wishes an older person wealth and long life. After the visitor has finished drinking, more tea is poured into the cup, as a symbol that there will be an increase in wealth, children, or years in life. When the visitor leaves, one has to leave two oranges and two tangerines as a symbol that there will be a continuing relationship.

At Chinese New Year we visit each other. At each home, we eat all over again the special New Year's monk's food, which may be described as a vegetable stew. Relatives whom we sometimes don't see for a whole year, we dine with at this time. . . . Eating and drinking together, we once again resume the family relationship, and at this time the old kindred spirit between the visiting relatives and the host is revived.

Even familyless migrants were included in these holiday activities—men who were actually relatives of a family and other friends of the father, who became, as it were, honorary uncles for these occasions. The claims of friends and relatives were taken seriously within the Chinese community:

> The first-generation Chinese families seldom invite their friends over to Sunday night dinner as the Westerners do. When they do give a dinner it is generally a ten-table affair and all their friends and relatives are invited so that no one would be left out. Woe be to you, if you forgot to invite a relative. He will never forget it and he will generally draw the conclusion that it is because he is poor that you neglect him, for who has heard of a wealthy relative being neglected?

Education of Children

One matter of particular concern to migrant parents of Hawaii-born Chinese was the education of their children—especially, at first, their sons. Most of the migrants who came before Annexation had little formal education. The economic hardship most of them had lived with during their childhood had thwarted any possibility of securing even elementary schooling. This very background, however, coupled with the improved economic position of immigrant heads of families in Hawaii and the age-old Chinese tradition that positions of highest prestige went to the most erudite scholars, led migrant fathers to try to secure for at least some of their children a good Chinese education.

In Chinese villages, beginners' schools were usually supported by clans and held in the ancestral hall under the supervision of a literate clan member. Villagers who did not belong to a clan prosperous enough to maintain such a school, or members of a family too poor to pay even the minimal expenses involved in sending a child to the clan school, could not take advantage of this schooling. For several reasons clan schools were never established in Hawaii, and Chinese families had been in the Islands several decades before it occurred to migrants of various clan and surname identities that they could jointly establish Chinese-language schools for their children. Between 1870 and 1910 the number of Chinese children in Honolulu between six and fifteen years of age grew from not more than a dozen or so to more than 1,700 and in all of Hawaii from less than a hundred to more than 3,500. Few formal schools were established by the Chinese themselves during this period, however. Most migrant families dealt individually with their children's education. Hundreds of Hawaii-born boys, especially eldest sons, were sent back to China to live in the villages with their fathers' relatives and attend the clan schools. During late adolescence, and commonly after being married in the village, the young men returned to Hawaii to work in their fathers' businesses or enter some other occupation. Sometimes boys who returned in their teens attended English-language schools in Hawaii to obtain the advantages of a dual education in Chinese and English, even though their learning in each might be limited.

A larger number of Hawaii-born boys and most Hawaii-born girls were not sent back to the villages, especially as the years passed and migrants changed from sojourners to permanent residents. It was the growing number of these children who remained in Hawaii that led ultimately to the organization of Chinese-language schools. Before such schools were established, some parents arranged to have their children privately tutored at home by one or another migrant who had enough knowledge of the Chinese classics to give lessons.[11] At least one teacher was brought from China, as an employee of a local Chinese businessman, "to open a private school in Honolulu for Chinese" in 1893, but no record of such a school was found.[12]

More important as precursors of the language schools were the mission schools established by Caucasians in or near Chinatown. The first of these, apparently, was the Bethel Mission School which opened as an evening school in 1869. Others established during the next forty years included the Chinese Children's English School (also known as the Chinese Mission Day School), Fort Street Mission School (later renamed Iolani School), Mills Institute (later called Mid-Pacific Institute), St. Louis College, and the Honolulu Anglo-Chinese Academy. At first these schools attracted China-born adolescents and young adults who realized the economic value of learning to speak, read, and write English. According to a report published in January 1881, some 248 of the 265 students enrolled in evening classes of the Bethel Mission School over the preceding eleven years had been Chinese.[13] An 1882 government report mentions Tang Peng Sum as "teacher of Chinese" "with Adela M. Payson as principal" in the Chinese Children's English School, which had been given $404.50 in 1882 "for the education of 50 boys and two girls in the Chinese and English languages."[14]

Classes held in nearly all the Chinese Christian churches in the Islands were less formally organized than the mission schools, but instruction in Chinese (both Cantonese and Hakka dialects) was given by Chinese ministers, with Caucasian Christian volunteers teaching

English. The Chinese YMCA located near Chinatown in Honolulu also organized classes for instruction in English and Chinese. In 1891 Lee On, who had been a teacher at the Chinese YMCA in the 1880s, was issued a permit in Hong Kong to reenter Hawaii where he was "required by the YMCA to resume his duties in the education of the Chinese boys."[15] Most mission schools admitted only boys, but girls from Chinese Christian homes who reached school age in the 1880s and 1890s began to receive schooling in the classes held in the churches. Some Chinese girls did attend the Kawaiahao Female Seminary in Honolulu, which later merged with Mills Institute to form the Mid-Pacific Institute, but there were not many and their schooling was primarily in English.

While children from non-Christian as well as Christian Chinese families were admitted to the church classes and the mission schools, many non-Christian Chinese parents disliked having their children educated under Christian missionary influence. A missionary magazine, *The Friend,* clearly stated in 1882 the objective of missionary education of Chinese youth: "It is one of the most useful agencies now in operation for Christianizing and elevating of the Chinese in our Islands."[16] C. K. Ai tells of the quarrels between Sun Yat-sen, his close friend and classmate at the Fort Street School, and Sun Yat-sen's older brother, Sun Mi, because of Sun Yat-sen's attraction to Christianity. According to C. K. Ai this issue "split the Chinese community in these islands."[17]

An alternative to the mission schools was offered by the government schools, which by the 1890s were taught entirely in English. The 1896 census reported that 475 Chinese pupils—351 boys and 124 girls—were attending independent schools and 140—117 boys and 23 girls—were in government schools. After Annexation, when the American public school system spread to the Islands, the majority of Hawaii-born Chinese children were enrolled in the public schools or Protestant and Catholic schools. At first, higher proportions of boys than of girls attended school: in 1900, some 802 boys and 423 girls between the ages of five and twenty were in school; in 1910, the enrollment was 1,924 boys and 1,317 girls. In 1910 about 80 percent of the boys five to twenty years old, and about 65 percent of the girls, attended school.

The fact that two-thirds of the Chinese girls between ages five and twenty were attending school in 1910 is remarkable in view of the low value traditionally placed by Chinese on the education of daughters. To be sure, school attendance was legally compulsory for girls as well as boys, but enforcement was weak for several years after Annexation. Quite probably Chinese girls went to school in such high proportions because non-Christian as well as Christian Chinese parents acquiesced in the wider community view that it was desirable to educate both boys and girls. Chinese parents quickly realized that well-paid jobs were available to educated women, and since Hawaii-born Chinese girls were not betrothed or married at as early an age as in China, it was to the benefit of the girls' families to see that their daughters could qualify for those jobs. It was also easier to find husbands for girls who could earn money.

The development of an extensive system of private and tax-supported public schools relieved Chinese parents of the necessity of operating schools for general education at their own expense, as overseas Chinese did in most of Southeast Asia and elsewhere. Nevertheless, since these schools were taught in English and within the Western, specifically American, cultural tradition, there was a widening gap between migrant parents and their Hawaii-reared and Hawaii-educated children—a gap that sometimes led to serious family conflicts. In his study of the Chinese-language schools in Hawaii, Kum Pui Lai concludes that the migrant generation's primary objective in organizing such schools was to prevent or retard "deculturization" or "deracialization" of their children. He translates, from a statement prepared by the founders of a language school opened in 1911, a passage that speaks of Hawaii-born Chinese children becoming "foreignized":

> Our youths of school age number several thousands. Because they are brought up here in an American cultural milieu, their speech, contacts, and experiences tend to be foreignized. Concerning Chinese customs and manners they possess no knowledge, and we are forced to bear seeing the process of a racial transformation.[18]

Concern about the Hawaii-Chinese children's knowing their ancestral culture was not the only impetus for opening two language schools near Honolulu's Chinatown only a few days apart in 1911. These schools—Wah Mun School and Mun Lun School—were opened by rival Chinese political movements, a development which is discussed in Chapter 12. Neither was a clan school like those in the villages; both accepted students of all surname identities and both accepted girls as well as boys. These two schools are still the largest

Chinese-language schools in the Islands. Over the years more than twenty others were opened in Honolulu, and at least three in rural Oahu, three in Hilo, three on Maui, and two on Kauai. Some of these, like the first two, reflected political viewpoints among the migrants; others were begun because of dialectical, factional, religious, and commercial interests. All were designed to supplement American schooling by providing institutions where Chinese boys and girls could be taught, after regular school hours and on Saturdays, the rudiments of written Chinese and some appreciation of their ancestral history and cultural heritage.

In the early 1930s children of migrant parents still made up about one-third of the students in the classes Kum Pui Lai studied at Mun Lun School; the other students were children of Hawaii-born Chinese parents. At that time from a third to a half of the Chinese children five to fifteen years old in Honolulu were attending Chinese-language schools.[19] In spite of the factional differences between their founders and supporters, the first two language schools played an important role in the organization of Honolulu's Chinese into a community, and they illustrate the significance of the family in this process.

Marriages

Through marriages, both of migrants and of Hawaii-born Chinese, relationships between members of Honolulu's Chinese community were strengthened and new connections were set up. Prosperous migrants arranged marriages for economically successful unmarried *heung li* with women in their home villages or districts; a migrant with children still living with their mother and grandparents in the village or Hawaii-born and Hawaii-reared was likely to be interested in the children of other migrants from his home district as prospective mates for his sons or daughters. These potential spouses might also have been living in the home district or they might have been members of a family established in Hawaii. Several hundred early second-generation young men went back to their fathers' home villages to be married to brides selected for them by their elders. Fewer of the Hawaii-born girls of the early second generation went back: many of them would be married to their fathers' *heung li* in Hawaii.

Betrothals and weddings in the villages and in Hawaii were occasions for gift exchanges between the families of the young couple as well as for the giving and receiving of gifts among *heung li*, friends, and business associates. Weddings in *wah kiu* families in the villages were far more elaborate than most nonmigrant families could afford. Accounts of these weddings in China circulated among migrant *heung li* in Honolulu, and the arrival of a village-reared bridegroom to join his father's circle of friends and acquaintances, or the return of the Island-reared bridegroom, was celebrated in Chinatown. If the bride came to Hawaii later than her husband, there were further celebrations after her arrival. After her arrival in Hawaii, the China-born bride often lived with her husband's family in Honolulu much as she would have done had she married someone in a neighboring village. A third-generation Honolulu girl described the situation of her parents' generation:

> When grandpa's sons were old enough to marry, he took them to China where he made the arrangements for each son's wedding. He selected his daughters-in-law with the help of matchmakers. For each son's wedding there was a large wedding feast to which the whole village was invited. Grandfather also paid for each daughter-in-law's passage fare to Honolulu. For many years all the sons and daughters-in-law lived together with grandpa and grandma in the same house. During these days they had no freedom nor authority to make any decisions. Grandpa supported the family; therefore, he was the ruler and the head of the family. Mother and the other daughters-in-law had to do all the cooking, ironing, washing, and other household duties for the whole family. The women never had an opportunity to go out alone. If ever they went out, grandma chaperoned them. Mother, who was only sixteen when she was married, was naturally very much afraid of grandpa and grandma. She was brought up with the idea that she was to obey and respect her husband's parents.

Marriages between Hawaii-reared Chinese girls and Chinese migrants in Hawaii also helped to forge bonds within the migrant community. Many of these marriages were "matched," often as the girl was reaching late adolescence, by a go-between who also assisted in the marital arrangements and acted as a sponsor of the marriage. This type of marriage was an approximation of traditional village customs —there was nothing like a Western courtship and the bride and groom saw little of one another before the wedding. In the earlier decades it was possible for parents to arrange economically more promising marriages for their daughters with migrants than with Hawaii-born young men. Migrants were more likely to have established themselves occupationally and to have saved enough to set up a home. For migrant parents who had themselves come to Hawaii for economic reasons, financial security would have been a major consideration in selecting a son-in-law. Apart from the economic security the successful bridegroom could offer his bride, there were often other business and financial advantages to be gained, on both sides, from such an alliance. One immediate advantage was that the unmarried migrant who married a Hawaii-Chinese girl saved the cost of a trip to China. On their side, Hawaii-born girls of the early second generation, themselves trained in Chinese ways, acquiesced in such matchmaking.

Marriages brought about further interlinking of the Chinese population of the Islands, new reciprocal obligations, new lines of mutual control. Betrothals, like the baby ceremonies, typically involved dozens of people, and weddings even hundreds. Gifts exchanged between the bridegroom's and bride's families were selected with an eye to family appraisal and comment from other members of the Chinese community. There were farewell dinners in the home of the bride and congratulatory dinners in the home of the prospective bridegroom and his parents if he was a Hawaii-born Chinese. An elaborate wedding reception and banquet was attended by relatives and friends on both sides. Gifts of money were presented, representatives and friends of the couple's families made congratulatory speeches, and there was much merrymaking and joking with the bride. Old-world customs were revived and sometimes expensively elaborated. Non-Christians worshiped at a temple, and if the bridegroom's family had a shrine in Hawaii the couple visited it and carried out rites honoring his ancestors. If the bridegroom's parents lived in Hawaii, the bride dutifully carried out the traditional ceremonies honoring them.

Each succeeding wedding increased the circle of interrelationships among these residents of a new world—even though, as time and acculturation went on, the pattern of the marriages themselves lost much of the old village character and took on a modified Western form. Because of these interrelationships Chinese children in Honolulu, instead of living in a world of Chinese strangers, had direct or indirect kinship ties with a great number of other Chinese. The widening circle of relationships in which individual Chinese were involved is illustrated by genealogical data given by thirty-six Hawaii-born Chinese who were students at the University of Hawaii in 1937 (Table 12). They were asked to list by kinship those persons

Table 12
Relatives Listed by Thirty-Six Hawaii-Born Chinese: 1937

Kinship	Living Relatives[a]			Deceased Relatives		
	Residing in Hawaii	Residing in China	Residing Elsewhere	Died in Hawaii	Died in China	Died Elsewhere
Paternal great-grandparents	—	—	—	5	3	—
Maternal great-grandparents	1	—	—	3	2	—
Paternal grandparents	14	3	—	13	33	—
Maternal grandparents	21	4	—	17	18	—
Father	26	1	—	7	2	—
Mother	34	1	—	1	—	—
Stepfather	—	—	—	1	—	—
Stepmother	1	—	—	—	1	—
Brothers	96	5	2	4	2	—
Sisters	108	3	—	3	1	—
Brothers-in-law	31	2	—	1	—	—
Sisters-in-law	12	5	2	1	—	—
Nephews	50	4	1	—	—	—
Nieces	39	1	2	—	—	—
Relatives through father's brothers	210	133	14	7	26	5
Relatives through father's sisters	127	65	2	14	3	—
More distant relatives of father	18	9	—	1	2	—
Relatives through mother's brothers	230	34	6	3	9	1
Relatives through mother's sisters	281	42	33	14	2	—
Total	1,299	312	62	95	104	6

a Hawaii-born relatives who were students in China, on the U.S. mainland, or elsewhere were classified as living in Hawaii.

they recognized as relatives, living or dead, in Hawaii, China, or some other part of the world. Twenty-two of the informants had China-born fathers and either China-born mothers (twelve) or Hawaii-born mothers (ten). Fourteen had Hawaii-born fathers and either China-born mothers (three) or Hawaii-born mothers (eleven).

Of the 1,299 relatives listed as residing in Hawaii, 92 were of part-Chinese ancestry and 25 were non-Chinese who had married Chinese relatives of the informants. Since the total Chinese population in Hawaii in 1937 was only about 28,000, it is impressive that this small group of 36 Hawaii-born Chinese, mostly in their early twenties, identified as relatives nearly 1,300 Chinese in Hawaii. This number, in fact, falls far short of the total number of Chinese in Hawaii with whom these informants could have traced family connections. For one thing, the information they gave omitted several hundred Chinese in Hawaii with whom they would have had an indirect kinship through their 31 brothers-in-law and 12 sisters-in-law living in Hawaii. Moreover, they could have found family connections with hundreds of other Chinese married to siblings of great-grandparents or grandparents who had settled in Hawaii or to descendants of those siblings. The rapid multiplication of connections with each generation is indicated by the fact that informants with one or both Hawaii-born parents listed 742 (86 percent) of the 866 relatives living in Hawaii who were identified in the last five categories of the table. Of the 1,673 living relatives listed, 1,299 (77 percent) were living in Hawaii, only about 20 percent in China, and less than 4 percent in other parts of the world. Of those living in Hawaii, more than 80 percent were in Honolulu. With marriages and births adding new familial connections each year, it is probable that by the 1950s Hawaii-born Chinese in Honolulu had to be very cautious about criticizing one another—in any gathering of Honolulu Chinese, one or more of those present would probably be related in some way to the person being criticized.

One indication of the differences between the Chinese village community and the Honolulu Chinatown community is the finding that more relatives living in Hawaii were identified on the mother's side than on the father's side. In the informants' ancestral culture, for countless generations, a highly institutionalized patrilineal kinship system had prevailed, and in the villages it is likely that most of those recognized as kin would have been connected with the father's side of the family. The fact that in Hawaii relationships on the mother's side were at least as well recognized as those on the father's side indicates not only that Western ideas were influencing the Hawaii-born Chinese but also that interfamily connections were more elaborate than they would have been in China.

The data in Table 12 lead one to infer that the informants' families were settlers rather than sojourners and that Hawaii was the major locale of their familial world. Very few of the informants' brothers or sisters had gone to China to work and live; even fewer were residents of the U.S. mainland or other parts of the world. The informants' Hawaii-born cousins who were employed had also remained in the Islands. Of 267 such cousins identified by the informants, 91 percent (242) were employed in Hawaii, only 6 percent in China, and 3 percent in the mainland United States. While the families of the 36 Hawaii-born students providing this information are not necessarily representative of the Hawaii-Chinese population, the data do illustrate the trend toward a Hawaii-Chinese community made up of a complex network of interrelated families.

Honoring the Elders

Among families that had been maintained in the Islands over several decades it was possible to celebrate an elder's fifty-first, sixty-first, seventy-first, and later birthdays according to Chinese custom. Though many familyless migrants in Hawaii also reached these traditional milestones, few would have been honored on these occasions in the way that parents and grandparents were honored by their children in Hawaii. Even families of limited means, even when times were hard, observed these occasions within their homes. In the 1930s a Hawaii-born Chinese girl described how her father's mother was honored by children and grandchildren:

> When my paternal grandmother was sixty-one, all her sons and daughters and their children came to the birthday party. Old grudges against each other were supposed to be forgotten, and everyone was merry and on good terms with those present. Early that morning, grandmother had paid her respects and thanks to the gods and ancestors who had let her live such a long life. She had the priest bless some bowls and chopsticks and some metallic emblems of her family name —all these things were later distributed to the guests. At this rare occasion all her children and grandchildren were gathered. We all took turns to pour her tea. Poor grandmother, how she must have been filled with tea—there were over fifty such faithful descendants who poured for her. She, in turn, gave us money wrapped in red paper as a sign of good luck.

In families that followed Taoist practices, the priest or priestess at a temple might be consulted for auguries to determine whether such a day as the fifty-first birthday was auspicious or whether the celebration should be postponed. The sixty-first birthday, regarded as the beginning of a second life, was celebrated more frequently than the others. On the morning of the banquet the elder might worship before the family shrine or go to the temple to thank the ancestors and the gods for having been permitted to live such a long life. Before the banquet it was customary for all the descendants, beginning with the eldest son, to prostrate themselves one by one before the honored elder and the elder's spouse, to wish them eternal happiness, to offer cups of tea ceremoniously, and to kowtow again as the elders drank. Before the banquet long strings of firecrackers were usually set off, and a Chinese orchestra might have been engaged to play during the feasting and drinking. Guests offered salutations and gifts and received gifts in return. Such a celebration in the 1930s was described by a third-generation Chinese girl:

> I remember a relative of ours who was honored at a birthday party given by his sons and daughters. He was celebrating his eighty-first birthday. Many people were invited and nearly everyone made an effort to come as this man was admired by many as having a "long, long life." The Chinese believed that if you ate something that pertained to an old man you too will have a long life. Everybody was merry. People went up to him and wished him eternal happiness. After the dinner each person was given a bowl, a pair of chopsticks, some honored "long life" buns, and a string of gilded square-holed copper money. It was an honor to receive these things from an aged person. When mother and father came home with these gifts they gave them to the two youngest ones in the family and told them to take good care of the bowls and said, "Use these bowls whenever you eat because it will bring you long life." As for the buns, mother divided them among all the members of the family so that everyone could have a taste of the "long life" and live as long as the owner or longer.

Funerals

The funeral of an immigrant grandparent or parent in a family established in Hawaii—in contrast to the generally simple burial procedures for a familyless migrant—became a complicated social ritual. Folk beliefs and customs were observed fully and conscientiously by Chinese families in Honolulu forty or more years ago. These beliefs and customs were concerned with successive phases of dealing with death: what should be done as a family member was dying; what should be done at home between the time of death and the wake; participation of priests, musicians, and even professional mourners along with relatives and friends at the wake, in the funeral procession, in the burial ceremonies; return of family members from the cemetery to the home of the deceased elder; ceremonies each seventh day for forty-nine days; varying mourning periods for relatives of varying degrees of kinship ("the five degrees of mourning"). Two Hawaii-born Chinese, writing in the 1930s, describe funeral practices followed in their families:

> The morning after [father's] death, we began the period of mourning. In the morning friends and relatives came over to the house. Most of these people were familiar with our customs and everything was de-

cided by them—the clothes we were to wear, the kind of funeral, and the million and one things that were to be done.

> [Grandmother's] descendants were gathered at her funeral. Priests chanted day and night. . . . Her immediate relatives were dressed especially for her sake. . . . When the hour before the funeral came, everyone gathered around the corpse and cried, wailed, chanted, and what not. My oldest aunt would start something like this: "Oh mother dear, life is just like a package of salt thrown into the ocean, the salt dissolves, and life is just like that." This is only my poor translation of the original in Chinese. When she was through with the verse, the whole mass joined in the chorus, which I could not make out. This was a very sad event; still it united the kinsmen, and seeing each other, gave each one more spirit to face this loss.

At the funeral of the head of a family, the immediate descendants, dressed in white mourning clothes, were expected to walk behind the coffin part or all of the way to the cemetery, the eldest son leading the group, perhaps carrying the ancestral tablet or a large portrait of the deceased. One young Hawaii-born woman wrote about her father's funeral in 1937:

> The mourning garments were made out of the cheapest grade of unbleached muslin. My mother and us girls wore triangle covers which were long enough to cover the face and the head. My mother's cover was white to indicate that she was married; my sisters and I wore blue covers which indicated that we were unmarried. Around our heads were tied pieces of white muslin. We wore cheap straw slippers. We wore mourning crepe on our right arms. My brothers wore the same attire but minus the head covers. . . .
>
> As a duty of filial piety and because of social expectations each member of the family had to walk part of the way to the cemetery. "What happens if we don't walk?" I asked my aunt. "If you don't you would be the subject of gossip in town. People will say that you lack reverence and love for your father," she replied. Due to the expectations of society we walked from the undertaker's until Washington Place on Beretania St. From there on we rode in automobiles to the burial grounds.

From Aggregation to Community

Settlement of Chinese families in the Islands and their concentration in Honolulu transformed the Hawaii Chinese population from an aggregation of sojourners, largely individuals, into a community of persons bound together by reciprocal relationships. As members of these families went through the phases of the life cycle, the observance of traditions carried over from Chinese village life (even though somewhat changed) formed a web of mutual expectations and moral obligations of which Chinatown was the psychological and cultural, as well as geographical, center. Whether or not they actually lived or worked within its limits, Honolulu's Chinese for several decades were part of a social world shaped by the cultural, institutional, and moral order of Chinatown.

CHAPTER 9

Group Identity and Early Migrant Organizations

FEW of the villagers who emigrated from China before 1900 had ever belonged to anything like a formally organized group such as a club, lodge, association, society, or political party. Most of them no doubt were aware that their village was part of an administrative system which ultimately culminated in the imperial government in Peking, especially because taxes were collected in their village by officials of that system, but they were unlikely to have had any sense of personal identification with the government, even on the district level. In their villages the main bases of group identification were families, lineage groups, and the clans made up of these lineage groups. Some migrants who came as traders had been associated in market towns with *kung si*, business companies that were essentially partnerships; others, who were artisans, had belonged to guilds. However, since most migrants had been agriculturists working on family-owned lands or for village landlords, they would have had little experience in organizations outside their kinship groups.

It is all the more remarkable, then, that wherever numbers of Chinese were located overseas, they formed themselves into a variety of groups that were based on common interests rather than upon kinship. More than two hundred groups were organized by migrant Chinese in Hawaii. Some of these did have connections with organizations in China; some, although not directly connected with organizations in China, were patterned after them; some were organizations formed to carry out functions that in the villages had been taken care of by family and clan. Others were set up to deal with problems the migrants faced in Hawaii as part of their experience as foreigners; still others emerged as the migrants and their descendants became a community within the Hawaiian community. Many of these organizations disappeared as sojourner migrants returned to China or died in Hawaii, as more of the migrants who remained in the Islands became settlers, and as Hawaii-born Chinese lost interest in continuing them. Others changed in character as the migrants themselves changed and as Hawaii-born Chinese took over leadership from the migrant generation. Some remained essentially the same in purpose though different in organizational structure; others which kept their original names and formal structures actually changed in purpose and function.

Several of the organizations founded by *wah kiu* in Hawaii had names that included the word *tong*. On the U.S. mainland and in Canada, especially in the late nineteenth and early twentieth centuries, non-Chinese associated the word *tong* with terrorist groups that struggled for power within Chinese communities, especially in large cities. The word had many of the same connotations in the minds of non-Chinese as the "mafia" has come to have in recent years. Such phrases as "fighting tongs," "highbinder tongs," and "tong wars," used in newspaper and magazine articles and in lurid books purporting to reveal "the secret world of Chinatown," became firmly fixed in the popular vocabulary. That the word *tong* was part of the name of many innocuous associations of law-abiding Chinese residents was rarely publicized. In its literal sense, *tong* refers to a hall. An organization that had, or planned to have, a headquarters or meeting place might signify this by using *tong* in its name, such as Fook Yum Tong (a Christian congregation), Hoy On Tong (a seamen's guild), or Lung Doo Chung Sin Tong (originally a benevolent society for migrants from Lung Doo district). Non-Chinese frequently confuse the word *tong* with the word *tang* (in Kuo Yu; *dong* in Chung Shan dialect), which refers to a political party, as in Kuomintang. Several other Chinese generic terms for organizations were used in Hawaii, with varying romanized spelling because of dialectal differences: *wui (wei, hui, hoey), wui goon (hui kuan, wei quan, fui kon), hong, kee loo, kee lok bow, kung si (kong si), say (sha, shah, sheh),* and *so (soh, saw, shaw).* Most of the groups which have used one or another of these terms have chosen variously the words "club," "association," or "society" when translating the names of their organizations into English.

Cemetery Associations

In view of the Chinese reverence for their ancestors and regard for spirits of the dead, it is not surprising that the earliest reports of cooperation among the migrants in Hawaii for other than business purposes refer to funeral services for *wah kiu* who died in the Islands. In the early days when there was only a small Chinese population in the Islands, a migrant who died there would not be likely to have clansmen nearby who could carry out burial rites for him in accordance with Chinese tradition; nor was it possible for his body to be returned to his village for burial. In these circumstances the small aggregation of "domiciled Chinese," even though of different clan, locality, and dialectical origins, combined to provide a ceremonial burial. An American trader in Honolulu noted in his journal in 1838 that "Chinamen made a great parade at the funeral of one of their deceased friends." And in 1841: "At 9 A.M. the Corpse of Ahtai was carried up to Manoa Valley to be interred after the manner and custom of the Chinese. . . . All the Chinamen were in the procession. Many residents were out to see the ceremony."[1]

Manoa Valley, which in the early 1800s was several miles beyond the outskirts of the port town of Honolulu, is the site of the earliest known Chinese grave in the Islands, dated 1835, of someone whose surname was Lau. In the years that followed, other Chinese were buried nearby on land owned by a Hawaiian. In 1854 a group of Chinese merchants formed the Manoa Lin Yee Wui, the oldest association, so far as is known, started by Chinese in Hawaii. The *wui* took charge of burials in the plot in Manoa Valley and bought several acres there for a Chinese cemetery. The association also put up a building and undertook the tasks of exhuming graves at auspicious times, usually during Ching Ming, cleaning the bones and preparing them to be returned to China for reburial. In 1889 the group received a charter of incorporation from the Hawaiian government under the name of Manoa Lin Yee Chung ("Chinese Cemetery Association of Manoa"), and in 1892 they obtained a clear title to the cemetery grounds. The 1835 grave, honored as that of the *tai gung* ("great ancestor") of Chinese in Hawaii, is the site of ceremonies held in early April each year to initiate the Ching Ming season.[2]

Other cemetery associations were formed later as the increasing Chinese population in Honolulu became differentiated into subgroups of different district, dialectal, and religious backgrounds. In 1872 land was purchased in Pauoa Valley (now, like Manoa Valley, a part of Honolulu) for burials of Hoklo people—migrants from the Swatow area of northeast Kwangtung, who spoke a Fukien-Chaochow dialect different from the Cantonese dialects spoken by most of the *wah kiu* in Hawaii. Three other cemeteries in the Pauoa area were developed in the 1880s. One was for migrants from Sam Yup districts such as Nam Hoy, Pun Yu, Shun Tak, Tung Kun, and Sam Sui which lie near the city of Canton (Kwangchow); another was mainly for Hakkas; the third was for members of the Ket On Fui Kon, a Hoong Moon (Hung Men) society whose members originally were mostly Hakkas. Two cemeteries for Chinese Christians were begun in Honolulu about thirty years later, one in Pauoa and the other in the Makiki section of Honolulu.

In the early plantation period Chinese laborers who died while working on sugar plantations were usually interred in a plot of land set aside by the plantation for burial of workers of all racial and ethnic identities. Ultimately, as the rural Chinese population increased, several Chinese cemeteries were established outside of Honolulu— at least three on Oahu, seven on the island of Hawaii, seven on Maui, and six on Kauai.[3] Most of these were developed by either a Hoong Moon society or a Chinese Christian congregation rather than by an association formed specifically for that purpose.

Hoong Moon Societies

The Tung Hing Kung Si, a Hoong Moon society, appears to have been the earliest organization, except for the Lin Yee Wui, formed by migrants in Hawaii. Little is known about this group, other than that it was started in 1869 by Hakkas and was located in the Koolau area of Oahu, at that time remote from Honolulu because it could be reached only on foot or horseback over a difficult mountain trail leading from Nuuanu Valley. With the appearance of the Tung Hing Kung Si, an ancient secret political and ritualistic society of China was transplanted to the Islands.

The parent organization, variously referred to as the Hoong Moon, Triad, or Three Dots Society, had been formed in the latter part of the seventeenth century after the invading Manchus established the Ching dynasty in 1644. The society's founders resented domination by an alien people and the Manchu decree ordering Chinese men to wear the queue as a sign of subjection. The avowed purpose of the society was to overthrow Manchu control and reestablish the Ming dynasty—*fan* Ching *fook* Ming ("overthrow the Manchus, restore the Ming"). The Manchu rulers, understandably, outlawed the organization but it continued as a secret society whose members could expect to be executed if they were apprehended. Members of the society in South China collaborated in the Taiping Rebellion (1850–1864), and when it became clear that the rebellion was going to fail many of them escaped capture by migrating to Southeast Asia, the United States, and Hawaii. The presence of these rebels in overseas Chinese colonies and the spread of the outlawed society overseas contributed to the Manchu government's indifference to the welfare of Chinese migrants, which in turn made it necessary for the *wah kiu* to organize to protect their own interests. In fact, overseas branches of the Hoong Moon society initially were little concerned with the overthrow of the Manchus in China. Instead they were preoccupied with the problems Chinese migrants faced in dealing with other Chinese migrants and with the "foreigners" under whose control they found themselves.[4]

The years of turbulence during the Taiping Rebellion weakened imperial control in Kwangtung, and one result was that fighting broke out between the Hakkas and the more numerous Puntis. By 1866 some 150,000 Hakkas are estimated to have been killed and more than that made homeless. Many of the homeless Hakkas emigrated, some of them to Hawaii.[5] It is probably not surprising that in Hawaii, where Puntis were more numerous and influential, it was a group of Hakkas who in the late 1860s banded together in a secret society. Between 1869 and 1910 more than thirty other Hoong Moon societies were formed in the Islands by other Chinese subgroups as well as by Hakkas. The societies had many names, the most common of which was Chee Kung Tong. Several thousand members, mostly illiterate agricultural laborers, were enrolled. Most of the societies were located in rural areas and small towns where such laborers were most numerous and where there was little contact with government officials. At least ten Hoong Moon societies were formed on Oahu, six on Maui, eight on Kauai, and eight on the island of Hawaii.[6] Several of them built clubhouses; others held their meetings in such places as rice mills.[7]

In their early years some of these societies, like the Tung Hing Kung Si, appear to have been dominated by Hakkas, others by migrants who spoke a See Yup dialect, still others by Puntis from Chung Shan district. The writer was told that when Ket On Fui Kon, a Honolulu society, began it was "for Hakkas," while two other Hoong Moon societies in Honolulu (which later merged into the Chee Kung Tong) were "for Puntis."[8] A Hoong Moon society established in Kohala, Hawaii, in 1886—Tung Wo Kung Si—was dominated by non-Christian Hakkas whereas Christian Hakkas and Puntis and non-Christian Puntis joined together in a rival society—Lock Shin Tong—with their own clubhouse within shouting distance across a gorge from the Tung Wo Kung Si clubhouse.[9] In rural areas where there was only one Chinese clubhouse—usually a Hoong Moon—migrants of different dialectal and locality origins in China found it worthwhile to cooperate in the local society's activities. This was especially common after Punti-Hakka antagonisms (which never became violent in Hawaii) declined. In 1931 a member of one of the Maui societies claimed that "before, about all the Chinese on Maui belonged" to one or another of the six Hoong Moon societies on that island. Another, recalling the men he lived with in plantation camps in the early 1900s, said: "All other fellows join. I join with the gang. Chinese want work together, have good times together, join all same society."[10] The Christian Chinese, however, having rejected Taoist beliefs, were less likely than non-Christians to participate in a Hoong Moon society with its Taoist rituals. For them a Fook Yum Tong (Christian church) was the place for social contacts and a source of mutual assistance as well as a religious center.

Although the original Hoong Moon society in China was organized to bring about dynastic change, it does not appear that the Hawaiian societies were politically active before 1900. They were primarily concerned with matters affecting their local members. Hoong Moon societies that did not have their own cemeteries nevertheless provided funeral services and burial for deceased members and made financial contributions if necessary. Far more important for the young familyless migrants were the social, recreational, mutual aid, and protective services they received through membership in these societies. Young migrants found themselves surrounded by migrants of other clans and other dialects who were almost as strange as the non-Chinese, the *fan kwai*, they had to deal with. The Hoong Moon society offered these young migrants a substitute for their kinship groups and at the same time inducted them into a new kind of communal world.

The migrant who joined a Hoong Moon society had to undergo an elaborate secret initiation by entering through the Hoong Moon (Hoong "gate" or "door") into the "Hoong family" or "Hoong brotherhood." These rites could take several hours, even an entire night. Although many, probably most, of the migrants who joined were illiterate, some of the leaders who were literate could read copies of the manual of dialogue, oaths, and regulations which had been brought from China.[11] In Kula, Maui, a Hakka, Ho Seong, who taught in the Chinese-language school there, served at one time as priest in the Ket Hing Fui Kon initiation rituals.[12] The initiate took thirty-six oaths in the course of the ceremony. According to a set of the oaths translated for Hawaiian government officials in 1884, one of these was: "After being admitted to the Hoong family, you shall treat the sworn brothers the same as your own brothers. If you do mischief to them you shall die in the cross roads." Another was: "After being admitted in the Hoong family, if your brothers of the same parents raise a controversy with our sworn brothers you must, without partiality, exhort them to peace; and if you aid and abet your own brothers to fight, you shall be drowned in the seas."

The initiation, then, seems to have been designed to transform unrelated individuals into a brotherhood with obligations as deep and powerful as those to one's own kinsmen. The initiate who had been alone amidst strangers was incorporated into a group that protected and controlled him as had his kinship group at home. This bond was symbolized by other oaths that stipulated: "If any of the sworn brothers, by giving a sign, desire to seek for a lodging for the night, you must welcome him" and "If you meet any sworn brother in the road who is on his way to make his fortune, and he gives you a sign, you must not rob him." The initiate was taught the signs by which he could recognize and be recognized by other society members.[13]

Significantly, this set of thirty-six oaths which was being used at the Hung Sin Tong, the Hoong Moon society then active in Hanalei, Kauai, had no reference to overthrowing the Ching dynasty and restoring the Ming, but the oaths prescribed several kinds of mutual aid among members. Among other things, members were obligated to deliver letters and money for a sworn brother, to care for any sworn brother's son "committed to you," to give financial aid to a sworn brother unable to support himself.

Hawaiian government officials came into possession of these oaths and other information about this society after "Chinese secret societies" were publicly charged with criminal acts. This was fifteen years after the first Hoong Moon society had been formed in Hawaii, and after others had been organized on all the main islands. Planters had been aware for several years of the existence of such societies in their localities, even where no clubhouse had been built, but had had no objections as long as the societies' activities seemed to be concerned with providing funerals for deceased Chinese and furnishing aid for ailing or impoverished Chinese laborers. In the early 1880s, however, local newspapers published the claims of some planters that "Chinese secret societies" on the islands of Hawaii and Maui were helping Chinese laborers on Caucasian-controlled plantations to escape their indentures, presumably to take employment on Chinese rice plantations or in other Chinese enterprises using Chinese laborers.[14] The editor of *Planters' Monthly* wrote in a front-page article of the May 1883 issue:

> Chinese are cunning, and quick to perceive their advantages, and to avail themselves of all the protection which civilized law affords, but they are able to evade the restraints of the law as no other people can. Their clannishness and secret organizations give them a power which is difficult to meet.

At about the same time the Reverend Frank W. Damon spoke against what he called "the evils of secret societies"; he regretted "especially to see what a strong hold the Chinese secret society, the 'Triad Organization', has on Kauai; it is a great hindrance to Christian work. When will our Government take energetically in hand the task of investigating and suppressing this baneful association?"[15]

In 1884 it was reported that "a serious riot" had occurred at Hanalei, Kauai, during which "a number of Chinamen—known to be connected with certain secret societies—threatened to take the life of the District Justice and Deputy Sheriff of Hanalei." Five men, presumably leaders of the Hanalei Hoong Moon society, were arrested and indicted for holding an unlawful assembly. According to the report the men "pleaded guilty to the charge, and received light sentences, with injunctions not to engage in any combinations to oppose the law." In connection with the arrests the sheriff of Kauai had seized several objects containing Chinese characters, among them the thirty-six oaths.[16]

The authorities were particularly disturbed by some of the oaths —such as the one requiring that "if any sworn brother who is in trouble shall come to your house you ought to harbor him, and you must not in any way inform the public officers and lead for his apprehension. If you do so, you shall be torn to pieces by (tying you to) five horses, and being dragged by them." Three other oaths dealt with protecting sworn brothers in trouble with the law. Observers of activities at the clubhouses mentioned that physical culture and Chinese arts of self-defense were popular among the younger members. This training might have had special significance in view of the oath requiring that "if any sworn brother create a controversy with other people in the streets, or in the markets, and gives a sign, you ought to aid him."

The government was warned of the danger of allowing these secret societies to exist, at least without some official control. Local newspapers called attention to the criminal activities carried on for decades by Triad secret societies in Borneo and the Straits Settlements before the Dutch and British colonial governments took steps to suppress or control them. Five months after the revelation that oaths of the Hanalei society required members to obstruct government attempts to impose law and order, the king signed an act "to prevent unlawful secret associations." This act was similar to the Dangerous Societies Suppression Ordinance the British had adopted in Malaya in 1869. After the act became law in Hawaii, secret societies already in existence or seeking to be organized were required to apply for a license. The application was to contain a statement under oath of the object of the group; the government might refuse to grant the license and licenses could be revoked; members of a secret society that continued to exist without a license could be imprisoned.[17]

The new law, of course, did not end the troubles with secret societies. A year and a half later a Honolulu journalist implied that the government had not really begun to "put the law into motion" and claimed that secret societies in Honolulu had been levying contributions on Chinese businessmen—"who dared not refuse for fear of reprisals"—in order to maintain "two or three thousand Chinamen in idleness in this city."[18]

In October 1888 something that had been widely assumed was publicly verified: the "social and recreational" activities in some if not all of the Hoong Moon meeting places included opium smoking. When a meeting place in Kaneohe, Oahu, was raided and police seized some opium, they were attacked by "a mob of about thirty Chinese armed with sticks." One Chinese injured in the melee died.[19]

Drastic action was taken in 1889 in a criminal case involving leaders of the Yee Wo Kung Si, a Hoong Moon society in Hilo. On 7 July 1888 some members of the society, allegedly bent on robbery at a Chinese camp on Waiakea Plantation near Hilo, were believed to be implicated in the death of a Caucasian employee of the plantation. Several suspects were arrested, but their supposed leader was reported by the attorney general to have "escaped to Honolulu, where he was taken under the care of a secret society formed in large part of Chinese criminals." A Chinese detective sent from Hilo to Honolulu to help apprehend this man "disappeared without a trace." A second Chinese "detective or informer" working on the case was murdered. The attorney general's report asserts that the murder of this man, in which "at least ten persons took part," was decided upon "in a meeting of the chief officers and some of the trusted members" of the Yee Wo Kung Si. The report goes on to say that some members went into the crime reluctantly feeling bound by their oaths and fearing to resist "the edicts of the society whose power they knew." The head of the society was convicted in a jury trial, sentenced to death and hanged. Two others tried with him were acquitted "for lack of direct evidence." The Yee Wo Kung Si apparently went out of existence.[20] No other reports of criminal acts by the Hoong Moon societies in Hawaii comparable to those of the Yee Wo Kung Si have been found in archival materials; nor is there a record of fighting between these societies such as occurred during the nineteenth century in Southeast Asia and in the continental United States.[21]

Concern about illegal activities by Chinese secret societies arose in the late 1880s when opposing factions in the Hawaiian and Caucasian population were challenging the Hawaiian government, which in 1889 put down the Wilcox insurrection. Government ministers suspected that Honolulu Chinese financed this outbreak.[22] A government report issued in October 1889 spoke of "the danger to the community by reason of the Chinese secret society organizations; their wanton disregard for human life; their concealment and assistance of criminals; and their reckless perjury in Courts of Justice."[23] The president of the Board of Immigration, in supporting importation of Japanese laborers in preference to Chinese, wrote in a similar vein in his 1890 report:

> The Chinese are secretive, systematically shielding and assisting Chinese criminals. It is but rarely that a Chinaman will testify against a fellow countryman, and perjury to rescue another from the clutches of the law is looked upon as a cardinal virtue.
> . . . The Chinese have the faculty of combination and organization developed to such an extent that their secret societies number many thousand members in the country. Their societies are criminal in

their objects and methods; their principal officers are criminals, and they do not hesitate at any crime to accomplish their ends. Three known murders and several suspected ones, during the past biennial period, are the direct work of these societies.[24]

While these reports exaggerated the occasional criminal actions of a few secret society members, it is true that the Hoong Moon societies did little, if anything, to discourage gambling and opium smoking among their members.

Most of the Hoong Moon clubhouses were built during the 1900–1912 period, after immigration of Chinese laborers had been cut off. The characteristic two-story clubhouses of the Hoong Moon societies in the small towns and rural areas cost more to build than ordinary members could afford. They could contribute their labor, but money for land, building materials, and furnishings were usually supplied by wealthy Chinese planters and storekeepers who wanted stable and peaceful relations among Chinese in their area. The clubhouse usually had on the ground floor a large hall which was used as a social and recreational center, open at festive events to the wives and children of members and to nonmembers. In 1928 three brothers held a banquet for some three hundred guests at the Tung Wo Kung Si clubhouse in Kohala, Hawaii, in honor of the ninety-first birthday of their mother, Mrs. Chau Ng, who had come with her husband to work in the cane fields of Kohala Plantation more than sixty years previously. Caucasians and Hawaiians as well as Chinese were among the guests.[25] In Kula, Maui, the Hoong Moon clubhouse, as described by Diane Mei Lin Mark, was a community center for the Chinese: "On Sundays, the society building was a bustling gathering place. People throughout the Kula region would lay down their labors for the day and go to the society to eat, drink, gamble, trade stories, and listen to news of China."[26]

A Chinese who grew up in Kula described the Sunday gatherings at the Ket Hing Society:

On Sundays my father and I (I'm the oldest) used to go over there [Ket Hing Society] and then there was a gambling joint there. All the men folks would be gambling. And they would all be listening to the storytellers. They would have a couple of people who had communication with China. This man would sit down and everybody would gather around him and he would be telling stories, especially of the history of China, of Confucius, and the Taoist way of life.[27]

Tin-Yuke Char also describes social activities at these clubhouses:

> Ground floors were used as school rooms for teaching the Chinese lan-
> guage, as game and recreational rooms, and as an assembly hall for fes-
> tive occasions like the Chinese New Year celebration when the wider
> community participated—haoles, Hawaiians, and others. The Tong
> Wo Society in Kohala conducted bazaars with tents out on the lawn to
> sell home-cooked Chinese food and homemade handicrafts. Of course,
> the familiar pig oven was worked overtime to produce roast suckling
> pig, duck, chicken, and *char-siu* ("barbecued pork").[28]

For many years, use of the upper rooms of the clubhouses was
restricted to members for such purposes as initiations and meetings.
One of the upstairs rooms usually had an altar with representations
of Kwan Dai, patron deity of the society, the five founders of the
parent organization, and such deities as the Heaven and Earth gods.
When families became established in areas far from Chinese temples,
images of deities worshiped especially by women were placed in the
clubhouses. On ceremonial occasions worship was carried out before
the altar. Some societies had a building behind the clubhouse for
gambling and for opium smoking, as well as another small building
on the clubhouse grounds to which an ailing member would be
taken when death was imminent, following a custom prevalent in
China.

Whether or not a society had a clubhouse, it had important values for the migrants. The ordinary member could expect the society
to help him when he came into conflict with other Chinese in a situation where he distrusted the officials of the "foreign" government,
and he was far from his kinship group which would have helped him
at home. In 1935 an elderly member in a rural area talked about this
role of the society:

> When a Chinese got in trouble with another Chinese, it was a good
> thing to belong to the society. If he belonged to no society at all, there
> was no way of getting help. If he did belong to the society, then he had
> the backing of the other men who were members. If both people who
> got in trouble belonged to the society, then they could bring up the
> matter before the headmen to settle it.[29]

Members generally knew that the society elders (the officers) would
arbitrate disputes between members, that the disputing members
would accept the elders' decision, and that it was better to settle such
disputes within the society than to go to court. Several of the oaths

taken at initiation specified appropriate relations between members, the duties of members toward elders, and the role of elders in settling disputes among members.

The situation was more difficult when a member of the society itself was in trouble with non-Chinese. A part-Hawaiian informant talked about this in 1931:

> Many of the disputes between the Chinese are settled at the meetings of their society. But in cases where the Chinese are in trouble with other races, they need someone who knows English. My brother used to handle many of their cases for them. He was one of the most outstanding lawyers [on Kauai]. . . .
>
> About [twenty-five] years ago, Governor Carter threatened to close up some of the Chinese societies, because there seemed to be a feeling that there were too many illegal things going on in them. The societies were unable to defend themselves because they had no members who could speak English well, and who could get a hearing. That was how I happened to be asked to join the Chee Kung Tong. I was sent personally to the governor, and with the governor we toured the island of Kauai. We went into all the Chinese organizations. It was at the time that there were the most Chinese on Kauai. There were five branches of the Chee Kung Tong—at Hanalei, Kapaia, Kapaa, Lawai, Hanapepe. The charge against them was gambling. The governor had also threatened Kamehameha Lodge, too. After this tour on Kauai, he withdrew his threats.[30]

After Chinese laborers were no longer brought to Hawaii and the Hoong Moon societies became increasingly made up of older migrants, the societies' welfare functions became more important, especially in the rural areas. Among the thousands of members were hundreds who had never made the fortunes for which they had come to the Islands and who had, in fact, become destitute. Some had never earned very much; others had lost fortunes at the gambling tables or had spent their earnings on opium. Sick members were given temporary care at the clubhouses and aged and impoverished members were allowed to live there permanently. Collections were taken up to return indigent members to China or to provide burial for indigent deceased members.

Meeting the costs of these welfare activities became increasingly difficult as more and more of the successful migrants returned to China or left the rural areas and towns for Honolulu. Some of those who moved to Honolulu shifted to Hoong Moon societies there;

others simply dropped out altogether. Even as early as 1909 one of the Honolulu Hoong Moon societies, in a Chinese newspaper, begged members to pay their dues. As time went on, clubhouses in rural areas were no longer centers of Chinese community life and became the residences of the few aged Chinese remaining behind after most of the other Chinese had left. In 1935 when the writer visited Kohala, Hawaii, five elderly men were living on very meager means in small buildings behind the Tung Wo Kung Si clubhouse. Few Chinese were left in this district where more than a thousand Chinese had once lived, and members of some of the remaining families claimed that providing for the welfare of indigent Chinese in the district was becoming increasingly burdensome.

Of the more than thirty Hoong Moon societies once active in the Islands, only two continue to hold even annual meetings. And neither of these carries out many of the societies' earlier functions. Both are in Honolulu; both have incomes from rental property and other investments; both have clubhouses where members, usually descendants of the original members, can gather to chat, play mahjong or cards, read, have something to drink. Some of the income is still used for welfare purposes, some for entertainment. The Ket Hing Fui Kon clubhouse at Kula, Maui, is maintained by former members' descendants who still live in the district. The Tung Wo Kung Si clubhouse in Kohala, for a time abandoned, has been renovated but there is no active organization of Hoong Moon society members to maintain it. In other places most of the clubhouses that have not disappeared are dilapidated, looted, and abandoned, with no members left to care about them or their history.[31]

The China Fire Engine Company

When Chinatown was becoming the center of the migrants' business and social life, Honolulu itself was still a frontier town even though it was the capital of the Hawaiian kingdom. Public services and utilities were gradually developing, but fires were still fought by private volunteer groups. Fire was always a danger in Chinatown and it was against this threat that the Chinese of Honolulu first organized themselves for mutual protection.

As early as 1847 Samsing & Co. brought the first fire engine to Honolulu. It was to protect their own property, but they made it available to others for a small fee. This hand-pumped contraption with water placed into it by a bucket brigade did not, however, prevent losses of about $25,000 to Afong and other merchants in a fire in 1855.[32] Steps were taken in the 1850s to establish a fire department in Honolulu, and a few volunteer fire companies were organized among the Caucasians, but the inadequate protection they provided was demonstrated by a fire in the Caucasian business district in December 1877 which caused over a quarter million dollars' damage. Two weeks later one of Afong & Achuck's stores on the edge of Chinatown burned down with losses of about $30,000. Before the end of January 1878 a number of Chinatown's leading merchants met and decided to undertake their own fire protection. One reason for this decision was the particular vulnerability of the Chinese quarter. Since most of the early migrants considered their stay in Hawaii to be temporary, they did not invest in buildings that would be fire-resistant and insurable. Not only were most of their stores and shops flimsy wooden structures but Chinatown lots were crowded with cookhouses and lodging quarters adding to the fire hazard. A further reason for the Chinese to organize their own protection was their doubt that they could rely on the Caucasian fire engine companies in a conflagration affecting both Chinese and Caucasian establishments.

Early in February it was announced that the Chinese were to introduce the first "steamer" in Honolulu, a steam fire engine manufactured by a New England firm. When this became known, the Caucasian-controlled newspapers urged that government (not the Caucasian residents) also purchase a steamer so that Honolulu might "be amply provided for emergencies." The legislature appropriated money for such a purchase and an engine of the same make arrived on the same boat as the one ordered by the Chinese. A new company of Caucasians known as Honolulu Fire Engine Company, No. 1, manned the government-owned engine. A group of about fifty Chinese who had formed themselves into a "Chinese Fire Company" shortly before their engine arrived sought to be recognized as part of the Honolulu Fire Department. They received this recognition and for a while the company was known as China Engine Company, No. 2. A Chinese-Hawaiian was selected to direct the operation of the engine. When the fire department held its annual parade in February 1879, the Chinese company was the last but largest in the procession, and a newspaper reported that "the Chinese Company looked particularly well dressed in their new uniforms."[33]

Recognition of this company as part of the Honolulu Fire Department was granted on condition that it adopt a constitution and bylaws and govern itself in accordance with these formal provisions. During 1879, therefore, a constitution and bylaws similar to those of the Caucasian fire engine companies were drawn up. These documents included, among other stipulations, a detailed account of the duties of each officer and the penalties to be levied for failure to carry out these duties; annual elections of officers; the frequency of regular meetings and drills; obligations of members and the fines to be imposed for their neglect; the method of making amendments; and two pages describing the rules of order.[34]

Such items were familiar to Westerners acquainted with the constitutions and bylaws of formal organizations, but for the Chinese migrants all this documentation was entirely new. Chinese villagers were accustomed to acting on the basis of unwritten tradition rather than written regulations. They were more likely to meet their obligations because of personal claims than because of formal penalties; attempting to compel behavior by fines or threat of expulsion was quite foreign to their tradition. To be sure, hundreds of immigrants were joining Hoong Moon societies during this same decade, but these societies were not then structured along Western lines. Even the formal oaths, though written down, were based upon a kinship pattern, not a contractual relationship. It was not until after the act of 1884 requiring secret societies to register that Hoong Moon societies undertook to state their objectives for public scrutiny and to draw up constitutions and bylaws. Even then, the English versions of their statements may not have conveyed the intended impression or the real purpose of the societies. A Hoong Moon society on Oahu, for instance, stated in 1899 that "the objects of said association shall be to care for, protect, and support with comforts of life the indigent, decrepit, and imbecile Chinese in the Hawaiian Islands."[35]

It is significant that immigrants were introduced to the Western pattern of organization partly as a result of their desire to deal with a problem faced by all the residents of Chinatown, whatever clan, village, district, or dialect group they had come from. At the same time, the formal structure of the engine company, one of the earliest organizations in Chinatown, came about because of the Chinese residents' effort to cooperate with other groups in a multiethnic community; in this effort they used as a model the pattern set by the Caucasians upon whom they drew for counsel.

For several years the China Engine Company was the most colorful part of the annual firemen's parade. The *Daily Bulletin*'s report of the 1886 parade, which took place during the Chinese New Year period, gave the details of the Chinese participants:

> The Chinese Company's decorations, besides several curious Mongolian fancies, consisted partly of the irrepressible and ubiquitous triangular yellow dragon flags. . . . A jolly Chinaman wearing an enormous mask representing the head of a lion, followed by some half-a-dozen attendants bearing a gorgeous train representing the body and tail of the monster; standard bearers carrying aloft banners and flags; companies of halberdiers and trident bearers, were features of the Chinamen's (No. 5) turnout that created a furore of excitement, particularly among the small boys, all along the route of the procession. The force turned out altogether about 150 strong.[36]

Whatever its place in the community's fire protection services (its fire-fighting efficiency seems to have been questionable),[37] the China Engine Company appears to have been important in developing community consciousness and contributing to the growth of other organizations among Honolulu's Chinese. The experience of drawing up a constitution and bylaws acceptable to the government was highly useful in the following decades when an elaborate network of Chinese organizations came into existence. Any organization wanting to buy property and build a clubhouse *(wui goon)* needed a charter of incorporation for which an acceptable constitution and bylaws had to be submitted. Contacts between members of the engine company and government officials provided further experience which was particularly useful to those Chinatown organizations, such as the United Chinese Society, which dealt with relations between the Chinese and other groups in the community at large. Lau Cheong (Lau Chong Kong), for example, who was the intermediary between the China Engine Company and Fire Department officials for many years, was one of the organizers of the United Chinese Society and its first treasurer.[38]

The United Chinese Society

In the same period that the China Engine Company was formed to deal with disasters originating within Honolulu's Chinatown, the United Chinese Society emerged in response to developments threatening the Chinese from the wider community and from the Hawaiian government. Chinese migrants, who had been welcomed when the booming sugar industry desperately needed laborers, were becoming targets of suspicion, antagonism, and discrimination—especially from Caucasian residents who were not directly involved in sugar production and from certain sections of the Hawaiian population. To meet increasing demands for restriction of Chinese immigration and also to encourage the importation of laborers of other ethnic origins, the Hawaiian government in 1877 inaugurated a policy of differential treatment of Chinese immigrants. Bonuses for importation of Chinese laborers were stopped although the government continued to spend millions of dollars to assist the importation of Portuguese, German, Norwegian, Russian, and Japanese workers. Special regulations which were imposed on ships arriving from plague-infested ports of South China required disembarking Chinese to submit to health inspections and treatment not imposed on other migrants. At the same time, Chinese businessmen were being subjected to new regulations designed to restrict their activities.

These discriminatory regulations eventually led the Chinese to organize a united front in order to cope with the new hostility. The initiative for this movement, however, did not arise within the Chinese migrant population, which for more than a decade had been too divided to take concerted action. In fact the initiative came from the Chinese government, which formerly had been indifferent to its overseas subjects. After the Burlingame Treaty of 1868 with the United States, the Chinese government became more interested in its relations with foreign countries and also in the Chinese living in these countries. In 1877 the imperial government appointed Ch'en Lan-pin as envoy extraordinary and minister plenipotentiary to the United States of America, Spain, and Peru, with legation headquarters in Washington, D.C.

Ch'en was aware of the mounting difficulties facing the Chinese in Hawaii. In addition to reports of Hawaiian official actions affecting Chinese immigration, complaints from some undetermined source in Hawaii had reached Canton and Peking that Chulan & Co., a Honolulu Chinese firm which recruited contract laborers for sugar and rice plantations, had "obtained Chinese to be used . . . as Coolies or slaves" and the governor of Canton had arrested the son and brother of Wong Kwai, a major partner in Chulan & Co., major rival firm of Afong & Achuck.[39] One of Ch'en's commissioners was sent to Hawaii to investigate conditions in the Islands. China had no treaty relations with the Hawaiian kingdom, but Chinese authorities, on the basis of the commissioner's report, decided to appoint a Chinese resident of Hawaii as "Commercial Agent" *(shang tung)* "for the Chinese Empire in the Hawaiian Kingdom" with authority to report on Chinese matters to Minister Ch'en.[40]

Afong (Chun Fong), who was appointed to this post in 1879, was probably the wealthiest Chinese in Hawaii, but it appears that many Chinese as well as some of the government's cabinet members did not regard him as the leader of the migrant group. His personal connections were at least as close, if not closer, to people outside the Chinese group as to those within it. He lived with his Caucasian-Hawaiian wife, of an elite family, and their children in a residential district of wealthy Hawaiian and Caucasian families. He appears to have been particularly close to Hawaiians near the throne. As an importer of Chinese goods and laborers he also had many dealings with Caucasian government officials, particularly those in the Ministry of the Interior, the Board of Immigration, and the Customs Office.[41]

Little is known about Afong's service to the Chinese community during the two years or so that he served as commercial agent. He was involved in a dispute concerning the signing of contracts by several hundred laborers who arrived unexpectedly and were forced into quarantine because of smallpox aboard their ships. Sometime after Afong's appointment as commercial agent, the Board of Immigration had appointed two Puntis as "shipping masters" to recruit more Chinese contract laborers for sugar and rice plantations, whereupon Hakkas protested in a petition to the Board of Immigration. They said they had not been consulted in these appointments and that because of the differences between Puntis and "the Ha Ka clan" a Hakka shipping master should also be appointed. Afong, whom the Board of Immigration referred to as "the head of the Pun Ti clan," recommended that the Hakkas' petition be granted. This apparently did not dispel the Hakkas' distrust of Afong. When he tried to act on behalf of the quarantined laborers, the Hakkas claimed that since he was only a commercial agent, not a consul, he had no right to intervene in the matter. Afong's report to Minister Ch'en in Washington led Ch'en to report to the governor-general at Canton that there was "a real slave trade" in Chinese laborers in Hawaii which should be investigated. This report, together with a letter Afong had written to a Chinese newspaper in Hong Kong, led the Minister of Foreign Affairs for Hawaii to write his consul in Hong Kong, denying that Chinese had not been properly treated in Hawaii. When Afong sought to be appointed Chinese consul in 1881, the Hawaiian government was unreceptive and early in 1882 Afong ceased to be commercial agent. Apparently he had little effect in uniting the Chinese community. He seems to have inaugurated an organization called the Hak Seong Wui Goon ("Guest Merchants' Association"), but it was dissolved when he was no longer commercial agent.[42]

When Minister Ch'en passed through Honolulu on his return to China in 1882, he talked with several Chinese migrant businessmen about conditions facing Chinese in the United States and Hawaii. He also contributed a thousand dollars toward building a headquarters in Chinatown for community affairs. Later in 1882 his successor sent to Honolulu two commissioners who were familiar with the organization of the Chung Wah Kung Saw—the Chinese Consolidated Benevolent Association, the so-called "Six Companies"—in the San Francisco Chinatown. The commissioners urged that a similar society be formed in Honolulu to coordinate and represent the interests of the entire Chinese community.[43]

A benevolent organization called the Wah Yun Lin Hop Wui ("Chinese Union"), which had been formed in 1880 and which held its meetings at the building of the China Engine Company, apparently was the nucleus for the more formal and inclusive organization that seemed to be needed. A meeting of some twenty-five leading Chinese merchants, both Hakka and Punti, at the Chinese fire station in late 1882 was the beginning of the Chung Wah Wui Goon in Honolulu. This organization, referred to at first in English as the "Chinese Union," later as the "United Chinese Society," was to play the leading part in Chinese community affairs for at least half a century.[44] A Punti, C. Alee, was chosen as president and a Hakka, Goo Kim, as vice-president. It was understood that the commissioners and the minister in Washington would recommend that the Chinese government appoint these officers as commercial agent and vice–commercial agent in Honolulu. The society also elected a secretary and assistant secretary, a treasurer and assistant treasurer, and twenty-four directors. One of the English-language newspapers, in an article about the society's organization, reported that "all Chinese are eligible to join this club provided their conduct is upright and respectful."[45]

The selection of C. Alee (Ching King Chun) and Goo Kim (Goo

Kim Fui) as the chief officers of the society reveals the organization's role in the emerging Honolulu Chinese community. The choice of a Punti and a Hakka signifies development of a "we-consciousness" that included all Chinese immigrants regardless of dialect, kinship, or native locality. These old-world identifications were still important within the Chinese community, but migrants who had lived in Hawaii for several years had come to realize that such differences meant little to other groups and that discrimination affected all Chinese as belonging to the same category. They had become aware, also, that quarrels between the Puntis and the Hakkas weakened their defense against such categorical treatment. In the selection of C. Alee and Goo Kim the society recognized as leaders two men who were both long-time residents of Hawaii and who had vested interests in gaining respect as well as toleration and equal treatment for the Chinese as a group.

At the same time, Alee and Goo had quite different backgrounds and roles in the Chinese community. Alee was a partner in the firm of Chulan & Co., which had been established by his relatives about 1860 and which in the 1860s and 1870s was one of the two largest Chinese businesses in the Islands. He was one of the first Puntis to bring his wife from China and establish a family in Honolulu. Goo was more of a self-made man. After coming to Hawaii in 1866, he had worked first in a machine shop owned by a Caucasian and then gone into business for himself and established several successful enterprises. Unlike Alee, Goo had married a Hawaiian woman, though he remained closely identified with his fellow Chinese. He was an active leader in the Chinese Christian community of Honolulu. Both Alee and Goo had the goodwill of influential Caucasians and Hawaiians, which made them valuable as intermediaries between the immigrant Chinese and the Hawaiian government.[46]

More than a year after the organization's first meeting Alee and Goo submitted to the government a petition for a charter of incorporation for the United Chinese Society. Although the society actually had broader objectives, the petition stated that its primary purposes were benevolent and charitable. The following arguments were advanced for granting the charter:

By reason of the difficulties in the way of intercourse between their countrymen and the Hawaiian and English population of the country, there is much needless misunderstanding and actual suffering on the part of poor and sick Chinese; which suffering, and in some cases deaths, might be controlled or avoided were there means at hand for intelligent alleviation.

Petitioners respectfully represent that it is their opinion and belief that the organization of a Chinese Benevolent Society may result in great good to their people, that to some extent such organization already exists, but it is imperfect, and not yet developed to its fullest usefulness.

. . . The principal place of business of said society when incorporated will be the City of Honolulu, but the field of its operations shall extend throughout the Kingdom.

. . . That the object for which a Charter of Incorporation is asked is for the purpose of cultivating friendly feeling among the Chinese, and for acts of benevolence and charity among those of Chinese descent . . . in the Hawaiian Kingdom. . . .

The king in Privy Council was extremely cautious in granting the charter. Correspondence from Alee and Goo indicated that apart from approaching the government as commercial and vice–commercial agents of the Chinese government they would be representing a society which would bring about "friendly feeling" between the Puntis and Hakkas in the local Chinese community. The government was disturbed, however, by the proposal for a new Chinese society at a time when officials were confronted with unlawful activities, and allegations of such activities, by Hoong Moon societies that had been formed without the government's knowledge and approval. The government's concern was not allayed by the Chinese name given in the petition for the United Chinese Society, Chung Wa Hui Quon, or by the statement that it was to be a benevolent society. The name was similar to the Chinese name for the Chinese Consolidated Benevolent Society in San Francisco—an organization known to non-Chinese as the "Chinese Six Companies" with a reputation for having a powerful hold on Chinese migrants and for protecting, if not actually engaging in, criminal activities among the Chinese.[47]

A special committee consisting of the attorney general and two other Caucasians was appointed to investigate the application for a charter and to examine the proposed constitution and bylaws. These had been prepared by the society's officers in collaboration with a Caucasian lawyer. Upon the recommendation of the committee, some unusual provisions were written into the charter: the annual elections of officers were to be subject to the veto of the Minister of

Interior; his approval was to be secured before the Board of Trustees could remove any of the officers from their positions; he was empowered to examine at any time a certified copy in the English language of the original minutes of all meetings and of all records; any changes in the bylaws and constitution were subject to his approval; and he might "require the officers in control of the property of the corporation to give and file with him proper bonds." Even so, it was six months more before the king in Privy Council approved the granting of the charter. Only two days later King Kalakaua signed the act passed by the legislature "to prevent unlawful secret associations."

While waiting for the charter, the officers of the society bought a lot in the Chinatown area and proceeded with their plans for a two-story *wui goon*—clubhouse or headquarters. Work on the building began in May 1885, but the formal opening ceremonies were not held until the following February, on the first day of Chinese New Year holidays.[48] According to one account, "the streets in Chinatown were transformed into beautiful vistas of chromatic light, from thousands of lanterns ranged in mathematical lines from above and below the everlasting verandahs." At the clubhouse "a magnificent triangular yellow flag, with an enormous dragon spread on it—the Chinese Imperial flag—floated from the tall flagpole on the roof. . . . Over the doorways were hung Hawaiian and Chinese flags, tastefully arranged. The rooms [on the upper floor] were handsomely furnished." The Royal Hawaiian Band and the Reformatory School Band furnished music for the gala occasion. The most spectacular part of the day's ceremonies was the dragon dance:

> The clamor of a hundred Chinamen on Nuuanu Street . . . announced the coming of the Chinese dragon. The procession stopped in front of the principal houses, and while batteries of firecrackers were exploding, the dragon would rush forward with mouth open and fangs projecting, as though to destroy imaginary victims, but retreating at the fantastic movement of a magical wand in the hands of a coolie.

The guest list for the formal opening luncheon shows that a major objective of the organization was to raise the status of the Chinese as a group in the Hawaiian community. The guests included H.R.H. Princess Liliuokalani, ministers of the Hawaiian kingdom, the attorney general, the justices of the Supreme Court, the ministers, commissioners, consuls, or other official representatives of the United

States, Great Britain, France, Germany, Italy, Denmark, Sweden, Norway, Netherlands, Belgium, Peru, Spain, and Japan, a number of lesser officials of the Hawaiian kingdom, and other prominent Caucasians and Hawaiians. These guests were presented to and entertained by officers of the United Chinese Society who were "gorgeously costumed" in silk mandarin gowns and hats. Members of the society were assisted at the reception by the Reverend Frank Damon, the Caucasian most active during this period in smoothing relations between Chinese and others. The guests were served "a splendid collation"—"turkey and other meats, salads, sandwiches, wines, and tea."

President C. Alee had prepared an address which he delivered to the guests in Chinese, and an English translation was read by C. Winam, a Hakka who was the English secretary of the society. The speech, published in the two leading English newspapers of Honolulu, reveals that the society was intended to serve as mediator between the Chinese and others in Hawaii and as an agency for mutual help and control among the Chinese themselves. Alee's appeal to his non-Chinese listeners for understanding is apparent, especially in his closing remarks:

> Our object in forming this association is to exercise a care and supervision over such of the Chinese residents as shall connect themselves with this Society; to make them acquainted with the laws and ordinances of the Hawaiian Government, particularly with those laws and ordinances which concern in any way our Chinese residents; to render assistance and advice to such as may stand in need thereof, especially to sick Chinese and those in destitute condition; to prevent and settle disputes among Chinese if possible, and to prevent, as far as it may be in our power, all unlawful combinations or posting of seditious or otherwise objectionable placards, and to render such aid to the Government as they may request or authorize in matters pertaining to the Chinese residents in this Kingdom. All the future funds for maintenance of this Society are to be raised from the Chinese residents. We therefore trust that the purposes of this Society shall be attained, that it will grow in its benevolence and usefulness, and that its officers shall ever administer its affairs in the spirit in which it was founded, that it may be of advantage not only to ourselves but to the non-Chinese residents of this community, and that through it you may obtain true glimpses of Chinese customs and manners. We, by virtue of the official position delegated to us as President and Vice-President of the United Chinese Society, declare this hall open.

CHAPTER 10

Migrant Organizations and Community Crises

THE development of the United Chinese Society in the early 1880s could hardly have come at a more crucial period for the Chinese in Hawaii. Anti-Chinese agitation was building to its peak, anti-Chinese groups such as the Workingmen's Party were pressing the government for action, and the government itself was putting into effect discriminatory measures against the Chinese. Although the United Chinese Society had no real power itself or backing from the Chinese imperial government in dealing with the Hawaiian government, it did nevertheless undertake various defensive measures against threats to the Chinese migrants and the Hawaii Chinese community.

Reaction to Immigration Policy

Most important to the migrants were laws and regulations designed to restrict the right of Chinese to enter the country. Only a few months after the organizational meeting of the United Chinese Society, the government took the most drastic action against the Chinese that had occurred up to that time. When several thousand unrecruited Chinese men—some infected with smallpox—had arrived unexpectedly early in 1883, the government asked authorities in Canton and Hong Kong to allow no more emigrant ships to leave those ports for Honolulu. Later in the year the government permitted the entry of more Chinese laborers asked for by sugar and rice planters, but the men were to come only in ships approved by the Board of Immigration and landed first at a quarantine station in order to prevent the spread of smallpox.

With these events, the officers of the United Chinese Society became concerned about the future status of Chinese immigrants and immigration. This concern was expressed in the first communication of Alee and Goo, "representing the Chinese Union," to the Minister of Foreign Affairs. This letter, sent in September 1883, expressed satisfaction "that there is a likelihood of a speedy reestablishment of Chinese immigration" but went on to say:

> Facts, connected with the admission of Chinese arriving at Honolulu from China, during the early part of this year, naturally lead to inquiries in reference to the conditions under which future immigrants will be allowed to land, as to whether these will be the same as are applicable to all nationalities, or whether the Chinese are to be subjected to other or special regulations. Especially are we desirous of learning the amounts of fees which individual immigrants will be obliged to pay before permission is given them to land, and the nature of regulations relative to their detention at the Quarantine Station or other given places. . . .
>
> We would avail ourselves of this opportunity to express the hope that the plans now proposed for Chinese Immigration may tend to strengthen the friendly relations already existing between the Hawaiian and Chinese peoples.[1]

The minister's reply was probably not very reassuring to the new society's officials:

> Whilst the Government is desirous to place all immigrants on the same footing without reference to the existence or absence of Treaty stipulations on their behalf, yet, in regard to your fellow countrymen, in view of their all coming from ports infected by diseases (from the importation of which the people of this Kingdom have suffered so much), also in view of the fact that the ordinary immigration from China consists almost wholly of males, it is necessary that the Chinese should be treated in an exceptional manner. . . . It appears necessary to impose a short quarantine, probably not exceeding, in the best cases the period of three (3) days, in order to enable the physician of the Board of Health to make that thorough general examination which cannot be made on board, and also for the purpose of proper fumigation. This will involve some small charges on the immigrant, enough to meet the costs of their food and medical attendance, and pay of guards. Beyond this, and the usual passenger tax, the Government recognize no fees or expenses whatever, as chargeable to the immigrants.[2]

About four months after receiving this reply, Alee and Goo submitted the petition for a charter of incorporation of the United Chinese Society. The following month (March 1884) the government issued new regulations restricting the number of new Chinese immigrants to twenty-five per vessel but providing for "outward passports" and "permits to return" to be issued to Chinese residents who wished to return to Hawaii after visiting China. Three months later more than eight hundred Chinese, including entrepreneurs who needed more workers, joined other Hawaii residents who were dissatisfied with various government policies in signing a petition demanding that the government ministers resign.[3] The cabinet did not resign, but when ships arrived in 1884 and 1885 with thousands more Chinese the immigrants were allowed to land.

After it seemed that Japanese contract workers would fill the sugar planters' labor requirements, new regulations and frequent revisions of regulations on Chinese immigration were issued between 1885 and Annexation in 1898. Throughout this period government officials knew that Chinese anxious to come to Hawaii and Chinese residents in Hawaii anxious to bring other Chinese to the Islands were using various means to evade the regulations. At first any Chinese resident could obtain the outward passport and permit to return for one dollar. The authorities soon became convinced, however, that sojourner migrants, especially laborers, who did not intend to return to the Islands were selling their passports and return permits in China to men who wanted to emigrate to Hawaii. The Hawaiian consul general in Hong Kong was instructed in 1885 not to "accept an outward passport as proof that any individual has resided formerly in these Islands. . . . Any case of real hardship (if any can arise) caused by this return to a literal enforcement of the Regulations can be dealt with through the Chinese Commercial Agents here Messrs. C. Alee and Goo Kim (Ching King-Tum and Ku Kum-fai)."[4]

Later that year, when evasions continued, the authorities restricted outward passports to well-established Chinese immigrants who owned property in Hawaii assessed at a thousand dollars or more and could show receipts for taxes paid upon it. After a meeting of the United Chinese Society, Alee sent a protest against the regulation to the Minister of Foreign Affairs. He received the following one-sentence reply: "For your information I desire to state that I am not prepared to grant return passports to any Chinese, whatever may have been his occupation, who cannot show his tax receipt for taxes on real or personal property within the Kingdom."[5] The United Chinese Society was able to obtain only a minor concession, and that was with legal help. Almost fifty years later a Chinese migrant recalled this situation and the feelings it aroused:

We Chinese in Hawaii who live far away from home must look towards others for a living. Therefore, discriminating laws are never ceasing and oppressive laws are always being passed. Before 1900 a regulation was passed stating that a Chinese must have properties amounting to $1,000 before he can receive a return passport. This oppressive law did not stop at this. It also placed a charge of twenty dollars for this passport. This Society, at the request of the Chinese people, held a meeting and hired a lawyer to dispute the law. In the end this law was slightly changed. The twenty dollars charge was reduced to five dollars.[6]

In 1887 the government and the United Chinese Society worked out an arrangement by which a Chinese seeking a passport first obtained an official "Chinese Commercial Agent's Certificate" from C. Alee. This certificate was also referred to as the "Chinese Benevolent Society's ticket" and as the "Chinese passport."[7] The Minister of Foreign Affairs informed the consul general in Hong Kong that the Chinese commercial agent charged three dollars for this passport and that two dollars of this was "paid to the funds of the Chinese Benevolent Society."[8] This system probably did eliminate some of the fraudulent evasion of the regulations, because the government dealt with individual Chinese migrants only after they had been certified by leaders of the Chinese community who were officially recognized by the Chinese government and generally trusted by the Hawaiian authorities. Apparently the cultural and social distance between the government officials and most of the Chinese residents was so great that officials found it easier to use the Chinese organization for carrying out regulations than to enforce them directly. To this extent the United Chinese Society was tacitly recognized as a government within the government, with some of the functions of an extraterritorial system.

United Chinese Society finances improved greatly through the fees it collected for issuing the certificates. More important, this arrangement enormously enhanced the prestige of the Society and its leaders among the migrants and consequently accelerated the organization of the Chinese community. It also gave the Society, whose membership was made up of the more responsible and wealthier migrants, a mechanism for controlling migrants who could not leave the Islands until they had met their obligations to other Chinese. In this way also, it had a quasi-governmental function. A Chinese editor remarked that "in the first place, the United Chinese Society has been like a 'government of a small country'"—primarily in Honolulu's Chinatown, secondarily among the entire first-generation Chinese population.[9]

As leaders of the United Chinese Society, Alee and Goo tried to ease relations between the migrants and the government by serving as a channel for communicating information about government regulations to the Chinese affected by them. Frequent changes in the regulations made it difficult for migrants who read neither English nor Hawaiian—or Chinese for that matter—to keep posted, and this was even more true of prospective immigrants in the Chinese villages. In a letter to the Minister of Foreign Affairs Alee and Goo indicated their awareness of this role:

> It is, as Your Excellency will readily perceive, of the very greatest importance that exact information should be obtained upon all such points, in order that those proposing to immigrate to these Islands may do so with a knowledge of what awaits them, and the conditions of admission. In this way much inconvenience may be spared such immigrants, and possible causes of complaint and dissatisfaction removed.[10]

The government's willingness to use the officers of the United Chinese Society in this way is shown in the numerous letters to the heads of the Society during the 1880s and 1890s asking them to inform the Chinese of changes in the regulations affecting migrants. One letter begins: "His Excellency the Minister of Foreign Affairs will be obliged to Mr. Goo Kim if he will cause to be notified to all Chinamen intending to apply for passports from this Department authorizing reentry to this Kingdom that . . . ."[11]

Several modifications of the regulations restricting Chinese immigration point to the influence of local Chinese. Late in 1887, for example, when sugar plantations were importing Japanese laborers but Chinese rice plantations needed Chinese laborers, the law was changed so that three hundred Chinese workers per quarter would be issued permits for entry. Moreover, "special classes" of Chinese, including merchants and travelers, could obtain permits to enter the country for a six-month period under $500 bond. Children under fourteen (with parents in Hawaii) and women could obtain entry permits. That same statute also showed the influence of local Caucasians in that permits were to be issued to Chinese servants for non-Chinese employers.[12]

These were politically turbulent years. In 1887 a reform legislature, controlled by Caucasians and a few Hawaiians, brought about a constitutional monarchy which reduced King Kalakaua's powers. Then an unsuccessful countermovement led by a part-Hawaiian in 1889 was followed by events leading to the deposing of Queen Liliuokalani, the formation of a provisional government in 1893, and another unsuccessful revolt led by a part-Hawaiian in 1895. There was widespread dissatisfaction with the Republic of Hawaii established under the control of pro-American Caucasians who succeeded in bringing about annexation of Hawaii to the United States. During these years Chinese residents, including some officers of the United Chinese Society, were occasionally suspected or accused of conspiracy and bribery—that is, attempting to influence Hawaiian members of the legislature and giving financial help to Hawaiians in the unsuccessful counterrevolutions.[13] Neither the president nor vice-president of the Society was involved directly in these charges, however, and they sent a letter recognizing the provisional government on the very day it was proclaimed.[14]

For years the president and vice-president of the United Chinese Society, in their joint capacities as Chinese commercial agents, met the ships bringing Chinese immigrants, observed the disembarkation, and interceded for men who had grievances. During the 1895–1898 period, when the proplanter officials of the Republic of Hawaii allowed more than fifteen thousand Chinese arrivals, this was a particularly onerous task. In January 1897 President Goo Kim asked for government permission to send Chinese "deputies" to the quarantine grounds where Chinese laborers were disembarking and signing labor contracts. This request was granted and representatives of the two main speech groups, Hakka and Punti, were appointed.[15]

When Annexation was imminent, the United Chinese Society employed a Caucasian lawyer to represent Chinese interests before authorities in Washington. There were two objectives. The first, which was not attained, was to prevent American laws excluding Chinese from being applied to Hawaii when it became a U.S. territory. The other, which Japanese groups also supported, was to ensure enforcement in Hawaii of American legislation against contract labor—thus freeing several thousand Chinese and Japanese laborers from the contracts under which they had been brought to the Islands during the three years preceding Annexation. The latter objective was achieved. Several thousand Chinese who might have been returned to China under conditions imposed by the republic were allowed to remain in Hawaii.

A Caucasian lawyer was again retained by the Society in 1899 when American immigration officials refused to honor return permits issued by the Hawaiian government before Annexation. According to *The Friend*, 482 Chinese were "cruelly detained at the quarantine station . . . for several months . . . while holding the permits of the Hawaiian government to return to their former residences in Hawaii." The case was pushed through to a favorable decision from the Hawaiian Supreme Court. The Society then sent the lawyer to Washington, where authorities finally recognized the validity of the Hawaiian reentry permits.[16]

In 1908 and again in 1916 and 1921 the Society sent delegates and Caucasian legal representatives to Washington in the interest of securing congressional legislation which would exempt Hawaii from application of the American laws barring Chinese labor immigration. In its petition to Congress in 1916 the Society asserted that "all we ask is to be treated the same as people of other oriental nations. Is it justice to single out the Chinese for exclusion? We fear this has an effect of lowering China in the eyes of the world."[17] None of the three attempts succeeded.

Reaction to Economic Restrictions

Legislation aimed at restricting their businesses and occupational competition was the greatest threat to Chinese sojourners who had already gained entry and were attempting to make the most of the economic opportunities on the Hawaiian frontier. The two most vehemently anti-Chinese organizations in the mid-1880s, the Anti-Asiatic Union and the Workingmen's Party, held meetings at which they protested Chinese competition, especially in skilled jobs. Other Caucasian and Hawaiian residents, though deploring the extreme rhetoric of these organizations, also favored legislation that would restrict Chinese economic activities. It was said that Chinese were "threatening to overrun the country"—from the late 1870s to the mid-1880s Chinese males had increased from about one fifth to about half of the adult male population. Chinese businessmen were said to be "ubiquitous," and it was felt that too many Chinese were in Honolulu and other towns as artisans or as "vagrants" instead of working on the sugar plantations.

To counter the mounting anti-Chinese agitation and legislation proposed by the reform legislature, representatives of the Chinese community met at the United Chinese Society clubhouse in 1887 and formed a special organization: the Bow On Guk ("Self-Defense Society" or "Protective Bureau" as it was variously called in English by Chinese spokesmen). Members were urged to contribute a dollar or more depending on ability to pay and merchants were asked to contribute twenty-five cents for each hundred dollars their firms handled in business that year.[18] Articles in the Chinese newspaper *Lung Kee Sun Bo* urged Chinese to join and help finance the new organization; handbills were distributed with the same objective. One of the handbills, as translated into English stated:

> We Chinese in Hawaii left our home villages to make our fortunes. At first we lived peacefully and happily, but later on conflicts arose among ourselves as we cut each other's skins. And because of this weakness we were frequently subject to foreign exploitation. Fellow countrymen, don't say that a spark of fire cannot burn a large plain nor that a tiny cloud cannot cause a rainfall, for drops of water will form a river and a little work each day will move a mountain. If we are not harmonious among ourselves and promote friendship among our countrymen, how can we protect our property and life? This is why the establishment of a Protective Bureau in Hawaii is the most pressing need. Remember the massacre of Chinese in Peru, also the driving out of Chinese in the United States and the burning of stores there. Beware that we don't fall into the same trouble. Although we see that the interests of the Chinese should be protected here, we cannot go on without financial support. Let all our fellow countrymen come together to defend themselves. Since we need money urgently, we are sending people to canvas for funds. We sincerely hope that all countrymen, no matter how rich or poor, open their purses that this worthy work might be accomplished. The fur patched together becomes a coat; the pollen gathered by the bees becomes honey. May we all be in accord with one another, cooperate, and eliminate all suspicion. If we can accomplish this, we can protect ourselves and live happily. This is the purpose of our organization. Please sign your name.[19]

Several thousand dollars were collected and a two-story building in Chinatown was bought as headquarters.

According to one Chinese account of this period there was fear that anti-Chinese agitation would lead to physical attacks on the Chinese residents or their places of business. Honolulu Chinese held meetings to plan self-protection. Some rifles were bought and watchmen were hired to patrol the Chinatown area at night. Leaders urged their countrymen to refuse to do business with members of the Workingmen's Union and Caucasian firms most active in the anti-Chinese agitation.

Actions of the 1888 session of the Legislative Assembly alarmed the Chinese community even further. One law promised to be particularly disadvantageous to Chinese businessmen, the group which provided most of the leadership of the United Chinese Society and the Bow On Guk. This act required all licensed businessmen to keep accounts "in the English, Hawaiian or some European language." While not explicitly mentioning Chinese businesses, the act in effect was aimed at them since most Chinese migrants in that decade would not have been able to meet this requirement, and there were few other businessmen in the Islands who could not have kept accounts in at least one of the required languages. While the assembly was still in session, Chinese petitioned for repeal of the act. The petition was discussed but rejected. One legislator claimed that because "Chinese have perpetrated frauds against their creditors" the bill was "made necessary by the Chinese themselves." The assembly overrode the king's veto of the measure, but the act was later declared unconstitutional when Caucasian attorneys brought a test case before the Supreme Court.[20]

Even more threatening was a constitutional amendment recommended by a special legislative committee on Chinese and Asiatic restriction. It would give the assembly authority to limit, even prevent, Chinese employment in occupations "in any line whatsoever" as specified by legislation, except that the assembly could not disbar Chinese from engaging in the rice and sugar industries. The amendment would also have allowed the assembly to limit the right of Chinese to acquire and hold land and deny Chinese the right to remain in the country for more than six years. The proposed amendment also provided that "no such laws shall be declared unconstitutional because confined in their operation to Chinese or any body or class thereof."

The intensity of the Chinese protest against such discriminatory legislation and the unity of the Chinese community in the protest are apparent in the *Daily Bulletin*'s long report of a mass meeting held on 30 August 1888 at the Chinese Theater. According to the report, "Every business house in Chinatown was closed, and almost every Chinaman turned out to the meeting. The building was jammed full . . . and . . . there was a crush outside of people unable to gain admittance." The chairman of the meeting, W. S. Akana, said that the proposed legislation would "be ruin to the Chinese; therefore they should do their best to protect themselves." C. Monting, a leader among the Hakkas who said he had come to the Islands ten years earlier as a rice cultivator, was the first speaker. His remarks, like those of all the other speakers, were interpreted into English for the benefit of reporters from the English-language press. According to the *Daily Bulletin*'s report:

> C. Monting said that when he came to Hawaii the islands were not as prosperous as they are now. The Chinamen had done much to bring the country to its present condition of prosperity. They went to work on waste and worthless lands and . . . made them productive and profitable. The Chinamen leased lands from white men, to whom they paid rent. He paid $3,000 a year in rent and taxes. The revenue of the Government is $1,200,000, of which amount the Chinese pay $500,000, or more than one-third of the whole. They do not grumble at this, but pay their taxes cheerfully. . . . Chinamen pay taxes as well as others, then why should they not have the same rights? . . . The speaker sat down amidst deafening applause.

C. Monting was followed by sixteen other speakers, including nine merchants, a teacher, a watchmaker, a carpenter, two drivers, an ex-policeman, and a cook. At the end of the meeting "a committee was appointed to wait upon the legislature." Two members of the committee were officers of the United Chinese Society; the others were all Honolulu businessmen and probably members of the United Chinese Society.

Six days later the committee submitted to the Legislative Assembly a "memorial" written in English pleading for justice. After saying "we understand the great pressure which has been exercised inducing a part of the members to make laws without regard to justice and forbearance," the memorial goes on:

> But we have at all times looked forward with confidence that the sentiment of fairness which lives in the educated white men, as well as the natives, would prevent the passing of any laws to drive us from the country or to take from us the right of earning a living by honest labor. . . .
>
> We have lived among this people whom you represent for years and will not and cannot believe that any injustice done to us would be approved by them. . . .

There is a saying written on the wall of your chamber, "Let justice be done though the heavens fall." We ask not to be favored only that the protection which justice gives us be not taken away from us.

Shortly before the assembly was to vote on the amendment, the *Bulletin* noted that "the Chinese attorneys [Caucasian attorneys employed by the Chinese] appear to be satisfied with the amendment." Presumably this was because in its final form the amendment stipulated that provisions regarding occupations, property ownership, or deportation would not apply to Chinese already residing in Hawaii. Faced with already enacted legislation that restricted Chinese immigration, the Chinese residents apparently decided to concentrate on the new threats posed by the amendment. The memorial had expressly stated that the question of restriction on further immigration was not the immediate concern, "excepting that it will be carried out . . . without oppression or cruelty, and expecting confidently that all legislation concerning us, our position and our property will be just, temperate, broad and magnanimous."

The Chinese did not rely entirely on their petition for justice and fair play. Four days after the mass meeting the *Bulletin* reported that "twenty to thirty representative Chinese were present in the Legislative Hall this morning" and sixty were there the day the memorial was read. The amendment was defeated when it was voted on the following day. Two days later the attorney general charged that several Hawaiian members who had voted against the amendment had been bribed. One accused man who admitted to taking a bribe informed on others, saying that "one day we went to Ahlo's store and a Chinaman said he would pay $50 to each native voting against the amendment. . . . [After the vote] I received a $50 Spreckels certificate." Loo Ngwak, a partner in Sing Chong Co., was also implicated. Three of the accused Hawaiian legislators were expelled from the House and a fourth severely censured. According to the newspapers this was the first time legislators had been expelled for bribery, although it was by no means the first time legislators were known to have been bribed. Newspaper reports contained no mention of any Chinese being charged with paying the bribes, although the penal code made the bribing of a legislator or government official a criminal offense.[21] Bribery would not have been regarded as particularly corrupt or unusual by the migrants themselves. In the villages of China from which they came government officials were regarded as generally venal,[22] and in Hawaii migrants became aware that government employees were frequently receptive to bribes.

A rather pathetic attempt to impress legislators with the Chinese power to retaliate had been made by one of the speakers at the mass meeting, but his point was not included in the memorial to the Legislative Assembly:

> Foreigners seem to think that the Chinese Government does not care for us, and that they can do as they like. China has plenty ships of war, cruisers, whose business it is to go around the world and protect her people. . . .
> . . . A little country like Hawaii thinks it can drive the Chinamen away. All nationalities come and settle here, and whether there be a treaty or no treaty they should be treated alike. . . . The laws against the Chinese are not right. A memorial has been sent to the ambassador at Washington and another to the Viceroy of Canton, and it is believed they will takes steps to render help.[23]

The Chinese leaders in Honolulu knew as well as Hawaiian government officials that little help could be expected from China or its representative in Washington. In moments of frustration, Tin-Yuke Char tells us, migrants were likely to say *"yat poon sarn sa* (China is like 'a pan of loose sand')."[24] The Minister of Foreign Affairs was well aware of the Chinese government's unwillingness to intervene on behalf of the *wah kiu* as indicated in a confidential message from the Hawaiian minister in Washington:

> As to the Chinese treaty the Chinese minister told me privately that the Viceroy said that if they made a treaty with Hawaii, and then any trouble grew up, they would be obliged to enforce the rights of the Chinese and that might lead to trouble, that now if a Chinaman complained they could say well, you know we have no treaty there, and so avoid trouble. He said that the Viceroy was evidently disgusted with foreign treaties and thought that Chinese had better stay at home.[25]

Although the proposed constitutional amendment was defeated, there was no letup in anti-Chinese legislation and regulations. One common and effective countermove by Chinese leaders was employing Caucasian attorneys to assist in drafting petitions and protest statements, to lobby at the legislature, and to take test cases to the courts (through to the Supreme Court if necessary). Recourse to the Supreme Court in order to have anti-Chinese legislation declared unconstitutional was the counterattack that anti-Chinese legislators had tried to block by provisions of the defeated constitutional amendment. A similar constitutional amendment, adopted along with accompanying legislation at the 1892 session, specifically prohibited additional Chinese from going into trade or mechanical occupations, but the overthrow of the monarchy soon after the session ended delayed enforcement.

Early in 1894 the Provisional Government considered a "licensing act" to achieve the objectives of the 1892 anti-Chinese legislation. The act would require "all Chinamen to pay one dollar each for a license before engaging in any trading or mechanical occupation" and would forbid "such licenses to be issued to any Chinaman not previously so employed."[26] Within a few days Chinese leaders called another Chinese mass meeting; more than 2,500 Chinese men were reported as gathering inside and outside the Chinese Theater for the heated two-hour meeting.[27] According to the *Hawaiian Star*, "As a mass meeting the event was in every way a success. . . . The proceedings throughout riveted the attention of all. There were frequent outbursts of applause and positive expressions from the audience. Half a hundred of the leading Chinese had seats on the stage." The *Star* was apparently alarmed by the belligerent tone of some of the speakers, but the cabinet of the new government would not have been worried by the remarks of the first speaker: "If [the new government] will not listen to us, let us instruct our representative to communicate with the Chinese minister at Washington and ask him to write the home government about our troubles." The next speaker, more realistically, "said they were assembled to see if all were of one mind respecting the situation." Other speakers expressed the indignation and humiliation that Chinese residents felt at being discriminated against:

> "I have been in this country for fifteen years," said Ching Ling Him, a clerk for the Hawaiian Hardware Company, who says he hopes to become a merchant. . . . "If this bill passes no man can do business except the one allowed him by the law. The Chinese pay most of the taxes, and were it not for us the white merchants of Honolulu would be ruined. I cannot be a rich man if this law passes, and we are treated worse than dogs. . . . We must stick together. . . ."
>
> Chung Kim, a lawyer's clerk, who brought his speech from C. W. Ashford's office, said . . . the Chinese have been extremely patient. They have borne oppression which would from almost any other race have provoked revolution. The Government seems to have formed the opinion that no injustice heaped upon the Chinese will be opposed

or resented. This is a mistake. Even a worm will turn when trodden upon, and so it may be with the despised Chinese should the oppression be carried too far. . . . By what right do our white-skinned brothers lord it over us to say that we shall do business and trade and live and breathe only by their consent? Is it only because our skins are brown and theirs are white? The Government is glad enough to collect taxes from the Chinese, but when it comes to finding a class upon whom the spite of all cranks shall be expended, they at once light upon the patient and long-suffering Chinaman. . . . The Hawaiian constitution declares that the Government is established for the equal benefit of all men and all classes, but if the Chinese license act shall pass it will show that the Government intends to deny to us the equal benefit of the laws. . . .

Lee Chu, a carpenter, is a radical. Said he: "We are descended from great fathers. Why should we be treated differently from others? I say that if we do not do our best to overcome this law we will show that we have no blood in us."

A committee of thirteen was selected to transmit a set of resolutions to the Minister of Foreign Affairs. Some of these resolutions stated feelings that had been expressed by many speakers at the meeting:

We, the Chinese residents of Honolulu . . . do solemnly protest against the injustice, degradation, and insult threatened to be imposed upon us and our race. . . .

. . . We respectfully assert our right, under the principles of enlightened justice and the provisions of the Hawaiian constitution, to dwell in Hawaii and be accorded the protection of the law upon terms of equality with those of other nationalities here sojourning.

. . . While we ask for nothing more than equality with other residents of equally good behavior, we shall be satisfied with and shall support and respect nothing that accords to our race a lesser degree of consideration and justice than residents of other nationalities enjoy.

Again the committee members selected to transmit the resolutions to government officials were mostly businessmen, several of them officers in the United Chinese Society. During the same crisis a petition was drawn up at a meeting of the United Chinese Society "praying that the councils refrain from enacting into a law the pending anti-Chinese bill." This petition, signed by some hundred and fifty leading Chinese in the city, was submitted to the government. The bill did not become a law.

Nevertheless, the government did revive a law that had been enacted in 1892. It did not affect Chinese already residing in the country but applied to some ten thousand new Chinese contract laborers brought in during 1895–1898 on condition that unless they worked in the rice and sugar industries or as domestic servants they were to be returned to China. As some Caucasian planters had anticipated, these new workers turned out to be more troublesome than the Chinese contract laborers of earlier decades. The latest contract laborers were recruited mainly from the same districts of Kwangtung as most of the earlier ones, Chung Shan and See Yup, but these young men were more sophisticated than their predecessors. Most of them came from villages which had been influenced by *wah kiu* returning from Hawaii and the continental United States. Many were kinsmen of migrants already in Hawaii. They knew more about life on the Caucasian-controlled sugar plantations and about the rights of laborers; they also had more information about the money to be made away from the plantations if they could escape their contracts.

The head of the United Chinese Society during this period pressed the authorities in Honolulu several times to intervene when he felt injustice had been done to indentured Chinese plantation laborers. Complaints by the workers, often quite at variance with reports by plantation managers and local government officials, were sent through him to the Minister of Foreign Affairs and to the attorney general. Goo Kim complained about the treatment of Chinese laborers at Lihue Plantation, Kauai, and asked the Board of Immigration to investigate the causes of a riot there in which a Chinese contract laborer had been killed. Goo also transmitted to the board complaints he had received from Chinese contract laborers at Olowalu Plantation on Maui. In both cases the complaints were found to be justified and the secretary of the Board of Immigration, who investigated them, took corrective action.[28] Later in 1897, at the suggestion of the Chinese minister in Washington, Goo asked the Hawaiian government to make "a general investigation by a government official of the condition of Chinese laborers in this country."[29] A denial by the government that such an investigation was necessary brought a request for letters of credentials for seven Chinese, appointed by Goo, to conduct an investigation for him. Also in the interests of the indentured laborers, Goo and the United Chinese Society, together with Japanese leaders, had succeeded in getting their contracts declared void and the men permitted to remain in the Islands.[30]

Defense of Political Rights

The provisions of the new constitution of 1887 which most offended long-term and well-established Chinese residents had to do with voting rights. Article 59 specifically gave Caucasian male residents who met certain property qualifications the right to vote whereas male residents of Asian birth were denied this right, even those who had become naturalized Hawaiian subjects. Apparently the Chinese were offended not so much by denial of the vote as by the blatant differentiation between Caucasians and Asians. A Chinese in 1913 wrote: "They [Chinese migrants] had not meddled with politics; they were peace loving and law abiding, and all they had ever expected was the right to engage in commerce and trade without molestation."[31] Concerned Chinese were embittered by the fact that while naturalized Asians were denied the franchise, Caucasians could qualify to vote without becoming citizens of Hawaii. C. Monting, one of the Chinese who attended a mass meeting of people opposing the new constitution for various reasons, spoke against the provisions affecting persons of Asian birth, asking for equality and fair play. Eventually one concession was made: the constitutional provisions were interpreted as allowing the vote to Hawaii-born Chinese and other Hawaii-born Asians, but probably less than a hundred Hawaii-born Chinese were old enough to vote in the late 1880s.[32]

After the monarchy was overthrown and while the proposed new constitution for the Republic of Hawaii was being considered, Chinese leaders were even more offended because Japanese migrants but not Chinese were to be given the franchise on the same basis as Caucasians and Hawaiians. Obviously, Japan's having a more powerful government than China, together with treaty agreements between the Japanese and Hawaiian governments, gave Japanese migrants more political leverage.

Nearly four hundred "leading Chinese merchants" signed a petition to the Council of the Provisional Government asking that Chinese be given the franchise and also representation on the council. Goo Kim, in an interview to the press, stated why Chinese in Hawaii had earned the right to the franchise much more than had the Japanese, but he added that the Japanese would not be mentioned in the petition. Although Goo, by right of his presidency of the United Chinese Society, was recognized as Chinese commercial agent, this position did not enable him to make a protest on behalf of the Chinese government; the petition itself contained a plea for renewal of efforts to get a treaty with the Chinese government. The petition ended with a request that the Chinese be given "equal rights with those of all other alien residents, subjects or citizens."

An editorial in the *Pacific Commercial Advertiser* conceded that a number of long-time Chinese residents might have a good case, but asserted that "the overwhelming majority of Chinese migrants are not . . . identified with Hawaii's interests, social, as well as material." When the constitution was adopted it did not extend the franchise to the Chinese.[33]

Following annexation to the United States, Chinese and others who had become naturalized subjects of Hawaii achieved full American citizenship, as did Chinese born in Hawaii, but American laws barred further naturalization of alien Chinese, with few exceptions, until 1943.

Concern about Civil Rights

Most Chinese migrants were wary of the Hawaiian courts and law enforcement agencies. Apart from the villagers' age-old distrust of government officials, migrants generally were not convinced that they could get justice under the Hawaiian legal system. Experience on the Haole-controlled sugar plantations led them to believe that sheriffs, constables, police, and the courts were agencies of the planters, used to enforce plantation contracts and regulations. Afong, the Chinese commercial agent in 1881, expressed this opinion in a letter to the Chinese minister in Washington: "The interests of all the Judges of the Island are in Sugar Plantations; consequently, there is no possibility of the case being decided impartially."[34] The converse of the Chinese attitude was the belief of many Caucasians, during the first decades of Chinese immigration, that Chinese testimony in court was not reliable. In March 1892 the Supreme Court of Hawaii declared that a juror was "not disqualified to sit on a case of a Chinaman charged with selling opium, who says that Chinamen are not to be equally credited with a Hawaiian or a white man, provided his other answers show that he will not disregard the testimony because it is from a Chinaman, and bears the impress of truth, but would weigh it without prejudice."[35]

The social distance between Chinese migrants and other groups helped account for these feelings. Communication between the Chi-

nese and officials was difficult; few government functionaries understood the Chinese language, Chinese attitudes, or Chinese traditions.
Chinese newcomers were baffled by Western principles and methods of justice. The migrants' distrust of the courts was sometimes
reinforced when older Chinese residents used Western procedures to
take advantage of other Chinese. Even the government's attempt to
facilitate law enforcement by employing Chinese detectives, police
officers, and court interpreters aroused some animosity among
migrants; those who accepted such positions were often regarded as
informers and traitors.

Chinese commercial agents and leaders of the United Chinese
Society knew that in many respects Chinese migrants were discriminated against by law enforcement agencies and in the courts, and
from time to time they appealed for fairer treatment. Quarantine
regulations, for example, that were applied to Chinese—not only
new immigrants but returning Chinese residents—and not applied to
Caucasians were galling. Chinese representatives tried to speed up
the release of Chinese from quarantine when the government maintained that differential treatment was necessary for health reasons.
When regulations adopted in the late 1880s required Chinese residents to submit profile and full-face photographs for a passport and
return permit not required of persons of other nationalities, the regulations were contested but unsuccessfully.

It was commonly felt that Chinese were arrested and convicted
on gambling charges more frequently than Caucasians or Hawaiians
involved in gambling. Even the *Pacific Commercial Advertiser*, no advocate for the Chinese, recognized this situation: "Gambling among
Chinese is put down by the strong arm of the law whenever an opportunity arises, but it very rarely happens that gamblers of other nationalities are interfered with by the police."[36] There were cases in
which it seemed clear to the Chinese community that Chinese
charged with criminal offenses or violation of some law were convicted on insufficient evidence. In other cases it appeared that non-
Chinese, particularly Hawaiians and Caucasians, were not punished
for offenses against Chinese persons or property. Even when a Chinese was murdered and the evidence seemed conclusive, the offender sometimes escaped penalty. Some of the complaints sent by
leaders of the United Chinese Society to the government in the
1890s were concerned with these indications of unequal regard for
the lives of Chinese residents.[37]

Nevertheless, the Society did assist the Hawaiian government in some serious criminal cases. In April 1892, for example, Alee, as president of the United Chinese Society, offered a reward for the arrest of "the parties" who had murdered a Chinese. Similarly, in October 1893 Goo Kim, then president of the Society, added $200 to the $100 reward the government had offered for the capture of a Chinese who had been identified as the murderer of a Chinese farmer on Oahu. Offering a reward, of course, was meant to encourage action different from that of the Hoong Moon societies whose oaths required members not to inform on each other. In the 1893 case the "Chinese murderer" was apparently sheltered for several days by Chinese who recognized him and then helped him to board a ship for the island of Hawaii; it was on that island two weeks later that another Chinese helped capture him.[38] Whatever the motivations of individual Chinese in such situations, the aim of the United Chinese Society was apparently to bring about a more favorable attitude toward the Chinese as a group by cooperating with the authorities in these criminal cases.

Defense of Personal and Property Rights

During the last decades of the nineteenth century Chinese migrants sometimes felt, with some justification, that their property rights were disregarded and their personal rights ignored in a humiliating way by government officials. The outstanding instance of what Chinese felt to be gross disregard for their personal and property rights occurred during the plague of 1899–1900 and the Chinatown fire connected with it. According to Li Ling Ai, her father, Dr. K. F. Li, diagnosed the first case of bubonic plague and reported it at once to the government health officials.[39] When this and two other cases proved fatal later the same day in Chinatown (12 December 1899), the Board of Health immediately started daily house to house inspections and the next day the whole Chinatown area was declared under quarantine. The area was divided into fifteen districts for cleansing and disinfection. On the fifteenth no one was allowed to enter or leave the area, and soldiers were posted along the borders of Chinatown to prevent anyone from doing so. According to one source:

Many of the restrictions . . . were placed exclusively on Orientals or were framed with the Asiatic in mind. This resulted, generally, from associating the Chinese and Japanese with slums and squalor—as revealed in Chinatown—and from the belief that the filthy environment of the Oriental was a breeding ground for plague germs. Many cases of plague originated in Chinatown, and the restrictions thus gained a logical support. Whether necessary or not, the regulations certainly displayed the Board of Health's power during the epidemic.[40]

One of the first measures to arouse Chinese protest was the cremation on the quarantine station grounds of the bodies of all those who died of the plague.[41] Even though the board knew that Chinese opposed cremation, the protests were ignored. The board's next step, which also violated Chinese feelings, was taken because a Sanitary Commission report led the board to conclude that Chinatown conditions were so unsanitary that it was impossible to disinfect the area by "ordinary means." The board resorted to burning buildings in which persons had died of the plague. Between 31 December and 19 January several fires were set. According to *The Friend*, these were "admirably handled" by the Fire Department. According to the account Dr. Li and his wife passed down to their daughter, the guards and inspectors were rude and intemperate. When someone died, others living in the building were herded into the streets. Their clothing was removed and burned, and the evicted residents were forced off to detention camps.[42]

One account of the plague reports that before the first fire was set the residents' belongings and goods from the stores were removed by the Board of Health and stored until the quarantine was lifted.[43] Correspondence between the Chinese consulate and the government shows that the United Chinese Society and the Chinese consul protested what they regarded as indiscriminate destruction of merchandise of Chinese stores and personal belongings in the lodging quarters, along with the burning of the buildings. The Minister of Foreign Affairs replied that the Board of Health had "summary powers in cases of this kind to order the removal or destruction of anything that is a cause of sickness, nuisance, or pestilence."[44] Chinese who did not wish to have their property destroyed should provide a suitable building where their goods could be fumigated, arrange for transporting such goods to the place, and store their belongings in warehouses outside Chinatown until the plague was over and the quarantine lifted. Many Chinese regarded these measures as unnecessary and too expensive. More protests were made when fires designed to burn certain condemned buildings also destroyed neighboring buildings not condemned, but the Minister of Foreign Affairs said little more than that the merchants had been warned "to pack their goods so that the same could readily be removed."[45]

Other effects of the quarantine added to resentment among people confined in Chinatown. Chinese and Japanese merchants not forced out of business by having their premises burned sustained heavy losses because they could not carry on normal business. Unemployment increased in Chinatown and contributed to decline in trade. Plantation laborers, servants in Haole homes, and other people who happened to be in Chinatown when the quarantine was imposed were confined there, jobless and without income.

After the pestilence had continued for more than a month, authorities decided to try to end it by burning buildings more quickly after deaths from the plague occurred in them. It was anticipated that this measure would increase the claims, but the cost would be more than balanced by earlier resumption of normal business activities. Financial losses outside Chinatown were also mounting. Business was almost at a standstill while quarantine in the city and between the islands was in effect and shipping between Hawaii and the rest of the world was disrupted. Shortly after this decision was made a fire on 20 January destroyed the buildings on about thirty-eight acres and nearly completed the burning of the entire Chinatown area. Although the government contended that the fire got out of control because of a sudden shift in the wind, it was widely believed among the Chinese that the authorities had purposely allowed their quarters to be burned out. Excerpts from the report in *The Friend* indicate some of the conditions on the day of the fire:

By the unexpected conflagration of Chinatown, nearly 4,500 persons were driven hastily into the street from their burning dwellings. It was a distressful and panic-stricken mass of humanity. This feature of the great disaster far exceeded every other. . . .

To a great extent, these crowds were in a state of panic, as well as of anger at the whites who, as they believed, had deliberately burned them out. In their fright they had saved little of their belongings from the flames which so rapidly swept down upon them. Among them were many violent men who urged their fellows to attack the armed guards who were controlling their movements. . . . Wives were often separated from husbands and children from parents, and wailing in distress. . . .

The citizens of Honolulu rose at once fitly to the situation with rapid and efficient organization. Several hundred citizens were at once armed with improvised clubs such as pick-handles, to assist the military and police. Forming in lines along the streets, the frightened crowds were driven between the brandished clubs, but without a blow struck, to the large Kawaiahao church yard, a distance of three-fifths of a mile. The weaker women and children were carried on drays. The men were loaded down with their effects. . . . Most happily there were no losses of life, and scarcely an injury to person.[46]

Years later a Chinese woman who was among those evacuated told about the handicaps of the women with bound feet:

Before we knew it, the fire was upon us. We were taken to the quarantine station in trucks [wagons?] but the men had to walk. . . . We were in the same building with Mrs. Y—— and Mrs. T——. [They], and many others, who have bound feet, were perfect nuisances, for they had to be helped across many muddy spots. I was never so thankful for being born of poor family as I was then.[47]

The Friend, a missionary paper generally more pro-Chinese than other English-language publications, tried to convey the attitudes of the authorities and Caucasian residents toward the "panic-stricken mass of humanity" being herded away from Chinatown:

These people must be controlled, calmed and comforted. They must be placed in safety. They must especially be prevented from scattering, to disseminate through the city the germs of plague from their insanitary and infected abodes. They must continue to be quarantined, as they had been for weeks before, having been guarded from leaving the district.[48]

While some residents of the city would do nothing for the homeless people in the detention camps for fear of contracting the plague, others who saw the need for compassion and aid volunteered help. *The Friend* reported the response of those who felt that people in the detention camps must be made "as comfortable as circumstances would permit. They must be fed, and in many cases, clothed. All of the bright Sunday the work of relief went on. The women of Honolulu organized to prepare clothing for the destitute women and children for whom the sewing-machines buzzed all day throughout the city, instead of Church or Sunday School."

Lana Iwamoto also tells about aid from many sources:

Citizens spontaneously offered supplies of all kinds; merchants liberally gave food, clothes, cash, and the use of vehicles to convey goods.

On Sunday, the day after the fire, the women of Central Union Church organized relief work and committees and assisted the public authorities in the work of meeting the needs of the destitute refugees. And a number of Nuuanu Valley ladies started a sewing bee to make women's and children's clothing for the homeless. They eventually produced 350 articles.[49]

Japanese, Chinese, and Hawaiian societies also actively helped the needy. According to a Chinese source, "the unfortunate people, old and young, raised their cries to Heaven, and proceeded to the United Chinese Society headquarters."[50] Shortly after the fire, when the private resources of many of the homeless were exhausted, Chinese again went to the United Chinese Society and proposed a charity drive. A committee soon raised more than twenty thousand dollars. Free food was distributed; emergency assistance was given. The Society interceded for impoverished Chinese who wished to enter claims for their losses but were deterred by the requirement of a fifty-dollar deposit for court costs, and the requirement in these cases was waived. The Society also provided legal assistance for carrying these cases through court. For his efforts on behalf of the Chinese at this time, the president of the Society was awarded a gold medal by Chinese residents. The Chinese consul was similarly rewarded.[51]

The United Chinese Society in Other Chinatown Crises

During the late nineteenth and early twentieth centuries when Chinatown was growing most rapidly, migrants concentrated there went through many critical times because of the hazardous conditions under which they lived. They had to be largely self-reliant in dealing with fires, accidents, and sickness. Under ordinary circumstances the migrant whose building collapsed or burned, or who was sick, might get help from kinsmen in Hawaii, *heung li,* or other personal sources. When, however, large-scale disasters struck Chinatown, or when migrants had no personal ties in the community, these sources were usually unavailable. Government assistance was limited because health and welfare agencies had not yet been organized. Often the United Chinese Society took over functions that generally, in the Western system, would have been handled by government authorities. Two such situations were the 1886 Chinatown fire and the cholera epidemic in Honolulu in 1895.

The 1886 fire broke out less than three months after the newly organized China Fire Engine Company had participated in the annual firemen's parade. Although the company reached the scene before other fire companies, it could not stop the fast-moving flames. The *Advertiser* commented caustically that any other company could have done so. The fire destroyed buildings over about thirty-seven acres —most of Chinatown—and caused losses, estimated at $1,500,000, sustained mostly by Chinese. Authorities were unable to handle the catastrophe in an orderly way; hundreds of terrified Chinese and other residents of the area were not restrained from frantic efforts to salvage their belongings or from crowding the streets. This disorder interfered with efforts to control the fire, which were hampered anyhow by the maze of temporary, flimsy buildings in the area.[52]

The United Chinese Society building, which had been opened with elaborate ceremony only two and a half months earlier, was burned, but the Society continued to function. Some of the several thousand homeless Chinatown residents went to live with people in other parts of Honolulu, the Chinese particularly with Chinese farmers in the Honolulu district. The president of the United Chinese Society secured permission from the government for Chinese who could not be taken care of otherwise to camp on the immigration depot grounds. In response to an appeal from the Society for funds to assist the many who were left penniless, the government granted ten thousand dollars, of which three thousand went to Hawaiians and seven to Chinese. The Chinese Christian Church, along with other church groups, provided meals and lodging for many of the fire victims.

The Legislative Assembly enacted laws to regulate the rebuilding of Chinatown in accordance with fire and sanitary precautions, but though many of the old wooden buildings were replaced with brick structures, new frame buildings were put up in violation of government rules The United Chinese Society still owed several thousand dollars for its first headquarters, which the treasurer, Lau Cheong, was charged with having neglected to insure, but the Society decided nevertheless to erect a new Chinese community building "in order to promote the feelings of the people from the same villages." The new building, similar to the first, was opened with a banquet in the spring of 1887.[53]

In August 1895 a number of deaths in Honolulu raised fears of a cholera epidemic. Health authorities carried out a plan for "city cleaning . . . with liberal use of lime and disinfectants." Newspaper accounts of inspectors' reports focused on conditions in Chinatown. According to one item, "many foul places were cleaned out, especially in Chinatown. . . . One of the bad places was the ground under the floors of the old fishmarket." Another article said that "the Japanese quarters were found to be very much cleaner than those of the Chinese, the latter being in an extremely filthy and altogether disgusting condition." In parts of Chinatown, it was said, "the ground reeks with contagion. . . . It is a shame that human beings should have to live in such close proximity . . . to pestilential exhalations." One newspaper, referring to a few malodorous buildings in one part of Chinatown, stated that "Chinese, Japanese and Hawaiians are so crowded together . . . that there cannot be immunity from tainted air."

Later, as more people died, certain sections of Honolulu, including Chinatown, were divided into districts in which every resident was to be inspected twice a day in order to identify and remove those who had become sick; no one was permitted to leave the city or spend a night away from his residence without a written permit. Church services and other large assemblies of people were forbidden for a three-week period.[54]

The United Chinese Society formed a special bureau to help Chinese who were in distress because of the epidemic. The Society contributed $250 and a committee raised an additional $850 from wealthy Chinese. Two meal tickets a day, each worth ten cents, were given to those who applied for them. The tickets could be used at any Chinese restaurant, which would be reimbursed in cash for all tickets returned to the bureau. Any Chinese who could not afford to buy medicine could have the bureau sign a prescription which would be filled at any Chinese drugstore. The United Chinese Society was asked by the Board of Health to provide Chinese doctors to assist the Caucasian physicians who had been appointed to supervise daily inspections. At a meeting of the Society ten Chinese doctors (herbalists) were selected to serve.[55]

A makeshift hospital was set up at the quarantine station to which individuals diagnosed as being sick from cholera were taken. Soon items appeared in the papers regarding complaints about the facilities and the handling of patients at this hospital, while health authorities repudiated the grounds for the complaints. Most of the deaths were of Hawaiians (seventy-seven of eighty-five), especially those living in the Iwilei section of Honolulu, an area about half a mile away from Chinatown. Many Chinese, as well as some others including a German physician, did not believe that cholera was the cause of the deaths, and it was not until the epidemic was over that reports of laboratory tests from the United States confirmed that the deaths had indeed been caused by cholera infection.[56]

Probably because of complaints among Chinese about the hospital at the quarantine station, the United Chinese Society decided that there should be a place under Chinese management where sick Chinese could be taken care of, especially in emergencies. A committee was appointed to discuss the matter with the other general Chinatown organization, the China Engine Company. A petition circulated among leading Chinese was submitted to the legislature, with 327 signatures, asking for a grant of land "in or near Honolulu" upon which the Society might erect and maintain, under government supervision, "a hospital for the care of the sick and also in connection therewith a home for the aged, infirm and helpless Chinese." Land in the Palama section of Honolulu was granted. A campaign was organized to raise money; the China Engine Company donated $1,950, the United Chinese Society bureau formed during the epidemic contributed its remaining funds, and other money was collected among Chinese and Caucasians.

In March 1897 the Wai Wah Yee Yuen, or Chinese Hospital, was opened by Goo Kim, still president of the United Chinese Society, at a ceremony attended, according to *The Friend*, by "the leading Chinese merchants and officials together with some thirty whites including most of our prominent Christian workers." The ceremony included "the Doxology and two anthems played by the Hawaiian Band, a prayer, a hymn, a reading from the Bible, a closing hymn and benediction," in addition to the main talks by Goo Kim and the Rev. F. W. Damon. The writer for *The Friend* noted that "the peculiarly Christian character of the opening exercises is largely due to the great influence of Mr. Goo Kim, so well known as an early convert and a long and able Christian worker, as well as a successful merchant."

Some of the regulations indicate how the hospital was intended to operate:

> Any Chinese who is sick and desires to enter this hospital must have a certificate from the president and vice-president of the United Chinese

Society and the director of the hospital. These will make investigations of where the patient came from. If the patient is found to be poor and has nobody to depend on, all services in the hospital are free to him. . . .

Patients who unfortunately die in the hospital may be taken out and buried by the relatives. Otherwise, the hospital undertakes this procedure, for which a sum of fourteen dollars is paid by the relatives. If the deceased is exceedingly poor and has nobody to depend on, the hospital buries him at a lesser price.

The Manoa Chinese Cemetery will be the burial ground. The province of the deceased together with his names will be recorded.[57]

C. K. Ai, president of the United Chinese Society from 1901 to 1906, reports that during those years he became deeply concerned about the wisdom of continuing to maintain the hospital. After a good start "the Chinese doctors in charge relaxed their discipline and the hospital became discredited." Chinese had spent more than ninety thousand dollars on a hospital which was being used as a "house of death" and as a burial society for indigent Chinese. Moreover, because of the great losses to Chinese merchants caused by the 1900 Chinatown fire, Chinese contributions to the hospital had decreased. In Ai's words:

The hospital was very unfortunate from the very start. No Chinese ever brought in a patient until it was too late for the physician to do anything. We tried to teach our people to bring the sick in earlier, so as to give the doctor a chance to help them, but all to no avail. Therefore, practically all those admitted into the hospital as patients went out in coffins. To hide this sad sight from living-dead, I had a high fence built behind. . . .

. . . In 1906, I called a meeting of the hospital committee and announced my decision to discontinue taking charge of the hospital. I told the committee there was no sense of carrying on a hospital when only those were brought in that were about to die. . . . Our hospital had really been nothing more than a mortuary or morgue. The other committee members finally came to my point of view.[58]

The Wai Wah Yee Yuen was closed later that year.

Group Consciousness and Organized Action

The United Chinese Society, it is apparent, was only partly successful in defending Chinese migrants against discrimination, but it symbolized and to some extent made effective a basic change in the orientation of migrants in Chinatown. Migrants who had come to Hawaii, especially during the earlier years of immigration, with almost no sense of identification with Chinese of other villages or districts, found themselves categorized and treated as "Chinese." In this situation migrants developed a willingness to act with other Chinese in their common interest and supported the United Chinese Society. Every new act of the government which imposed special requirements or restrictions upon the Chinese intensified their sense of oneness—their "we-consciousness." In Chinese mass meetings, on handbills, and in the Chinese newspapers appeals were made to "fellow countrymen"; speakers and writers talked about "we Chinese." In addition to *sook jut* ("uncle-nephew"; that is, kinsmen) and *heung li*, a new phrase came into use among the migrants: *tung bau* ("fellow countrymen"). The new feeling was expressed in the slogan, "Unity is what we want and must have—unity in mind and action. If we unite we will gain our point."[59]

Having been organized originally to voice the protest of Chinese migrants against discrimination and to take whatever collective action was possible in coping with it, the United Chinese Society was ready to organize other kinds of mutual assistance in times of crisis. It became important not only because it acted on behalf of the migrants but because, representing all elements of the Hawaii Chinese population, it was a centripetal force in the emerging Chinese community.

CHAPTER 11

Differentiation and Integration

THE Chinese migrants, fending for themselves in an often hostile world, could well appreciate the value of a United Chinese Society which could speak, and sometimes act, in their common interest. At the same time, the migrants who made up the Hawaii Chinese population were by no means a homogeneous group with strong personal loyalties to one another. Hakka and Punti, Sam Yup and See Yup, Christian and non-Christian, of this or that clan, of one village or another, from different districts—these and other identities were the bases for subgroups within the Chinese community. Unlike the situation among Chinese on the U.S. mainland, especially in California, the United Chinese Society preceded the evolution of formal organizations based on these varying old-world identities, but development of a sense of affinity with *tung bau* did not replace older and deeper subgroup loyalties.

The first district association was formally organized in 1890, eight years after the beginnings of the United Chinese Society; the first village club came in 1897; the first surname society in 1889. Eventually migrants organized more than forty societies based on these subgroup affiliations, but even then such societies were only a minority of the more than two hundred formal organizations developed by the migrant generation.[1] Associations founded on old-world subgroup loyalties multiplied most rapidly as anti-Chinese agitation in Hawaii was dying down, but this was also the period (1889–1930) when Chinese political organizations appealing to *tung bau* loyalty were most active.[2]

The District Associations

Among the strongest and most important of the migrant organizations were the district associations, most of them established between 1890 and 1907, mainly a sojourner period. Each district association was made up of members who had migrated from or were somehow identified with a specific geographic locality in Kwangtung province. Some of these districts covered only forty or fifty square miles, but from one small area, with a population of more than 100,000, migrants came to Hawaii from at least eighty-three different villages.

Chinese migrants came to Hawaii from just a few districts of Kwangtung province (Table 13). In fact, more than half the contract laborers arriving during the years 1895–1897 came from See Yup— the "Four Districts" of Sun Ning (Toi Shan), Sun Wui, Yen Ping, and Hoi Ping (see Map 1, on endpapers). A little less than one-third came from Chung Shan district, but Chung Shan had been the chief recruiting ground for laborers for more than a generation before this, and it is likely that a large majority of the six thousand Chinese "free immigrants" who arrived in the Islands during the same three years came from Chung Shan. Probably one-tenth of the contract laborers

Table 13
Origin of Chinese Contract Laborers (1895–1897) and Chinese Women (1893–1898) Granted Permits to Land in Hawaii

Area of Origin	Number of Chinese Contract Laborers (1895–1897)	Number of Chinese Women Migrants (1893–1898)
Heung Shan (Chung Shan)	2,269	190
See Yup districts		
Sun Ning (Toi Shan)	2,132	15
Sun Wui	778	10
Yen Ping	607	—
Hoi Ping	414	2
Hok Shan	23	2
Hakka districts		
Sun On (Pao On)	436	54
Kwai Sing	109	19
Tung Kun	90	25
Other Hakka districts	36	3
Other districts	60	16
Unidentified	143	73
Total	7,097	409

Note: Data tabulated under the direction of the writer from records of the Board of Immigration now filed in the Archives of Hawaii. The records for men refer to Chinese brought in under "conditional permits" as contract laborers, mostly for the Haole-controlled sugar plantations. The figures for women refer to permits issued to Chinese women by the Board of Immigration validating their right to land. Not all the women actually arrived in Hawaii.

in these years were Hakkas. The number coming from all other districts of Kwangtung was negligible.

The local origins of the Chinese women immigrants closely approximated the origins of all Chinese migrants in Hawaii—the largest element from Chung Shan, the Hakkas more numerous than the See Yups, with an insignificant remainder of Puntis from other Kwangtung districts, including some in and near the city of Canton.[3] The district associations organized in Hawaii by the Puntis reflect, in their number and nature, this distribution.

Because of the general illiteracy and immobility of Chinese villagers for generations, considerable dialectal and cultural differences existed even between areas as small and close together as these districts. A modern Westerner can scarcely comprehend the social distance between migrants even from neighboring villages, much less between those of different districts. As one migrant stated, the district had been the universe for the ordinary Chinese villager and like most universes it contained conflicting groups—in the Kwangtung districts and villages these were competing clans. However, migrants who would have had little to do with each other at home in China were drawn together in Hawaii by their common local origins. Abroad, old-world rivalries, distrust, and feuds became subordinated to the fellow feeling among those who spoke the same dialect, observed the same local customs and had similar childhood memories.

The first three district associations formally organized in the Islands were for migrants from three of the ten *doo* (subdistricts) of Chung Shan district, and all but three of the other district associations were also organized by migrants from Chung Shan.[4] (See Map 2.) The other three district associations were formed by migrants from See Yup ("The Four Districts"). Because they spoke a different dialect of Cantonese and were culturally different in other ways from the numerically and economically predominant Chung Shan migrants, See Yup migrants tended to be a separate group apart from the main Chinese community. Chung Shan people generally claimed to be closer dialectally and in other ways to the city of Canton, the cultural center of Kwangtung province, than the See Yup people whom they regarded as more rustic than themselves. Heavy migrations of See Yup contract laborers to the sugar plantations between 1895 and 1898 were important in making the See Yup Wei Quan the second largest association in the Islands, at one time claiming three thousand members. Factions led to the formation of the other two associations:

Map 2. Chung Shan District

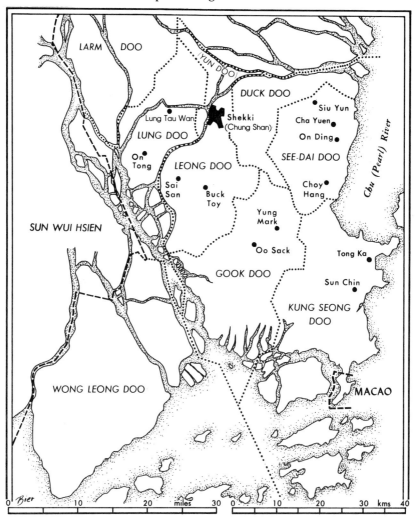

Source: Tin-Yuke Char, *The Sandalwood Mountains* (Honolulu: University Press of Hawaii, 1975), p. 17

Yee Yi Tong open to migrants from all four of the See Yup districts and Kong Chau Wei Quan open only to migrants from Sun Wui. The following list presents the district associations organized in Hawaii. In some cases the year given is only the approximate year of founding:

Honolulu

1890	Chuck Sing Tong (Wong Leong Doo) ("Wong Leong Doo Chuck Sing Tong")
1890	Duck Doo Kee Loo ("Duck Doo Society")
1891	Lung Doo Chung Sin Tong ("Lung Doo Chung Sin Tong Benevolent Society")
1897	See Yup Wei Quan ("See Yup Benevolent Society")
1901	Yee Yi Tong ("Yee Yi Tong")
1901	See Dai Doo Wui Goon ("See Dai Doo Society")
1907	Leong Doo Wui Goon ("Leong Doo Society")
1907	Kong Chau Wei Quan ("Kong Chau Benevolent Society")
1930	Kung Seong Doo Luen Heung Wui ("Kung Seong Doo Society")
1930	Gook Doo Sam Heung Tung Heung Wui ("Gook Doo Sam Heung")
1950	Chung Shan Tung Heung Wui ("Chung Shan Association")

Hilo

1904	Wong Leong Doo Kung So ("Wong Leong Doo Benevolent Society")

Membership in the district associations was open to any migrant whose "native place" was a village in the district. Every association had an admission fee, generally two or three dollars, but no annual dues. Most associations required that migrants returning to China subscribe an additional sum, generally two dollars. Representatives of the association would be at boatside at embarkation time to collect the admission fee if it had never been paid, as well as the departure contribution. Indigent migrants being helped to return to China were exempt from these fees. As an association's expenses increased, especially when a headquarters building was put up, admission fees were sometimes raised and special assessments levied against affluent members. Sometimes admission fees were lowered later and a scale of fees for admission of sons of members was adopted. Wealthy members who made voluntary contributions in addition to the regular fees were formally recognized. The See Dai Doo Wui Goon had this bylaw on special donations:

> Each . . . member who makes an extra donation of $50 or more shall be rewarded with a first-class silver medal, and his portrait shall be hung on the wall of the meeting hall to show him respect; each . . . member who makes an extra donation of $25 or more shall be rewarded with one first-class medal; and each . . . member who makes an extra donation of $10 or more shall be rewarded with a second-class medal; each . . . member who makes an extra donation of $5 shall be rewarded with a third-class medal.

The Lung Doo Chung Sin Tong, the largest association, illustrates the nature and functions of the district associations. In the mid-1930s it had more than 4,250 members—about 15 percent of the Hawaii Chinese population at that time. When this society applied for a charter of incorporation in 1905 the fifty-six petitioners stated that they were "by occupation, merchants."[5] Like most migrant organizations, it was to have a president and vice-president, a Chinese secretary and assistant secretary, an English secretary and assistant secretary, a treasurer and assistant treasurer, two auditors, and a board of directors. The forty-eight board members were all to be appointed by the officers who were to be elected annually. It appears that in this as in most of the other associations the board or executive committee members were mainly *yau ming mong* (a name looked up to: "big names"), prominent members, and large contributors who were given the prestige of the position without being expected to take on routine chores of the organization which were left to the officers. Only twelve of the forty-eight were needed for a quorum in a meeting of the board. Concentration of power in the hands of the officers is indicated by a bylaw providing that "thirty members shall constitute a quorum at any meeting of the Society, where notice is given by posters." Lists of officers submitted annually to the Hawaiian government by this and other district associations commonly showed the same names year after year, sometimes moved from one office to another. Chu Gem, for example, was president of the See Yup Wei Quan from its incorporation in 1897 until his death in 1924.

The Lung Doo association, like many others, began informally when successful merchants and other clansmen of the district were approached for help by migrants from the district who were in distress. In the 1930s the president of this association, who had known several of the founders, gave his version of how it got started:

> The men who started this society were all merchants and were all living in Honolulu at the time. I think about ten or twelve of them got together and decided that the Lung Doo people ought to have their own society. Before they have society, if a man need kokua ("help"), maybe he go to one of the businessmen in Honolulu who is Lung Doo man, ask him to kokua him. Maybe he from the same village in Lung Doo. By and by the men who give all this kokua have meeting of these people. By that time some of them are getting old, they get sick, they don't want to go the hospital, they have all kinds pilikia ("trouble"). Then they start Lung Doo Chung Sin Tong. This society do all kind welfare work. At the first time, they have no building. They have meetings 'round different places—maybe in store of one of the members.[6]

District associations, in the constitutions filed with the government when they applied for charters of incorporation, affirmed that their main or sole object was to be benevolent societies. The Lung Doo constitution stated: "The Lung Doo Chung Sing Tong Benevolent Society is founded for the purpose of aiding, assisting, and supporting disabled, sick, and indigent Chinese." The bylaws of this association were more explicit than those of some other associations in stating its benevolent objectives and how they were to be implemented:

> All persons of Chinese nationality and descent who are not members of the Lung Doo . . . Society, arriving in Honolulu from any part of the Territory of Hawaii other than the Island of Oahu, and who have no shelter or work or means of subsistence, shall, on their arrival at Honolulu, be furnished by the Society with lodging, for a period not exceeding two weeks. . . .
>
> Any member who is ill, and wishes to stay at the Society for treatment, or who desires temporarily to reside on the premises, must first make his intention known to the Secretary. The records must show that such member has paid his initiation fee before he can be allowed to lodge there. . . .
>
> All members of the Lung Doo Benevolent Society in good standing and of good moral character, who are infirm from illness or old age, or indigent or unable to earn their subsistence by labor, shall,

upon application to the Society, be furnished with means to return to their homes in China, and with such further assistance as may be needed, provided the Executive Committee of the Society shall so determine. . . .

If any member shall die within the Territory, the Society will undertake to defray the expense of collecting his remains and ship them back to China.[7]

At first most of the district associations rented buildings in Chinatown for their headquarters, which became known as the societies' *wui goons* ("clubhouses"). After the Chinatown fire of 1900 the larger associations bought land and built clubhouses in the area to the north and northeast of the old Chinatown quarter. Most of these buildings had three stories. The first floor was rented, usually to a member, for business purposes, the rents going toward the upkeep of the entire building. The second floor was equipped as the society's headquarters—a large room, with an altar in the rear, where members could gather for gossip, exchange of news, tea, friendly games, and individual worship at the altar, and where general meetings or meetings of the officers could be held. The third floor had rooms where temporary lodgers could stay, sick members could be cared for, or indigent members could live. Sometimes buildings were also put up behind the headquarters, including a cook house and additional space for lodgers.

A few associations lent surplus funds to members, but most invested these funds in real estate in areas where many Chinese lived, at a time when Honolulu's land values were low. Some built and rented tenements. One of the wealthier associations was reported in 1931 to own property valued in excess of $100,000 and to be collecting between $6,000 and $7,000 annually from rentals. Members of a society were given preference as renters in its tenements; in the beginning such tenements were occupied mainly by Chinese single men and families coming from the same district. Members unable to pay their rent were often allowed to accumulate large debts to the society, many of which were never paid.

Providing rooms at the clubhouse where sick migrants could be cared for appealed particularly, of course, to members without families or relatives in Hawaii to care for them in times of distress. Though the Chinese hospital in Honolulu existed for several years, its general unpopularity was implied by one district association when speaking of the advantage of membership in its own organization:

The main purpose in establishing this Wei Quan is to provide a temporary place of stop-over . . . and as a temporary resting place for those
who are sick.

   In the earlier days there was no Chinese hospital; and although
"under the eyes" [at present] there is one now, individuals find it hard
to come out and go in freely. Here, our Wei Quan functions like a hospital for our fellow villagers; and the conveniences and comforts provided are well known to every friend.[8]

For sick members unable to meet the expenses of their illness, the association would engage a Chinese doctor or herbalist and buy the
prescribed medicines at a Chinese drugstore. There were always men
living at the clubhouse who could prepare medicinal brews, cook
meals, and care for other needs of the sick.

Opium addicts who were becoming physically and financially
helpless and faced dependency upon some public institution commonly found a more tolerant attitude toward their affliction at the
district clubhouse than elsewhere. Here, in a place rarely entered by
non-Chinese or by Chinese from other districts, the addict would feel
secure from molestation by outsiders and at the same time be among
people willing to meet his needs. District associations did not as a
rule use their funds to supply penniless addicts with opium, but individual members sometimes helped them secure the drug.

By the 1930s Hawaii-born Chinese physicians whose fathers or
grandfathers had come from the members' districts were contributing medical services and thus reducing the cost of caring for the sick
in the district association clubhouses. Such services appear to have
been not entirely gratuitous. Some Hawaii-born Chinese physicians,
like other Western-trained professionals, realized that their success
depended considerably upon the confidence and goodwill of the
older generations, at least until the elders were no longer influential
in the Chinese community. Partly for this reason, some Hawaii-born
Chinese physicians and dentists were active in immigrant institutions
such as the district associations and agreed to serve as officers or on
the charity committee, as well as contributing their services to indigent members.

One way the Lung Doo association tried to help migrants "infirm from illness or old age, or indigent or unable to earn their subsistence by labor" was by arranging their return to their native villages
where, it was assumed, they would be cared for by their clans. The
association did not pay all the traveling expenses for such a man but

contributed a certain amount, perhaps ten or twenty-five dollars. Moreover, officials would prepare a document, stamped with the society's seal, giving the man's name, indicating his desire to return to China, designating the amount the society had advanced, and asking members and friends to contribute. The migrant then took the document from member to member, from person to person of his own surname, from store to store, and had donors sign the document and the amount of their donations. Shortly before the man left for China, a notice of thanks would be published in one of the Chinese newspapers with the names of the contributors and the amounts they gave.

By the mid-1920s a growing proportion of indigent migrants were disinclined to return to their native villages in South China. They had been away thirty or forty years or longer; parents, uncles, brothers, in fact most of the relatives they had known before leaving home were dead or were themselves overseas. The aged migrant would return to strangers; a younger generation of relatives might be contemptuous of an elderly, broken-down migrant who had spent a lifetime in the "Sandalwood Mountains" and had returned penniless and dependent. Migrants came to realize that moneyless returned *wah kiu* were not likely to enjoy their last days in a village, even in one where old age had been traditionally respected.

Few migrants, at the time they joined the district associations, would have expected to remain in Hawaii the rest of their lives. Many of the unsuccessful ones, however, postponed their departure time after time as various misfortunes used up the savings with which they had planned to reestablish themselves in the village; others who were improvident had saved nothing for their old age. Some had become eligible for pensions from plantations or other employers; others had personal claims upon Chinese in the Islands who had fared better than they and were more likely to be of help than unknown relatives in the village. Public relief agencies were avoided for a long time by the Chinese, but in the depression of the 1930s hundreds of elderly Chinese applied for old age assistance. It is significant that they preferred even meager public relief to asking the district associations for help in returning to China. Remaining in Hawaii, they were spared the loss of face they would suffer by returning impoverished to their home villages.

Consequently, the district associations were asked in the 1920s and 1930s to provide shelter and subsistence for many of their aged, indigent members. In fact, more needy members remained in Hawaii than most of the associations could or would provide for. Some penniless old members were allowed to build shacks on grounds owned by the associations and then to shift for themselves as best they could. The demands of others were often simply ignored. When the 1937 legislature enacted legislation making Hawaii eligible for federal old age assistance, the increased monthly pensions gave further help to indigent migrants, and several district associations continued to shelter elderly members until the old men died.

Another charitable function referred to in the Lung Doo association's bylaws had to do with sending the remains of any member who died in Hawaii back to his clan and village. The sentiment of wishing to be buried near one's childhood home or with one's relatives is common enough the world over, but the desire of the Chinese migrant to be buried near his native village was more than this. It was intimately connected with the Chinese villager's conception of a person's spiritual life after death. The spirit of each dead person must be cared for and propitiated—not only for the comfort of the spirit but also for the well-being of living descendants. Hence the great desire for a line of male offspring who would assume responsibility for carrying out the proper rites for dead ancestors. The spirits of the dead were believed to return to the place where the bones lay at the times of the festivals for the dead. To die without male heirs was terrible in itself; to be buried in a spot unknown and uncared for by any relatives was to be condemned to an eternity of being a wandering spirit—a much more terrifying thought.[9] It is difficult to exaggerate, therefore, the reassurance the migrant received in joining his district association, knowing that if he died in Hawaii instead of in his village the association could be depended upon to dig up his grave a few years after his death and burial, collect his bones, place them in a container with the correct identification, and transport them to China for delivery to relatives for the proper rites of a final burial.

This purpose of the district associations, at least until the Peoples' Republic of China established control over South China in 1949, probably was carried out more conscientiously and more continuously than any other objective for which the associations were organized. For the poorer members some associations expanded the scope of this service to include partial or complete payment of the burial expenses. A few associations owned sections in the Chinese cemeteries; others provided a free plot in a cemetery for a poor member. Some of the poorer migrants were members in funeral societies organized by undertaking establishments serving the Chinese group. For one who had made no such provision and without relatives to pay the funeral expenses, the association to which the migrant belonged commonly paid for a minimum-priced funeral. By the 1930s, however, some associations were avoiding such expenditures by arranging for a county burial and simply furnishing a plot in a Chinese cemetery.

With increasing concern among Chinese over status and appearances in Hawaii, group participation of association members in funeral rites became an important activity. Particularly when the deceased migrant had had superior status in the Chinese community or in the association, members would march with the mourners in the funeral procession and otherwise assist in the burial rites. One of many notices of thanks appearing in a Chinese newspaper in 1909 concerned this aspect of the district association's activities:

> We wish to thank See Dai Doo Wui Goon, Wing Lock Hong, Kwock On Wui friends for contributions for the medical care of our uncle during his illness. Unfortunately the drugs were inefficacious, and on the tenth of this month he died.
>
> Thanks to See Dai Doo Wui Goon, Wing Lock Hong, Kwock On Wui members, and to relatives and other friends, for contributing funeral expenses.
>
> We also like to express appreciation to the different *wui* friends, uncles and cousins, for directing the funeral affair and for participating in the funeral on the day of the procession.[10]

Punti migrants from districts of Kwangtung other than Chung Shan and See Yup were so few that the only organizations they formed in Honolulu were two cemetery associations already described—one for Hoklo people from districts around the port city of Swatow and the Tung Sin Tong by Chinese from districts around the city of Canton.[11] Chinese from over twelve districts belonged to the latter *tong*, which had about two hundred members in the mid-1930s. As well as participating in funerals for deceased members at their cemetery in Pauoa Valley, members were invited to take part in ceremonies and a feast at the cemetery grounds during Ching Ming (April) and on the fourteenth day of the seventh month and the fifteenth day of the ninth month. At some of these occasions the births of sons to society members were recognized.[12]

The district associations provided their members another form of mutual aid through religious services. Apart from the deities and spirits he associated with home and clan, the Chinese villager generally believed that every district had a "place god"—a deity who was particularly concerned with the district's *fung shui,* good or bad fortune. When the earlier district associations built clubhouses, the place god of the association's home district was given a position of great honor among the images of other deities on the altar in the meeting room. Thus installed in the heart of the immigrant colony overseas, the deity was expected to look after the fortunes of the Chinese of the district who were temporarily on foreign soil in the midst of alien gods. Oil lamps were kept burning before the altar and incense sticks were placed there morning and evening by the caretaker. Migrants could come to the altar of their district association whenever they pleased; anniversaries of the gods were celebrated and other religious occasions observed. Chinese immigrants, it is true, like most immigrants usually found little time for their gods, and the longer they were away from their home district the less they seemed concerned about the gods they had left behind. In the clubhouses of the 1930s, with the altars rarely visited and the images barely lighted enough by small oil lamps to reveal the accumulated dust, the gods appeared to be almost forgotten.

Various other benevolent services were undertaken by the district associations as occasions arose. They tried to help relatives in China and elsewhere locate migrants who had not been heard from for years, or find out if they had died and under what circumstances. The estate of a migrant from the district who had died in Hawaii but had no relatives in the Islands was sometimes turned over to the district association with the understanding that the association would serve as administrator and deliver whatever balance remained, after debts and other expenses were paid, to the man's nearest relatives in China.

Though their ostensible purpose was to provide benevolent services, district associations controlled migrants from their districts in China in some ways that could hardly be called benevolent. Leaders of these associations during the 1890s and early 1900s included employers of large numbers of migrants, especially in the rice industry; some were labor recruiters and labor contractors. "Free" migrants (that is, men who had not been recruited on contracts to the sugar plantations) were met at the boat on arrival and housed temporarily by an association. Members of the association could then employ the newly arrived migrants in one of their enterprises on terms the immigrants would feel obliged to accept. Many new arrivals actually were already indebted to *heung li* who were members of the association and who had advanced money for their passage.

The government unwittingly strengthened the district associations' control over their members when, in 1887, it arranged to issue passports and return permits only to migrants who had obtained a "Chinese Benevolent Society's ticket." Since leaders of the district associations were also leaders in the United Chinese Society which issued these tickets, district association officers could be alerted when *heung li* from their district were about to leave the Islands. This made it possible to bring more pressure on the departing migrant to pay any debts he might have to association members and other Chinese than a creditor alone could exert—the migrant might not get his ticket until the Society was satisfied he had repaid as much as he could.

A more openly acknowledged role of the older and stronger associations was that of arbitrator of disputes between members. The scope of disputes accepted by a society for arbitration and the machinery and regulations by which it was to be carried out are set forth in the bylaws of the Lung Doo association:

> Natives of LOONG DOO DISTRICT, HEONG SAN, who have come to the Territory of Hawaii for any lawful purpose, whether resident in the City of Honolulu, or in any part of the Islands, shall treat each other fairly, and in their transactions with each other, shall deal honestly and justly; they . . . shall peacefully carry on their various pursuits; they shall endeavor to avoid any conversation which may cause trouble; if any trouble occur through the conversation of any member, the Society shall not uphold such member in his wrong doing.
>
> Any members whose actions may cause others to attack him, without fault on his part, may lay his grievance before the Society. . . . Where complaint is made, the Society shall decide, according to the evidence, as to the best course to be pursued under the circumstances, but is not bound to pursue any specific course. . . .
>
> Whenever any member having a controversy with a fellow-member has made complaint to the Society, he must abide by the decision of the Society as to such controversy.
>
> Should any member not abide by the decision of the Society as to his controversy, the Society shall nevertheless do its utmost to reconcile the differences of which complaint has been made. . . .

Most disputes brought to the association were economic, and successful arbitration depended largely on the prestige and power of those chosen as arbitrators. The disputants' willingness to accept the arbitrators' decision was influenced by the arbitrators' clan and ancestral village connections as well as by their status in Chinatown. The number of disputes handled by the associations steadily diminished, however, and arbitration had little part in the activities of district organizations established after 1920. In 1931 the president of the Lung Doo association described arbitration in his society:

> Many years ago, the society used to settle lots of disputes—plenty of them, but now not many. Now the people go to the courts. But last year we had some members in pilikia who came to the society to complain. Most of the time they come because some member doesn't want to pay what he owes to the other member. This year already we had one case. A man was having trouble with his wife; they came to the society and we told them what to do. I think now they take it to court.
>
> When a Lung Doo man has pilikia with another Lung Doo man over a little thing, he brings it to the society. He doesn't want to take it to the courts. If you go to the court, you have to pay for a lawyer, and it costs you lots of money—maybe more than the man owes you. The society does this for nothing. . . .
>
> When a man comes to our society with his pilikia, the notice is sent out to all the officers and the committee and they are all supposed to come. Most of them look at the notice and say, "It's just a little thing, I don't want to go." Only a few will come—more than two or three, but not many. Whoever comes, helps to decide what ought to be done.[13]

The associations' bylaws usually stated specifically that migrants from their district should be law-abiding and that the society would not handle the cases of law violators. It might even expel such members if the violations were serious. The Lung Doo association's bylaws on this point stated:

> Natives of Loong Doo District . . . shall observe the laws of the Territory of Hawaii and of the United States of America. . . . No member shall have the right to lay before the Society any grievance arising from the keeping of houses of prostitution, or from gambling, or from any breach of the law.
>
> . . . Any member guilty of a serious violation of the laws of the Territory of Hawaii, or of other grossly immoral or dishonest conduct may be expelled from the Society by a 3/4 vote of the Executive Com-

mittee, but only upon notice to such member, and after he has been given ample time and opportunity to be heard in his own exculpation.[14]

Village Clubs and Lineage-Village Clubs

In 1935 a Hawaii-born Chinese, talking about the way migrants identified themselves, said: "When there were only a few Chinese, a man would say with pride that he came from such and such a district—say Heung Shan, perhaps the district in which people spoke his dialect; when more Chinese came from that area, he began to speak about coming from such and such a *doo*, such as Lung Doo; then after many more migrants from that district came to Hawaii he would answer the question 'Where are you from?' by saying he was from such and such a village, such as Lung Tau Wan or On Tong."

Migrants from Chung Shan were numerous enough to organize and support several village clubs as well as seven district associations. In contrast, the less numerous migrants from See Yup organized only the three district associations and no village clubs. In the mid-1930s, when the Lung Doo association listed over four thousand persons on its membership rolls, the members came from families in eighty-three villages. One village was represented by 445 persons, five villages by 200 to 299, nine villages by 100 to 199, and nine villages by 50 to 99. In this same period the See Dai Doo Society had almost 1,200 members who came from forty-nine villages: eight of the villages had 50 or more members each—one village had 111. There undoubtedly were other migrants from these villages who had not joined their district's association. Buck Toy village, for example, was said to have about 350 emigrants in Hawaii at that time, but only 125 of them were on the district society's membership list.[15]

Typically, village clubs evolved from the gatherings of *heung li* at Chinatown stores. Stores remained the main social centers for migrants from most villages, but nearly a score of village clubs were formally organized and three of them—the Buck Toy Villagers' Club, the Oo Sack Kee Loo Society, and the On Tong Villagers' Club—had clubhouses in Honolulu. All of the following clubs except one —Poo Get Tung Heung Wui—were formed by Chung Shan villagers (in some cases dates of formal organization are only approximate):

Village Clubs

1897	Oo Sack Kee Loo (Gook Doo) ("Oo Sack Kee Loo Society")
1898	Buck Toy Tung Heung Wui (Leong Doo) ("Buck Toy Villagers' Club")
1890s	Yung Mark Kee Loo (Gook Doo) ("Yung Mark Society")
1921	Siu Yun Quon Chark Say (See Doo) ("Siu Yun Villagers' Club")
1926	Lung Tau Wan Tung Heung Wui (Lung Doo) ("Lung Tau Wan Villagers' Club")
1930	Poo Get Tung Heung Wui (Pao On district) ("Poo Get Pao On Association") (Hakkas)
1940s	Lung Tong Tung Heung Wui (Lung Doo) ("Lung Tong Villagers' Club")
1950	Choy Hung Tung Heung Wui (Dai Doo) ("Choy Hung Village Club")
1950s	Kong Tow Tung Heung Wui (Lung Doo) ("Kong Tow Society")
1950s	Chung Tau Village Club (Lung Doo)

Lineage-Village Clubs

1926	Lum: On Tong Tung Heung Wui (Lung Doo) ("On Tong Villagers' Club")
1927	Chun: Cha Yuen Wai Bok Say (See Dai Doo) ("Cha Yuen Villagers' Club") (Also includes Chuns from Poo Shan and Sing Tong villages)
1931	Ching: On Kai Say (On Ding village, Dai Doo) ("On Kai Society")
1931	Mau: Mau Shee Tung Heung Wui (Kung Seong Doo) ("Mau Club of Hawaii") (Hakkas)
1940s	Pang: Ling How Hing Pang Tung Heung Wui (Lung Doo) ("Ling How Pang Society") (Pangs from Ling How Hing village)
1940s	Young: Sun Ming Ting Tung Heung Wui (Lung Doo) ("Sun Ming Ting Association") (Youngs from Sun Ming Ting village)
1954	Au: Cho Pu Tow (village) (See Dai Doo) ("Au Clan")

Each of the seven organizations listed as lineage-village clubs was made up of persons who had come from a village where all the residents, except perhaps the storekeepers and a few other "outsiders," had the same surname. In some villages the residents belonged to a set of genealogically interrelated lineages best denoted by the term clan. Some of the clubs included members of the same clan who came from neighboring villages. One important reason for the organization of village associations, especially those of the lineage-village type, was the distrust between migrants from different parts of Kwangtung, even from different villages within the same *doo*, and the carryover into Hawaii of rivalries between different clans. Antagonisms between clans of the same or neighboring villages were endless, notorious, and often devastating. Strong clans took advantage of weak clans; villagers from other parts of the trade area surrounding a market town were wary of one another. One migrant gave as his reason for coming to Hawaii the ruin of his formerly wealthy clan because of a feud with another clan in his village. As late as the 1930s an informant attributed the recurrent factionalism and discord within the district associations to clan rivalry.

Village clubs had some of the same functions as the district associations—among them, mutual aid and settlement of disputes—but carried out much more informally. Village clubs did not usually stipulate in their bylaws the kinds of assistance they would give members or under what conditions; members were helped according to needs as they arose. Financial matters were also handled more personally. Whereas the district associations usually forbade loaning their funds to members, specifying that surplus funds were to be deposited in banks or invested in real estate, village clubs would often circulate surplus funds among members as loans. At first club members were not usually required to sign notes for such funds or give any form of surety for repayment; members were expected to meet their obligations without such formalities—and in the earlier years they usually did.

Similarly, settlement of disputes by formal arbitration would have been incongruous in an organization made up of people with close personal ties both in the home villages and in Hawaii. When there was trouble between *heung li* they took the problem to respected leaders of the village club for solution rather than to officers of the district association. Not only would they have more confidence in people from their own village but other *heung li* would press them to settle squabbles within the village club rather than let them be talked about in Chinatown. This concern about avoiding gossip, not only in Chinatown but also back in the village, made it easier for club leaders to persuade the quarreling parties to accept a solution. Nevertheless, a club composed of members from several clans could have trouble in getting consensus:

> It must be hard for one who is not a Chinese to realize how strong the family ties are. This is the reason, I think, why the ——— Villagers' Club was never very strong. There are twenty-one clans represented. The ———s and the ———s are the strongest; families always stick together, which means that the club never had very much solidarity itself. The different families couldn't get together.[16]

An informant provided another clue to the reasons for discord within village clubs. He said that the strongest family in the club in which he was a member was more successful than other families in getting loans from club funds.

The Hakka Association

For over fifty years the distinction between Hakkas and Puntis was the most keenly felt division within the Hawaii Chinese population. "Hak-ka" is a combination of two Chinese characters which mean "people who are guests"—in this context, "outsiders." Among Puntis the term had many derogatory connotations signifying a despised, low-status, aggressive group. Among Hakkas in turn Punti was often used in a pejorative way as indicating oppressive people with a superiority complex and unclean personal habits. "Pun-ti" literally means "the root of the ground" and designated the "natives"—the original (more accurately, earlier) Chinese settlers in Kwangtung as distinct from the Hakkas who began migrating into Kwangtung in about the thirteenth century. In Hawaii Punti was generally an in-group term referring to any Chinese originating in Kwangtung who was not a Hakka.[17] While there were dialectal variations among the Cantonese-speaking Puntis, Hakkas belonged to a quite different speech group, speaking a form of Chinese nearer the Mandarin spoken in northern and central China and completely unintelligible to the Puntis. Since Hakkas were latecomers to Kwangtung and of lower status in the districts from which most Puntis came to Hawaii, they had to learn enough Cantonese to communicate with Puntis, few of whom made any effort to learn the Hakka language.

Migrants brought to Hawaii attitudes that had developed during generations of rivalry, economic struggle, persecution, and periodic warfare between Hakkas and Puntis. Though there is no record of open, violent conflict between Hakka and Punti migrants in the Islands, there were tensions from time to time. When the Hawaiian government in 1881 introduced a new immigration policy that gave the Puntis, perhaps unwittingly, a monopoly of labor agent licenses, Hakka merchants and labor recruiters stated in a complaint:

> There are now in this Kingdom about four or five thousand of the members of the said Ha Ka clan whose language, manners, customs, prejudices and feelings are wholly distinct from those of the Pun Ti, and other clans, and that from time immemorial, irreconcilable differences have existed between them. . . . Owing to the said differences, it is quite impossible for members of this clan to have business dealings with members of the other clans in regard to the shipping of contract laborers, without engendering suspicions which cause long continued discontent and ill feelings.[18]

One might have expected that since Hakkas made up over a fifth of the migrant population they would have formed their own association when the district associations were being developed by Punti migrants, but there was no general Hakka society until 1921. There were several reasons for this. In the first place, Hakkas did not come from only a few districts as most of the Puntis did, and there was no large number from a single district. They came from at least twenty-one districts in Kwangtung, from the extreme northeastern section of the province to districts south of Canton.[19] A few migrated from Chung Shan and See Yup districts where they lived in generally poor Hakka villages near the villages from which Puntis migrated to Hawaii. In the second place, Hakka migrants did not concentrate in Honolulu as heavily and rapidly as the Puntis. Even though the rural Hakka colonies eventually were depleted by movement to Honolulu, this took a long time. For many decades there were not enough wealthy, influential Hakkas in Honolulu to provide the initiative and leadership needed to organize an Island-wide Hakka association.

Even more important, perhaps, was the fact that Hakkas became acculturated to Western beliefs and practices more rapidly than the

Puntis and began to give up Chinese ways earlier. Christian missions were markedly more successful among the Hakkas than among the Puntis. The movement toward Christianity is at once an index of acculturation and a means through which it took place. From the 1880s to the 1910s, when Puntis were organizing so many migrant associations, a larger proportion of Hakkas than of Puntis were becoming Christians and helping to organize Chinese Christian churches and the Chinese YMCA. Proportionately the Hakkas were more active than the Puntis in groups that were oriented toward fitting into the multiethnic community structure, such as the American Chinese Federation and the Chinese-English Debating Society.

A movement—mostly by Hawaii-born Hakkas—to establish a Hakka association finally got under way after 1910, but the response among the Hakkas was not very encouraging. Although as many as five or six thousand Hakkas may have been in the Islands at the time, several years went by before as many as nine hundred agreed to join.[20] The organization was called the Nyin Fo Fui Kon ("People Peace Association") after an all-Hakka organization of the same name established several decades earlier in San Francisco. It was formally launched in June 1921. The objectives set forth in its constitution indicate an orientation quite different from that of the more inward-looking district associations:

> A. To promote closer unity and sympathy and to exchange knowledge among the Chinese in Hawaii in general and the Hakka people of the Chinese race in particular, and to cooperate with all the Hakka organizations throughout the world.
> B. To encourage and promote education, charity, and benevolence.
> C. To aid and succor all members of this Society against poverty, injustice, and oppression.

Through the 1920s the organization continued to have trouble enlisting support for a program of activities. Years passed without prospect of raising enough money to build a clubhouse. In 1931 a new set of leaders petitioned for a charter of incorporation as a preliminary step to putting up a building. Another six years went by before the association opened headquarters—not in a clubhouse but on the second floor of a building in the center of Chinatown. In that year, 1937, the organization also changed its name to Tsung Tsin Association "to correspond with [Hakka] associations in other cities throughout the world which are devoted to the welfare of the Hakka people."[21]

Surname Societies

As is generally known, Chinese social structure is unusual in that China, with hundreds of millions of inhabitants, has fewer than 450 surnames.[22] There were only fifty different surnames among the 4,254 Chinese on the membership list of the Lung Doo association in the mid-1930s. Just ten of these surnames—Lee (582), Lau (455), Young (428), Lum (306), Chong (278), Pang (273), Siu (245), Chun (188), Wong (175), and Yee (163)—accounted for more than 3,000 of the 4,254.

According to ancestral cult tradition, persons of the same surname, whether or not common lineage could be traced genealogically, were bound together by reverence for the common ancestor believed to be the founder of the surname and also by worship of a patron deity.[23] Because of such folk beliefs, migrants in Hawaii found themselves mystically connected to people of the same surname from different districts, speaking different dialects, with whom they would have had no contact before leaving the home village. For most sojourner migrants of a given surname the mystical bond of a common ancestor from centuries, even millennia, earlier was too tenuous a connection to serve as a basis for organization in Hawaii. Their various backgrounds, diverse origins, and cultural differences, however minor, hindered the development of cohesion and loyalty among them. Common district and village origins were much stronger bonds.[24] Although several surnames were shared by large numbers of migrants in Hawaii, only three surname societies were established by the *wah kiu* before 1920: the Lum Sai Ho Tong in 1889, the Wong Kong Har Tong in 1902, and the Lung Kong Kung Shaw in 1919. Several others were organized after 1935, mostly initiated by Hawaii-born Chinese.[25]

The Lum Sai Ho Tong was established by and for migrants with the surname Lum (Lam, Lim, Lin). In 1932 this group reported members from sixty-four villages in Kwangtung; thirty-three of these villages were in Chung Shan, twenty-nine in the See Yup districts, and two in the Sam Yup districts. The Wong Kong Har Tong for migrants with the surname of Wong (Huang) claimed about 1,200 members in 1930, a year in which the Chinese population in Hawaii was about 27,000. The Lung Kong Kung Shaw, commonly called the Four Brothers' Association or the Society of the Four Families, was open to persons of four surnames: Chong, Chu (Chiu, Chew), Lau, and Quon (Kwon).[26] Despite the diversity in their memberships, these early surname societies attempted to foster harmonious relations and mutual aid among their members, as indicated in the by-laws of the Lung Kong Kung Shaw:

> The objects of this association are to establish and promote peace and love among the members thereof, to continue the good principles inculcated by the forefathers of the members, to encourage the coming generations to practice the virtues and good principles of our ancestors, to give aid and assistance to the needy and infirm members of the society and the widows and children of deceased members, and generally to promote the welfare of the community. . . .
>
> The Motto of this Society shall be Righteousness and Peace. If any member of this society shall intentionally violate any of the rules, regulations, or bylaws of this Society, he shall automatically cease to be a member.

In many respects these surname societies tried to carry out the same functions as the district associations. All three, through admission fees and special donations, collected enough money to build clubhouses which were gathering places for members during leisure hours and also offered them temporary lodging. They bought other property and buildings which were rented to members, bringing income to the society. They tried to help their sick, needy, indigent, and aged members. When an aged, impoverished member wanted to return to China, his society would issue a document certifying his intention and asking members to contribute individually for this purpose. The societies contributed toward the burial of indigent members; funerals of prominent members would be attended by representatives of the society. There were annual banquets when officers were installed. An altar in the headquarters honored the "first ancestor" and the patron dcity of the surname group, and annual ceremonies were sometimes combined with a feast. Members performed religious and ancestral rites during the periods of the "feasts for the dead," particularly Ching Ming. During the Feast of Lanterns, about two weeks after Chinese New Year, lanterns hung before the altar announced the birth of male children during the previous year and a feast celebrated the occasion. Members sometimes performed pri-

vate rituals before the altar, such as a father's presentation of a recently born child to the ancestors.

The three early surname societies were formed during a period
when arbitrating disputes among members was still an important
function of migrant organizations. In each surname society officers
were likely to come from different districts for which there were also
district associations, and the surname society could arbitrate disputes
between members of the same surname but from different districts.
In the late 1920s and early 1930s officers in each of the three groups
came from all seven *doos* of Chung Shan for which there were also
district associations in Honolulu. Although the surname societies ar-
bitrated disputes between members who came from different *doos* of
Chung Shan, the rosters of officers available for arbitration were
such that disputes between Puntis from Chung Shan and See Yup, or
between Puntis and Hakkas, were not likely to be handled. Two officers of the Lum Sai Ho Tong in the period mentioned did come
from Sun Wui (a See Yup district), but none appeared to be of Hakka
identity. All the officers of the Wong Kong Har Tong were Puntis
from one or another *doo* of Chung Shan. In the 1930s an informant
named Wong said that while some Hakkas might have become
members of the Wong Kong Har Tong, they would not have participated actively or had much opportunity to become officers. Most officers of the Lung Kong Kung Shaw were also from Chung Shan,
though a few were from Toi Shan—a See Yup district—and two
(both with the surname Lau) were Hakkas.

The Guilds

Unlike the district associations, village clubs, and surname societies,
the *hongs* ("guilds") formed in Hawaii by Chinese craftsmen, traders,
and workers had other bases than old-world identities. True enough,
a few migrants had been members of guilds in such cities as Macao,
Canton, and Hong Kong, and in urban centers of Chung Shan and
See Yup like Shekki, Sun Wui, and Toi Shan, and they took the lead
in organizing similar guilds in Honolulu.[27] It is unlikely, however,
that many of the migrants who joined in Honolulu had been guild
members in China. In Honolulu, the guilds developed to meet the
needs of Chinese who were competing for jobs and trade in circumstances where they were sometimes at a disadvantage with members
of other ethnic groups. From 1890 to 1930 eleven guilds were orga-

nized, all but three of them by 1904 (year of founding is in some cases approximate):

1890	Wah Hing Tong (laundrymen)
1901	Quon On Kwock (cooks and waiters in hotels and restaurants)
1903	Hoy On Tong (employees on interisland boats)
1903	Seong Gar Hong (carpenters)
1903	Job Yee Tong (painters and varnishers)
1903	Wing Lock Ngue Hong (fish dealers)
1904	Bark Yee Hong (dressmakers, makers of white uniforms)
1904	Kum Yee Hong (tailors)
1922	Kutt Hing Kung Soh (actors, musicians)
1924	Luen Hing Kee Lock Bo (cooks, servants, especially in Haole homes)
1928	Ngow Yuk Hong (beef and pork dealers, butchers)

The *hongs* were more like European craft guilds than like nineteenth- or twentieth-century trade unions. For one thing, employers as well as employees were members in most of them. In some of them employers were the most influential members because they were most likely to be knowledgeable about conditions in the community at large and could therefore be the *hongs'* spokesmen. The *hongs* were not collective bargaining organizations, but they were concerned with securing favorable competitive conditions for their members. Such guilds as the Seong Gar Hong and Job Yee Tong tried to regulate, as far as possible, the conditions under which Chinese craftsmen competed with Caucasians in the same trades. Chinese depended upon their willingness to accept lower pay in order to get work, but the *hongs*, by controlling the number of Chinese entering an occupation and by regulating competition among Chinese, attempted to maintain a balance by which the Chinese would all have work while receiving an income as close as possible to that demanded by Caucasian competitors with a higher standard of living.

Most of the *hongs* served as employment agencies—acting as intermediaries between Chinese employers and workers and at the same time regulating the conditions of employment. The Kum Yee Hong had explicit bylaws stating the methods by which it imposed its controls on employers and employees. Chinese proprietors of tailoring firms were permitted to join the guild but without voting rights:

> Any employer who wants to employ a tailor must first report to the committeeman on employment. The latter will find a member for him and upon trial if that member does not suit him, say by the end of the first week, is not satisfactory to the employer, the same committeeman will try to find another member for him. And in case the employer does not want to use any of our members and does employ one or more who are not members of our Society, a meeting will then be called for the purpose of taking such steps as will tend to enforce him to employ our members.
>
> Twenty per centum of the total amount received by each member for wages received for working over time or extra work will go to the Treasury of the Society; and such amount as it may be, large or small, shall be paid in to the Treasury at the first regular meeting; those violating this Article without showing any proper cause shall be fined $2 for the first offense, $4 for the second offense and shall no longer be regarded members if it occur the third time. Any member who knows of another member's failure to live up to this article, and does not report the same punctually to the committee, shall, if found out, be fined 50¢.

Hongs were often effective, at least for some time, in maintaining Chinese control of certain occupations. The Hoy On Tong, for several years, virtually monopolized the jobs of stewards, cooks, and waiters on interisland ships owned by Caucasian-controlled corporations. The shipping companies learned that it was wise to have the Chinese stewards select new Chinese employees for the ships. Less successfully the Luen Hing Kee Lock Bo tried to protect Chinese employees against competition for positions in household employment when other groups, especially the Japanese, began increasing their numbers in that field. Perhaps most successful in that respect was the Wing Lock Ngue Hong, which included fish dealers, workers, and apprentices. Organized in 1903 after Japanese fishermen had largely replaced Chinese in supplying the Honolulu market, the guild was formed by Chinese fish dealers to maintain their control of sales in the fish markets. Members of the guild, who retained major control through the 1930s and 1940s, not only limited the entrance of Japanese into this area but also restricted Chinese participants largely to those who, like themselves, were of Lung Doo origin.

Hongs dealt with disputes among members and also attempted to help members who were being treated unjustly by outsiders. The bylaws of one guild stated that "whenever any member meets with adverse circumstances and is oppressed, he shall report the matter to the secretary, who shall call a meeting of the members to find out the truth of the matter, and if it is necessary to employ counsel to defend said matter, the expense shall be subscribed for by the members. . . . The Society must see to it that justice is done to said member." A notice in a Chinese newspaper in 1909 reveals the indignation in a guild when members did not deal with their grievances within the organization:

> Attention: Since the establishment of this *Hong*, it has been our policy to settle all questions arising from public business or pertaining to rules through discussion at meetings. This procedure each member has peacefully followed in the past. However, yesterday there appeared notices in the *Chee Yow Sun Bo* and the *Sun Chung Kwock Bo* by Lee ———, Pang ———, Yee———, and Pang ———, four people saying that they are withdrawing from this *Hong*. Their words bewildered us, for when did those four people notify this *Hong* that they were going to withdraw, and when did they turn their duties over to others? Since they voluntarily joined this *Hong*, they ought to join in a good manner and quit in a good manner. . . . This *Hong* has never forcibly used restraint, so why write public withdrawal notices that are inconsistent with their actions? This matter is an injustice to this organization, and for that reason we specifically desire to inform the public.[28]

Apart from their primary activities of promoting the occupational and economic interests of their members, the *hongs* undertook many of the same benevolent, mutual aid, and social functions as other Chinese organizations. Usually they had headquarters where familyless members could pass the time when they were not working. Some had rooms where members could live and the sick could be cared for. They provided for the needy, the aged, and the burial of deceased members. At one time or another, for example, the Quon On Kwock, besides serving as an employment agency and arbitrator, carried out several other activities. It rented the lower floor of its headquarters building to a member for his business; it rented rooms on the upper stories to single men and families; it converted one part of the building into a hospital ward for members.

Members of the Quon On Kwock could hold their weddings in the main room, and newly wedded couples were allowed to live in the building for three months without rent. Wedding gifts of at least two dollars, five hundred firecrackers, and "a pair of hangings with antithetical sentences written thereon" were given to each member who married. Upon the birth of his first male child after joining the society, a member received a congratulatory gift of two dollars. A member returning to China was given the thirty dollars he had been assessed (at a dollar a month) for this purpose, and each member of the *hong* was assessed fifty cents as a gift for the departing member. If a member was refused reentry by immigration authorities after a trip to China, he was to be given a purse made up by contributions of at least fifty cents by each member "to show that the Society did its best for him." A member received a gift of at least two dollars from the *hong* upon reaching his fifty-first birthday and gifts on each subsequent tenth birthday. When a member died in Honolulu, surviving members were each required to contribute fifty cents toward the funeral expenses and all who were able were expected to participate in the funeral procession or pay a fine of one dollar. The society could furnish "two carriages for the officers on the occasion of the funeral of the deceased," but the other members were expected to pay for hiring their own carriages. (When most of these bylaws were written —1903 to 1905—wages of migrants in trades were only about a dollar a day.)

Just as the district association had an altar honoring its place god, and the surname *tong* had its first ancestor and patron deity, the *hong* generally had an altar at which the legendary founder of the occupation and its patron deity were venerated. Most members, however, were probably not much interested in this aspect of the guild. An elderly migrant who had been a member of his guild for nearly thirty years and one of its main officers for several years expressed an apparently common attitude: "Hoy On Tong has certain days when they have worship. One of the members has charge of that. On those certain days he takes care of the worship. Any of the members can go if they want to. I never went on those times. I don't even know what the days are."[29]

Most of the *hongs* had shorter lives than the district or village associations. Many members withdrew as they moved into other occupations, and attrition occurred through return to China and by death. By 1930 four of the guilds—those for laundrymen, cooks in private homes, dressmakers, and tailors—no longer existed. The most recent list of Chinese organizations issued by the United Chinese Society includes only two guilds: the Seong Gar Hong and the Kutt Hing Kung Soh. The former, made up of carpenters, had bought property in its early days and put up buildings from which it secured rental income. By 1927 it had formed a subsidiary realty company, probably because of problems concerning the guild's tax status as a benevolent society. Income from rentals and the increased value of its property have provided incentive for continuing the guild even though the days of migrant carpenters have long since gone.

The Evolving Community

After the early 1880s, when the United Chinese Society was one of the few migrant organizations in Honolulu, the increasing number of groups based on old-world attachments or new-world interests changed the character of the Chinese community. In fact, they may be said to have *created* the community as a complex of differentiated but interlocking groups.[30] Chinatown in the early years really had no unified community spirit except when faced with external hostility. Among themselves migrants were typically factious, exploitive, and suspicious of one another. The United Chinese Society was a step toward the evolution of community consciousness among the *wah kiu* in Honolulu, but it was only in times of crisis that it enlisted the active support of any large number of Chinese residents in its early years. The less inclusive organizations, often based on in-group sentiments and out-group antipathies, had more homogeneous memberships than the United Chinese Society and therefore developed more personal ties and greater unity among the members. At the same time, since these organizations had overlapping memberships and some of their officers were commonly leaders in the United Chinese Society, they helped to integrate the Chinese population in the emerging complex community.

The relationship between differentiation and integration is illustrated by the ways disputes were settled within the Chinese community. Because the migrants, even many of the early Island-born Chinese, were reluctant to enter suits in the government courts, the United Chinese Society from its very beginning undertook the role of arbitrator. President Alee, in his address at the opening of the Society's headquarters in 1886, said that one of the Society's objectives was "to prevent and settle disputes among Chinese if possible."[31] The Chinese minister to Washington, in a report to the Chinese government in 1898, mentioned this as one of the chief functions of the Society.[32]

Cases brought to the Society stemmed most commonly from

migrants' refusal to pay debts or going into bankruptcy to avoid payment, going back on promises in business deals, and trying to take unfair advantage of Chinese competitors. Unlike village quarrels, which were usually within or between kinship groups, most of the migrants' disputes were between individuals and Chinese partnerships. Many an overseas migrant dealt with other Chinese, sometimes even with members of his own clan, in ways he would never have attempted at home. Opportunism was less restrained in Hawaii because so many of the Chinese with whom the migrant came in contact were individuals to whom he had no traditional obligations and whose opinion meant nothing to him. The United Chinese Society and other immigrant associations therefore sought to impose limits on opportunism.

The leaders in the United Chinese Society who acted as arbiters in disputes were not clan elders or legally trained judges, but they included the wealthiest and most prominent immigrant businessmen in Chinatown. Though they had no legal authority, they could use their influence among the migrants to secure agreement to their decisions. Furthermore, while a migrant might be willing to take advantage of fellow migrants who had no control over him, he also was in a position to be exploited, so it was in his interest to accept the Society's judgment even if it might be against him.

After district, village, surname, and guild associations were organized they took over much of the arbitration that the United Chinese Society had handled, but not all of it. Disputants belonging to the same society generally preferred to settle their differences through the leaders of their society, but these organizations were less successful in arbitrating controversies between their members and members of other societies. Such cases could be taken to the United Chinese Society as the organization of broadest representation in the Chinese community.[33] One former executive secretary put it this way:

> The reason for the United Chinese Society is that it . . . is for all the Chinese. No matter whether you pay money to become a member or not—if you have trouble and you want to make a complaint, you come to the Society. This Society is not for just certain Chinese. If you are Chinese man, no matter where you come from, or what dialect you speak, or what political party you belong to, or what your surname is, you can bring complaints to the Society.[34]

A similar relationship between the United Chinese Society and other Chinatown organizations existed in benevolent activities. The less inclusive groups which gave various forms of help to their members relieved the United Chinese Society of much of the responsibility of caring for individual migrants. At the same time, the United Chinese Society coordinated and in other ways aided the benevolent work of the different organizations. Thus the United Chinese Society, representing the Chinese community as a whole, succeeded during the depression of the 1930s in securing a 25 percent reduction in steamship fares for aged Chinese who were being helped to return to China by various societies. The Society also persuaded the territorial government to waive payment of delinquent poll taxes by these old men. When the Palolo Chinese Home was proposed, the United Chinese Society cooperated with various Chinese organizations in getting it established.

The interlocking leadership of the Society and the other organizations is another indication of differentiation and integration in Chinatown. From the first, the leaders of the Society represented the diverse origins of the migrant Chinese population. The first president was a Chung Shan Punti; the first vice-president was a Christian Hakka whose ancestral home was in northeastern Kwangtung; another long-time president was a See Yup Punti from Toi Shan. The sixteen leaders (officers, trustees, and executive secretary) in 1930 included eight Chung Shan Puntis, three See Yup Puntis, one Punti from Shun Tak district, and four Hakkas. They came from twelve different surname groups. All except two had their main businesses in Chinatown. Generally, leaders of the United Chinese Society have also been leaders in other influential Chinatown organizations. When issues concerned only one segment of the Chinese community, officers of the United Chinese Society who were identified with that segment took the lead; when the whole community was concerned, they worked with the other officers of the United Chinese Society.

A New Moral Order

As migrant organizations proliferated, the *wah kiu* were transformed from displaced individuals in an alien world into persons with roles, obligations, and interests in the developing Chinese community of Honolulu. The societies based on old-world identifications were particularly effective among the sojourner migrants because they provided a transition from the clan and village world to the new-world community. While they did not replicate the family, clan, and village world in which the migrants had grown up, they did serve some of the same functions by providing personal relationships and meeting needs in times of crisis. Migrants who might never have considered associating with anyone outside their own clan became members because of the social and physical security the societies offered.

At the same time, the societies brought the migrant into a moral order something like that from which he had come—where the individual undertook responsibilities, recognized obligations, and asserted claims because of group expectations rather than because of legal coercion. Once a member of a group, he was drawn into helping other members. He came to pay initiation fees, contribute to various causes, and participate in the group's activities whether or not he was personally inclined to do so. As a member, moreover, the migrant was likely to become concerned about how the Chinese community at large regarded his behavior. He thus became part of the new moral order emerging in Chinatown.

CHAPTER 12

From Familism to Nationalism

IN common with many other immigrant groups from peasant backgrounds, the Chinese migrants had little national consciousness before going overseas. Their world was that of the family and clan embedded in the traditional village community—outside contacts usually reached no further than the district market town. It is understandable, then, that for some time after emigration the migrant's concern remained centered in his home village, particularly when he had left wife and children as well as parents there.[1]

While anticipating his eventual return to live there permanently, the sojourner migrant looked forward to visits home where he would be treated as a *tan heung shan hak* ("guest from the Sandalwood Mountains"). On his visits he would be expected to bring gifts and enough money to entertain his kinsmen as well as to spend several months at leisure before returning to the Islands. A migrant who could afford to do so would invest in land for his family and hire tenants for the family farms, have a better house built for his parents, wife, and children, and bring servants into the home. Sometimes a migrant brought back the bones of *heung li* who had died in Hawaii for burial near the village.[2] A financially successful *wah kiu* might give money for the repair or enlargement of the ancestral hall (*chi tong*) and have his name and the amount of his contribution conspicuously displayed in the building. A wealthy Honolulu Chinese was reported in a Honolulu newspaper to have provided in his will for posthumous veneration in his home village:

> A provision that a part of the income from an estate valued in excess of $500,000 be devoted to the celebration of Chinese rituals and to the purchase of a parcel of land in China to serve as a family inheritance, was contained in the will of the late Young Ahin, Chinese capitalist. . . .
>
> . . . The instrument . . . provides also that a fund not to exceed one-sixth of the income from the estate shall be used for "days and oc-

casions recognized by Chinese customs, for appropriate rituals at my grave and such shrines and temples as was our custom to worship." Rituals for the widow [after] her death are provided for.

The parcel of land to be purchased in China is to be "held according to Chinese law as family inheritance, the income to be spent for the well-being of my soul," for that of his wife, the children who have died, and "for the prosperity of my living descendants."[3]

When members of one clan in a village club made up of different clans cooperated with *heung li* of other clans, these *wah kiu* took a step, however small, away from individualistic family concerns. The formal organization of village clubs in Honolulu helped the migrants do collectively what they were not likely to do individually. One of their aims was to provide security for the villages in the absence of adequate protection by the Chinese government. The coastal section of China in which the migrant villages were located was periodically raided by bandits and pirates. Government protection, if any, was usually insufficient; in fact, police and military forces themselves frequently robbed the villagers. The migrant districts were particularly vulnerable. Fewer able-bodied men were there to protect them and, at the same time, they were more worth looting than other districts because of the money and goods sent back by the *wah kiu*. Apart from building stronger houses for their own families, migrants could see the advantage of collective measures to protect a whole village; village clubs raised money to repair or heighten village walls and to build watchtowers and small forts. Village clubs also supported protective armed forces and night watches.

Other projects for village improvement were carried out as well. One club reconstructed village temples and paid the temple keepers, built a modern elementary and secondary school, paid young educated men of the village to teach in the school, funded an open-ditch sewage system, paved, named, and numbered village streets, constructed a wharf leading to the nearby canal so that villagers need not travel through a rival village to use its wharf, and helped finance the construction of a corporately owned bus road between the village and Shekki, seven miles away.[4]

The Migrant and the Home District

Rivalry between village groups was stimulated when projects like these became the subject of comment among migrants from the same district and were publicized in Chinatown newspapers. On their visits home the *wah kiu* were likely to travel around their native districts more than they had ever done before migrating, often to visit other *wah kiu* they had known in Hawaii who had retired to other villages. Reports about improvements elsewhere in the district made migrants in Hawaii even more responsive to appeals for contributions toward village projects. The migrant was coming to identify himself with a social order that was larger than his kinship group and home village. He contributed to these projects not only out of concern for the welfare of his family and *heung li,* but also to raise the status of his village (and his own) in the eyes of migrants from other parts of the district.

Membership in a district association led a migrant to participate in matters affecting the whole district to which his village belonged. Migrants from Lung Doo, for example, became interested in a proposed public highway that would supplement the canal system and replace narrow, rough ricksha paths in their district. A campaign in Honolulu, with more than fifty Lung Doo men from various villages working on subscription teams, raised several thousand dollars in 1928 for this project. Chinatown newspapers published the contributors' names and the amounts they gave. One Chinese merchant subscribed HK$10,000 and several others pledged between HK$1,000 and HK$5,000.[5] A few years later Chinese in Hawaii from this same district raised over $10,000 from contributions and from its own treasury to help build a junior high school in Lung Doo. Similarly, Chung Shan Chinese in Hawaii cooperated with Chung Shan migrants in other overseas areas to help establish a hospital, Western-equipped and staffed by Western-trained medical personnel, in Shekki. In 1936 Chung Shan Chinese in Hawaii raised funds to build a Chung Shan District Library in Shekki.[6]

Somewhat different in character was the Chung Shan migrants' concern about a change in the location of the district's administrative headquarters. The district magistrate in 1931, a national figure, had moved the headquarters from Shekki to his ancestral place, Tong Ka, a market town in the southeastern part of Chung Shan. Opinion among Chung Shan migrants in Hawaii was divided: those from villages near Tong Ka favored the change; those from villages closer to Shekki protested strongly. Representatives of both sides held meetings on the matter and sent cables to Chinese officials. The general weight of opinion in Honolulu favored returning the headquarters to Shekki and there was evident relief when the return was effected.[7] Migrants were not only becoming district-conscious but were also taking an interest in the district's government, which formerly they had regarded as alien to them. (By this time, of course, the Manchu government had been replaced by the Republic of China.)

The Migrant and Kwangtung Province

With his mental horizon expanded beyond the limits of kinship and village, the migrant was exposed to new appeals for moral and financial support. He was frequently asked as a "fellow Cantonese" or "fellow provincial" to support some cause, movement, or institution in Kwangtung outside his home district. Chinese in Honolulu were usually approached by someone from China through such organizations as the United Chinese Society or the Chinese Chamber of Commerce of Honolulu. With their approval, committees would be formed to campaign for funds:

> In December 1929, Miss Wu Soo Cheu, principal of the St. Paul High School for Girls in Hong Kong, arrived in Honolulu from China to seek contributions from the Chinese here for the school. In January of 1930 a committee to raise funds for this purpose was formed. Mr. Chung Yee was made chairman and Wong Fook Mun treasurer. A sum of $2,194 U.S. money was raised. Miss Wu left on January 31 for the United States to appeal to Chinese there.[8]

A flood in Canton in 1931 brought an appeal to the United Chinese Society in Hawaii for aid. A committee organized to solicit funds raised HK$6,388 which was sent to Canton for relief. Conflicts between Communists and non-Communists in Canton in 1927 left many people destitute and homeless; Honolulu Chinese were told of "horrible" conditions in the area, pictures of "massacres" were displayed in Chinatown windows, and assistance was solicited for "fellow Cantonese." Chinese newspapers and posters on telephone poles and walls in Chinatown announced an open meeting to be held at the joint headquarters of the United Chinese Society and the Honolulu Chinese Chamber of Commerce; representatives of Chinese associations were especially invited. A *nan gau chai wui* ("calamity salvation organization" or relief committee) headed by Chinatown leaders was formed at this meeting. A month later $1,297.50 had been collected; $1,218.30 was forwarded to relief headquarters in Canton. (The rest was spent on "stationery and publication of the names of the subscribers in the Chinese newspapers in Honolulu.")[9]

The most generously supported projects in Kwangtung not specifically in the migrants' home districts were educational and medical institutions in Canton and Hong Kong. Among them, apart from the school mentioned above, were the Hong Kong Girls' Technical Academy, which received $2,925 from Honolulu Chinese in 1928; Lingnam University of Canton, $3,600 in 1930; Canton City Philanthropic Society, for a school in a Canton hospital, $3,500 in 1931; Canton Hon Chi Medical School, over $6,000 (Canton currency) in 1935; and Canton National Chung Shan University, $1,500 in 1936. The names of overseas Chinese contributors and the amounts they gave were published in Chinese newspapers, and rooms or other parts of the institutions were named in honor of groups of donors. An inscription on a plaque might say, for example, that a particular room was donated by and dedicated to the Tan Heung Shan Wah Kiu ("Hawaii Overseas Chinese"). A few Chinese migrants sent their children to these schools for part of their education, but more important motivations were the *wah kiu's* respect for education he himself had seldom received, the flattering recognition implied in the school's appeals to him, and his anticipation of enhanced status among his fellow *wah kiu*. Regardless of his motives, the migrant's contributions to causes that did not involve his own family, clan, village, or district indicate that he was becoming a part of a much larger Chinese world than the one from which he had emigrated.

The Rise of Nationalistic Societies

The migrants' early experiences overseas prepared them to be drawn into nationalistically oriented societies and activities. On the one hand, the *wah kiu*, who had so many different group identities among themselves, were treated categorically as a single group ("Chinamen") by people who were antagonistic to them and by the Hawaiian government's restrictive laws and regulations. On the other hand, some migrant leaders believed that the discrimination suffered by Chinese immigrants was a consequence of the weakness of the Chinese government in dealing with foreign powers. To improve their own status as immigrants, it was argued, the power of the Chinese government needed to be strengthened. Personal interest, therefore, was important in the rise of national consciousness among the *wah kiu*.

Although migrants generally came to agree that something had to be done to strengthen China as a nation, there was no unanimity on how this could be achieved. Different Chinese rallied around different standards. Political discussions were heated, rival political groups were set up, and conflicting views among leaders disrupted the functioning of more than one migrant organization.[10]

Hing Chung Wui—The Revolutionists

The first political group in Chinatown was initiated by Sun Yat-sen when he visited Hawaii in 1896, nearly twenty years after he had first come to the Islands as an adolescent. Dr. Sun's older brother, Sun Mi, was an early migrant to Hawaii. Their father was a farmer in Choy Hung village in Chung Shan district. Sun Mi was successful in Hawaii and by 1879 had persuaded his parents to let his thirteen-year-old younger brother, then known as Sun Tai-cheong, come to Hawaii. Realizing the value of knowing English in Hawaii, Sun Mi arranged for Tai-cheong to enter the Anglican school in Honolulu now known as Iolani School. Sun Mi must have been gratified three years later when Tai-cheong won an English prize at the school, but he was infuriated when he learned in 1885 that his brother wanted to be baptized a Christian. Tai-cheong was summarily sent back to Choy Hung where he angered the elders by publicly mutilating images in the village temple. During the next decade he attended school in Hong Kong where he was baptized along with Tong Phong, a former schoolmate from Honolulu; he completed a medical degree and practiced briefly in Macao and Canton; he took the name of Sun Yat-sen.

In 1894 Sun Yat-sen made a trip to Hawaii where he discussed the need for national revolution with old friends. He became the leader of a secret anti-Manchu movement innocuously named "The Education Society" and became a refugee after government forces raided the movement's headquarters in Canton and captured and executed five of his colleagues in the movement. A year after his first return from Hawaii his family had arranged a marriage for him with a girl from a nearby village, and now his wife, children, and widowed mother, to avoid reprisal, were taken to live with Sun Mi in Hawaii.

During his 1896 visit Dr. Sun spent several months in Honolulu advocating revolutionary overthrow of Manchu rule. Few migrants were interested in his proposals, but thirty or so attended a meeting at the home of a former school friend, Ho Fon, at which they took oaths to work together in a revolutionary movement. Although Dr. Sun spoke at public meetings arranged for him, only fifty or so of the five thousand adult Chinese males then in Honolulu were willing to become founders of the revolutionary group organized as the Hing Chung Wui ("Save China Society"). Apparently these early supporters were mostly young men who, like Sun, had been brought to Hawaii as adolescents by older relatives and received some Chinese education in China and some English education in Hawaii. Others were early second-generation Chinese who had some education in both Chinese and English. Of the names identified, more were Hakka than Punti—Ho Fon, Li Cheung, Yap See Young, Chang Chau, William Kwai Fong Yap, among others—but some, like C. K. Ai, Luke Chan, and Tong Phong, were Punti. Most of these men had become Christians after attending mission schools in Hawaii. Li had attended Queen's College in Hong Kong and had been employed by the Hawaiian government as a court interpreter. He and Ho Fon had collaborated for several years in publishing the first Chinese newspaper. These young men were among the few intellectuals in a predominantly money-oriented immigrant community.

The Hing Chung Wui was the first of hundreds of revolutionary societies formed among overseas Chinese in support of Dr. Sun's program during the succeeding fifteen years. In a proclamation it declared:

> China is weaker day by day. Those who are invested with the central power are indifferent and unscrupulous while the masses are ignorant and incapable of any deep thought. Unnecessary indignities and insults are suffered from many foreign nations, while Chinese civilization and culture are undervalued. With a population of 400,000,000 and several million *mous* of rich land, this country can be the strongest nation in the world, but due to the misrule of the Manchus, it has fallen to this pitiable condition. At the present time China is surrounded by strong neighboring countries who are envious of her abundant metals, of her richness in products. The aggressive actions of the foreigners have increased to such an extent that patriots cannot help but make a move to rescue the population from peril. The Hing Chung Wui has been organized solely for the purpose of saving the country, and hopes that its sympathizers will help to accomplish its aim.
>
> . . . This *wui* is established to promote the interest and to uphold the dignity of China. The country has been accepting insults at the hands of foreign nations, while her people could not complain of the

tyrannous rule. For the purpose of eliminating these evils, we have linked together the Chinese at home and abroad by the Hing Chung Wui. . . .[11]

Before Dr. Sun left Hawaii to plead the revolutionary cause among *wah kiu* in the continental United States and in Europe, his supporters in Hawaii raised about six thousand dollars which they turned over to him. The newspaper published by Ho and Li was to become an active instrument for propagating revolutionary ideas. Some of the more zealous members of the Hing Chung Wui began military drill in the Rev. Frank Damon's yard with a Hakka, William Yap, as captain and C. K. Ai, a Punti, as lieutenant. Ai refers to this activity, which did not continue long, as "Tiger head, snake tail"—an optimistic beginning, a dismal ending.[12] Nevertheless, members remained enthusiastic and recruited others, especially young men, into the movement.

Bow Wong Wui—The Constitutional Monarchists

In 1900 Hawaii's Chinese community came under the influence of a rival movement initiated by Liang Ch'i-ch'ao, a famous Chinese scholar, persuasive speaker, and political reform advocate from Kwangtung province. After China's defeat in the Sino-Japanese war, he and K'ang Yu-wei had interested Emperor Kuang Hsu and some of the emperor's advisers in reform measures designed to strengthen the government of China. Before these measures could be carried out the empress dowager, Tz'u Hsi, had put the emperor under confinement in the palace and deprived him and his advisers of power. K'ang and Liang had escaped to Japan where they organized the Bow Wong Wui ("Protect Emperor Association") among overseas Chinese there.[13] Liang came on to Hawaii where he recruited supporters for a branch of the Bow Wong Wui in Honolulu. The Wui's immediate goal was to return Kuang Hsu to power so that he could put into effect reforms that would strengthen the government without eliminating the Ching dynasty.

Liang arrived in Hawaii at a critical moment in the Chinese community—the time of the 1899–1900 plague and Chinatown fire. He seized upon the situation to emphasize the existing Chinese government's weakness in helping its overseas subjects and to advocate organization of the Wui. According to *The Friend*, "some of the oldest and most responsible Chinese in the country" formed the nucleus of the Wui,[14] but as a matter of fact several prominent Chinese, who were conservative leaders and businessmen in Chinatown organizations, refused to have anything to do with it. Nevertheless, Liang did recruit other successful and somewhat less cautious businessmen who were among the leaders in the United Chinese Society and other migrant societies to take charge of the Bow Wong Wui. Members and other interested Chinese gathered on Sunday evenings and listened to fervent talks on the need for political reform in China and to heated attacks on the proposals of other groups. With some of his Honolulu followers Liang visited Chinese communities on the other islands where branches were formed and several thousand members enrolled. Within the first three months the Wui collected more than thirty thousand dollars in initiation fees and contributions. Euphoric officers claimed that 80 or 90 percent of the migrants joined the organization.

Wui leaders applied to the territorial government for a charter of incorporation with a view to building a headquarters and clubhouse. Territorial officials refused to grant the charter but did not outlaw the Wui. A meeting place became available when a newspaper, the *Sun Chung Kwock Bo (New China News)*, was started with the help of Bow Wong Wui members sent from the Orient by Liang. The paper's objective was not only to promote political reform in China but also to counter the propagation of Dr. Sun's revolutionary approach by the *Lung Kee Sun Bo (Hawaiian Chinese News)*. Literate migrants like Dr. K. F. Li found a new interest in writing polemical articles for the *Sun Chung Kwock Bo* and attacking the arguments presented by writers for the other paper.[15]

Chung Wah Tung Ming Wui—Successor to Hing Chung Wui

When Dr. Sun returned to Honolulu in 1903, he found that several of his earlier followers had been drawn into the Bow Wong Wui, but loyal supporters arranged public meetings on Sunday afternoons and he spoke to enthusiastic crowds at the Chinese Theater. Reports in the *Pacific Commercial Advertiser* referred to Dr. Sun as "the famous revolutionist," "an orator of considerable power" able "to sway his audience at will," his speech "frequently punctuated with applause." To emphasize the difference between his movement and the Bow Wong Wui, he stressed the idea that the Manchu rulers were a decadent alien race who must be overthrown. He said that though the Chinese had great "pride of race" it was difficult to rouse in them "a spirit of nationalism." "Once this spirit can be awakened in the dormant minds of the conquered Chinese race which has submitted to the Manchu yoke for centuries, Dr. Sun believes that the Chinese nation will rise in its might of four hundred millions of people and overturn the Manchu dynasty forever."[16]

The Hing Chung Wui was renamed the Chung Wah Tung Ming Wui ("Chinese Together Revolution Society") to express more openly its revolutionary objective. Its motto was translated as "Drive away the Manchus, restore China, establish a republic, equalize rights; and if there is regret from any one, may the public punish him." Many Hawaii Chinese withdrew from the Bow Wong Wui and within a year it was claimed that the Tung Ming Wui had more than a thousand members. The societies supporting Dr. Sun and the revolutionary cause came to have the largest though not the wealthiest membership in the Islands. Hawaii Chinese raised a larger sum than during Dr. Sun's earlier trip to finance a revolutionary army; bonds were sold which were to be redeemed after the establishment of the republic.

Hoong Moon Societies and the Revolutionary Movement

During his 1903 stay in the Islands Dr. Sun visited his family on Maui, and Chinese in Kula claim that while he was there he joined the Ket Hing Fui Kon, the predominantly Hakka Hoong Moon society at Kula.[17] This would have been consistent with his goal of enlisting the support of the Hoong Moon societies which had thousands of poor, illiterate or semiliterate members who had no reason to expect any benefits from the Manchu government. Such members had no business interests that would incline them toward the less disruptive political reform movement supported by the wealthier migrants.[18]

Dr. Sun undertook to convince Hoong Moon leaders in the Islands that they should revive their revolutionary objective of overthrowing the Manchus—but in order to establish a Chinese republic rather than revive the Ming dynasty. During the years immediately preceding the 1911 revolution in China some of these societies did cooperate with Dr. Sun's revolutionary organizations in Hawaii. The Hoong Moon branches in Honolulu seem to have been the most active in the cause. Shortly before Chinese New Year in 1911 members of one of these branches announced that they were taking the defiant step of cutting off their queues—as Dr. Sun had done in 1896—thus "severing . . . the badge of servitude to the Manchu dynasty." (They may have been worried a few months later when a Hawaii-born Chinese physician living in Nanking sent word that hundreds of Chinese without queues had been executed at the order of a Manchu general whose troops had retaken that city.)

Dai Kwock Hin Jing Wui—Successor to Bow Wong Wui

With the death of Emperor Kuang Hsu the name of the Bow Wong Wui ("Protect Emperor Association") was no longer appropriate so it was changed to Dai Kwock Hin Jing Wui ("Constitutional Monarchy Society"). Even though the organization was really political, it obtained a charter of incorporation as a charitable society from the territorial government in 1908. A clubhouse built on a lot owned by one of the members was the meeting place and headquarters. Despite several name changes during the next twenty years this organization continued to be referred to by Chinese in the Islands as the Bow Wong Wui.

Chinese Politics and Migrant Organizations

Just as important as the formation of overtly political societies was the penetration of political issues and controversies into the immigrant associations which had been organized for other reasons. District associations, village clubs, surname societies, guilds, Chinese Christian churches, even the United Chinese Society itself, were all affected. Some of the most hotly contested elections during this period were really concerned with the efforts of each political faction to get control.[19] Supporters of unsuccessful candidates often tried to discredit the motives of those who had been elected.

Moreover, events within the societies were interpreted politically, as shown by a controversy within the See Dai Doo district association. Upon the deaths of Emperor Kuang Hsu and the empress dowager in 1908 many Chinatown societies displayed the imperial dragon flag at half mast. The See Dai Doo association, however, did not do so. Choy Hung village, Dr. Sun's birthplace, was in Dai Doo and many migrants from See Doo and Dai Doo were his ardent supporters. A member of the See Dai Doo association who belonged to the Bow Wong Wui charged that the See Dai Doo Wui Goon and its officers had become revolutionists. He was suspended from the association and the officers wrote an open letter to the *chi li* ("fellow district men") published in the Chinese newspaper that sponsored the revolutionary cause:

> This action on Wong's part caused a meeting to be held immediately, at which time it was decided that Wong believed the *wui goon* to be insignificant and powerless and had accordingly insulted the whole membership. . . .
>
> On the ninth day of this month he printed an article in the *Sun Chung Kwock Bo* falsely and maliciously accusing the president of making trouble without reason. His two ideas were that the president belonged to the revolutionary society, and that this *wui goon* had already begun to split into cliques and factions. . . .
>
> No doubt our broadminded and wide-visioned *chi li* will ignore such accusations, and will dismiss them at first thought as being unworthy of the attention of learned people. It is only because this whole affair concerns the name of this *wui goon* as well as that of the members that this article is printed in the press for the protection of our self-interests.
>
> That article stated that all the *wui goon* in town raised their flags at half-mast. Is it not known that while many *wui goon* raised their flags, not a few also did not raise their flags? Regarding this situation, will the government [Chinese] lose its prestige merely because some *wui goon* failed to raise their flags at half-mast?
>
> As for Wong, he himself has failed to observe the rules of mourning, and that ought likewise to brand him as a revolutionary follower. He claims to be an educated Chinese, a former teacher of the Chinese-English Academy of this town. If a country's mourning period is as important as he claims, why does he not observe mourning customs? Rules for mourning are that there should be no hair-cut within one hundred days, clothes should be in white, school and offices are to be closed during the period—why didn't he as a learned individual, observe these rules and in that way set an example for our *wah kiu*? A few days after the message [the death of the emperor] came, Wong had his hair cut, dressed contrary to the mourning customs, and attended to his school work as usual. Without observing mourning rites a *hou* [ten cents] he himself deserves the title of revolutionary follower.[20]

Through the first decade of this century and until the 1911 revolution in China, most officers of the United Chinese Society were passively if not actively promonarchy, and several were leaders in the Bow Wong Wui. Nevertheless, nationalistic enthusiasm in Hawaii following the founding of the Provisional Republic of China in December 1911, with Dr. Sun as its president, led to the election in December 1912 of officers in the United Chinese Society who supported Dr. Sun, even though General Yuan Shih-k'ai had replaced him. The election the following year was a tumultuous affair. Determined to keep control of the Society, Dr. Sun's followers filled the hall on election night with their sympathizers, newly registered as members. Having lost the election, promonarchy migrants unsuccessfully contested it in court. Followers of Dr. Sun won another Society election in 1914, but by this time Dr. Sun was losing support in Hawaii. In 1915 migrants willing to back General Yuan gained control which they kept until after the Northern governments were replaced by Chiang Kai-shek and the National Republic of China in Nanking in the late 1920s.

While the struggle for control of the United Chinese Society was going on (1912–1915), there was another conflict over leadership which was ultimately to bring about the eclipse of the Society as the leading Chinese organization in Honolulu.[21] The importance of the *wah kiu* to the Chinese government having become apparent, officials of the Manchu regime, during its final months, made plans for cooperation between the government and migrants. Every large center of overseas Chinese was advised to organize a Seong Wui ("Merchants' Association") with a constitution and bylaws supplied by the Chinese government. From then on communication between the Chinese government and overseas Chinese would go through the consul and the Merchants' Association. The Merchants' Association would serve as a general society representing "all the Chinese" in the area.

The unexpected happened in Honolulu where two rival organizations were formed in response to this proposal. United Chinese Society leaders, who had just succeeded in getting rid of a vindictive consul, organized the Chung Wah Chung Seong Wui ("Chinese Merchants' Association") in August 1911, with the same president and vice-president as the United Chinese Society. Before the year was out the Manchu regime was overthrown and Dr. Sun's followers organized a separate merchants' organization, the Wah Kiu Seong Wui ("Overseas Chinese Merchants' Association"), hoping the republic would recognize it in place of the rival organization. General Yuan's government, which took over from Dr. Sun so quickly, granted a charter to the Chung Wah Chung Seong Wui, however; the Wah Kiu Seong Wui, ignored by the Yuan government, dissolved.

The consul appointed by General Yuan's government ignored the reception on 1 January 1913 held by the United Chinese Society, at that time controlled by officers supporting Dr. Sun. Instead he attended the reception of the Chinese Merchants' Association, which had been recognized by his government. That reception was also the only one attended by other diplomatic representatives and by officials of the territorial and federal governments. This happened again at New Year's in 1914 and 1915. By July 1915 the United Chinese Society was controlled by the same group of men who controlled the Chinese Merchants' Association. Cooperation in joint activities resulted in an almost complete merger of the two organizations, with interlocking officers and boards of directors. The Merchants' Association, which changed its name to the Chinese Chamber of Commerce of Honolulu in 1926, raised money for an addition to the United Chinese Society building that became headquarters for both organizations. In 1929 the Chinese consul in Honolulu, who was pro-Northern government and anti-Chiang, resigned and took over much of the work of the two organizations.

Clashes with Chinese Consuls

During the time that agitation for political change in China was creating controversy among the Island Chinese, the *wah kiu* were having trouble with consuls sent to Hawaii by the imperial government of China. Even though migrants had often bemoaned the indifference of the imperial government toward the problems they faced in the Islands, some of the consuls sent from China after Hawaii was annexed to the United States in 1898 caused even more problems.[22]

The first consul, Yong Wei-pin, was a young man of See Yup origin whose wealthy father had built wharves for the British in Hong Kong. For the first few years of the consulate Goo Kim, who had been president of the United Chinese Society since 1892, was the official vice-consul, and officers of the Society served as consular staff. Gradually they were replaced by a consular staff of men sent from China who had risen in the Manchu government but who were sent to Hawaii without much regard to how fit they were to deal with the problems of the migrants in the Islands. Some of them who were from provinces other than Kwangtung did not understand any of the dialects spoken by the migrants, they had more education than the migrant leaders in Chinatown, and they made little effort to disguise their contempt for the mostly illiterate migrants.

At the time of the 1900 fire Yong was commended in the English-language press for his work, especially in convincing some three hundred angry homeless Chinese to accept the authorities' plan to move them from the Kawaiahao Church grounds to a detention camp. The same newspapers, however, criticized him for his protests while authorities were trying to control the Chinatown fire. (The Japanese consul was commended for his forbearance on that trying day.)

It was not long after the fire that Liang Ch'i-ch'ao came to Honolulu and the Bow Wong Wui was organized. Enthusiastic members of the Wui were dismayed when Consul Yong successfully opposed the incorporation of the group by the territorial government—and they were alarmed when they learned that the consul had petitioned his home government to arrest and punish family members of a migrant in Honolulu in whose home Liang had been living. Word came to Honolulu that the man's mother and grandmother had been imprisoned and tortured, that his mother had committed suicide, that his grandmother had died in prison of shock.

Wong Leong, the first president of the Bow Wong Wui, also suffered retribution even though his family was with him in Honolulu and he was an American citizen through naturalization in Hawaii before Annexation. The consul could not take the same kind of vindictive action against Wong's family, but he did have the magistrate of Wong's home district—Chung Shan—seize the ancestral temple of Wong's clan and require the clan to redeem it by paying a fine. The clan's spokesman then demanded reimbursement from Wong, amounting to about $1,250, threatening to remove his name from the clan's genealogical records if he refused. Many migrants who had joined the Bow Wong Wui or contributed to it repudiated their connections for fear of reprisals. The consul assured nonreprisal to those migrants who filed a certificate with the consulate (at $5.25 each) attesting that they were not members of any society opposed to the Chinese government. Hundreds of Chinese were reported to have filed these certificates.

Sometime after the Boxer Rebellion in mid-1900 Consul Yong proposed that about $9,500 left over from $25,000 locally contributed to the United Chinese Society at the time of the Chinatown fire be sent to Peking for repairs to the empress dowager's Summer Palace. Migrants thought this was a move by the consul to get a special award to himself from Peking. According to C. K. Ai, who became president of the United Chinese Society before this issue was resolved, the consul claimed that as the servant of the emperor of

China he had control of 80 percent of the money and therefore a right to use it for such a purpose. Ai reported that the older merchants, at the meeting of the Society Yong had called to make his proposal, "dared not oppose" the consul. The Society's treasurer, Yim Quon, who had not joined the Bow Wong Wui, supported the consul. President Ai, at that time a Bow Wong Wui member and its first treasurer, employed Caucasian lawyers to file an injunction that prevented the consul from getting control of the money which had been deposited in the Bishop Bank. Ai's supporters induced Secretary Hay of the U.S. Department of State to request the territorial governor to investigate charges brought by Chinese-Americans in Hawaii against the consul.[23] In the name of the United Chinese Society, President Ai also wrote to the American minister in Peking seeking his assistance in presenting a petition from the Society to the imperial government asking that Consul Yong be recalled. Yong left the Islands late in 1902.

Tension in the community rose again in 1904 when Yong's successor sent names of Dr. Sun's supporters in Hawaii, along with names and addresses of their relatives in Kwangtung, to the viceroy in Canton. But the most disturbing controversy involving a consul occurred shortly before the revolution against the Manchus broke out in China in early 1911. The consul in this case was Liang Kuo-ying, a wealthy young official reported to have a "palace" in Canton but whose native place was Tong Ka in Chung Shan. Chinatown leaders dutifully joined federal and territorial officials in attending the reception Consul Liang held soon after he arrived in January 1910, but resentment of the consul's actions began when he announced that his office would take a census of Chinese in Hawaii and that each person enumerated would be charged $1.25. He refused to reply to questions about his authorization for the census and the charge. When asked what the money was to be used for, he replied that twenty cents would go to the secretary of the census, five cents to the consulate office, and one dollar to China for official uses. Hawaii Chinese called this an unauthorized tax, and there was a movement to refuse cooperation with the census. The consul was accused of graft because it was thought he would keep the dollar a head instead of sending it to China. The consul then said that the census would be limited to children between five and twenty years of age and the dollar would be used locally for educational purposes. The issue of the census and the fee had not been resolved before the *Chee*

Yow Sun Bo published the news that Consul Liang had sent the names of eight Chinese—Dr. Sun and seven Honolulu men—to his home government as "dangerous revolutionary characters." Fears for the relatives in China of the seven migrants spread through Chinatown.

In April 1910 Dr. Sun had come to Honolulu under an assumed name and had spent several weeks conferring with his followers. By this time there was a reported price of several hundred thousand dollars on his head. Most of his activities in Honolulu were kept secret, but he did give an interview in the office of the *Chee Yow Sun Bo*, in which he predicted that Chinese soldiers in the imperial army would soon revolt and overthrow the Manchus. The interview was reported at length in the *Pacific Commercial Advertiser*. Dr. Sun also gave one revolutionary talk to a large, responsive audience at the Chinese Theater. A copy of the consul's report, which had been published in a Canton newspaper, reached the editors of the *Chee Yow Sun Bo* early in December. To local Chinese the report made it clear that the consulate had been spying on them at a time when the revolutionary spirit was spreading in Honolulu and elsewhere in Hawaii—branches of the Tung Ming Wui were active on the islands of Maui and Hawaii as well as on Oahu.

A committee of the United Chinese Society called on the consul to request that he send word to Peking retracting his charges against the seven Honolulu men. He refused to do so unless the seven would swear allegiance to the emperor and the government in China; he threatened that more Honolulu Chinese would be reported to Peking and their relatives in China hunted down if the Society persisted in opposing him. When the committee reported this at a meeting of the Society, it was decided to petition the Chinese minister in Washington and the government in Peking for the consul's removal. Rumors spread that the consul had sent about a hundred names of Honolulu merchants to Peking, and signatures were collected at a mass meeting on a petition that the consul be withdrawn. Despite strong feeling in the Chinese community that the consul should leave, some of the more conservative merchants continued to support him, even to the point of getting him to have Hee Fat, a popular Chinese who had spoken at the mass meeting, arrested and sued for libel.

Antagonism against the consul surged when the *Chee Yow Sun Bo* reprinted the full text of Consul Liang's report to the viceroy of Kwangtung. The consul had added more names to his list and charged that between 80 and 90 percent of Honolulu Chinese were revolutionists—of these, he claimed, about 10 percent were members of the Bow Wong Wui (Hin Jing Wui) and about 10 percent were in the "Sam Hops" (Hoong Moon societies). The rest, presumably, were supporters of Dr. Sun. Consul Liang is also reported to have decided that no Chinese with American citizenship would be allowed to visit China unless he himself certified that they were not revolutionists. A delegation from the United Chinese Society demanded an explanation of his alleged reporting of local Chinese as revolutionaries. He refused on the grounds that the Society, as an unofficial body, had no right to question his official acts.

Former adherents of the consul among the local merchants withdrew their support. A mass meeting called by the United Chinese Society was reported by the *Advertiser,* which said that "five thousand Chinese roared at Aala Park last night. . . . Speaker after speaker drew applause." The shouts of the throng were translated as "Aie! Aie! Send him back! Send him to hell!" When a petition "to get rid of him" was presented, "a forest of hands shot up . . . and each throat yelled . . . Aie!"

The consul had already lost face in the Chinese community when his libel suit against Hee Fat failed and the Caucasian judge admonished him for using methods "foreign" to American views. Speakers at the mass meeting derided him for placing himself under the jurisdiction of the American courts by filing the suit.

The Chinese minister in Washington sent a commissioner to Honolulu. He conferred with the consul, met at his hotel with "United Chinese Society leaders and other Chinese merchants" wearing "their full costumes of flowing silk, not everyday garb," and later talked with local Chinese at a meeting at the Society's headquarters. Word circulated that Chinese officials in Washington had known nothing about the census and the $1.25 charge until they received complaints from Honolulu. Chinese New Year celebrations were more jubilant than usual when news came that the Chinese ministry in Washington had asked the consul to resign.

Revolutionary Enthusiasm and Disillusionment

The staff of *Chee Yow Sun Bo* was the first group in Honolulu to display confidence in the success of the revolution by flying the revolutionary flag—white sun on a blue field—after fighting broke out between imperial forces and revolutionary troops in Hupeh on 10 October 1911. As victory after victory of the revolutionary forces was reported, and a few days before the emperor formally abdicated, the United Chinese Society decided to adopt the new flag, which was raised on 20 November at its headquarters in a public ceremony.[24] That evening a lantern parade was followed by a mass meeting directed by the staff of the *Chee Yow Sun Bo* and other enthusiastic leaders of the Tung Ming Wui. It was reported that members of the Bow Wong Wui thought the parade was premature and refused to take part in it. Nevertheless "thousands gathered," students from several Chinese-language schools carried lanterns and banners through Chinatown, and "queues were conspicuous by their absence. . . . Chinese musicians, up to now always in Chinese clothes, wore haole clothes like everyone else."

A surprising new feature of Chinatown's political activities appeared a few days later when "flaming red posters in Chinatown" and Chinese and English newspapers announced that the United Chinese Society was inviting Chinese women to meet at the Society hall and organize a local Chinese branch of the Red Cross. Both men and women attended the meeting but instead of organizing a Red Cross branch they initiated a new type of fund drive. Two committees of Chinese men—executive and finance—were formed. Twenty-four "prominent Chinese ladies" in groups of six, carrying "a red cross banner as the symbol of their errand," would call on Chinese merchants to solicit funds. The money would be sent to China to aid wounded soldiers of both the Ching and revolutionary forces. Chinese and non-Chinese women would meet daily "to prepare bandages under the direction of American trained nurses who have volunteered their services."

A few weeks later the bandage-making ended when news arrived that Dr. Sun had been made president of the Provisional Republic of China. There was another noisy celebration with firecrackers, horns, boys parading through Chinatown with flags, banners, and portraits of Dr. Sun. Also paraded through the streets was an effigy of the editor of the promonarchical paper, *Sun Chung Kwock Bo,* being hanged. A committee of Chinese-Americans cabled Washington asking for congressional recognition of the Provisional Republic. The *Advertiser* carried a long article on Dr. Sun's wife who had lived for more than ten years in Hawaii, mostly at Kula on Maui. There was speculation about what this village woman from Chung Shan would be like as First Lady of the former empire. (Three and a half years later the *Advertiser* and Chinese newspapers were to carry the news to a bewildered Chinese community of Dr. Sun's marriage to his private secretary, Miss Soong Ching-ling.)

President Sun ordered that his revolutionary parties, no longer outlawed in China, change their name to Kuomintang ("National People's Party"). The Tung Ming Wui branches in the Islands complied and became branches of the American division of the Kuomintang with headquarters in San Francisco. The Hin Jing Wui ("Constitutional Monarchy Society") was temporarily eclipsed.

Chinese in Hawaii soon realized that "overthrowing the Manchus" was one thing, establishing a peaceful and stable government quite another. The betrayal of the revolution by General Yuan Shih-k'ai brought the resignation of President Sun, after he had been in office less than seven weeks, and the election of Yuan as president. Subsequently Yuan attempted to have himself made emperor under a constitutional monarchy. In Hawaii he was supported by the pro-monarchy merchants who had belonged to the Hin Jing Wui. On instructions from North China this group changed its name to Kuo Min Hsien Cheng Tang ("National People's Constitutional Party") and for several years enjoyed the prestige of being aligned with the strongest government force in China.

Dr. Sun's organizations were again outlawed and driven into secrecy in China, and again he appealed to his followers overseas to support another revolutionary cause—this time to wrest control of the Chinese government from "overbearing warlords and greedy politicians." Honolulu followers changed their name once more, this time to Chung Wah Kuo Ming Tang ("Chinese National Revolutionary Party"). Several hundred Chinese in the Islands allied themselves with this movement and supported it by buying bonds to raise funds for overthrowing the "usurpers."[25]

Continued civil strife in China kept the migrants interested in Chinese national affairs, but they were even more divided over the reconstruction of China than they had been before the Manchus were overthrown. Every new turn of events brought advocates and critics; rival newspaper editors kept up the stream of charges and countercharges. Some migrants who had supported the revolution deplored the civil war and refused to respond to Dr. Sun's pleas for funds to carry out a new revolution. They felt the main task had been accomplished when the Manchus were driven from power, and they were disposed to support any strong Chinese government. As civil strife in China wore on, migrants began to doubt whether the money collected in the seemingly perpetual campaigns was getting sufficient results to compensate for the personal sacrifice called for. In 1930 one old migrant who had spent thirty-four years in an isolated plantation community on Maui bitterly bemoaned the political confusion in his homeland:

> In China now time all time fight, fight. I no like see fight in China. I no like Kuomintang because all time want to fight. In Hawaii, Kuomintang all time have Chinese give money. Some head man put plenty money he pocket. Rest money, send China, buy guns, fight, kill own China brother. If have war with Japan, allite, I give plenty money fight Japanese, but give money fight China brother—I no can. Ah, bad t'ing. China too much fight. . . . Kuomintang man in Hawaii, all time must give money, all time pay, pay, head man take plenty. You know Ah Fook at Kahului? Before time, he Kuomintang man, but he pay and get out—he say all time too much pay.

Nevertheless, the main old-world identification of most of the Hawaii Chinese was with Kwangtung where Dr. Sun and his forces attempted from about 1915 on to control the provincial government independently of the Northern government. This was the part of China where the relatives of most of the migrants were living, where migrants wanted to visit, retire, die. Tacit if not active support of Dr. Sun was safe because the Northern government was unable to control South China, and the consuls sent to Honolulu were not in a position to threaten noncooperative migrants with persecution of their families in Kwangtung.

Many Chinese in Hawaii regarded Dr. Sun's death in 1925 as a great setback to the Nationalist cause, just when the success of his forces in the Canton area seemed to promise a reunited China. News of the death of a great national leader whom so many Chinese in Hawaii had known personally brought about more unity of sentiment in Honolulu's Chinatown than had been felt for years. The memorial services in Honolulu testified to the pride Honolulu Chinese took in honoring a man for whose greatness they could themselves feel partly responsible.

Before Dr. Sun's death his revolutionary party had once more become a public organization and had been renamed the Chung Kuo Kuomintang ("Chinese National People's Party"). Hawaii Kuomintang groups had sent representatives to the first "national" meeting of the Kuomintang held in Canton in 1924. At this meeting the Hawaii Kuomintang organization was given the status of a province with its own headquarters, no longer subordinate to the San Francisco headquarters, and on a par with Kuomintang provincial divisions in China. The Hawaii provincial organization, with branches on the islands of Oahu, Maui, and Hawaii, set up headquarters in Honolulu. After Chiang Kai-shek rose to power following the Northern expedition in 1927, however, the Kuomintang in China split between pro-Chiang members backing the Nanking government and anti-Chiang members who had largely been supporters of Dr. Sun. By 1928 this split was reflected in the Hawaii Kuomintang membership and the appearance of a pro-Chiang newspaper: *Chung Wah Kung Bo (United Chinese News)*. That year pro-Chiang Kuomintang leaders in Hawaii, in an action ironically reminiscent of Consul Liang's actions in 1910, sent to Nanking a list of Hawaii Kuomintang members "believed to be counterrevolutionists."[26] The following year a rival organization of the Oahu branch of the Kuomintang secured recognition from the Nanking government.

Honolulu Chinese were shocked in 1931 when Wong Buck Hung, on a trip with his wife and children to his village in Lung Doo, was arrested as his ship arrived in Shanghai. Wong, a prominent merchant, banker, and leader in several migrant societies, was active in the anti-Chiang wing of the Kuomintang. It was widely believed in the Chinese community that his arrest had been instigated by the pro-Chiang group in Honolulu, but leaders of that group denied the charge. The Lung Doo Society, the United Chinese Society, and the Chinese Chamber of Commerce all held meetings to plan a strategy for getting Wong released. One Lung Doo Society leader expressed the fears circulating among the Honolulu Chinese:

> We know he is in jail, and you can't tell what the Chinese government will do. We think maybe the government will kill him. If you are arrested by the American government you know you will not be killed, but if you are arrested by the Chinese government, you don't know what will happen. You might have your head taken off, and your relatives won't hear about it until after it is all done. . . . We decide to send a cable to Ng Ung-sun, who is high up in the Nanking government. We think maybe he will be able to save Wong. He used to be editor of the *Liberty News* about twenty years ago.[27]

Cables were sent from Honolulu. Wong was released, apparently without explanation.

Conflict between pro-Chiang and anti-Chiang wings of the Hawaii Kuomintang continued while the South China provinces of Kwangtung and Kwangsi maintained their own governments independent of the Nanking regime. Meanwhile the local Hin Jing Dong (Hsien Cheng Tang) continued to oppose the Kuomintang, especially through its newspaper, *Sun Chung Kwock Bo*. After the Kuomintang under Chiang Kai-shek became dominant in North and Central China, the Kuo Min Hsien Cheng Tang changed its name again, this time to Chung Kuo Hsien Cheng Tang ("Chinese Constitutional Party"), but from 1930 on the group's political activities waned and eventually all but disappeared, although the *Sun Chung Kwock Bo* is still published. The once-large membership dwindled to a small group of conservative migrants, some quite wealthy, who prided themselves on the occasional recognition they had received from the Manchu government or postrevolution Northern governments. One elderly Chinese, from time to time reminding listeners that he was the grandson of a "mandarin," was reelected president year after year. The group turned from current politics to Confucianism and study of the classics. Professing Confucianism as its origin and human welfare as its end, the group in the 1930s announced its six basic principles:

1. To build up the morality of the people by a return to practice of Confucianism
2. To establish the people's rights on the basis of morality and justice
3. To strengthen the country by basing it upon a strong constitution
4. To protect and safeguard the people's rights by constitutional rights
5. To make the nation an instrument for world peace
6. To promote human welfare by universal peace[28]

Shortly after the Provisional Republic of China was proclaimed, the Yee Hing Chung Wui, a Honolulu Hoong Moon society known today as the Chee Kung Tong, started the *Hon Mun Bo* ("Han People News") to promote a third position on political change in China, although Hoong Moon leaders in Hawaii had sided with the Kuomintang in opposing Yuan Shih-k'ai's attempt to become emperor in 1915.[29] Hoong Moon leaders in China tried unsuccessfully in 1922 to develop a political party opposed to the Kuomintang under the name of Chee Kung Tang ("Towards the Public Good Party"). None of the Honolulu branches adopted this name, although the *Hon Mun Bo's* editorial opposition to the Kuomintang went on until the paper discontinued publication in 1929. A few moderately wealthy Hoong Moon members, having once committed themselves to this position, refused to back down for fear of losing face in the Honolulu Chinese community. Some Hoong Moon members were active in other political organizations, mostly the Kuomintang, while hundreds of members with no strong political attitudes continued to use the Hoong Moon clubhouses for nonpolitical activities.

The Chinatown Press

Expanding nationalistic feelings among the Hawaii *wah kiu* were largely responsible for the growth of Chinatown newspapers. By background and training most migrants were no more newspaper readers than they were political party members. At home gossip had provided the important news of their immediate world; news of the larger world had come mainly by word of mouth on market days. Even if they had been interested in papers or literate enough to read them, they would have had little access to them in the nineteenth century.

Predecessors of the Chinatown newspapers were the posters pasted on the walls at the busiest corners of Chinatown. A red piece of paper, covered with boldly written black characters, might announce a festival, temple ceremony, or association meeting; a pink poster might give notice of a business transaction of interest to debtors and creditors of a Chinatown firm; a handwritten yellow poster might inform Chinatown of plans for the funeral of a prominent resident recently deceased. The rules of some Chinese societies decreed that important business transacted at special meetings would be void unless such meetings were announced by posters "in the usual places" in Chinatown.

The newspaper now generally considered the first in Chinatown appeared in 1881.[30] Titled the *Tan Shan Sun Bo (Hawaiian Chinese News)*, it was started as a commercial and literary venture by young Chinese migrants who had received some schooling in the Chinese language and classics. Two of them were Hakka Christians, one educated in Hong Kong, the other in a church school in Honolulu. They had no printing press for the difficult Chinese characters; it appears that they turned out a handwritten four-page paper by means of a duplicator. Two years after it started Ho Fon became manager of the paper, which was then issued twice a week with the bilingual name of *Lung Kee Sun Bo* ("The New Prosperous Business News") and *Hawaiian Chinese News*. The early numbers were filled mostly with Chinese classical literature and compositions written in the conventional and difficult "rhyme prose."

Dr. Sun gave the first strong push to newspapers in Chinatown during his 1894 visit. Among the young men with whom he discussed the need for revolutionary changes in China were the publishers of the *Lung Kee Sun Bo*. From then on the paper carried articles expressing Dr. Sun's political views, and when he returned to Hawaii in 1896 he made the paper's office his headquarters. Books by Chinese authors advocating revolution became sources for subsequent articles, and Dr. Sun himself wrote articles for the paper. The difficulty of increasing the paper's circulation without a printing press led the Hing Chung Wui, Dr. Sun's organization in Honolulu, to solicit funds to buy a hand-printing press from Hong Kong in 1900.

Members of the Hawaii branch of the Bow Wong Wui financed the purchase of a similar printing press from Hong Kong at the request of Liang Ch'i-ch'ao, and the first numbers of the *Sun Chung Kwock Bo (New China News)* appeared before the end of 1900. Liang wrote some of the leading articles in these early issues; after he left the Islands others were based upon his publications and those of K'ang Yu-wei.

From then on a battle of words was kept up between editors and contributors to papers representing opposing political views. As political groups formed, named and renamed themselves, split, reorganized, and sometimes dissolved, so newspapers aligned with them were started, their editorial policies were formulated and reformulated, and they were continued or discontinued as their support continued or declined. Table 14 lists the Chinese newspapers in Honolulu and indicates their sponsorship as well as their duration.

Nine of these papers were supported by groups promoting one or another program for political change in China. The *Tan Shan Sun Bo* started as a literary paper like the *Wah Ha Bo*, but during its most flourishing period it was a political organ. Most members of the corporation publishing the *Hawaii Chinese News* were Hawaii-born Chinese, with some China-trained young men on the staff to prepare the Chinese half of the weekly edition. This paper appealed for sub-

Table 14

Chinese Newspapers Published in Honolulu

Chinese Name	English Name	Year Started	Year Discontinued	Supporters
Tan Shan Sun Bo[a]	Hawaiian Chinese News	1881	1907	Dr. Sun's followers, Hing Chung Wui, after 1894
Wah Ha Bo	"Chinese Times"	1893	1907	Christian Chinese (literary, nonpolitical)
Lai Kee Bo	"Beautiful News"	1895	1900	Literary, nonpolitical
Sun Chung Kwock Bo	New China News	1900	1980	Promonarchy, constitutionalist party (Bow Wong Wui, later Hin Jing Dong)
Kai Ming Bo	"Enlightenment News"	1905	1905	Hoong Moon societies
Mun Sang Yat Bo	"Livelihood News"	1908	1909	Conservative element of Hing Chung Wui
Chee Yow Sun Bo	Liberty News	1908	1938	Radical element of Tung Ming Wui; later, Kuomintang
Kai Chee Sun Bo	"Instruction News"	1909	1910	Liberal element of Hing Chung Wui
Wah Hing Bo	"Progressive China News"	1909	1923	Successor of Mun Sang Yat Bo; after 1911, Chinese Merchants' Association; pro–Yuan Shih-k'ai; pro–Northern governments; intermediate between Kuomintang and Hin Jing Dong papers
Hon Mun Bo	"Han People News"	1911	1929	Hoong Moon societies
Tan Wah Sun Bo	Hawaii Chinese News	1927	1937	Hawaii-born Chinese active in territorial politics; mostly Republicans but paper run as "independent"
Chung Wah Kung Bo	United Chinese News	1928	—[b]	Pro-Chiang Kuomintang
	Hawaii Chinese Journal[c]	1937	1959	Hawaii-born Chinese

Note: Chinese titles are translated into English if the newspaper had no English title. Thrum's Hawaiian Annual for 1898 (p. 196) and the Pacific Commercial Advertiser (28 February 1902) both mention a paper called the Chinese Chronicle (Yuen Chu Ho, editor) but no further information about it was found. Passing reference is made to a paper published in Hilo, Sun Wun Yat Bo, in Chinese of Hawaii, 1929, p. 79.
a Later Lung Kee Sun Bo.
b Still published.
c After 1957, Hawaii Chinese Weekly.

scribers among the younger, Hawaii-born element of the Chinese population. It gave more attention to local news, both general and Chinese, than to political events in China; about one-fourth of the four-page English section carried news about local Chinese society and another fourth about local sports. By the mid-1930s, when the two large Honolulu dailies were carrying more society news about Chinese residents than they had done earlier, the *Hawaii Chinese News* was losing circulation and had to discontinue publication because it could not get enough advertising. Two other Chinese newspapers published only in English, the *Hawaii Chinese Journal* and the *Hawaii Chinese Weekly*, had the same fate.

Most of the newspapers published by the *wah kiu* did not depend upon income from subscriptions and advertising. As organs of political groups they continued as long as their sponsors were willing to give them financial support. Party members contributed to these papers in addition to paying for subscriptions, and they were expected also to demonstrate their loyalty to the party's cause by buying advertising space in the paper. Sometimes the same advertisement by a Chinese firm would appear for months. Notices by Chinese organizations, such as lists of officers, might be repeated issue after issue because, having once been painstakingly prepared by hand-picking the Chinese characters from countless boxes of type, they were already made up and could fill space between new articles. In such ways a larger and more impressive paper could be issued than would have been possible with the usual small staff. There was little money for cabled news from China; Honolulu Chinese papers depended for news on mail, including newspapers published in China, on translations from the Honolulu English-language papers, and on fertile imagination.

Like many immigrant newspapers, those published in Chinatown before the *pai hua* ("colloquial language") movement of the 1920s were not written to communicate with the general migrant population. The editor and his staff were hired to plead a particular cause and most editors tried to do this as eloquently as possible, demonstrating their erudition. Hence most newspapers were written in a style that few Chinese in Hawaii could read readily or understand. Since these newspapers were in the same category of group symbols as flags, badges, and bands, the papers' supporters had little objection. Though the difficult style is almost untranslatable into English, the following excerpt illustrates the partisanship and nationalistic attitudes of the writers:

The *Liberty News* was born this day one year ago. The days and months pass by as quickly as the spinning machine and as rapidly as flowing water. With a sigh, I reflect that in our native country mountains and rivers remain as of old; people are well with no sickness; but the Han people just let their time pass away. They know not that they lost their national state long ago; their bodies have become those of slaves; and they are worse off than horses or cattle.

Happily, in recent days there has appeared a person who is thinking deeply [Sun Yat-sen], who knows and feels the toothless shame of calling an alien person [the Manchu Emperor] "father." Accordingly he has raised the racial question and advocated the rise of our [Han] race. Wash away and purify ourselves of that shame. Annihilate the other race. Together we will sing the Song of Revenge. That is the policy of this newspaper. Our meaning is one and identical.

We think of our native country—endlessly worrying about it like the Gi insane one of old. We know not when our dreams will come true; when, with hot blood spraying over Manchu heads, we can fight till the end. Already we see the dying influence of the Manchu regime and we know it won't be long.

Henceforth we will struggle till death if necessary; we'll brightly restore the Han "family" to its original position. Heaven's hand will turn to help us. Remake the prestige of our nation. Until that day, this newspaper's name will be "Liberty."[31]

The Chinese-Language Schools

Rivalry between the Bow Wong Wui and the Tung Ming Wui also entered into the founding and functioning of the two largest Chinese-language schools in Honolulu, which, not accidentally, opened only four days apart on 4 February and 8 February 1911.

During Dr. Sun's visit to Hawaii in 1910 he had urged his followers in the Tung Ming Wui to start a language school for Hawaii-born Chinese children because education in the Western-oriented, English-medium schools was weaning them away from their cultural heritage. He pointed out that hundreds of Hawaii born Chinese were growing up without a Chinese education and argued that they must be given the opportunity to learn the Chinese language and to know Chinese culture. He is reported to have said to the editor of the *Chee Yow Sun Bo:* "Although we have the newspapers to be our propaganda agents, we must also cultivate the future generation to uphold our revolutionary ideals. We ought to establish a Chinese school in Honolulu, for it will be of help to us."[32]

Following this suggestion, several of Dr. Sun's supporters each pledged a hundred dollars for the establishment of such a school. Several United Chinese Society leaders favored this project and a meeting was held at the Society to enlist the help of prominent Chinese in the community. The president, who like many other members by this time had his family in Hawaii, was enthusiastic about the idea and not only contributed heavily himself but also worked hard to get support from other Chinese. A building in a district near the center of Chinatown was bought for five thousand dollars. Two Chinese teachers were engaged and the school opened shortly after Chinese New Year with more than a hundred pupils. Students went to the Chinese school in the late afternoons after attending American schools as usual.

The school's name—Wah Mun School ("Chinese People's School")—was suggested by Dr. Sun.[33] Its close connection with the revolutionary movement is indicated by the fact that the man who became principal in the fall of 1911 was the editor of the *Chee Yow Sun Bo*. As the school expanded, other members of the newspaper's staff were added as teachers. After Dr. Sun's death the school was renamed in his honor Tan Shan Chung Shan School ("Hawaii Chung Shan School") and, still later, Sun Yat-sen School.

After the revolution, supporters of this school were generally regarded as Kuomintang sympathizers. Students sang the Kuomintang party song on ceremonial occasions. Instruction was patterned along lines suggested by Kuomintang leaders in China, and textbooks prepared by Kuomintang writers were imported from Shanghai. The *San Min Chu I*, Dr. Sun's book setting forth the "Three Principles" of government, was basic in the school's curriculum. With the promotion of Mandarin as the national language in the effort for national unity, the school tried for a while to teach in Kuo Yu. In a Cantonese immigrant community, however, this was almost useless, and since the school had difficulty in getting teachers who could teach in Kuo Yu the effort was dropped. Nevertheless the school was registered with the Nanking government and for several years received a subsidy from that government's Commission on Overseas Affairs. Students were encouraged to take part in parades, fund-raising campaigns, and benefit performances for nationalist Chinese causes.

The Bow Wong Wui had become interested in starting a Chinese-language school about the same time as Dr. Sun's group.[34] Some of its members were in the Moo Hock Kee Lock Bo, a group of young intellectuals interested in classical Chinese education and also involved in publishing the *Sun Chung Kwock Bo*. The Moo Hock Kee

Lock Bo turned over its clubhouse for use as a school building, and the Mun Lun School ("People's Ethical Training School"), with two teachers from a Chinese-language school sponsored by the Bow Wong Wui in Yokohama, officially opened on 4 February 1911, four days before the Wah Mun School. Mun Lun School became the largest and best-equipped Chinese school in Hawaii. Its program was oriented toward traditional Chinese cultural and classical education rather than toward the combination of revolutionary and Western ideas in the Wah Mun School's curriculum. Prerepublic textbooks were brought from China and others were written by the school's teachers to fit local needs of the "overseas student." For a time the history of the Chinese revolution of 1911 and subsequent events was taught without reference to Sun Yat-sen or Chiang Kai-shek. For several years the school used the five-bar flag of the Northern governments instead of the National Republic's flag, and the Mun Lun song referred to the "five races of the Republic."

The school, registered with General Yuan Shih-k'ai's Chinese government in 1914, displayed prominently a motto in Chinese characters translated as "a bright light overseas" written and presented to the school by Yuan's minister of education. The school received some financial aid from subsequent Northern governments and boasted of scrolls presented by President Li Yuan-hung in 1917 and by President Hsu Shih-cheng in 1922. During this period the school was also favored by consuls sent to the Islands by these Northern governments. The pro-Kuomintang Wah Mun School, of course, scorned these connections and was not officially registered with the Chinese government until the Kuomintang was returned to power in 1926. Wah Mun School, renamed Hawaii Chung Shan School in 1927, enjoyed greater prestige with the Chinese government through the 1930s and 1940s. As most *wah kiu* came to recognize the Kuomintang regime as the legitimate government in China, the directors and teachers of Mun Lun School tended to emphasize that their policy was cultural rather than political. Their aim, they said, was to train Chinese youth in China's cultural heritage, not to promote a particular political cause. Nevertheless, the school continued to be managed by members of the Moo Hock Kee Lock Bo and the Bow Wong Wui's successor, the Constitutional Party, and affairs of the Mun Lun School were communicated to the migrants through the *Sun Chung Kwock Bo* rather than either of the Kuomintang newspapers.

Relief Projects

The migrants' awakened sense of identification with China led not only to their participation in Chinese party politics but also to concern about famine and other disasters in parts of China outside their home districts or province. As early as 1878 a few *wah kiu* in Hawaii contributed two thousand dollars—then a large sum—to help famine-stricken inhabitants of North China. In this early period, however, migrants engrossed in trying to make their own fortunes were little concerned about the misfortunes of Chinese living in a part of China that was almost as foreign to them as India or Europe. Identification with Chinese outside of Kwangtung as *tung bau*—fellow countrymen—evolved slowly. Sojourner Chinese were usually led to respond to appeals coming from other parts of China by migrants who had lived in Hawaii longer than they had and who were directly or indirectly connected with the Chinese government.

The famine relief fund of 1878 had been raised at the initiative of Chun Fong, who was appointed the first Chinese commercial agent in Honolulu shortly after he had forwarded the relief money to imperial government officials. Leaders of the United Chinese Society after its formation in the early 1880s were responsible for most of the appeals to the local Chinese for help to unfortunate countrymen and for contributions to causes in the home country. A typical appeal was made in 1892 when the United Chinese Society received word of a severe drought in central China causing hundreds of thousands of Chinese to starve. Officers led a campaign which raised five thousand dollars for a relief fund. The imperial government recognized this "act of charity" by awarding the United Chinese Society a large wooden plaque carved with the characters *Wai Kup Chung Chow* ("Your Charity Reaches to China"). This plaque, along with others awarded on similar occasions, was conspicuously displayed in the Society building.

Officers sometimes received personal awards from the imperial government: Hat of the Sixth Order, Hat of the Ninth Order, and so on. Personal awards to leaders of fund drives for aid to China during national calamities became a matter of contention after the turn of the century when political divisions within the Chinese community began to affect elections of officers in the United Chinese Society. When one political group held control, those with other political affiliations were inclined to be indifferent to appeals made by the Society. An article in the *Chee Yow Sun Bo* in 1909 reflected cynicism among opponents of the imperial government about the Society's relief activities at a time when its officers were cooperating with the Chinese imperial consul:

> Yesterday on the street, I saw a United Chinese Society long red notice, saying: "Four District flood; officers already sent to various islands to solicit contributions from *wah kiu* for relief." Just think, the United Chinese Society has recently become a private organization, with no connection with the *wah kiu* of the Islands. . . .
>
> The United Chinese Society originally was a public organization of our *wah kiu;* the land was bought and the building constructed, from the blood-sweating money of our *wah kiu,* not from money given by the Ching Government. For this reason, the United Chinese Society really ought never to become an aristocratic Society. Now, no matter what happens, the Chinese Imperial Consul meets with the Society officials at the headquarters; no matter on what official business, he sends a letter to inform the Society as if it is the "united society" for all the *wah kiu* in the various parts of the Islands.
>
> Our *wah kiu,* scattered abroad, receive no protection from the Chinese Government. Now the government, no matter what happens, never fails to ask our Chinese here to contribute money. Everyone of our *wah kiu* knows the love of our *tung bau;* and we *wah kiu* should open our pockets to give aid to our *tung bau* in distress. However, we *wah kiu* can send the relief money back to the interior ourselves. Why is it necessary for the relief money to go through the hands of a consul? While the Ching Government loudly advocates the adoption of a constitution, says it truly loves its people, it uses up $6,000,000 to bury Kwang Hsu, the dead king. If the Ching Government really loved the people, the money it used in the burial of one dead king would be more than adequate for relief aid in the Four District flood. Our country men are taxed bloodily for government protection; now, in the time of flood, it ought to be able to perform its protective duty, without coming to our Chinese in Hawaii to ask us to open our pockets to give aid.
>
> It would be well for our *wah kiu* to seek an effectively lasting solution, to improve our country politically so that the people can receive government protection, and not need to spend money endlessly on relief like a kind-hearted woman. . . .[35]

During the most intense rivalry between political groups for control of the United Chinese Society (1912–1915) no large campaigns for relief projects in China were carried out, but after 1915 the Society and the Merchants' Association (later the Honolulu Chinese Chamber of Commerce) cooperated to raise funds for such projects. As tensions between traditionalists and modernists, "constitutionalists" and "revolutionists," gradually relaxed, these societies and a few others continued to provide leadership for movements to ameliorate suffering in China. Although the number of migrant men decreased greatly until they made up only about one-fourth of the Chinese adult male population in 1940, substantial funds were raised even during the worst years of the depression of the 1930s. Table 15 shows some of the projects carried out during the six years 1930–1935 by *wah kiu* in Hawaii, with Hawaii-born Chinese as well as migrants contributing.[36]

Patriotic Activities

Migrants' participation in activities that were more patriotic than charitable demonstrated their growing nationalism most clearly. Even during the 1890s, when few of the early migrants were concerned about national affairs in China, the defeat of China in 1895 in the Sino-Japanese war stirred up bitter feelings among the *wah kiu*— chagrin at the weakness of the Ching government and resentment against the Japanese. These feelings were intensified in the Islands by the Hawaiian government's policy of assisting Japanese immigration in the decade prior to 1895 and restricting immigration from China. Some tenseness between Chinese and Japanese migrants in Hawaii during the war must have been evident because notices in the English-language press asked the two groups to "keep quiet" over the affair.[37]

Local conflict between the two groups did break out in 1896 on one of the sugar plantations. In a bloody fight between Japanese and Chinese laborers, three Chinese were killed, others injured. The immediate cause apparently was a personal quarrel between a Japanese and a Chinese laborer, but the developing *tung bau* identification among the Chinese migrants, as well as the feelings stirred up by the Sino-Japanese war, probably exacerbated the situation.[38]

The Boxer Rebellion in 1900 aroused another emotional storm among the Hawaii Chinese. The Chinese government's inability to control the rebellion and prevent retaliatory measures by foreign powers signified to many *wah kiu* the need for governmental change, though others disagreed. The Chinese community was divided over

Table 15
China Relief Projects Carried Out by Hawaii Chinese: 1930–1935

Year	Amount Contributed (in Mex$)	Cause	Location in China	Sponsor
1930	$ 11,000	Flood-famine	Honan, Konsu, Shensi	Chinese Chamber of Commerce and United Chinese Society
1930	146,056	Flood-famine	North China (especially Shensi)	United Chinese Society and Island-wide community
1931	72,224	Flood	Sixteen provinces	Chinese Chamber of Commerce
1933	10,000	Famine	(North East Relief Organization)	Chinese Chamber of Commerce and United Chinese Society
1933	2,580	Flood	Yellow River region	Chinese Chamber of Commerce and United Chinese Society
1935	1,500	Flood	Yellow River region	Kuomintang Headquarters
1935	12,000	Flood	Yellow River region	Chinese Chamber of Commerce and United Chinese Society
1935	3,932	Flood	Yellow River region	Tan Sing Dramatic Club (benefit show)
1935	240	Flood	Yellow River region	Chinese First Church of Christ
1935	224	Flood	Yellow River region	Chung Shan School student body

a request from Peking, forwarded by the Chinese minister in Washington, asking for contributions toward the reconstruction of imperial buildings that had been destroyed by foreigners. The request came in 1901 while Chinese businessmen were trying to recoup their own losses in the 1900 Chinatown fire. This was the time when Consul Liang proposed sending to Peking the money remaining from the funds collected to aid victims of the fire. Although United Chinese Society leaders blocked this action, other Chinese businessmen who did not wish to oppose the consul collected 4,870 ounces of silver which were sent to Peking.[39]

With feeling against the imperial government growing strong among the *wah kiu* in Hawaii, Chinese patriotism was expressed more often by financial support of the revolutionary movement than by actions supporting the Ching regime. After the revolution, appeals to migrants for contributions to patriotic causes continued. Examples taken from a list reported by Kuomintang societies in Hawaii between 1912 and 1928 show the types of appeals to which Chinese in the Islands responded:[40]

1912	Purchase of bonds issued by Dr. Sun's "Canton Army Government"
1912	Contribution to Honolulu headquarters
1913	Campaign for local organization funds
1914	Funds for Dr. Sun Yat-sen in Tokyo
1915	Funds for Lin Sen in America
1915	Funds forwarded to Kuomintang's American headquarters in San Francisco
1916	Funds for memorial to "Seventy-Two Heroes"
1916	Purchase of bonds of Chinese Revolutionary Party
1916	Funds for Chinese aviation schools in America
1917	Funds for Chinese army supplies
1919	Campaign for National Heroes Monuments at Wong Fa Kong in Canton
1920	"Save Canton" campaign
1922	Funds to Canton for airplanes and other army supplies
1922	Funds to Shanghai for "national welfare"
1923	Funds to Jup Sun School, in Canton, erected in honor of national hero
1924	Funds for cotton-padded coats for Chinese army
1924	Funds for erection of tomb for General Dang Sang-pa

1924   Funds for local Kuomintang building
1925   Funds for May 30 Affair, Shanghai, Canton
1926   Funds for Northern Expeditionary Army
1928   Contributions to Kong Yet Kow Kwock Wui, anti-Japanese organization

Participation of *wah kiu* in the new regime in China was not confined to financial contributions. Some migrants returned to China to take an active part in the government; others encouraged their sons to secure official appointments in the Chinese government and helped them financially to do so.[41] One wealthy migrant who had given refuge to political exiles from China sent his son, whom he had named after Sun Yat-sen, to the mainland United States for training as an aviator so he could serve in China. Several fathers showed their new political loyalty by giving their sons nationalistic instead of traditional names.

The more patriotic of Honolulu's Chinese community reacted strongly to international events concerning China.[42] The "Twenty-One Demands" of the Japanese upon China in 1915, the plan to give to Japan the German rights in Shantung after World War I, the reported massacres of Chinese by British and Japanese in 1925—these and other events had repercussions in Honolulu. The first of these prompted a group known as the Young People's Oratorical Association to lead an anti-Japanese campaign; the second led to the formation of an Overseas Chinese Patriotic Organization with the purpose of arousing concern about another "national disgrace" being perpetrated against China and agitating for better treatment of China by international powers; after the third of these events another association, the People's Foreign Relations Club, was started to express indignation against the "atrocities." A group calling itself the National Diplomacy Supporting Association was formed in 1928 at the time of Japanese military actions in Shantung.

When the Japanese invaded Manchuria in 1931, Chinese in Hawaii were not much concerned at first because Manchuria, beyond the Great Wall, was outside the boundaries of China proper and was controlled, moreover, by a warlord of whom Chinese in Hawaii were contemptuous. Nevertheless, the resistance of General Ma's army against the Japanese won the admiration of Hawaii Chinese, who sent money to him directly, as well as money and clothing to the Shanghai Northeast Relief Organization.

When undeclared war broke out in the Shanghai region in 1932, it was inevitable that Chinese in Hawaii should be concerned. Shanghai was in China proper. Cantonese troops—the 19th Route Army under its Hakka leader, General Tsai—showed the strongest resistance to foreign invaders that Chinese forces had ever made. Furthermore, the worst fighting and greatest destruction by the Japanese was in the district of Shanghai inhabited particularly by Cantonese, some of them close relatives of Chinese in Hawaii, and several Hawaii Chinese businessmen had investments in Shanghai firms. Within a few months Chinese in the Islands raised and sent to China some HK$350,000.

Old political divisions among the Hawaii Chinese were subordinated to patriotic concern. Former constitutionalists and Kuomintang members worked together to aid Chinese resistance. During the early period of the 1931–1932 Sino-Japanese conflict a Wah Kiu Kau Kwock Wui ("Overseas Chinese Save the Country Organization") had been formed by the most active members of the pro-Chiang Kuomintang group, with headquarters in the Kuomintang clubhouse, but the Chinese community as a whole contributed toward the HK$24,000 raised by this group. When the conflict in Shanghai broke out, a mass meeting led by the anti-Chiang faction of the Kuomintang was held at the United Chinese Society building, and after this two other "Save China" organizations were formed, with officers who were also leaders in the United Chinese Society, the Chinese Chamber of Commerce, and the Kuomintang. During the peak of the 1931–1932 fighting between Chinese and Japanese armies, other Chinese organizations, already established, raised money for the Chinese forces by campaigns among their own members. Among them were several district associations, two of the guilds, the Mun Lun, Chung Shan, and Hoo Choo schools, and the Chinese-English Debating Society. Young Chinese in Honolulu formed a "Chinese Students Save China Dramatic Club" which staged benefit plays—nationalistic, of course, rather than classical Chinese drama. "Save China" organizations that were set up on the islands of Hawaii, Maui, Kauai, and Molokai raised substantial amounts to assist Chinese forces.

Feelings against Japan were strong throughout the Hawaii Chinese community, among ordinary working men as well as among leaders of nationalistic groups. A letter sent in May 1932 by a waiter in the Lau Yee Chai restaurant to a friend who was a cook in Hong Kong expressed these feelings:

The dwarf Jap invade our territory. When I heard about it my hair stick up. I really feel regretful to see my country devastated by internal strife and foreign invasions and the miserable condition of the people. My only hope is to have all us to work together and struggle and boycott Japanese goods and make the dwarf Jap kill themselves.[43]

When the fighting in Shanghai ended, however, and routine news from China replaced dramatic reports of conflict, patriotic fervor among the Hawaii Chinese died down. The "Save China" organizations wound up their business and published their final reports in the Chinese newspapers. Ardent Chinese nationalists continued to plead for assistance to China's economic and military development, but aside from a few gestures, such as a contribution toward buying airplanes as a birthday gift to General Chiang Kai-shek, there was little participation in patriotic causes until the Japanese invaded China in 1937.

As Japanese forces moved down into South China, another set of relief groups was organized by the Hawaii Chinese.[44] The Western-educated Chinese consul, King-Chau Mui, who was of See Yup origin, had established good relations with Chinese organizations since coming to the Islands in 1930 and got the cooperation of the leaders in the program he suggested. Doo Wai Sing, the president of the United Chinese Society in 1937, chaired the Chinese Relief Association, which sent some $350,000 to China in the first two years of its appeals; he also chaired the China Women's Relief Organization. S. H. Tan, the executive secretary of the United Chinese Society and Chinese Chamber of Commerce, was executive secretary of both relief organizations. Chinese Liberty Bond committees on each island encouraged migrants to invest their money in Chinese military activities.

By the mid-1930s Hawaii-born Chinese outnumbered the migrants, but they joined in on these war-relief enterprises. A Hawaii-born Chinese physician who was active in migrant organizations headed a China Emergency Medical Relief Committee, and he also chaired a committee of the Chinese University Club, an organization of Hawaii-born Chinese which collected and shipped large quantities of clothing to China. Funds were raised among Hawaii Chinese by other organizations such as the Aid to Chinese Wounded Soldiers and Refugees Committee, the Aid to South China Refugees Association, and the Overseas Chinese Chungshan Relief Association. Efforts to assist war-torn China continued through World War II and after, until the People's Republic under Chairman Mao extended its control over all of China, including the migrants' home districts.

Recognition for Nationalistic Activities

Patriotic idealism seems to have been not the only motive for the devotion of so much time, money, and effort to nationalistic causes. Undoubtedly the stirring appeals by various political leaders for a greater new China were effective in developing new attitudes among the fortune-seeking *wah kiu,* but the migrants also came to realize that China's international status affected their own personal interests.

For many decades the humiliating treatment of Chinese migrants in foreign countries and the imposition by foreign powers of extraterritorial rights for their own nationals in China were perennial topics of editorials in Chinese newspapers. Both these situations, it was argued, resulted from China's weakness. In one moment of optimism Chinese in Hawaii joined with those on the mainland in a movement to prevent renewal of the labor treaty between China and the United States under which the Chinese exclusion acts operated and which were to expire in 1905. An organization formed for the purpose, Mun Sing Tong, raised some ten thousand dollars for action; the objective was to exert pressure on the United States government by mobilizing a boycott in China of American-made goods.[45] The ineffectiveness of this movement and the continuation of Chinese exclusion were disheartening. Experiences like this convinced most Chinese in Hawaii that discrimination could be eliminated only by persistent efforts to change public opinion in foreign countries and by strengthening the power of the Chinese government in international relations.

Meanwhile, migrants also came to realize that generous contributions and untiring work as organizers and leaders in patriotic activities were bringing tokens of recognition from the Chinese government in power: appointments to imperial orders, certificates, tablets, plaques. And, moreover, publicity through newspapers and by word of mouth about these awards enhanced the status of the migrants receiving them as "outstanding Chinese" within the Hawaii Chinese community—a sought-after form of recognition once migrants were no longer solely preoccupied with amassing a fortune they could take back to their ancestral villages.

Hawaii Chinese received more recognition from the govern-

ments that followed the 1911 revolution than the imperial government had given them. Chinese in the Islands had special pride in their
close connection with Dr. Sun, a pride that is still felt by many
Hawaii-born Chinese. Hawaii is frequently called "the birthplace of
the Chinese revolution" partly because the first overseas revolutionary group, the Hing Chung Wui, was organized in Hawaii by Dr.
Sun and his followers. The help that Hawaii Chinese gave to Dr. Sun
during his years of revolutionary effort is often recalled. Memories
and mementoes of Dr. Sun's visits to Hawaii have been cherished,
particularly by those who had some personal connection with the
Tsung Li ("Leader").

Migrants who worked steadily for the revolution and closely
with Dr. Sun were especially esteemed and their descendants continue to enjoy the honor given their families. One such migrant was
Luke Chan, born in Dr. Sun's native village, who helped Dr. Sun's
family to escape possible arrest by imperial officials and who served
for a time as Dr. Sun's personal bodyguard. He was sent to Nanking
as Hawaii's representative at the dedication of the Chung Shan mau-
soleum in 1929, and until his death in 1952 was an honored guest at
local nationalistic celebrations. Another was Young Kwong Tat from
Buck Toy village in Chung Shan district, who was an ardent suppor-
ter of Dr. Sun and a leader in some of the struggles for control of the
United Chinese Society between supporters and opponents of Dr.
Sun. In 1922, a year after returning to China, he was rewarded by being made chief magistrate of Chung Shan district, which was in the
area controlled at that time by Dr. Sun's forces.

Conservative migrants who collaborated with the Northern
governments from 1912 to 1930 were recognized many times
through awards to them personally and to the organizations they
represented, including the United Chinese Society, the Chinese
Chamber of Commerce, the Mun Lun Chinese School, and the Constitutional Party.

For a few years after Chiang Kai-shek established the National
government in Nanking in the late 1920s, Chinese in overseas communities could achieve recognition by nominal participation in the
Chinese government itself. This recognition was especially satisfying
to loyal Kuomintang members in the Islands after the Hawaii Kuomintang was given provincial status and could send elected delegates
to the party meetings, the National People's Convention, and the National Congress in China. In 1936, for instance, several candidates for

election as delegate to the congress were sponsored by coalitions of Chinese societies. Candidates gave campaign speeches thanking their sponsors and pledging, if elected, to do their utmost to benefit the Chinese people of Hawaii. The winner in such an election in 1929 was Lau On, a restaurant owner in Hilo, who had been active in the Tung Ming Wui before the revolution and then a leader in the Hilo branch of the Kuomintang. After attending the congress in Nanking he was appointed sheriff and magistrate of his home district from which he had migrated to Hawaii in the 1880s.[46]

Awards like the following, issued after the Sino-Japanese hostilities of 1931–1932, show how individuals and societies in Hawaii were officially recognized by the Chinese government:

Awards to Chinese People of Hawaii from the National Government

(1) Tan Shan Wah Kiu Kwock Nan Kau Chai Wui (Hawaii Overseas Chinese Save China Organization)—President Wong But Ting—a gold tablet and certificate No. 29.

(2) Tan Shan Wah Kiu Ju Kwock Kau Chai Tin (Hawaii Overseas Chinese Save Country Organization)—President Doo Wai Sing—a silver tablet and certificate No. 35.

(3) Chung Wah Jun Chai Wui (Chinese Save China Organization)—President Ching Chau—a silver tablet and certificate No. 70.

(4) Tan Dou Wah Kiu Kau Chai Wui—a silver tablet and certificate No. 77.

(5) Wah Kiu Kau Kwock Wui (Overseas Chinese Save Country Organization)—President Y. K. Lee—a silver tablet and certificate No. 78.

(6) Hilo Jun Chai Wui (Hilo Save China Organization)—a panel with inscriptions and certificate No. 107.

(7) Maui Chung Wah Jun Chai Wui (Maui Chinese Save China Organization)—a panel with inscriptions and certificate No. 191.

(8) Mr. Chun Hoon—a silver tablet and certificate No. 46.

(9) Mr. Young Sung Kee—a panel with inscriptions and certificate No. 144.

(10) Mr. Chun Hoon—a special award for his contribution to Chinese schools.[47]

Although Hawaii-born Chinese sometimes regarded them as too dearly attained, such awards were treasured by migrants of the older generation.

CHAPTER 13

Personal Prestige

MIGRANTS changing from sojourners into settlers gradually shifted their social orientation from their native villages, districts, and country to the Island community of which they were becoming a part. Even activities concerning matters in their homeland were strongly influenced by the desire for personal prestige among other Chinese in Hawaii, especially in Honolulu. Status in Hawaii had at least two aspects for the migrant: individual prestige among other Chinese and the prestige of the Chinese as a group in the interethnic Island society.

Three worlds became interlinked in the migrant settlers' social universe—the China of his newly developed nationalism; the Chinese community in Hawaii; and the Island society at large. Which of these social areas was most important to the migrant would be impossible to discern. A migrant who gave a large donation for famine relief in China might have been responding to three concerns simultaneously: compassion for the plight of the *tung bau* with whom he had come to feel a nationalistic identity; desire to gain face with his fellow *wah kiu* in Hawaii; and interest in demonstrating to the non-Chinese in Hawaii that Chinese were philanthropic and humanitarian as well as commercially oriented. Only arbitrarily can the migrant be considered as having acted with reference to his nationalistic concerns at one time, his status in the local Chinese community at another, and his identity with his ethnic group in the Island society at another. All three concerns were interrelated in the complex society into which the migrant settler was becoming inducted.

Status through Migrant Organizations

The migrant who stayed in the Islands for several years without joining at least one association was an anomaly. The general participation in migrant organizations is all the more striking since few of the Chinese adults who emigrated before 1900 had belonged to formal associations in the old world. With the kinship group dominating almost every phase of life, there was little need or opportunity to join formal associations.

And yet the two facts appear to be closely related. The Chinese villager was accustomed to thinking of himself not as an independent individual but as a member of his clan. Belonging to a weak clan was tragic; belonging to a powerful one was fortunate. In the new world formal associations took over the role of the clan in the migrant's life, slowly but virtually completely. In the village a man's status had depended more upon that of his family and clan and his role within them than upon how outsiders regarded him personally. In Hawaii the time came when the status of a migrant in the Chinese community depended largely upon the number and types of societies he belonged to and his standing in them. Biographies of migrants in the Hawaii Chinese "who's who" publications detailed the organizations to which they belonged and the offices they held in them. The biography of one migrant who had been brought from Chung Shan as an infant and reared in Honolulu listed nearly forty organizations to which he belonged and in many of which he had been an officer.[1] Obituary notices of migrants who had become prominent in Honolulu carried similar information about organizational affiliations.

The status that the early migrant organizations conferred upon their members was important in the formation of similar associations later on, after most of the migrants remaining in Hawaii had become settlers. Thus, for example, the prestige in the Chinese community of district associations such as the Lung Doo Chung Sin Tong and the See Dai Doo Wui Goon motivated migrants from other *doos* of Chung Shan district to organize their own district associations—one as late as 1930, toward the end of the period when the earlier ones had been of real value in helping the migrant make the transition from old-world community to new. It would seem that establishing such an association in this late phase of the migration process was essentially an effort to add to the prestige of its founders.

The status conferred by a Chinese organization seems to have been an important consideration among the Hakkas in Honolulu who organized the Nyin Fo Fui Kon in 1921. Sponsors of this new organization were concerned that the Puntis, more numerous than Hakkas in the Islands, looked down upon the Hakkas. They wanted a society under their own control, one that the Chinese community would recognize as representing the Hakka people, an organization to which individual Hakkas could turn for help, but even more so one that would bolster their self-respect. Although it was sixteen years before the Nyin Fo Fui Kon got its headquarters, participants in the dedication ceremony in 1937 included the Chinese consul general, a Punti from Toi Shan district, as well as representatives of a dozen or so organizations headed by Puntis. The daughter of an officer of this organization commented, shortly after the dedication:

> The opening was held on George Washington's birthday. It seems each Chinese group wants to have a headquarters to show how important they are. Many delegates were sent from other Chinese societies. Each of them made a speech, also Consul Mui. The consul made the best speech. My mother said the speeches by most of the others were terrible. All each man could do was to stand up there and talk about all the things he had done—I, I, I, all afternoon. Another funny thing was that although it is a Hakka society, none of the speeches made by the Hakka speakers were in Hakka—all in Punti. I suppose this was because the delegates from the other societies could not understand Hakka.[2]

Status through Leadership

When Chinese societies began to multiply in the Islands, the migrants were mostly young men between twenty and thirty-five, with a few older Chinese who had preceded the major migration. Chinese merchants with longer residence in Hawaii were generally the organizers and officers of the societies. For several reasons merchants continued to provide most of the leadership in migrant organizations from the 1880s into the 1930s. Most important was the fact that the officers were generally successful businessmen, affluent if not wealthy, and as such they were respected by the younger money-oriented migrants. Wealth was a great advantage for officers in other ways. Most of the societies depended upon nominal admission fees, assessments, and campaigns for funds, but most ordinary members paid only admission fees and limited assessments while the wealthier migrants usually paid big assessments and took the lead in fund-raising campaigns. Having contributed more than most members, they were likely to assert more right to determine policy and claim more voice in choosing officers. Wealthy migrants could give face to an organization by large contributions to Chinatown fund drives, by lavish entertainment, and by importing ceremonial robes to wear on public occasions. With well-established businesses, often with several enterprises on different islands, they could employ subordinates to handle details of management and devote much of their time to the affairs of their societies.

Chinese merchants in the Islands were also likely to be much more secure, legally, than the ordinary laborers who made up the bulk of the migrant population. Merchants, generally exempt from most of the immigration restrictions imposed on laborers, were likely to take up long-term residence in Hawaii, bring in their wives and children, and establish a family identity in the Island community. With extended residence and many business activities they often became well known to local government officials and to Caucasian firms with which they had dealings. In connection with their commercial enterprises they became experienced in employing Caucasian attorneys before Hawaii-born Chinese went into law; these attorneys were occasionally called on to help the officers of the Chinese societies in dealing with the government and other non-Chinese sections of the Island community. The merchants' experience, then, prepared them to serve as intermediaries between the less sophisticated sojourner migrants and other ethnic groups in Hawaii.

The dominant role of the merchants as leaders in Chinatown was a marked contrast to the situation in their home districts. Traditionally the merchant class was not a highly respected part of the Chinese social structure, being quite subordinate to the literati. Few migrants belonged to China's educated elite, however, and those who did had usually been brought to Hawaii to edit newspapers subsidized by merchants or to teach in language schools heavily financed by merchants. If these educated *wah kiu* were active at all in migrant organizations, they usually held the position of Chinese secretary, translating documents and handling correspondence and records in Chinese.

On their part, the merchants saw many personal benefits in organizing and officiating in migrant associations. Not only were they able to exercise control over ordinary migrant laborers to their own financial advantage but, even more important in the present connection, they could advance their own social status through their roles in the associations. From the first, most early leaders in these societies enjoyed high prestige in the Chinese community. As the societies multiplied, they came to form a hierarchy of status based largely on size and wealth. This stature in turn reflected on the prestige of their leaders. At the top of the hierarchy for several decades was the United Chinese Society, semiofficially recognized by both the Hawaiian and the imperial Chinese governments. The status of the leaders of this society thus extended beyond the Chinese community; for over twenty years they acted as representatives of the imperial government, which recognized, by personal awards, their position and work among the *wah kiu*. They were also among the Chinese most respected by Hawaiian officials and Caucasians who dealt with Chinese in business or civic affairs. They were referred to in the English press as leaders in the Chinese community. They stood, therefore, at the top of the scale by which prestige was measured in the three areas of primary concern to status-conscious migrants: the national society of China, the Chinese community in Hawaii, and the Island society at large. From time to time a migrant who was not a leader in the United Chinese Society or the Chinese Chamber of Commerce might have had higher prestige in one of these areas but not in all three, at least during the period from the early 1880s to the 1930s.

As the migrant associations multiplied, relationships among them operated to enhance the personal status of their leaders. After 1900, for instance, when the position of president of the United Chinese Society became elective, one of the first men elected to this office had for several years been president of the See Yup Wei Quan, one of the most powerful district associations. Subsequently the United Chinese Society presidency was filled by men who had previously been presidents of two other strong district associations, the Lung Doo Chung Sin Tong and the See Dai Doo Wui Goon.

Socially ambitious migrants deliberately sought office in less influential societies with a view to using these positions as stepping stones to more prestigious positions. Migrant societies which had outlived their purpose were often prolonged by members who wanted to be elected to offices and have their names appear in Chinese and English-language newspapers and on posters in Chinatown. By the 1930s inactive members or former officers of more than one society were saying "The society is only for the officers." Attempts to revive moribund societies suggest that some individuals were interested in gaining face for themselves through publicity. A group trying in 1931 to revive the Lum Sai Ho Tong, a surname society formed in 1889, published statements which illustrate such an effort:

About 100 years ago people of our clan with a pioneer spirit, progressive mind, crossed the sea and came to this place from Kwangtung. We, the posterity, should revere the pioneer spirit of our clan people, which can rival that of Columbus and Magellan. If we don't have an organization to bring our clan people together, friendship will be diminished and we'll treat each other as strangers. It is, therefore, evident that our clan needs an organization in order to bring all of our people together. . . .

We must have past history as a model for the present. . . . The establishment of the Lum Sai Ho Tong was initiated by Say Yip and Lop Soi and some others. They saw that the people of our clan in Hawaii were increasing in number, and that all were engaged busily at work. Although they are "brothers" of the same clan, they cannot get rid of conflicts between themselves. For this reason, Say Yip gave his property for a place to build a clan clubhouse. . . . Since the establishment it has now been several decades. As time goes by, all the deeds they have done are buried. All the records have been lost. . . . Therefore, when the directors met on the twentieth year of the Republic [1931], July 15th, they passed a resolution to have registration. The directors elected humble me as the Chairman. . . . Within a short period of two months, the work was completed. . . . Posterity looks to the present, just as the present looks to the past. I sincerely hope that posterity in the future will uphold the same principle to build up an everlasting memory. This is my humble, sincere hope.[3]

Similarly, the promonarchical Chinese Constitutional Party was kept in existence for years after the end of the Ching dynasty by a small group of well-known conservatives serving as its officers. They continued to finance their newspaper, *Sun Chung Kwock Bo (New China News)*, even though by the 1930s the members had generally come to accept the Republic of China, had contributed financially to the Nanking government's opposition to Japanese invasion of China, and had come to have only contempt for the Manchu Pu Yi who abdicated as emperor in 1911 but became a "puppet ruler" for the Japanese in Manchukuo in the 1930s.[4]

Many migrant associations contributed to the status-seeking efforts of some members, and recognized the status already achieved by others, by having large boards of directors who were mainly honorary. The bylaws of the Lung Doo Chung Sin Tong, mentioned earlier, authorized the eight officers to appoint forty-eight members to the board of directors; the duties of the board were not clearly stated and only twelve were needed for a quorum. The Chinese Chamber of Commerce bylaws called for the election of fifty directors in addition to the officers; only fifteen constituted a quorum at a board meeting. The United Chinese Society had a board of fifteen trustees and an advisory council first of fifteen members, later of forty-five. Members of the advisory council could give advice at executive meetings but had no vote. By appointing or electing directors the societies could give prestige to members whose cooperation and financial support they wanted; they could honor members who had served for many years as active leaders; they could add lustre to their own organization by having eminent members of the community on their boards. They could also give directorships to promising, active young men who might later be elected to offices in which they would serve not only as leaders in the societies' own affairs but as their representatives in the Chinese community.

Sometimes Chinese who wanted social recognition in the Chinese community but thought they had little chance of getting it through established Chinese societies set out to organize new associations in which, as sponsors, they would have leading roles. Such considerations fostered new district associations, surname societies, village clubs, patriotic organizations, physical culture clubs, oratorical, debating, music, dramatic, and literary societies. They could count on receiving publicity in the Chinese press, perhaps also in the English-language newspapers, as well as attention on the Chinatown grapevine-telegraph. Elections of officers, annual banquets attended by officers of other associations, clubhouse dedications, participation in Chinatown relief campaigns—all provided possibilities for personal publicity for the associations' founders and leaders.

The various associations in Chinatown eventually formed a network within which leadership in one organization brought recognition from all. Leaders were generally asked to represent their organizations at public gatherings sponsored by a particular society whose leaders in turn would appear as honored guests at functions sponsored by the other societies. Guests of honor at the annual dinner of a district association, for example, would often be leaders of other district associations, the United Chinese Society, and the Chinese Chamber of Commerce, all of whom would be asked to speak. The formal opening of a new clubhouse was a typical occasion when a society would invite representatives of other societies to be guests of honor. Many societies held open house at Chinese New Year not only for their own members but also for officers of other associations.

The United Chinese Society and Chinese Chamber of Commerce, acting jointly after 1929, held New Year receptions attended by civic leaders in the general Island community as well as by officers of other Chinese societies.

It was at events sponsored by the Chinese community as a whole that the social status of leaders of various organizations was made most evident. When a public reception was held for a distinguished Chinese visitor at the United Chinese Society headquarters, association officers had a prominent part in the affair. After 1912, when mass meetings were held each 10 October—Double Ten Day ("Chinese Independence Day")—to celebrate the establishment of the republic, leaders of societies that were nationalistic in sympathy were on the platform, wearing badges and making speeches. Graduation exercises at Chinese schools became occasions for praising public-spirited members of the Chinese community. Prominent Chinese led the most solemn community ceremonies each year: the rites for the spirits of the departed at the Spring Festival (Ching Ming). All such occasions have been part of a complex of social behavior related to status in the Chinese community and indicative of the use of leadership in immigrant societies as a way of gaining prestige by individual migrants.

Status through Philanthropy

Increasing individualism and ambition for personal status among the migrants, the inevitable results of their release from restricting kinship ties, are clearly seen in what some members of the Chinese community called "buying face"—gaining recognition and prestige by donations to Chinese community projects. In this connection one must keep in mind that most migrants came to Hawaii primarily to make money and the majority of those who migrated before 1900 were illiterate and unschooled. Few, even of those who accumulated the largest fortunes, could read or write more than a simple form of written Chinese. They could most easily bid for status with money. Hence most migrants participated in Chinese nationalistic causes mainly by giving financial support to other Chinese who provided the leadership. Some of the drives in support of nationalistic causes were the most highly publicized, strongly advocated, and aggressively promoted enterprises undertaken by the *wah kiu* in Hawaii. Heavy contributions, as a consequence, gained "big face" in the local Chinese community in addition to recognition from the government in China.

Two local projects illustrate how buying face was facilitated by fund-raising techniques: a campaign in 1929 to collect money for adding classrooms to Mun Lun School, and another in 1933 to buy the Makiki residence of the late Y. Ahin for use as the Chinese consulate.

Because of Mun Lun's eminence as one of the first two Chinese-language schools, and as the largest, and also because its supporters were in favor with the governments controlling China from 1912 to 1929, directorships on its board carried almost as much prestige as offices in the United Chinese Society and Chinese Chamber of Commerce. The campaign procedure shows how effectively the committee used the desire for face to get large contributions. Executive officers were chosen to head several committees, and more than seventy-five Chinese were appointed to campaign positions. Before the main drive started, four leading supporters of the project headed the list of contributors, two subscribing $1,000 each, another $800, and the fourth $500. The rules governing contributions show how carefully the committee graduated the recognition to be given to donors in terms of the size of their donations:

> (1) The names of all those who contribute less than ten dollars will appear in the newspapers.
> (2) The names of all those who contribute more than ten dollars and up to one hundred dollars will be displayed permanently in the guest room.
> (3) Those who contribute between one hundred and five hundred dollars will have their pictures framed and hung in the guest room.
> (4) Those who contribute between five hundred and seven hundred fifty dollars will have their pictures framed and hung in the guest room and *classrooms* will also be named after them.
> (5) Those who contribute more than seven hundred fifty dollars will have the larger classrooms named after them besides having their pictures hung in the guest room.[5]

The success of the campaign and subsequent events were recorded in the school's twenty-fifth anniversary publication:

> As a token of appreciation to all those who donated some money, the school hired a troupe of actors to put on a Chinese play at the Oahu Theatre [in the old Chinese quarter]. . . . Before the play started, there

was singing by the students. Speeches were made by Yee Chun, president of the school; Chun Quon, president of the campaign; and Chang Yum-Sin, principal of the school, who thanked and commended the spirit of the Chinese people. Afterwards the names and pictures of those who contributed more than one hundred dollars were flashed on the screen. . . .

On September 29, noon, the opening exercises of the school were held. At this time works of the students pertaining to composition, letter-writing, penmanship, and art were exhibited. . . . To add to the gaiety, the Royal Hawaiian Band was on hand to play. . . . On the four walls of the reception room hung the pictures of the members of the Ching Nin Moo Hock Kee Lock Boo and also the pictures and names of the contributors, as mentioned in the rules above. . . .

The amount of money from contributions was $16,320.50; the net income from the benefit shows was $6,084.90; a total of $22,405.40.

This publication also noted that twelve of the school's classrooms had been named after the following donors: Chun Quon, Dai Yen Chang, Yee Chun, Chun Kam Chow, Wong Goon Sun, Yee Mun Wai, Chun Kwai Hin, Leong Bew, Chun Hoon, Wong Wai Wing, Hee Yau Kun, and Chong Pak Shun. Five of the classrooms were named after firms making substantial donations: C. Q. Yee Hop Company, City Mill Company, King Street Fish Market, Castle and Cooke Company, and Alexander and Baldwin Company. One room was designated the Alumni Room, another the Ching Nin Moo Hock Kee Lock Bo Room.[6]

Similar methods of giving face to donors were used in the campaign to raise money for the permanent Chinese consulate, as shown in the fund-raising committee's constitution:

> I. Name of the Committee: The name of this committee will be the "Committee to Raise Funds for the Purchasing of the Consulate Quarters."
> II. Publication of Campaign Results: After the campaign, the names of those who contribute money, as well as how the money was used, will be published in a special commemorative book.
> III. Special Awards to Contributors:
>   A. Anyone who contributes more than five hundred dollars will have a whole page in this book, containing his photograph and a history of himself.
>   B. Anyone contributing more than two hundred fifty dollars

will have half a page in this book, containing his photograph and a brief history of himself.

C.   Anyone contributing more than one hundred dollars will have a fourth of a page in this book, containing his photograph and his occupation.

D.   All those contributing more than fifty dollars will have their photographs published in this book. . . .

IV. Commemoration Plaque: The committee will try to place a commemoration plaque within the consulate's quarters, on which the names of all those who contribute more than fifty dollars will have their names inscribed for memory.[7]

This campaign was kept within the Chinese community; no Caucasian firm or other outside sources were solicited for funds. Individual Chinese, business firms, and organizations of Hawaii-born Chinese as well as migrants cooperated. The committee's goal of $15,000 was exceeded by more than $2,500. A commemorative book published a list of the 1,417 contributors with the amounts they gave, photographs of those who donated fifty dollars or more, pictures and biographies of the larger contributors, and brief histories of associations and firms giving fifty dollars or more. The commemorative volume also mentioned those who sent gifts or congratulatory messages for the opening ceremonies of the building.

Such activities reveal not only the concern migrants came to feel about their status within the Chinese community, but also the values that were becoming dominant in their new social world. To an extent that never existed in the old world, status in the Chinese community became identified with individual wealth and with liberality in contributing to community enterprises. But wealth alone did not assure the migrant of esteem within the Chinese community. The way he accumulated his wealth was considered, although not always as it would have been in a typical American community. It was common knowledge among Island Chinese, for instance, that several of the wealthiest Chinese men of the older generation had made part of their fortunes in activities the Hawaiian government defined as illegal and some Caucasians regarded as immoral, but this knowledge did not particularly damage their reputation or that of their descendants among the Chinese. Some were known to have made thousands of dollars helping Chinese enter the Islands fraudulently. Others were reputed to have made their fortunes in the opium trade. A founding officer of the United Chinese Society was arrested and tried in 1896 for helping "hundreds of Chinamen" enter the Islands with false papers. Another prominent merchant was arrested in 1896 on a charge of trying to bribe an inspector at shipside to allow some migrants to remain in the Islands illegally; several years later he was president of the United Chinese Society.[8]

But the Chinese merchant or entrepreneur who owed his wealth to deliberate exploitation of his fellow migrants was held in contempt by the Chinese community. And a wealthy migrant who was indifferent toward Chinese community projects or refused to contribute liberally to nationalistic causes was looked down upon as miserly or selfish. One such migrant was described in the 1930s by a Hawaii-born Chinese as a misfit:

> A "misfit" member of the Chinese Chamber of Commerce is ———. The mere mention of his name to other Chinese will reveal that he is regarded as "different." . . . He is a well-known business man and could almost be called a Chinese millionaire. He has become a member of the chamber just to have his store listed as a member, but he does not participate in its activities. To him, his business is more important than organizations. In spite of his riches he is seen walking on the street in his everyday cheap Chinese working clothes. He runs his own business. In fact he works as though he were very poor. It is very true that he does not adapt himself to organization. He does not even mingle with his own people. He does not have any spare time. His business is running all the time. Deliveries are made in the night as well as on late Saturdays. . . . During the famine drive, he was approached by one of the chamber team captains. He readily told the man that he was giving fifty dollars. The solicitor tried to give a good speech in order to persuade him to give more. But ——— frankly said that he had decided how much to give the night before. . . . After giving the check he went on with his business and just ignored whether the solicitor remained or not.

On the other hand, spending money solely to gain face was not a sure way to get it. This was demonstrated when an enterprising group of young Chinese men undertook in 1928, as a commercial venture, the publication of a book called *Tan Shan Wah Kiu* ("Overseas Chinese of Hawaii"). Descriptive and historical articles were written in Chinese on the Hawaiian Islands, Island history, economic activities of Chinese in the Islands, and Chinese associations and institutions. Seven short articles in English, three of them written by Caucasian professional men, were also included. No advertising was solicited or included in the publication, but the promoters capitalized on the desire of Chinese migrants for recognition by including an unselective "who's who" of Chinese in Hawaii. Any Chinese who paid twenty-five dollars for a page could have his picture printed together with a brief biography written in both Chinese and English or in Chinese alone. The final publication was largely made up of the 207 pages devoted to the 198 Chinese men included in the who's who section. Most of the prominent Chinese migrants in the Islands were among the 198, but many of the others were not regarded in the Chinese community as worthy of such recognition. The inclusion of these "nobodies" and social climbers was the subject of caustic comment; several of the men who had bought pages were ridiculed. Many Chinese who had been impressed by the ostensible purposes outlined by the promoters saw the volume as the commercial venture it was—and were so disillusioned that when a second volume on the Chinese in Hawaii was undertaken in 1935 few Chinese leaders paid to be included. The who's who in the second volume was regarded by Island Chinese as even less representative of eminent members of the community than the first.

Status through Family

It was not simply coincidental that most of the migrants who became leaders in the Chinese community were men who sooner or later established families in Hawaii. Those who brought their wives and children from China, or married in Hawaii and had Hawaii-born children, were generally the more successful migrants, and with their families in the Islands they were the ones most likely to settle there rather than return to China. At the same time, the presence of their families gave them opportunities for social recognition not open to familyless migrant men no matter how well off they might be financially.

The family home became one of the most obvious symbols of affluence in Honolulu, and the location, style, and furnishing of houses took on considerable social significance. Sojourner migrants had been little concerned about housing once their basic needs for shelter and cooking facilities had been met. Intent on making money as quickly as possible, they generally accepted the inconveniences of crowded, makeshift living quarters. Even the early families lived for the most part in sparsely furnished, crowded rooms on or near the family business premises. However, even before they finally gave up the idea of returning to China, many migrants responded to pressures from wives, children, relatives, and friends in Hawaii to buy homes in residential neighborhoods outside the business area of Chinatown. Chinese families in Honolulu began moving out of Chinatown much earlier than those in San Francisco or New York.[9]

A 1900 census report on home ownership showed that only 393, about 12 percent, of 3,247 Chinese heads of families owned the houses they lived in. Most of these houses and those bought by Chinese during the first quarter of this century were relatively inexpensive and modest in size and appearance, but as the idea of permanent residence in Hawaii replaced the sojourner outlook, rivalry for prestige within the Chinese community as well as concern about status in the wider Hawaiian society led to the building of larger and more impressive residences.

In the first English-language publication on successful Chinese migrants, in 1913, Chinese authors noted the beautiful and spacious homes several of these migrants owned outside Chinatown. Many large houses were built in anticipation that married sons and their children would live in them with their parents, after the style of well-to-do families in China. A middle-class residential development of the late 1920s and 1930s in which many second-generation Chinese bought homes together with their immigrant parents became popularly known as "Chinese Hollywood." Some years later a development of much more expensive homes was sometimes jocularly called "Mandarin Heights" because some of the wealthiest Chinese built houses there, though they made up less than half of the residents. House interiors as well as exteriors were used for competitive display —the lighting and plumbing were modern and Western, but the furnishings were often of the sort that wealthy families in China would have had, and in fact furniture was commonly imported from China. A Chinese consul who had traveled widely among overseas Chinese colonies, especially in the western hemisphere, said in 1931 that the Chinese in Hawaii had nicer homes than any other group of overseas Chinese he had visited.[10]

Housewarmings became elaborate affairs. By the late 1920s it was common for dozens, even hundreds, of guests—mostly Chinese but usually including Caucasians, Hawaiians, Japanese, and members of other groups—to be invited. These occasions revealed that owning a home, whatever other purposes it served, was a way of gaining face.

Children, especially sons, gave their migrant fathers further opportunity to gain face in the Chinese community. Apart from the traditional ceremonies attending births and the celebration of birthdays, well-to-do migrants could give their children educational advantages far beyond anything dreamed of by most of the earlier migrants. Sending sons back to the ancestral village for elementary education in schools that the migrants themselves often supported, or later to a college or university in China, was highly praiseworthy in the eyes of other migrants, especially the older ones. After Annexation, however, it became more usual to send sons to American colleges and universities, especially for business or professional training. "My son the doctor" was just as much a matter of pride to Chinese parents in Hawaii as to parents in other immigrant groups on the U.S. mainland. Honolulu newspapers carried articles on sons or daughters going to or returning from China or the U.S. mainland, there were parties to celebrate their return with diplomas or degrees, and the careers of Hawaii-born Chinese were followed with great interest. Migrants took pride in sons who came into the family business or branched out into new commercial fields, as they did in sons who entered professional, educational, governmental, or religious occupations.

Marriages of Hawaii-born children in migrant families were matters of great concern to the parents of prospective brides and grooms. Within the well-understood status structure emerging in the Chinese community, the selection of mates could enhance or, less noticeably, lower a family's status. Parents tried to arrange the best possible marriages for their sons and daughters, considering carefully not only the character of the bride or the prospects of the groom, but whether or not the marriage would bring about a favorable alliance between their families. In the early days, parents of Hawaii-born girls were in the fortunate position of having their daughters in demand by well-to-do older migrants who preferred not to send to China for a bride. A wealthy rice planter on Kauai, for example, could find Chinese parents in Honolulu willing and eager to arrange his marriage to their daughter twenty or twenty-five years younger. In turn, the parents would be seen by people in the Chinese community as connected with a highly successful migrant. When marriage arrangement gave way to the Western custom of romantic choice, parents tried to limit their children's associates to a circle within which a suitable choice would be made. Weddings became tremendously expensive affairs, even among less well-to-do families. Parents really unable to afford elaborate wedding banquets and receptions commonly passed on the debts incurred to the young couple, in the meantime enjoying the satisfaction of having impressed members of their own generation and gaining some face in the Chinese community.

Adult sons were often a help to leaders of migrant societies who wanted to maintain their status and that of their families in the community. Elderly migrant leaders often recruited their sons and those of fellow leaders to take over responsibilities in the societies. For their part, young progressive businessmen and professional men, such as lawyers, public accountants, and doctors, found it advantageous to their careers to devote time to these organizations. In a way, this process tended to crystallize status patterns established by the migrants and continue them in the Chinese community in succeeding generations.

As migrants reached their later years, celebrations of such birthdays as the sixty-first and seventy-first became occasions for demonstrations of respect from friends and acquaintances. Their children usually arranged banquets, often for several hundred guests, at which their achievements were recounted by personal friends and public figures who spoke in testimony to the qualities that had made them successful and esteemed. A Honolulu newspaper in 1928 carried an account of a somewhat exceptional example of anniversary celebrations held in China as well as in Hawaii. The host in Honolulu was a "son of two fathers," having been adopted by his uncle. Although his real name was Yuen Kwock, he was known locally as Fong Inn after the name of the store he had established in 1903, and his son took Inn as a surname. Yuen served as officer in several migrant societies in Hawaii, including the presidency of the United Chinese Society. The newspaper described the occasion:

> Yuen Jan Yock, 91, and Yuen Kee Yock, 89, aged brothers of Lam Bin Hee [Chung Shan] . . . were honored by prominent sons and grandsons in different parts of the world in a series of anniversary banquets, the last of the number being by Fong Inn and his son, Henry Inn, well-known local businessmen, at the Sun Yun Wo on Sunday of last week. More than 70 friends were the guests at the celebration held in this city.
>
> The honorees are the fathers of Fong Inn following an old Chinese custom. Fong Inn, who is the youngest son of Yuen Kee Yock, father of three sons, was adopted by his uncle, Jan Yock. . . .
>
> Fong Inn returned to China with his family, including his wife, a

daughter, Miss Kam Soo Inn, Mrs. Henry Inn, and four children of the latter in January of this year, to attend the grand double anniversary celebration in Lam Bin Hee. While they were in Shanghai, a banquet was held for relatives and friends residing in the metropolis of the east. More than 15 members of the family joined those from Honolulu to attend another celebration in Canton and, later, the final feast at Lam Bin Hee.

More than 2000 attended the Lam Bin Hee affair, people coming from a radius of 12 miles of the village. Many prominent officials of the Nationalist government sent gifts and attended the event.

The Lam Bin Hee birthday celebration was one of the largest of its kind in the Nom-long district. . . . With more than 50 male descendants, Jan Yock and Kee Yock Yuen are great-great-grandfathers.[11]

In the Chinese tradition it was on occasions like this that elderly Chinese women, who seldom had been seen at public affairs and who had had inconspicuous though important roles in their husbands' lives, were also publicly honored. Many articles in local newspapers have described banquets arranged by grateful sons and daughters on the occasion of their mothers' sixty-first, seventy-first, or eighty-first birthdays.

Even death, which in the village would have concerned the kinship group primarily, came to have status implications as it became a combined family and public matter among the migrants. It has been said of the Chinese that "the most important thing in life is to be buried well."[12] In village China, being buried well was mainly a matter of using *fung shui* in the selection of a propitious burial place, which would assure comfort to the spirit in the hereafter, and making provision for ancestor worship by descendants. In Hawaii, funeral services and burials became elaborate and expensive, reflecting not only the status of the deceased but also that of his family in the eyes of the community. Funerals had to be attended by priests, orchestras, friends and acquaintances, business associates, and representatives of the various Chinese societies to which the migrant had belonged. For several decades funeral services for prominent migrants were reported in detail in the Honolulu English-language newspapers as well as in the Chinese press. The status of the deceased was indicated by the status of the men who agreed to be honorary pallbearers. The *Honolulu Star-Bulletin*, 21 March 1931, announcing the forthcoming funeral services for the late Young Ahin, wealthy migrant and leader in several Chinese organizations during his last years, gave the names and affiliations of the pallbearers and other details about the services:

The pallbearers are C. K. Ai, vice-president of the Chinese American Bank; Doo Waising, president of the Honolulu Chinese Chamber of Commerce; Fong Hing, president of the United Chinese Society; Wong Lum, vice-president of the Chinese chamber; Dr. Kalfred Dip Lum, president of the United Chinese News; S. H. Tan, former Chinese consul; Ching Chow, manager of Wing Hong Yuen Co.; and Lau Yun Chee, retired merchant.

There will be three bands, one furnished by the family, another to be provided by the Bucktoy Villagers' club, of which Young Ahin was the president, and the third by the Wing Chong Lung and Kwong Chong Lung companies, in which the deceased was copartner.

About 100 automobiles will be in the procession. Those who will march all the way will be the members of the Bucktoy Villagers' club, members of the Kuomintang, and students of the Chungshan Chinese school.[13]

The cemetery chosen for the burial and the location of the burial plot also reflected upon the status of the deceased. At least until 1950, prominent Chinese families, especially those who were tradition-oriented non-Christians, regarded the Manoa Chinese Cemetery as the most prestigious. Prices of plots within this cemetery varied widely: the higher-priced plots were nearest the burial place of the *tai gung* ("Great Ancestor").

CHAPTER 14

Group Status

THROUGH most of the migrant period there was a certain ambiguity in the status of the Chinese as a group in the social order developing in Hawaii. Merchants, craftsmen, and servants in the urban areas, sugar and rice planters, farmers and laborers in the rural areas were sometimes welcomed and respected by other groups, sometimes rejected, and sometimes simultaneously welcomed and rejected by different sections of the Island population. During much of the same period, as nationals of a country which for a long time rejected and ignored or grudgingly acknowledged them, they lacked the protection of a government such as that enjoyed by nationals of other countries coming to the Islands during the nineteenth and early twentieth centuries. As a consequence, the status of the Chinese community in Hawaii had to be established by its own members. Through most of the migrant period their efforts in this direction had two interrelated objectives: to combat discrimination against them as a group and to raise their prestige as a group in the view of other groups in the Islands.

The need to cope with discrimination as a group did not arise during the first half-century of their presence in the Islands when Chinese, like other foreigners, were accepted as individuals by the indigenous Hawaiians. During this period, when Caucasians had not yet established their strong influence over Hawaiian rulers and the Hawaiian kingdom was not yet firmly controlled by a central authority, Chinese had close contacts with the Hawaiian *alii* ("nobles") in several parts of the Islands. Governors of the islands of Maui and Hawaii made lands under their control available to Chinese for sugar production and arranged for Hawaiian laborers to work in the cane fields. Marriages with Hawaiian women of chiefly rank demonstrated the cordial relations between these early Chinese migrants and the Hawaiian elite. By 1845 at least one Chinese migrant had been admitted to citizenship in the Hawaiian kingdom in accordance with regulations applying to all foreigners, and before the monarchy ended in 1893 at least 750 Chinese had become citizens of Hawaii. One, whose wife was Hawaiian, was repeatedly elected in the 1880s by a predominantly Hawaiian constituency to the position of district magistrate.[1]

It was not until Chinese came in larger numbers as indentured laborers and servants to work for Caucasians, and Caucasians were becoming the most powerful foreign group, that the earlier Chinese came to feel uncertain about their status in Hawaii. A ball given in 1856 by the still tiny group of Chinese merchants, on the occasion of the marriage of King Kamehameha IV, appears to have been an attempt to assert their place on the upper levels of the pluralistic Island society. The American diplomatic corps and businessmen had given a ball which was followed by one given by the Germans. Following suit, the Chinese merchants invited the king and queen and a large number of guests to their festivity, which the Honolulu English-language newspapers described at length:

> The idea which prompted the Chinese merchants to give some marked testimonial of their loyalty to the Sovereign of their adopted country, was a happy one, and showed that they were ambitious to equal at least their fellow citizens in "honoring the King." The "festival" consisted of a ball which took place on ... November 13 at the court house. An unusually large number of invitations had been issued, in conformity with the wishes of the Chinese merchants, that none should be omitted, and it is probable that over one thousand persons visited the hall during the evening.
>
> ... Visitors met and greeted the Chinese merchants, all dressed in the different styles of Mandarins. But when their Majesties arrived the long line of Mandarins bowed their heads very low, till they passed, which is the Chinese custom in the royal presence.
>
> On entering the hall, guests accosted the *Mandarins Anglais*, Weong Chong Hoffmann, Chong Fong Field, Ming Ching Reiners, and Weong Kong Waterman, dressed in Chinese costume, fans included, who were charged with the duties of Directors general—a ball being practically above the comprehension of a Chinaman. ...
>
> Among the distinguished guests present we noticed, beside their Majesties, H.R.H. the Premier, Princess Victoria Kaahumanu; H.R.H. Prince L. Kamehameha, their Excellencies the Ministers of Foreign Relations and of the Interior, John Ii, Esq., M.P.C.; the Commissioners of France and of the United States, all the resident Consuls; Captain Harvey and the officers of H.B.M.'s ship *Havannah*, Captain Gizolme and officers of H.I.M.'s ship *Embuscade*; and many others of the elite of Honolulu.

The ball was opened at 20 minutes to 9, Her Majesty having honored Mr. Yung Sheong by selecting him for her partner in the first cotillion; the King dancing with Mrs. Gregg. . . . Other couples were . . . Mr. Afong and Mrs. W. C. Parke; Mr. Ahee and Mrs. Coady; and Mr. Gee Woo and Mrs. Aldrich. . . .

The collation *(man in)* was perhaps the richest and most expensive part of the festival. It consisted of three tables across the Hall of Representatives, with seats for 150 ladies. The taste displayed in getting up this feast is a little ahead of anything we have ever witnessed here or elsewhere. . . . Two of the items we may mention . . . were six whole sheep roasted, and 150 chickens. The beautiful pastry was got up by the Chinese themselves, as were the decorations, which were in the most flowery style of the Flowery Kingdom. . . .

The cost of the ball, as we are informed, amounted to not far from $3,700. The opportunity to display their attachment and loyalty towards the Sovereign of the country in which they reside, and bear so high a name for regularity in their business habits and general observance of the laws, was seized on by the Chinese merchants in a way that will be long remembered by all those who had an opportunity to observe it. . . . The ball . . . was the most splendid affair of its kind that has ever occurred in Honolulu.[2]

All the elements of the Chinese concern about their status are implicit in the phrasing of the Caucasian reporters' accounts of this ball: its demonstration that the "Chinese merchants . . . were ambitious to equal at least their fellow citizens in 'honoring the King' "; the "*Mandarins Anglais* . . . charged with the duties of Directors general—a ball being practically above the comprehension of a Chinaman"; the elaborate "collation . . . a little ahead of anything we have ever witnessed here or elsewhere"; and "the opportunity to display their attachment and loyalty towards the Sovereign of the country in which they reside . . . seized on by the Chinese merchants." The implication is obvious. Though they bore "so high a name for regularity in their business habits and general observance of the laws," the Chinese merchants found it necessary to give an affair even more lavish than those given by other foreign groups.

Migrants as Representatives of China

Though the Chinese merchants continued for some time to be spoken of as a "quiet, honest, and peaceable class" and as "faithful and devoted subjects,"[3] the intemperate anti-Chinese agitation of the late 1870s and the 1880s changed the picture. The term "coolies" which at first was merely a descriptive word for unskilled laborers came to be used among other groups as a derogatory term and to symbolize a new set of attitudes toward the Chinese. It was in this new atmosphere that leaders of the migrant group tried to assert the dignity of the Chinese as nationals of a foreign country and to seek for themselves as representatives of China the formal recognition and public courtesies accorded to representatives of other nations in official Hawaiian circles. In 1884, shortly after being recognized as commercial agents of the Chinese government, C. Alee and Goo Kim informed the Minister of Foreign Affairs that the anniversary of the emperor of China would be celebrated by a display of the Chinese flag and a reception to which officials of the government were invited. Even though this was during the peak of anti-Chinese agitation when the government was restricting Chinese immigration, the minister replied that government officials would be pleased to attend the reception. Annually, until the first Chinese consul arrived in 1898, the Chinese commercial agents, assisted by other migrant leaders, held similar receptions at the United Chinese Society headquarters; each year the receptions were attended by officials of the Hawaiian government and diplomatic representatives of other nations.[4]

After Annexation these receptions in honor of the emperor gave way to receptions on the first day of the Chinese New Year with officers of the United Chinese Society cooperating with the Chinese consul at the Society's headquarters. Beginning in February 1912 the Chinese Merchants' Association replaced the United Chinese Society in assisting the consul in the annual reception. After the Merchants' Association was renamed the Chinese Chamber of Commerce in 1926 and moved into joint headquarters with the United Chinese Society in 1929, the official receptions were given by the consul and the officers of the two organizations. Throughout this period the migrant leaders had a semiofficial role at these receptions. Whoever was the Chinese consul at the time was of course the official representative of China; but the migrant leaders, long-time Island residents, were generally recognized as the link between the Hawaii Chinese and other sections of the Hawaiian population.[5]

Events in China sometimes impinged upon the migrants' concern for their reputation as an ethnic group in Hawaii. The Boxer Rebellion in 1900 was such an event. It broke out at a particularly crucial time when the American territorial government was being set up in Hawaii and there was still uncertainty about the legal status of Chinese under the new government. "Chinese citizens" held a mass meeting in Honolulu "in regard to the recent deplorable situation in China" and drew up resolutions denouncing the "Boxers" as "murderers and outlaws" and expressing "profound sympathy for the loss of life which has been inflicted upon the citizens of the United States in China by the 'Boxers'." A copy of these resolutions was sent to the Chinese minister in Washington to be presented to the American secretary of state, and another copy was presented by a committee of Chinese leaders to the governor of Hawaii.[6]

In contrast to the Boxer Rebellion, which Chinese in Hawaii felt reflected unfavorably upon them as a group, the establishment of the Republic of China was seen as an event that would raise the status of the *wah kiu* since it promised to be an effective, modern government that would make China a stronger power in the international world. The gala reception held on 12 January 1912 by the United Chinese Society, reported at length in the *Advertiser*, was attended by "nearly 2,000 Chinese and foreigners." Changes coming about with the new order were symbolized by the Western clothes worn by migrant leaders instead of formal Chinese dress ("not a queue was seen"), and for the first time the wives of migrant leaders joined them in the reception line. That same year migrants were active in drawing up petitions, signed by Hawaii Chinese who were American citizens, urging the United States to recognize the Republic of China.

When the republic did receive American recognition, the Chinese consul held a reception "for the American people" which was attended by the governor of Hawaii, the heads of American military forces in the Islands, and other American officials.[7] A few months later Hawaii Chinese published a forty-eight-page pamphlet, *The Chinese in Hawaii*, "to commemorate the recognition of China as a Republic by the United States." It was written in English and obviously for non-Chinese readers; on the cover were American, Hawaiian, and Chinese flags. Along with pictures and biographies of successful Chinese businessmen in the Islands, there were articles on different ways Hawaii Chinese had taken part in Hawaiian and American life: the taxes they paid, financial contributions to disaster relief in San Francisco in 1906, the education of Hawaii-born Chinese in Chinese-supported private schools, the participation of Hawaii-born Chinese in the National Guard, tours of Hawaii Chinese baseball teams around the United States, and other activities. The continuing grievance against the American exclusion laws was expressed in an article on the indignity and economic hardship those laws imposed on the Chinese.

In-Group Control

During the 1880s and 1890s, when anti-Chinese agitation increased the social distance between the Chinese and other groups in the Islands, migrants found ways to circumvent oppressive regulations—and this in turn led to charges that the Chinese conspired with one another in illegal activities of all sorts. Honolulu newspapers regularly carried notices of arrests of migrants for breaking one law or another, and there were occasional accounts of charges against established migrant businessmen. However, the very isolation created by mutual distrust between the authorities and the Chinese provided a measure of protection for migrants engaged in illegal practices. Even if such practices were not condoned by most migrants, it was difficult under the circumstances for Chinese to testify against one another.

The situation changed after anti-Chinese agitation died down. With migrants rising on the economic scale and settlement attitudes spreading, many practices that had been tolerated among the *wah kiu* were censured because they reflected unfavorably upon the whole Chinese community. Chinese societies made it clear that they would not protect members who committed crimes. An article in the United Chinese Society bylaws published in 1901 stated that "it shall be the duty of the Managing Committee to assist the Government in the investigation of any criminal charge against any Chinese [and] to assist Chinese of needy circumstances who may be wrongfully accused of crime or misdemeanors." Obviously, inner cohesion was not considered so important that the Chinese community would allow itself to lose face in order to save one of its own members. Even as late as the 1970s this concern for the good name of the Chinese community in Hawaii led United Chinese Society leaders to call in some newly immigrant Chinese youths and warn them that the Hawaii Chinese would not tolerate the sort of gang warfare that was starting up in San Francisco. Hawaii Chinese would not hesitate to cooperate with the police in dealing with the culprits.

In the earlier migrant period several community leaders were vigilant in preventing or at least controlling activities that had brought Chinese into disrepute elsewhere. Goo Kim, while he was president of the United Chinese Society in the 1890s, took action to prevent Chinese in the Islands from becoming involved in traffic in prostitution. There had been charges that American efforts to suppress the business among Chinese in the continental United States were being impeded by Chinese in Hawaii. Women who had been bought in China and then denied entrance to the United States were sent back to China—but, it was claimed, they were being taken off the boats in Honolulu and returned to the West Coast by Chinese confederates of the traffickers in the United States. Goo, a Christian who worked Sundays in a Chinatown mission, is said to have been alerted by Christian missions in California when girls were being returned to China and to have personally undertaken to see that they were not taken off the boats in Honolulu.

Opium smoking among the migrants was a particularly vexing problem to Chinese community leaders who, recognizing Chinese tolerance of the practice, were also concerned about the public disgrace it caused. For several decades opium smokers contributed the largest numbers of Chinese migrants arrested for violations of the law.[8] In 1907 the Chinese consul initiated a campaign against opium, and a young migrant businessman, Chun Kam Chow, with Leong Chew, a Hawaii-born relative, interested a number of migrants in organizing the Chun Moo Min Sun Gai Yin Wui, or Anti-Opium League. Chun, who had come to Hawaii in 1886 as a boy of twelve to join his father, a Honolulu merchant, operated a dry goods store in Chinatown. According to a son-in-law, Chun "was so ashamed at seeing his fellow Chinese arrested for smoking opium and being marched to the police station with their pigtails tied one to the other that he joined others to start an Anti-Opium League and was its first president. . . ."[9] Prominent Chinese and Caucasians interested in the movement took part in the league's opening ceremonies held on the second floor of a Chinatown grocery store. According to a Chinese account:

> The original purpose of the association was self-respect. In August a second meeting was called at the headquarters of the *Kum Yee Hong* [Tailors' Guild]. . . . At this meeting the scope of the work of the association was increased. Money was contributed by the members. Medicine was brought from Shanghai to help the opium smokers in suppressing and ridding their habits. Public meetings were held where speeches against the use of opium were made. Visitation committees were appointed to carry out the objectives.[10]

Articles published in the *Chee Yow Sun Bo* three years later showed the continuing interests and activities of the league:

> This *wui* is founded for the purpose of helping our *tung bau* break away from the "black-world." In the attempt to stop the use of opium, how-

ever, some individuals are handicapped because they are forced by necessity to toil during the day with the result that they do not have enough strength left after the day's work.

In such cases our *wui* feels deeply sympathetic, and we have especially provided a good method to help our friends in attaining their aims. Enter the hospital and rest while you stop using the drug. Our *wui* will help pay all the hospital expenses incurred in connection with the treatment. To all who have the ambition to quit using opium, please come and talk things over with either the president of this *wui* or with Mr. Leong Chew.[11]

We wish to express the appreciation of this organization to the owner of the Royal Theatre for letting us hold our public speaking contest there on January 5. We also appreciate the presence of friends from various vocations in taking part in voicing the evils of opium and, in doing so, convincing our *tung bau.*

We are happy to learn that our friends showed up in such numbers that no single seat was unoccupied. From this it can be readily seen that our Chinese people are uniting in a common patriotic cause against opium smoking.[12]

The main activities of the league appear to have been directed toward users rather than against the importers and dealers. One member, Dr. K. F. Li, is said to have gotten into trouble with the Chinese community by reporting the names of opium smugglers to the authorities.[13] The prevailing view seemed to be that apprehending those in the opium business was the responsibility of the authorities, not the Chinese community. As a matter of fact, there was a general apathy among nonusers toward getting opium smokers to break the habit. In a few years the Anti-Opium League went out of existence. Ultimately, with the passing of the generation of unattached migrants, opium smoking virtually disappeared.

Gambling, while certainly not peculiar to the Chinese, was another basis for criticism of the migrants. Almost from the beginning of their migration to Hawaii, Chinese had the reputation of being more addicted to gambling than other groups in the Islands. Caucasian Christian ministers and newspaper editors periodically raised their voices against the prevalence of gambling, especially among the plantation workers but also in Honolulu's Chinatown. Some Chinese residents complained about it from time to time, but no antigambling league was organized in the Chinese community.[14] Eventually, of course, the distinctively Chinese forms of gambling declined along with opium smoking as the migrant generation died off.

A matter of much graver concern to Chinese migrant business-men was the appearance of any threat to their reputation among Caucasians for honesty and reliability. Having it said that their "word was as good as their bond" was a great advantage in dealing with Caucasian firms, and any publicity about Chinese businessmen failing to meet their obligations created a scandal in Chinatown. Some of the Chinatown firms that lost everything in the fires of 1886 and 1900 had already been in debt and went into bankruptcy, but others that had built up a reputation for integrity were extended credit by Caucasian firms solely on the promise of payment. Stories about migrants like Chu Gem and C. K. Ai who succeeded with determined effort in repaying every dollar they owed Caucasian firms redounded to the credit of Chinese business.[15]

Chinese business leaders' regard for their group reputation in the Caucasian financial community was demonstrated again when a prominent Chinese businessman died in 1911, leaving behind debts he had incurred by questionable methods. The Chinese were particularly embarrassed because the man had been president of the United Chinese Society and during 1910 the English-language press had publicized his role as a leader in the movement to get an unpopular Chinese consul recalled by the Ching government. He died on 30 December, just about the time of year when by Chinese tradition debts were paid off. Two weeks after he had been given an elaborate funeral, a Honolulu English-language newspaper published a long article on stories circulating about the dead man's "high and frenzied finance" and the "forgery, misrepresentation, and abuse of old friendships" involved in "the disappearance of some twenty thousand dollars." It was hinted that the man whose word had been "as good as his bond" and whose "credit in the local banks was practically unlimited" had committed suicide. Endorsements on some of the notes at Caucasian-owned banks were reported to have been forged or obtained fraudulently. Chu Gem, who had succeeded him as president of the United Chinese Society, had been one of the endorsers. The newspaper article ended with the statement that the banks would not lose any money on their notes because Chu Gem and other Chinese would raise the money to meet the obligations.[16]

Cultural Compromises and Cultural Change

The Chinese migrants' increasing consciousness of their status as a group in the Hawaiian multiethnic society led them to abandon or modify some of the cultural practices they had brought with them to the Islands. They became sensitive to charges such as those expressed by the president of the Board of Immigration in 1890:

> A Chinaman is unprogressive. He remains a Chinaman as long as he lives and wherever he lives; he retains his Chinese dress; his habits; his method; his religion. . . . He . . . will not adapt himself to the country where he goes. . . . There are exceptions which but prove the rule.[17]

Chinese sojourners in their early years in the Sandalwood Mountains indeed had no intention of replacing their own customs with those they saw among other groups in the Islands. For a while language and social distance insulated the migrants from awareness of the way members of other groups judged them, but they came in time to realize they were being ridiculed and even condemned for practices that to them were natural and customary. True enough, many *wah kiu* remained indifferent to these "foreign" attitudes even after they became aware of them. Any inconvenience or even indignity they suffered could be accepted as a part of their temporary life overseas which would be left behind when they returned to China. Nevertheless, the time came, earlier for some and later for others, when indifference gave way to self-consciousness. Then changes were gradually made to reduce their visibility as cultural curiosities, to modify or eliminate practices regarded by other groups as immoral or inhumane, and to adopt Hawaiian or Western customs.

The most obvious changes were in personal appearance. Wearing the queue caused more ridicule of Chinese migrants than any other practice brought from China. Before the Manchus were overthrown, migrants who intended to return to China did not dare cut off their queues—to do so would have signified revolutionary sympathies. Chinese schoolboys suffered unmerciful teasing by other boys until their parents agreed to let them cut off their queues; mission schoolteachers offered gifts to Chinese boys to encourage them to overcome parental objection and to encourage fathers also to abandon the queue. The first migrants to have Western haircuts were those who had decided to remain in Hawaii rather than return to China and therefore did not fear reprisals by the imperial government. Dr. Sun's followers and members of the Hoong Moon societies were among the pioneers in cutting off their queues, which symbolized Chinese subjection to the Manchus, but conservative migrants resisted the change until after the revolution. Other characteristics of Chinese grooming, such as the cultivation of long fingernails by men not engaged in manual labor, disappeared more gradually and with less notice.

Changes in clothing were another visible sign of cultural accommodation to Western ideas. Migrants who gave up manual work or house-to-house peddling to become shopkeepers and skilled workers in the towns discarded the peasant's broad-brimmed, straw umbrella hats and coarse working clothes which fitted the coolie stereotype. A corresponding change took place among prosperous merchants who, in the 1880s and 1890s, had worn silk caps and mandarin-style gowns and shoes on formal occasions and for family photographs. When Chinese became tailors and shoemakers for Caucasians and the Hawaiian upper classes, the Chinese themselves began to wear Western clothes at public affairs and in family photographs as well as for business.[18] Passport pictures in the Archives of Hawaii show the transition from Chinese to Western clothing. At first all the Chinese men are in black Chinese blouses; then an occasional Western shirt and coat appears; and finally Chinese clothes have been entirely replaced by Western. By the 1920s, aside from unsuccessful older migrants who found Chinese clothing cheaper than Western, Chinese men no longer wore Chinese clothes in public. One exception was the visiting scholar who, as if to differentiate himself from the migrants and to impress local Chinese and Caucasians, appeared in public in the silk gown of the Chinese intelligentsia. Into the 1930s Chinese community leaders wore formal Western attire—silk top hat, full-dress suit, white gloves—for such ceremonial occasions as funerals and Ching Ming services.

Changes in clothing, hairstyles, and other matters of personal appearance were slower among the Chinese migrant women than among the men, probably because they were more isolated from contacts outside the home and Chinese community. A Hawaii-born Chinese reporter for the *Honolulu Advertiser,* in an article published in 1932, wrote about the wife of a partner in one of the largest Chinatown firms:

> She has made her home here 40 years, coming at the age of 12. . . . She is a short woman and typical of the Chinese lady who is wife of the wealthy, well-guarded from the conflicting environment of a mixed society. She dresses as a woman in China and does not speak nor understand English, Hawaiian, or the pidgin English of Hawaii. Her friendships and associations have only been among the Chinese. She has not acquired any of the mannerisms peculiar to people of Hawaii, all of whom are of a different racial and social standing.[19]

As late as 1936 it was not uncommon to see less affluent Chinese women such as those noted in December of that year near Liliha and School streets: "two elderly Chinese women, surely in their sixties, both dressed in pyjamas; unbound feet, Chinese hairdress; jade earrings; each with a paper shopping bag filled with Christmas packages."

One difference between Chinese and Western customs that was less visible than grooming or clothing but sometimes more confusing involved the migrants' names. Most of those who came in the early years of migration had seldom used their surnames (really clan names) in villages where everyone knew everyone else, and in the nineteenth century most of their personal contacts outside the migrant group were with Hawaiians who had not yet completely adopted the Western practice of family surnames. It was therefore common for migrants to be known only by a Hawaiianized version of their given names: for example, "Kan" became "Akana." This name, in turn, was frequently adopted by the migrants' children as their surname, especially when they went to school where Caucasian schoolteachers expected them to have surnames as well as given names. In the larger urban areas, particularly in Honolulu, migrants made more public use of their clan and generation names but continued the Chinese practice of placing them before the personal name rather than after: for example, Goo Kim Fui rather than Kim Fui Goo. Only a few of the migrant generation, like Dr. K. F. Li (Khai Fai Li), adopted the Western order which became accepted practice among Hawaii-born Chinese. The English spelling of Chinese names was sometimes confusing since the Chinese character for a name could be phonetically transcribed in several ways, such as Lum, Lam, Lim, Lin, or Len. A few migrants adopted the spelling closest to those of Western surnames, so that Lau, for example, would become Lowe.

Some practices that were conventional in Chinese tradition were regarded by many Westerners in Hawaii, particularly those in missionary circles, as not only strange but immoral or barbarous. Among these practices were concubinage, the *mui tsai* ("slave girl") system, and footbinding. As a matter of fact, none of these practices was widespread among the migrants and, except for footbinding, non-Chinese were seldom aware of them. Missionaries who had been in China were very much concerned, however, about migrants bringing these practices to Hawaii and called them to the attention of Hawaiian authorities and other groups in the Islands.

Polygamy and concubinage, while practiced to a limited extent by Chinese in Hawaii as well as in China, brought very little censure to the migrants during the nineteenth century, except for the occasional condemnation by missionaries. Liaisons between Hawaiian women and Chinese who had left their wives in China encountered little social or legal opposition. Other foreigners were rather lax in observing the sexual mores of their own cultures, and the unstable, mobile, predominantly male Caucasian group tolerated practices that would have been condemned in their home communities. As late as the 1870s the Caucasian members of the Hawaiian Supreme Court recognized the legality of a polygamous marriage where the second wife was a Hawaiian married to a Chinese who had a Chinese wife in China.[20] The fact that Chinese migrants, even those who eventually returned to China by themselves, generally provided well for their Hawaiian families contributed to the generally tolerant attitude. Even if a migrant had two Chinese wives in Hawaii, it was unlikely that anyone outside the Chinese community would know about it. Antibigamy laws were not strictly enforced until after Annexation. In 1910 a Honolulu English-language newspaper reported the case of a prominent Honolulu Chinese merchant who was arrested and convicted of bigamy by federal authorities.[21] While visiting See Yup and Chung Shan districts in 1932, the writer learned of wealthy returned *wah kiu* from Hawaii who were living in Hong Kong, Macao, or in their villages with a wife and one or more concubines, but by that time concubinage was rare in Hawaii and widely condemned in the Chinese community.

The *mui tsai* system was even more strongly condemned than concubinage by non-Chinese who learned about it. *Mui tsai* were young girls whose poverty-stricken parents, upon being paid a certain sum, bound them to work without wages in the households of their masters. *Mui tsai* were particularly in demand in families where wives and daughters had bound feet. Char says that in the early days "Chinese immigrants of better circumstances brought *mui tsai* with them to Hawaii. Some came posing as daughters or domestics of immigrants and were later consigned to their new employers as *mui tsai* either by prearrangement or by sale after their arrival."[22] Chinese custom demanded that a marriage be arranged for a *mui tsai* in her middle teens. The husband was required to pay a dowry of an amount usually larger than that originally paid for the girl.

After Christian missionaries became active among the Chinese in the Islands, in the 1880s, this practice was severely criticized by Caucasians, and occasionally an article in English-language newspapers brought a specific case to public attention. In 1895 a Chinese girl who was reported to have been "twice sold into slavery in Hawaii" and "treated cruelly" found refuge in a seminary for Hawaiian girls.[23] In 1900 a Honolulu newspaper reported a meeting of the Women's Board of Missions at Central Union Church at which a speaker condemned the "slavery" existing in Hawaii. A few months later a major Chinese organization was reported to have rescued a "cruelly used Chinese slave girl from her alleged owners" and to have filed charges against them.[24] In the 1920s a group of Chinese in Hawaii, mostly Christians, started a movement against the practice under the leadership of a Chinese Christian minister who had been born and raised in a See Yup district and who had been a minister in Chung Shan district.[25] By that time firm application of American immigration laws had made it difficult to bring *mui tsai* into the Islands and no new cases were being reported, but those in the movement hoped that the practice could be eliminated in Kwangtung and eventually all of China.

The missionary paper, *The Friend*, claimed in 1892 to know about "an occasional case of infanticide among the Chinese" in Hawaii, and in 1912 a Chinese migrant couple was charged with having murdered an infant daughter. Though some extremely poor families in the migrants' home districts did practice female infanticide, no other reference to it in Hawaii appeared.[26] However, many second-generation Chinese have reported that their parents thought that daughters were of little worth, certainly as compared to sons. In the 1930s the writer was told of a few cases of parents who gave young daughters to other Chinese families. Not all these parents were poor; some simply placed a low value on daughters. Chinese Christians were among the first to change this attitude, no doubt, but general change among the migrants was probably less a result of taking over Western attitudes than of coming to realize the practical contributions daughters in Hawaii could make to the family.

Footbinding was a matter on which migrants capitulated to the revulsion expressed by other groups and to legal action against it. Footbinding was by no means universal in the migrants' home districts in China. Hakkas did not practice it. Poor Punti parents who had no hope of arranging marriages with men in wealthy families did not bind their daughters' feet since girls who could not do farm work might not be able to get husbands. Most of the earliest Punti migrants did come from poor families, but footbinding increased in the *wah kiu* villages as they became more prosperous and families aspired to marrying their daughters to men from affluent families in neighboring villages or to wealthy *wah kiu*.

By the 1880s and 1890s Punti migrants to Hawaii and Hawaii-born Punti men who had been taken to China for marriage began bringing brides with bound feet to the Islands. When these women began to appear in public occasionally, footbinding became a subject of critical comment among non-Chinese. Some of these women began to bind their daughters' feet in anticipation of arranging their marriages when the family returned to China—or, in the Islands, to men who could make a large marriage settlement. This practice outraged the missionary group, whose feelings were shared in this matter by other non-Chinese. The practice became a public issue in 1895 when it was learned that a Chinese girl had died as a result of footbinding. The missionary journal, usually defensive of the Chinese, sharply attacked them on this practice:

> The question is forcing itself upon public attention, whether Chinese mothers in this country are any longer to be permitted to torture their young daughters by binding their feet. Their motive is to fit their children for good social position. They do it out of mistaken kindness, but it is notwithstanding a dreadful cruelty. It is a process of prolonged agony, and it makes its victims unhappy cripples for life.
>
> On April 12th a child in Fowler's yard died of lock-jaw after some weeks of torture. For several days her cries had been frightful. If Chinese enjoy the privileges of residence here, may they not be required to conform to our conceptions of the demands of humanity, and to abstain from obvious cruelties? . . . It would seem that this evil ought to be suppressed. If the Chinese cannot comply with civilized sentiments in this matter, let them betake themselves elsewhere.[27]

Later that year footbinding was made a statutory offense, and shortly afterward a Chinese father was charged with violating the law and fined twenty-five dollars.[28] Although Chinese succeeded in getting this law declared unconstitutional on technical grounds, footbinding was discontinued in Hawaii before it was outlawed in China. Hakkas joined Caucasian Christians in condemning it, and as Punti migrants came to regard Hawaii as their permanent family home they realized that footbinding was not only of no advantage but an actual handicap to improving their social status. A second-generation

Chinese student told how these considerations changed her own parents' attitudes:

> My mother's feet were bound since she was a young girl. It was a cus-
> tom of the Chinese people at that time. I am most thankful that my
> parents did not bind any of my older sisters' feet. Many of the Chinese
> who came to Hawaii kept up this custom and bound their daughters'
> feet. My mother opposed this custom of footbinding because of her
> own pain and sufferings. Very often she would remind us when we
> misbehaved, "You should be lucky that father and I did not return to
> China. Then we will have to bind your feet like mine." We would
> usually laugh, although very grateful at heart, and retort, "Why didn't
> you bind ours then? Mrs.——'s daughter is born in Hawaii and her
> feet are bound." "No," she would answer, "although I have broken one
> of the widely practiced rules of China, I would much rather see you
> standing on your natural feet. This is the Sandalwood Islands and not
> where your grandparents live!"

As with many other immigrant groups, including those from Europe, compulsory school attendance laws brought migrants into occasional conflict with authorities in the Islands, but the combination of traditional Chinese respect for education and desire for improving their status soon resolved this problem. Compulsory school attendance, initiated in the 1890s and more strongly enforced after Annexation, was resisted by some migrant parents who wanted their children, especially their sons, to help the family make money with which to return to China. Government officials persuaded United Chinese Society leaders to hear the Caucasian missionary working among the Chinese explain why parents should obey the law. Years later, when it celebrated its fiftieth anniversary, the Society made a point of the fact that the government had turned to it "to explain matters to the Chinese people and to encourage the carrying out of the law."[29] Whatever the Society's influence was, the percentage of Chinese school-age boys who did attend school rose steadily until it was the highest of all ethnic groups in the Islands, including the Caucasians. Somewhat later this was also true of Chinese girls.

Chinese migrant parents, like parents in almost every immigrant group in America, faced the demands of children who wanted to adopt modern ways, outside the home if not inside. Even though Hawaii-born Chinese of the early generations were regarded as models of obedience and respect for their elders and seldom rebelled openly against their parents' Chinese ways, they brought home the pressures they felt at school and at work to conform to patterns prevailing in the Westernized community. Children, especially the young adults, often appealed to their parents' desire for status in Hawaii to persuade them to modify or abandon Chinese customs.

Excerpts from two accounts of marriages written by students in the 1930s indicate the acceptance of traditional Chinese practices by Hawaii-born girls of an earlier period:

> I have five married sisters and two brothers who are married. Two of these marriages, of my oldest and third sisters, were through match-making. My oldest sister did not meet her husband until the day of her wedding. My third sister met her husband only after they were matched and agreed upon by the parents of my sister and her husband. There is at home today a set of pictures of my sisters which they used in match-making. These pictures show them dressed in their old-styled and best Chinese gowns with wide flowery laces around their sleeves and front. They did not smile but appeared reserved and sweet.

> My mother's bridal costume still retains memories of her old-fashioned marriage. Its gorgeousness aroused my imagination. To quote from my mother—"I wore a red mandarin coat and skirt. The matchmaker accompanied me over to your father's cousin's home where the wedding was to be held. The vehicle was decorated with two lanterns and a red sash. My head was covered with a large red handkerchief. After the short ceremony, I had to serve tea to everyone present. Then I changed my entire costume and the rest of the evening was spent informally—the interest being centered around me. They put me through all kinds of embarrassing stunts to entertain the folks."

An account of a marriage in 1937 involving two prominent Chinese families was reported in detail in the *Honolulu Star-Bulletin* during a decade when society sections of Honolulu's two main English-language papers were beginning to publicize society events of non-Caucasians along with those of Caucasians; the account documents acceptance by migrant parents of marriage practices more in accord with Western ways:

> Miss Esther Au, daughter of Mr. and Mrs. Au Tin Kwai, became the bride of Richard Q. Y. Wong, son of Mr. and Mrs. Wong Nin, at eight Wednesday evening at the Waialae Golf Club. About 3,000 friends of the young couple were present. The bride was given in marriage by her father. The Rev. Stephen Mark officiated. Mrs. H. L. Chung sang Because I Love You Truly, accompanied on the piano by Miss Juanita Lum-King.

Miss Au wore a gown of white lace with a train. The gown had an Elizabethan collar and the neck-line was cut low in front. . . . The bride wore a fingertip veil and carried anthuriums and orchids.

Miss Beatrice Lum, who was the maid of honor, carried talisman roses and wore baby roses in her hair. Her gown was of steel-colored lace made with a full skirt. . . .

The bridesmaids, Miss Mary Au and Miss Rosie Wong, wore pink lace. Their dresses also had full skirts. . . . Dressed in dainty white organdy were the little flower girls, Carol Wong and Irene Chinn. . . . Harold Wong was the best man, Albert Lai and Ah Tung Wong, ushers.

The ceremony was held in front of a latticework decorated with ti leaves and calla lilies. The side screens were of ti leaves and gardenias. On the center table were white larkspurs and white tapers. Tender melodies were played throughout the ceremony.

A reception and dancing were held later.

To welcome the bride at her new home, special firecrackers were imported from China. They fired off words of good fortune. . . .

Many prenuptial parties have been given for the bride during the past few weeks. . . . Her parents were hosts at a going away dinner party. . . . Invitations were sent to 300 friends and relatives of the bride's family.

The bridegroom's parents will be hosts at a dinner for 400 persons Sunday afternoon to honor the young Mr. and Mrs. Wong.[30]

An Ethnic Group in the Island Community

Participation as a distinctive ethnic group in community-wide activities defined the Chinese collective identity and status more clearly than did the less perceptible cultural compromises and changes made by individual migrants and their children. The Chinese migrant community gradually became part of the common life of the Hawaiian social world through the participation of their organizations in multi-ethnic social enterprises. Activities in which the Chinese took part as a distinct ethnic group were of three general types. The first comprised projects undertaken because of events elsewhere in the world —such as World War I—which aroused the concern of the people of the Islands. The second type, which had great influence in drawing the Chinese into the multiethnic society, had to do with cooperative efforts to deal with Island welfare problems. The third type included community-wide events to which the Chinese contributed as a distinctive cultural group.

The Island Community and the World

Following the San Francisco earthquake and fire in 1906, people in Hawaii undertook to collect funds for relief of the victims. Chinese in the Islands were also active in raising funds for this cause though their concern naturally was mainly for the plight of the Chinese in San Francisco. The United Chinese Society helped raise over $1,100, and funds sent directly to relatives by Chinese migrants in Hawaii added considerably to this amount. In 1913, when a disastrous flood occurred in Ohio, the United Chinese Society was one of the groups mentioned in Honolulu newspapers as helping to raise money for Middle West relief organizations. That same year Chinese contributed to relief for the *Titanic* survivors.[31]

World War I brought migrants to a sharper awareness of the ties that were binding them ever more closely to the common life of the peoples of Hawaii and to the United States, even though Hawaii was still a territory and most of them were not American citizens. The philosophy of democracy and antimonarchism which Dr. Sun's supporters had preached, as well as the commitment of the settler migrants and their Hawaii-born children to America, made them partisans of the Allied countries. Two companies of the National Guard had been made up entirely of Hawaii-born Chinese, even before World War I started, and they were well trained when America entered the war. Over a thousand Chinese in Hawaii enlisted in the military services—most of them Island-born but some young migrants also. Hundreds of migrant parents with sons in the armed forces inevitably became more identified with America, and other groups in the community became more aware of the Chinese as part of what had already become "American Hawaii." Chinese newspapers in Honolulu reported events of the war; many migrants and local-born Chinese were employed by the army and navy; teams of Chinese helped out in Liberty Bond drives. A few Chinese died in the service. Two who were killed in battle in Europe are still commemorated by the name of an American Legion branch—Kau-Tom Post No. 11—formed by Chinese veterans in Hawaii.[32]

The destructive earthquake in Japan in 1923 was the occasion for another relief campaign in the Islands in which the United Chinese Society helped to raise funds. In 1925 Chinese teams in a national fund drive for the Young Women's Christian Association collected $21,000. Five years later a Chinese committee working with a Caucasian committee in Honolulu raised $4,300 for the National Committee of the Young Men's Christian Association in China.[33] In that same year the Honolulu Chinese Chamber of Commerce enlisted the support of the entire Island community in response to appeals from the China Famine International Relief Commission because of an unusually severe famine in North China. A committee of two migrants and two Hawaii-born Chinese called upon the governor of the territory. According to a Chinese account:

> His Excellency, the Governor, was only too glad to give us his *kokua* [help] and immediately issued a proclamation, setting aside May 23rd, as "China Relief Day" and urging the people in the territory to do all they could to help the suffering millions in the sister Republic.
>
> With the wonderful support and cooperation from all the local newspapers and also those from other islands and with the hearty assistance of the Honolulu Chamber of Commerce, Japanese Chamber of Commerce, Japanese Merchant's Association, Department of Public Instruction, Catholic Churches, Federation of Churches, Hawaii Civic Club, all other Civic and Social institutions, and all the enthusiastic workers for the drive, the campaign was a great success. In less than two weeks, a total of $42,825.48 or $146,107.31 Mex. was collected and forwarded directly to the China Famine International Relief Commission in Peiping.[34]

Island Community Welfare

As early as the 1850s Chinese migrants became involved in a project designed to benefit all groups in Hawaii by raising money for the Honolulu Hospital. A subscription list dated 12 May 1859 shows that S. P. Samsing & Co. donated a hundred dollars, a handsome contribution at that time, and several other Chinese names were on the list. In the same period another prominent Chinese firm, Hungtai, was a "main pillar" of support of the Oahu Charity School.[35] Doubtless there were many such instances that were not publicized. In a later period several Chinese were among those listed by the *Pacific Commercial Advertiser* as subscribers to a fund for developing a park in Honolulu as a memorial to President McKinley.[36] In December 1910 the *Advertiser* publicized a Malihini Christmas Tree project in downtown Honolulu to which Chinese and Japanese organizations were asked to contribute. The *Advertiser* announced that Chinese, "led by the venerable Chinese merchant, Chu Gem," did contribute although a Chinese court interpreter, in turning over the money, made it clear that this did not mean that "Chinese recognize the religious significance of Christmas."[37]

In social welfare matters the relationship between the Chinese and the community at large eventually underwent important changes. Migrant leaders, anxious that their group be regarded favorably by others, had for years taken pride in pointing out that Chinese took care of their own needy. The Chinese petition sent to Washington in 1916 stated:

> The Chinese of Hawaii have always been a law-abiding race, no matter under what government the Islands have been. Tong wars have never been nor do they exist in Hawaii. Our Tongs or societies are purely benevolent and eleemosynary institutions, for without ever seeking aid beyond our own race we take care of our sick, needy, and aged, never burdening or having recourse to the charities of other races.[38]

It was only after World War I that numbers of the less fortunate migrants were reaching the age when they became permanently unemployed and dependent. By this time many of the successful migrants had returned to China and those who had settled in Hawaii were becoming less responsive to appeals for aid from migrants from their villages or districts—and even less to appeals from others with whom they had no traditional or regional ties. The number of dependents was increasing at a time when the organizations based on old-world sentiments were losing their solidarity, and few of these organizations had the financial resources to take care of those in need.[39]

When it became apparent that many indigent migrants were not receiving help from village, district, or clan societies, "all-Chinese" organizations such as the United Chinese Society and the Chinese Merchant's Association became active in dispensing charity. Indigents of any surname, dialect, district, or village were nonetheless *tung bau* for whom it was felt the Chinese community should assume responsibility. In 1910 a committee chaired by the Chinese consul and including such prominent men as C. K. Ai, Chu Gem, and the Reverend Y. T. Kong, a Christian minister, had been organized to consider ways of caring for penniless migrants who resisted return to China. The committee undertook to collect money from Chinese, and some of its members used their own money to help the neediest men. In 1918 the committee was enlarged and a Chinese Women's Committee was formed to work with it.

In spite of these efforts, a growing number of elderly Chinese men in dire want came to the attention of the Honolulu Social Service Bureau. After consultations between Chinese leaders and representatives of churches and social agencies, it was decided to establish a home for these men. In 1920 property in Palolo Valley (in Honolulu) was purchased after negotiations involving the Charities and Social Welfare Committee of the Honolulu Chamber of Commerce, the Chinese Merchants' Association, the Associated Charities, and the Hawaii Sugar Planters' Association. The initial purchase money was made up from $5,000 turned over from the defunct Wai Wah Hospital and a similar amount from the Hawaii Sugar Planters' Association. Contributions from the Chinese community added $1,500.

The first eight men moved into the Palolo Chinese Home in November 1920. As the number of elderly dependent single men increased and Chinese societies found themselves unable to pay the expenses of those in the Home as well as those still being cared for in the society clubhouses, the Social Service Bureau gave financial help as well as some casework service. Cecilia Chuck Hoy, the Hawaii-born daughter of a member of the Chinese Committee, was a caseworker for the Social Service Bureau who did some of the admissions work for the Home. In 1926, when about eighty men were living there, the Bureau paid $3,149 of the Home's $5,500 expenses; Chinese organizations and individuals paid the remainder. That year Dr. K. F. Li, the leading physician of the migrant generation and active in the Home's operation, announced that some way must be found to relieve the Chinese societies of paying for the men's care. It was agreed that the Social Service Bureau would assume responsibility for both the financial support of the Home and its administration, with the cooperation of the bilingual second-generation Chinese manager and an interethnic board of directors including some eminent migrant and second-generation Chinese. The Social Service Bureau would also give assistance to other needy migrants outside the Home. In return, the Chinese community was to become more active in the campaigns of the United Welfare Fund which supported the Bureau.[40]

Although the Social Service Bureau took over the main financial support and management of the Palolo Home, members of the Chinese community continued to help with special projects. In the 1930s and 1940s, for example, they funded several additions to the Home. Members of the migrant generation usually raised money by direct appeals to well-to-do Chinese and by sending delegations to Haole firms and wealthy Haole philanthropists. The younger generation of Chinese, acting through the Hawaii Chinese Civic Association, used different methods in a 1936 drive for funds to add another building at the Palolo Home:

The committee taking charge . . . decided . . . to sell benefit tickets, with the grand prize being a Ford V-8, as the means of raising funds. . . . Besides the car, additional prizes will consist of a refrigerator, a radio and an electrical washing machine. The committee also chose Consul General Mui to head the honorary committee which will consist of [follows the names of eminent Chinese of the migrant generation].[41]

Several Chinese organizations sold tickets to a benefit circus performance and operated concessions at the circus. There was also a benefit dance at a local golf club. These entertainments were widely advertised in the English-language newspapers, which also gave generous space to the progress of the drive. After these activities had raised about five thousand dollars a delegation was sent to selected Haole firms and Haoles who matched the sum with an additional five thousand.

Meanwhile, in carrying out their part of the arrangement by which the Social Service Bureau took over the operation of the Home, Chinese cooperated in the annual United Welfare Fund drives. For several years, beginning in 1927, the United Chinese Society and the Honolulu Chinese Chamber of Commerce jointly organized Chinese teams of migrant and Hawaii-born Chinese to solicit the Chinese community for donations and pledges. In 1936 nine teams of men and a women's team were appointed by the captain of the Chinese Division of the campaign. The one hundred sixty-eight names on these teams appeared to constitute the core of a Chinese who's who on Oahu that year. Over the ten-year period 1927–1936, Chinese teams secured annual contributions averaging about six thousand dollars, which did not include the money subscribed through non-Chinese firms and government departments by their Chinese employees.[42]

By the late 1940s the ethnic emphasis in the general welfare drive was reduced to ethnic teams for an "advance gifts" committee. In 1949 the Honolulu Community Chest asked the Chinese Chamber of Commerce to take charge of the Chinese Division of the Advance Gifts Committee. Two Chinese bankers on the Community Chest's board of directors served as liaison with the Chinese Chamber of Commerce and the United Chinese Society. Thirty-three "prominent Chinese businessmen" were appointed to the committee; sixteen of these attended a luncheon at Wo Fat at which four Haoles involved in the fund drive described the needs of the Red Feather agencies and asked for generous contributions from Chinese before the opening day of the drive. By that day the Chinese Division had reached only about half of its $10,000 goal, but the full amount was collected before the drive ended.[43] In the 1940s the board of directors of the Community Chest and some of its committees were still consciously interethnic—as were the boards of many of the Red Feather agencies such as the Young Men's Christian Association, the Young Women's Christian Association, the International Institute, the Hawaii Cancer Association, and the Honolulu Social Service Bureau.

The Chinese Chamber of Commerce which had participated jointly with the United Chinese Society in the welfare fund drives was the successor of the Chinese Merchants' Association. The change in its name suggests the accommodations being made by Chinese to the interethnic life of Hawaii. While one of the Chinese Chamber's stated objectives was "to promote Chinese commerce in Hawaii," another was "to inspire in its members a sense of civic responsibility and an active interest in all community affairs." Increasingly, promotion of Chinese commercial interests involved helping Chinese businessmen compete in an economy that was becoming less and less ethnically oriented. Relations between the Honolulu Chamber of Commerce and the Chinese Chamber of Commerce were friendly and generally cooperative. The Honolulu Chamber for a long time remained predominantly Caucasian even though, beginning in the 1920s, a few Chinese migrant and Hawaii-born businessmen were admitted to membership.[44] These Chinese members provided liaison between the two chambers, keeping the Chinese Chamber in touch with developments in the Honolulu Chamber and helping to coordinate the work of the two organizations on various community projects. The Chinese Chamber's attitude was expressed in the president's annual report for 1930:

> In closing, I wish again to remind you of the importance of our Chamber as a part of the local community. We are no longer isolated from the activities of other organizations and we must do our part in order to retain that high esteem and Aloha we now have. Our success or failure as an organization depends on each and every one of you. Give it your hearty support and cooperation in all its work and endeavor, and it will be successful. Be indifferent, and it spells defeat.[45]

Island Community Events

The time came when migrant Chinese leaders were asked to arrange for Chinese participation in community-wide public events planned by leaders in Caucasian or Caucasian and Hawaiian circles. Still later

Chinese leaders were included in interethnic committees planning such events. The earliest instance was the China Engine Company's appearance in the annual firemen's parade in Honolulu beginning back in 1879. In 1881 when King Kalakaua was welcomed back from his world tour the Chinese put a pagoda over an arch at King and Fort Streets in downtown Honolulu.[46] After Annexation the Chinese were represented in public celebrations of American national holidays. On George Washington's birthday in 1910 Chinese organizations, along with Japanese, took part in a parade sponsored by the Honolulu Chamber of Commerce, then a Caucasian group. A Chinese newspaper reported:

> The Haole paper yesterday commented that the Orientals of Honolulu are very enthusiastic over the celebration of Washington's birthday. Yesterday about 200 Chinese were discussing and making plans to deck out a Flower carriage [float] to represent China in the holiday parade. It is rumored that the Imperial consul has decided to sponsor a carriage also. His secretary met civic leaders to discuss plans yesterday.
>
> Japanese merchants are also attentive on the matter, and it is said that they will try to sponsor a better program than that of the Chinese.[47]

> On the 22nd day was the birthday of the first president of the United States. Consul Leong asked our tong members to participate in the ceremony with the lion dance and the flower car. Thanks to the stores, shops, and various organizations and *wui goon* for welcoming our lion dance with firecrackers. Lung Doo Chung Sin Tong.[48]

Two years later, when Chinese were asked to assist in Fourth of July ceremonies, ten Chinese women agreed to help decorate the pavilion on the palace grounds.[49] Probably the largest celebration held in Honolulu up to that time came in 1934 when President Roosevelt visited Hawaii. More than a dozen floats prepared by the United Chinese Society, the Honolulu Chinese Chamber of Commerce, other Chinese organizations, and Chinese firms were in an elaborate night parade climaxing the celebrations.[50]

There was a period in Hawaii when most sports were played by teams from different high schools or by amateurs organized by neighborhood or ethnic identity. Some Chinese teams were sponsored by Chinese firms, just as other ethnic and mixed teams were sponsored by firms and community associations. Migrants, especially those with children, became interested in the athletic events in which Hawaii-born Chinese were playing. The All-Chinese Baseball Team was so successful in 1912 and 1913 that sponsors sent it on mainland tours. An ACA (All Chinese Athletes) association organized other events such as the track meet held on Chinese New Year's Day in 1910 in which teams from McKinley High School, Oahu College, St. Louis College, and Central Grammar School as well as the victorious ACA competed.[51]

In such sports, of course, Hawaii-born Chinese were representing their ethnic group in a way that had nothing to do with their ancestral cultural heritage. The athletic events were not "cross-cultural" with each ethnic group contributing elements of its traditional culture. Baseball and track were American. The Chinese youths who participated in them generally had quite different interests from those of members of the Chinese Physical Culture Association who were practicing Chinese calisthenics and other forms of exercise. In fact, most Chinese youths tended to disparage "old-world ways"; they were more interested in the things they considered modern, the things that were popular in the Hawaii-American community. In a paradoxical way, however, the desire of the migrants' children to merge into the multiethnic social order of Hawaii brought about a new appreciation of Chinese traditional culture.

As Hawaii began to take pride in its ethnic diversity, China's ancient artistic, literary, and philosophical achievements became sources of prestige for the Island Chinese. Even though most migrants had come from poor families with limited knowledge of China's "high culture," Island Chinese encouraged Chinese scholars to come to Hawaii and began taking more interest in Chinese art, literature, and philosophy. The founding of the Honolulu Academy of Arts in 1927 by a member of a *kamaaina* ("Island-born," "established") Caucasian family played a considerable part in this development. The goal of the academy's founder was to encourage children and adults of all ethnic groups in Hawaii to appreciate the culture of their ancestors. Although the early donors were mainly Caucasians, local Chinese also contributed to the academy's Asian art collection. When the academy's educational department started programs to develop appreciation of the cultural practices of local ethnic groups, Hawaii Chinese gave performances and demonstrations at the academy during Chinese New Year. By the 1930s, when these programs started, some of the activities formerly associated with this and other festivals, especially in Chinatown, had almost disappeared.

The dragon dance was no longer performed and the lion dance was seen only rarely. In 1937 the academy persuaded the Chinese Physical Culture Association, whose members were mostly young men educated in China and former students of Chinese-language schools in Honolulu, to stage a lion dance at the academy for a largely non-Chinese audience. Other programs showed some of the features of the Dragon Boat Festival and similar celebrations.

The growth of the tourist industry in Hawaii after World War II gave an impetus to a rather different kind of Chinese cultural revival.[52] When the Hawaii Tourist Bureau (now the Hawaii Visitors Bureau) recognized the potential tourist appeal of the distinctive cultures of Asian ethnic groups in the Islands, advertisements in mainland publications began to include pictures of Oriental festivals and temples along with the obligatory beaches, hula dancers, and Hawaiian musicians. In the late 1940s, when the Bureau decided to promote Aloha Week each fall as a series of events to attract and entertain tourists, Chinese were asked to participate along with other ethnic groups in special "cultural" events. In 1948 one of these events was an International Lantern Parade in which the Chinese were represented by a lion dance, three floats, and some students carrying Chinese lanterns. The following year the United Chinese Society and the Chinese Chamber of Commerce, having been approached again by Caucasian representatives of the tourist industry, planned a more elaborate schedule of Chinese events: participation again in the Aloha Week lantern parade with floats, the lion dance, and marchers carrying lanterns as in the previous year, to be followed by a Chinese play in English by the Hawaii Chinese Civic Association on the Ala Moana Park stage; an all-day community-wide picnic in a Honolulu public park; a Narcissus Festival during the Chinese New Year season.

The Chinese part in the Aloha Week parade was praised in the press, as was the play which drew an estimated audience of fifteen thousand. Some seven thousand people went to the picnic, where there was both Western and Chinese entertainment. Chinese businessmen donated prizes for the young people's blindfold races and pie-eating contests; a lion dance and exhibitions of Chinese boxing and fencing were presented for onlookers. The big event, however, was the first public selection of a Chinese Beauty Queen. The winner, chosen from fifty-seven contestants, was given a two-week trip to West Coast cities where she would be entertained in the Chinatowns of San Francisco and Los Angeles and attend the Rose Bowl football game.

The Narcissus Festival events, which also included a beauty queen contest, emphasized features of Chinese culture that would interest tourists and local non-Chinese. The festival took its name from the South Chinese tradition of cultivating narcissus plants which bloom at the time of the lunar new year. For the first time in nearly forty years a 110-foot Chinese dragon, brought from Hong Kong, danced in Chinatown's streets along with lion and unicorn dances. More lanterns were imported for a parade through Chinatown by Chinese children and there was a fireworks display in Aala Park adjacent to Chinatown. The United Chinese Society–Chinese Chamber of Commerce hall had exhibits of narcissus, Chinese painting, calligraphy, scrolls, and screens. At the American Chinese Club the public was invited to a tea at which members, both men and women, received the guests and gave talks about Chinese teas, decorations, gowns, and other "things Chinese." Two Chinese plays were performed nightly, one in English, the other in Chinese. The beauty contest was judged in the largest downtown theater and the following evening a Narcissus Ball at the American Chinese Club's pavilion honored the Narcissus Queen and her court. The festival was acclaimed a great success in both English-language and Chinese newspapers. Chinese businessmen found it profitable enough to continue their support, and a Narcissus Festival has been held annually ever since.

By the end of the 1940s, of course, few of the early migrant men and women were alive to see these events, much less take part in them, and many of the activities would probably have been as strange to them as anything they encountered in nineteenth-century Hawaii. The ethnic distinctiveness of post–World War II Hawaii Chinese was far different from that of the migrant community. Hawaii-born Chinese were much more integrated, individually and collectively, into the community at large than most of their forefathers had been, and also much more so than most American-born Chinese of their generation in mainland U.S. cities. Nevertheless, many families continued to observe some ancestral customs and practices, many informal social groups as well as formal organizations were entirely Chinese in membership, and the presence of the Chinese as a distinctive group in Island community events demonstrated the persistence of Chinese group identity.

Appendix:

Population of the Hawaiian Islands by Racial and Ethnic Groups: 1853–1970

Group	1853	1860	1866	1872[b]	1878[b]	1884[b]	1890[b]
			Number				
Hawaiian	70,036	65,647	57,125	49,044	44,088	40,014	34,436
Part-Hawaiian	983	1,337[a]	1,640	2,487	3,420	4,218	6,186
Caucasian	1,687	1,900[b]	2,400[a]	2,944	3,748	16,579	18,939
Portuguese	87	85[a]	90	424	486	9,967	12,719
Other Caucasian	1,600	1,815	2,310	2,520	3,262	6,612	6,220
Chinese	364	816	1,306	2,038	6,045	18,254	16,752
Japanese						116	12,610
Korean							
Filipino	5						
Puerto Rican							
Negro							
All Other	62	100[a]	488	384	684	1,397	1,067
Total	73,137	69,800	62,959	56,897	57,985	80,578	89,990
			Percentage of Total				
Hawaiian	95.8	94.0	90.7	86.2	76.0	49.7	38.2
Part-Hawaiian	1.3	1.9	2.6	4.4	5.9	5.2	6.9
Caucasian	2.3	2.7	3.8	5.2	6.5	20.6	21.0
Portuguese	0.1	0.1	0.1	0.7	0.8	12.3	14.1
Other Caucasian	2.2	2.6	3.7	4.5	5.7	8.3	6.9
Chinese	0.5	1.2	2.0	3.6	10.4	22.6	18.6
Japanese						0.1	14.0
Korean							
Filipino							
Puerto Rican							
Negro							
All Other	0.1	0.1	0.8	0.7	1.2	1.7	1.2

Source: 1853–1960, Andrew W. Lind, *Hawaii's People* (Honolulu: University of Hawaii Press, 1967), p. 28; 1970, U.S. Census.

  a Estimate.

  b Based on Romanzo Adams, *The Peoples of Hawaii* (Honolulu: Institute of Pacific Relations, 1933), pp. 8–9.

  c Includes Spanish, not separately listed.

  d Includes Spanish and Portuguese, not separately listed.

  e Includes Spanish, Portuguese, and Puerto Ricans, not separately listed.

1896b	1900b	1910	1920	1930	1940	1950	1960	1970g
31,019	29,799	26,041	23,723	22,636	14,375	12,245	10,502	71,274
8,485	9,857	12,506	18,027	28,224	49,935	73,845	91,597	
22,438	26,819	39,158c	49,140c	73,702c	103,791d	114,793d	202,230e	301,429
15,191	18,272	22,301	27,002	27,588				
7,247	8,547	14,867	19,708	44,895				
21,616	25,767	21,674	23,507	27,179	28,774	32,376	38,119	52,375
24,407	61,111	79,675	109,274	139,631	157,905	184,598	203,876	217,669
		4,533	4,950	6,461	6,851	7,030		9,625
		2,361	21,031	63,052	52,569	61,062	68,641	95,354
		4,890	5,602	6,671	8,296	9,551		
	233	695	348	563	255	2,651	4,943	7,517
1,055	415	376	310	217	579	1,618	12,864f	13,316h
109,020	154,001	191,909	255,912	368,336	423,330	499,769	632,772	768,559
28.4	19.3	13.6	9.3	6.1	3.4	2.5	1.7	9.3
7.8	5.1	6.5	7.0	7.7	11.8	14.8	14.5	
20.6	17.3	20.4	19.2	20.0	23.0	23.0	32.0	39.2
13.9	11.9	11.6	10.6	7.5				
6.7	5.4	7.7	7.7	12.2				
19.8	16.7	11.3	9.2	7.4	6.8	6.5	6.0	6.8
22.3	39.7	41.5	42.7	37.9	37.3	36.9	32.2	28.3
		2.4	1.9	1.8	1.6	1.4		1.3
		1.2	8.2	17.1	12.4	12.2	10.8	12.4
		2.5	2.2	1.8	2.0	1.9		
	0.2	0.4	0.1	0.2	0.1	0.5	0.8	1.0
1.0	0.3	0.2	0.1	0.1	0.1	0.3	2.0	1.7

f Includes Koreans, Samoans, Micronesians, and American Indians, not separately listed.

g "Persons of mixed stock, including part Hawaiian, are classified either on the basis of self-identification or race of father. Many persons who would have been counted as part-Hawaiians under the former definition were classified as Caucasian, Chinese, Filipino, or some other race in 1970" (Robert C. Schmitt, *Historical Statistics of Hawaii* [Honolulu: University Press of Hawaii, 1977] p. 26).

h Includes Samoans, Micronesians, and American Indians, not separately listed.

Notes

ABBREVIATIONS

AH   Archives of Hawaii
PCA   *Pacific Commercial Advertiser*

CHAPTER 1

1. John Meares, *Voyages Made in 1788–1789 from China to the Northwest Coast of America* (1791; reprinted ed., New York: Da Capo Press, 1971); extracts in Bruce Cartwright, Jr., ed., *Hawaiian Historical Society Reprint No. 1*, p. 31.

2. "Log of the Chatham," *Honolulu Mercury* 2(December 1929):86; Captain George Vancouver, *A Voyage of Discovery to the North Pacific Ocean and Round the World*, 5 vols. (London, 1801), 5:112–113.

3. John Diell, *Sandwich Island Gazette*, 19 May 1838. The remaining "foreigners" comprised "some 200 to 250 Americans, 75 to 100 Englishmen, and a few French, Spanish, and Portuguese."

4. Vancouver, *Voyage of Discovery* 1:378–379.

5. L. L. Torbert, "Chinese in Sugar," *The Polynesian*, 31 January 1852.

6. Wai-Jane Char, "Three Chinese Stores in Early Honolulu," *Hawaiian Journal of History* 8(1974):10–38.

7. Peggy Kai, "Chinese Settlers in the Village of Hilo before 1852," *Hawaiian Journal of History* 8(1974):39–75.

8. *Hawaiian Annual*, 1888, pp. 28, 88–89; "A Model Plantation," *PCA*, 25 December 1880; *Honolulu Advertiser*, 2 August 1931. As with Chun Fong, called Afong in Hawaii, close relations between Chinese migrants and Hawaiians resulted in Hawaiianization of Chinese names, usually of a given name rather than of a surname; Chung Hung was known as Ahung, Wong Chun as Achun, Tom Wan as Awana, and so on.

9. *The Polynesian*, 30 October 1852.

10. Char, "Three Chinese Stores," pp. 20, 25, 27–28, 30–31.

11. Ibid., pp. 14–16, 18–19, 25–26.

12. Ibid., pp. 12–13, 15, 23–24, 28–29; Kai, "Chinese Settlers," pp. 53–54; *The Friend*, 12 December 1905, p. 12.

13. Arthur C. Alexander, *Koloa Plantation, 1835–1935: A History of the Oldest*

Hawaiian Sugar Plantation (Honolulu: Honolulu Star-Bulletin, 1936), pp. 10, 22, 37; *Hawaiian Annual*, 1890, p. 90.

14. *Report of the Hawaiian Immigration Society* (Honolulu, 1874), pp. 10, 19 (AH).

15. Tin-Yuke Char and Wai-Jane Char, "The First Chinese Contract Laborers to Hawaii, 1852," *Hawaiian Journal of History* 9(1975):128–134.

16. Clarence E. Glick, "The Voyage of the 'Thetis' and the First Chinese Contract Laborers Brought to Hawaii," *Hawaiian Journal of History* 9(1975):135–139.

17. "Arrival of Coolies," *The Polynesian*, 10 January 1852.

18. *Transactions of the Royal Hawaiian Agricultural Society*, vol. 1, no. 3 (Honolulu: Government Press, 1852), pp. 6–7 (AH).

19. Address of E. H. Allen to the Royal Hawaiian Agricultural Society. Quoted in *The Polynesian*, 10 July 1852.

20. *Transactions of the Royal Hawaiian Agricultural Society*, vol. 2, no. 1 (Honolulu: Government Press, 1854), p. 103 (AH).

21. 31 January 1852. The dialect spoken by Chinese from the Amoy area of Fukien is more appropriately known as Hokkien dialect.

22. *The Friend*, 19 August 1856, p. 58.

23. Char and Char, "First Chinese Contract Laborers," p. 133.

24. *Report of the President of the Bureau of Immigration to the Legislative Assembly of 1886*, Appendix, pp. 266–267 (AH) (hereafter cited as *Bureau* or *Board of Immigration Report*, depending on the name of the agency in different periods. It was first organized in 1865 as the Board of Immigration, changed later to Bureau and back again in 1890 to Board). Some of these arrivals were undoubtedly resident Chinese returning from trips to China. New arrivals and returning Chinese are not listed separately in the immigration reports. Some discrepancies appear in the statistics inasmuch as the census for 1860 reported 816 Chinese, 452 more than in 1853. Deaths and permanent departures would have occurred in this period and there could have been few children born since according to reports no more than five Chinese women came to Hawaii in the 1850s; children born to Chinese fathers and Hawaiian mothers presumably would have been put into the category of "half-castes" used in these early censuses.

25. The Hawaiian legislatures between 1864 and 1892 were reported to have appropriated $1,181,320.87 for the work of the government in the interests of labor immigration. See U.S. Senate, *Report of the Committee on Foreign Relations*, 1894, p. 1947. The most common procedure was for the government to license a few individuals and firms, including Chinese, to act as agents in the business of importing contract laborers. These agents were required to pay the customs fees and to subject the men to strict physical examination. See *Bureau of Immigration Report*, 1886, pp. 22–23 (AH).

26. This contract is quoted in full by Tin-Yuke Char, comp., *The Sandalwood Mountains* (Honolulu: University Press of Hawaii, 1975), pp. 275–277; he also describes (p. 319) assistance given by the Reverend William Lobscheid, at a mission in Kwangtung province, in the recruiting of these laborers.

27. *Hawaiian Annual*, 1898, p. 18.

28. During most of this half century the arrivals annually exceeded the number of Chinese leaving the Islands.

29. S. S. Hill, *Travels in the Sandwich and Society Islands* (London, 1856), p. 31.

30. *Incidents of a Whaling Voyage, 1841* (New York:Tuttle, 1969), pp. 212–213.

31. The writer, Stephen Reynolds, had been giving dancing lessons in this "Chinamen's Hall."

32. *PCA*, 23 October 1869; *Hawaiian Gazette*, 12 July and 8 August 1876; see also *PCA*, 8 October 1870; C. C. Bennett, *Life on the Sandwich Islands* (San Francisco: Bancroft, 1893), pp. 25–26.

33. *Bureau of Immigration Report*, 1886, pp. 77–78. At different periods this same argument was advanced in advocating importation of South Sea Islanders, East Indians, and Japanese. For favorable views of Chinese marriages with Hawaiian women see *The Friend*, March 1894, p. 24, and Romanzo Adams, *Interracial Marriage in Hawaii* (New York: Macmillan, 1937), p. 89.

34. *Hawaiian Monthly*, May 1884, pp. 99–100; July 1884, p. 163; *PCA*, 22 March 1878; *The Friend*, January 1880, pp. 5–6; Memorial to King Kalakaua, 29 February 1876, Department of Interior (AH); Bennett, *Life on the Sandwich Islands*, p. 30.

35. Bennett, *Life on the Sandwich Islands*, pp. 25–26.

36. *PCA*, 4 March 1876.

37. Ventures of this type were not always profitable. A ship chartered by the pioneer member of the Chung-Hoon family to bring between 200 and 300 Chinese to Hawaii was shipwrecked at the island of Molokai. C. K. Ai, himself a successful migrant from Chung Shan district, not far from Macao, relates that his wealthy grandfather in China loaned $60 to each of about seventy young men to migrate to North and South America and Australia with the expectation of being paid back $120; none of the men is known to have repaid any of the money. See Chung Kun Ai, *My Seventy-Nine Years in Hawaii (1879–1958)* (Hong Kong: Cosmorama Pictorial Publisher, 1960), pp. 16, 105. Throughout the text the author, whose surname was Chung, is referred to as C. K. Ai, as he was called in Hawaii.

38. *Bureau of Immigration Report*, 1886, p. 163 (AH).

39. The total number of males, fifteen to fifty years of age, of all origins was 35,506. Of the 15,798 females in these ages, 10,510 were Hawaiians.

40. *Board of Immigration Report*, 1890, pp. 88, 90; *Hawaiian Monthly*, May 1884, pp. 97–101; *PCA*, 17 May 1888, 6, 11 September 1889; Bennett, *Life on the Sandwich Islands*, p. 30.

41. J. A. Cruzan, "The Chinese in Hawaii," *The Friend*, 1 November 1882, p. 115.

42. Ibid.

43. *The Friend*, November 1885, pp. 3–4:

44. One of their champions, for instance, poured out invectives against the Chinese and the planters in a pamphlet called *The Planters Mongolian Pets, or Human Decoy Act* (Honolulu, 1884) (AH); *PCA*, 6 September 1889, 22 January 1892; *The Friend*, December 1892, p. 6.

45. During the next four years over 11,000 Chinese arrived, but the number of Chinese on the sugar plantations increased only 589 to a total of 5,626.

46. *Planters' Monthly*, May 1883, p. 26.

47. One hundred forty-eight Japanese came in 1868. During the height of the anti-Chinese agitation and beginning of restriction of Chinese immigration

the Hawaiian government sent a representative to Japan (1883) to arrange for the importation of Japanese contract laborers.

48. *Third Report of the Commissioner of Labor on Hawaii, 1905,* pp. 387–388. See U.S. Department of Commerce and Labor, Bureau of Labor Statistics, 59th Cong., 1st sess., 1906, House doc. 580.

49. According to a report of the Board of Immigration only 165 Chinese were on plantations under contract in 1894, but an additional 2,444 had remained on plantations as day laborers.

50. "Japan's 'Peaceful Invasion'," *Hawaiian Annual,* 1898, pp. 131–134; "Peril from Heathen Japanese," *The Friend,* May 1899, p. 34. Between 1886 and June 1894, some 23,071 men, 5,487 women, and 133 children had been brought in from Japan.

51. *Report of the Minister of Foreign Affairs,* 1897, p. 12 (AH).

52. This is the estimate made by Romanzo Adams, the most thorough scholar of demographic data on nineteenth-century Hawaii. See his *Interracial Marriage in Hawaii,* pp. 30–42.

CHAPTER 2

1. "An Act for the Government of Masters and Servants" in 1850 provided the legal machinery for enforcing labor contracts. See *Penal Code of the Hawaiian Islands* (1850), pp. 170–178 (AH).

2. *Bureau of Immigration Report,* 1886, p. 36 (AH).

3. Elizabeth Wong, "Leaves from the Life History of a Chinese Immigrant," *Social Process in Hawaii* 2(1936):39.

4. From one of the papers written by students in the author's classes, 1929–1937. Personal names and most place names in this and other un-published documents are fictitious.

5. Adapted from a record in the files of a Honolulu social welfare agency, 1937. Personal names and most place names in this and similar agency records are fictitious.

6. *Honolulu Advertiser,* 14 August 1932. A *mou* is about one-sixth of an acre.

7. These conditions were set forth in a contract signed on 23 June 1865 between Dr. Hillebrand and Wohang Company of Hong Kong. See Interior Depart-ment, Miscellaneous: Immigration—Chinese, 1864–June 1865 (AH).

8. From a student paper in the writer's files.

9. *Board of Immigration Report,* 1892, pp. 67–78; reprinted in Char, *Sandalwood Mountains,* pp. 75–80.

10. Koloa Sugar Co., Koloa, Kauai, to the secretary of the Board of Immigration, 6 March 1897. Board of Immigration. Letters, v. 1 (AH).

11. Labor Contract, 1870. Also in the Chinese language. See Interior Department, Miscellaneous: Immigration—Contract Forms (AH).

12. See translation of letter of 19 September 1891, Interior Department, Miscel-laneous: Immigration—Chinese (AH).

13. "Rules for the Government of Chinese Laborers on Waihee Plantation, April 1866," Interior Department, Miscellaneous: Immigration (AH). New Chinese laborers found poi disgusting. See Char, *Sandalwood Mountains,* p. 73.

14. *Board of Immigration Report,* 1899, p. 21 (AH).

15. See Char, *Sandalwood Mountains,* pp. 72–73.

16. *Hawaiian Board of Immigration Report of the Secretary,* 1879–1899, p. 8 (AH).

17. Letter from sheriff on the island of Hawaii to the marshal of the Republic of Hawaii, 22 January 1897, ibid., p. 62.

18. Wray Taylor, "Labor in Hawaii," U.S. Bureau of Foreign Commerce, Department of State, *Consular Reports* No. 620, 5 January 1900 (Hawaiian Sugar Planters' Association Library).

19. Based on records of the Chinese Bureau, Department of Foreign Relations (AH).

20. George N. Wilcox, whose experience in plantation management extended back into the 1870s, said in an interview in 1930 that he could not remember a Chinese woman having lived on his plantation—not even a Chinese storekeeper's or camp director's wife, often the only Chinese woman in a plantation community.

21. Adapted from a record in files of a Honolulu social welfare agency.

22. Bureau of Customs, *Report of the Collector General of Customs, Port of Honolulu, Hawaiian Islands,* 1874 (AH).

23. F. W. Damon, "Tours among the Chinese," *The Friend,* 7 July 1882, p. 76.

24. As late as the 1930s, long after most Chinese had left the sugar plantations, at least three-fourths of the work was still unskilled. See Andrew W. Lind, *An Island Community* (Chicago: University of Chicago Press, 1938), p. 253.

25. *Bureau of Immigration Report,* 1882, p. 12. Possibly even these three sugar boilers were on Chinese-owned plantations.

26. *Board of Immigration Report,* 1899, p. 36. By the 1940s the few Chinese employed on plantations were mostly Hawaii-born and fared much better in the competition for preferred positions.

27. *Bureau of Immigration Report,* 1886, pp. 175, 250. Contracts in 1870 stipulated six dollars a month for men, five dollars for women. The wages for day laborers did not include food.

28. *Board of Immigration Report,* 1892, p. 25.

29. Lind, *Island Community,* p. 256. (Filipinos were included with the Chinese in the figure for the latter date.) The migrants' objections to plantation work were similar to those expressed by Hawaii-born boys in the 1920s: "Prominent among the unfavorable conditions [mentioned] are low wages; early rising; the burdensome, grimy character of the work done under the hot sun and in the rain; lack of opportunity for promotion; racial discrimination in the better jobs; the way . . . laborers are treated by plantation foremen, police, and doctors, and in general, a type of plantation discipline which denies what the worker regards as reasonable freedom." The quotation is from Romanzo Adams and Dan Kane-zo Kai, *The Education of the Boys of Hawaii and their Economic Outlook* (Honolulu: University of Hawaii, 1928), p. 42.

30. In 1907 there were 3,245 Chinese workers on sugar plantations; in 1917 there were 2,129.

31. Interview, with the aid of an interpreter, at Tung Wo clubhouse, Kohala, Hawaii, 23 December 1935.

32. Adapted from a record in the files of a Honolulu social welfare agency.

CHAPTER 3

1.   John W. Coulter and Chee Kwon Chun, *Chinese Rice Farmers in Hawaii*, University of Hawaii Research Bulletin no. 16 (March 1937), p. 9; Ralph S. Kuykendall, *The Hawaiian Kingdom*, 3 vols. (Honolulu: University of Hawaii Press, 1938–1967), 2:151.

2.   The census report of 1896 stated: "As rice planters the Chinese have almost a monopoly, numbering 718 out of 844. In this line, the Chinese have been of great benefit to the country. Large areas of land which were unfit for ordinary cultivation, great reed-covered swamps, which were the home of the wild duck and the water hen, have been made productive by them and now yield a fine rent to the owners of the land and a revenue, in taxation, to the government." See General Superintendent of the Census, *Census of the Hawaiian Islands, 1896,* pp. 77–78.

3.   Charles K. Iwai, "The Rice Industry in Hawaii" (M.A. thesis, University of Hawaii, 1933), p. 28; A. S. T. Lund and K. Murata, *Third Annual Summary of Costs and Farm Efficiency Studies in Rice Production, Kauai County, 1934,* University of Hawaii Extension Circular no. 26 (April 1935), p. 3.

4.   *The Friend,* 1 April 1882, p. 36. A large portion of Damon's valuable observations on Chinese migrants in rural Hawaii in 1882 has been reprinted in Char, *Sandalwood Mountains,* pp. 200–217.

5.   *The Friend,* November 1892, p. 86; Supreme Court, *Hawaii Reports,* 4(1882): 457–459 (AH).

6.   *Board of Immigration Report,* 1890, pp. 78, 90; 1892, p. 73; 1897, p. 8; 1898, p. 13; 1899, p. 14.

7.   *Honolulu Advertiser,* 14 August 1932.

8.   Adapted from a record in files of a Honolulu welfare agency, 1937.

9.   Ibid.

10. *The Friend,* 1 April 1882, p. 37.

11. Coulter and Chun, *Chinese Rice Farmers,* pp. 162–169.

12. Adapted from a record in files of a Honolulu social welfare agency, 1937.

13. Ibid.

14. Ibid.

15. Compiled from interviews and a feature article by Ah Huna Tong, *Honolulu Advertiser,* 30 December 1931. Ho Yee, referred to earlier, was another rice planter who established a family. Ho Yee married his first wife on a trip to China in 1882, and he made two other trips to China in 1894 and 1911. Five sons and ten daughters were born to his first and second wives. For additional examples of Chinese rice planters and of Chinese migrant entrepreneurs in other rural ventures, see *Chinese Historic Sites and Pioneer Families of Kauai,* compiled and edited by Tin-Yuke Char and Wai-Jane Char (Honolulu: Hawaii Chinese History Center, 1979).

16. *Honolulu Star-Bulletin,* 4 March 1919; Iwai, "Rice Industry in Hawaii," pp. 48–49.

17. *PCA,* 27 September 1873.

18. Albert Rebel, *Survey of Hawaiian Industries* (Honolulu: Chamber of Commerce, 1930), p. 19; Chung, *My Seventy-Nine Years,* pp. 189–190, 205.

19. Compiled from interviews and biographies in *Chinese in Hawaii: A Résumé of the Social, Industrial, and Economic Progress of the Chinese in the Hawaiian Islands, with an Historical Sketch of the Events Leading to and the Foundation of the Chinese Republic* (Honolulu: Honolulu Star-Bulletin Print, 1913), p. 20 (hereafter cited as *Chinese in Hawaii,* 1913); *Tan Shan Wah Kiu* ("Overseas Chinese of Hawaii")—*The Chinese of Hawaii* (Honolulu: Overseas Penman Club, 1929), pp. 194–195 (hereafter cited as *Chinese of Hawaii,* 1929); *Honolulu Star-Bulletin,* 6 September 1930.

20. Compiled from interviews and biographies in *Chinese in Hawaii,* 1913, p. 27, and *Chinese of Hawaii,* 1929, p. 2. Chulan Kee was also referred to as Chulan Company, Chulan & Co., Chu Lan Lee Hook, and Chulan Brothers.

21. *Board of Immigration Report,* 1890, pp. 39–41; James W. Girvin, "Chinese in the Hawaiian Islands," *PCA,* 2 July 1903.

22. *Agricultural Census of Hawaii,* 1920 and 1930; Lund and Murata, *Third Annual Summary,* p. 3. By 1929 acreage in rice had declined further to 2,045 and by 1933 to 825.

23. "Petition to the Administrators of the Government of the United States of America for the Betterment, Conditions and Admission of Chinese Laborers to the Territory of the Hawaiian Islands," in *Hearings before the Committee on Immigration and Naturalization, House, 64th Congress, First Session on Petition by United Chinese Society for Admission of Chinese to Hawaii, Tuesday, September 5, 1916* (Washington: Government Printing Office, 1916), pp. 3–7. Among the thirty-two Chinese individuals or firms endorsing the appeal were Sing Chong Co., claiming to have already abandoned 1,923 acres of rice land, Y. Ahin (Young Ah In), 1,330 acres, Wong Wai and Ching Shai, 350 acres, and Wong Leong, 800 acres, all of Oahu; Leong Pah On, 250 acres, and C. Ako, 125 acres, both of Kauai.

24. Iwai, "Rice Industry in Hawaii," pp. 36, 43.

25. Diane Mei Lin Mark, *The Chinese in Kula* (Honolulu: Hawaii Chinese History Center, 1975), p. 1.

26. Y. Baron Goto, "Chinese Brought Most Plant Life to Hawaii," in Robert M. Lee, ed., *The Chinese in Hawaii: A Historical Sketch* (Honolulu: Advertiser Publishing Co., 1961), p. 26 (hereafter cited as Lee, *Chinese in Hawaii,* 1961). This publication was a fiftieth anniversary volume for the Chinese Chamber of Commerce of Hawaii.

27. U.S. Bureau of Foreign Commerce, *Consular Reports,* "Coffee Culture in the Hawaiian Islands," 17 January 1898, pp. 2, 8.

28. John Wesley Coulter, *Land Utilization in the Hawaiian Islands,* University of Hawaii Research Publications no. 8 (1931), pp. 108–109; *PCA,* 5 October 1894; Chung, *My Seventy-Nine Years,* p. 72.

29. Lee, *Chinese in Hawaii,* 1961, p. 87. For a biography of the founder of Wing Hing Company, Chong Sum Wing (known locally as C. S. Wing), see *Chinese of Hawaii,* 1929, p. 47. A biography of a major partner in the firm, Chong Song, appears in *Tan Shan Wah Kiu* ("Overseas Chinese of Hawaii")—*The Chinese of Hawaii: Volume II* (Honolulu: Overseas Penman Club, 1936), p. 19 (hereafter cited as *Chinese of Hawaii 2,* 1936). See also August Soren Thomsen Lund, "An Economic Study of the Coffee Industry in the Hawaiian Islands" (Ph.D. dissertation, Cornell University, 1934), pp. 233–235.

30. The leading export variety of banana for many years, known locally as the Chinese banana, was introduced into Hawaii about 1855. Another favorite in Hawaiian markets is the "apple" banana, brought by Chun Fong from China in 1868. See Willis T. Pope, *Banana Culture in Hawaii*, Hawaii Agricultural Experiment Station Bulletins, no. 55 (1926), pp. 23, 32.

31. Ibid., p. 21.

32. Chung, *My Seventy-Nine Years*, pp. 150–151.

33. Ibid., p. 215; *Chinese of Hawaii*, 1929, p. 19; Goto, "Plant Life," p. 26. C. K. Ai noted that Au Yong was growing sugarcane and bananas as well as pineapples in the 1920s.

34. Chung, *My Seventy-Nine Years*, pp. 217–246.

35. *Chinese of Hawaii*, 1929, p. 138; Lee, *Chinese in Hawaii*, 1961, p. 127. Wong Nin, a taro planter in Manoa Valley, Honolulu, in the 1890s, became wealthier when he turned his taro lands into residential property. See Chung, *My Seventy-Nine Years*, p. 230.

36. Goto, "Plant Life," p. 27.

37. Chung, *My Seventy-Nine Years*, pp. 64–65, 71–72, 96, 136, 163–168, 253.

38. If census data differentiating between rural and urban occupations by race were available for the 1860s and 1870s, they would show that even more than 80 percent of the migrants in those years were in nonurban occupations.

CHAPTER 4

1. Clarence E. Glick, "The Relation between Position and Status in the Assimilation of Chinese in Hawaii," *American Journal of Sociology* 47(1942):667–669. This article was based on data presented in Clarence E. Glick, "The Chinese Migrant in Hawaii" (Ph.D. dissertation, University of Chicago, 1938).

2. Louis Wirth, *The Ghetto* (Chicago: University of Chicago Press, 1928), pp. 25–27.

3. Interview, 14 October 1931.

4. Interview, 12 November 1930.

5. "Fifty Years of Hawaiian Commercial Development," *The Friend*, September 1893, pp. 66–67.

6. Lee, *Chinese in Hawaii*, 1961, p. 90.

7. *McKenney's Hawaiian Directory* (Oakland, California: Pacific Press, 1884), p. 300.

8. *Husted's Directory of the Hawaiian Islands*, 1896–1897, p. 404.

9. *Chinese of Hawaii*, 1929, Chinese section, p. 5.

10. The occupational index is generally obtained by dividing the proportion of a subcategory of employed people (say, Chinese males) in a given occupation by the proportion of the entire category of employed people (say, all males) in the same occupation for the same area and date. A quotient of more than 1 means that the group is overrepresented in that occupation; a quotient of less than 1 signifies less than statistical parity, or underrepresentation. See Lind, *Island Community*, pp. 245–264.

11. Idwall Jones claims that during the early Gold Rush days clothing was sent to Honolulu from San Francisco to be laundered; he also asserts that the first Chi-

nese laundry in San Francisco was started in 1851. See "Cathay on the Coast," *American Mercury* 8(1926):4.

12. Hawaiian Kingdom, *Session Laws*, 1890, pp. 18–19. The Supreme Court declared the law constitutional during the same year. In June 1898 *The Friend*, p. 48, reported that "the unsanitary practice in Chinese laundries of spraying clothes from the mouth for ironing has been made a misdemeanor, with a fine of ten dollars."

13. *Fan kwai* ("foreign devil"), a term commonly used in China in reference to Caucasians, especially during the nineteenth century. *Fan wah* ("foreign language") here means English. See Bung Chong Lee, "The Emigrants as a Social Force in a Chinese Village: A Study in Social Contacts" (unpublished manuscript, 1936), p. 5.

14. See, for example, Chung, *My Seventy-Nine Years*, pp. 181–182.

15. Ho Pan, after twenty-one years as a yard man and gardener for George P. Castle, was given a trip to China and assured of a pension for the rest of his life. See *Honolulu Advertiser*, 8 January 1930.

16. Hsieh T'ing-Yu (Tin-Yuke Char), "Origin and Migrations of the Hakkas," *Chinese Social and Political Science Review* 13(1929):204. The article is reprinted in Tin-Yuke Char, *The Bamboo Path: Life and Writings of a Chinese in Hawaii* (Honolulu: Hawaii Chinese History Center, 1977), pp. 78–93.

17. Adapted from a record in files of a Honolulu social welfare agency, 1937. Several cooks and restaurant operators who were more provident established families in the Islands.

18. *Board of Immigration Report*, 1890, p. 69.

19. By 1950 there were 388 salaried or self-employed women operating "eating and drinking places" in addition to the 694 men. By 1970 women held 699, nearly half, of the 1,470 jobs in this category. The ethnic identity of employed persons was not reported in the 1970 census; casual information suggests that Hawaii-born Chinese women were well represented in this occupation.

20. *Tan Shan Wah Kiu* ("Overseas Chinese of Hawaii")—*The Chinese of Hawaii Who's Who, 1956–1957* (Honolulu: United Chinese Penman Club, 1957), pp. 11, 159 (hereafter cited as *Chinese of Hawaii Who's Who*, 1957); Lee, *Chinese in Hawaii*, 1961, p. 87.

21. *Chinese of Hawaii*, 1929, pp. 5, 46; conversations with Chong Pang Yat during the early 1930s.

22. The ethnic identity of the 6,975 women employed in 1970 as waitresses is not supplied by the census. Given the popularity of Chinese restaurants among tourists as well as local residents, and with third- and fourth-generation Chinese women seeking employment, it is quite likely that Chinese women now have statistical parity in this occupation. Chinese men and women of alien status who have migrated to Hawaii from Hong Kong and Taiwan since 1950 are undoubtedly overrepresented in this type of work. See David Fu-Keung Ip, "Motivations and Adjustments: An Assimilation Study of Chinese Immigrants to Honolulu" (M.A. thesis, University of Hawaii, 1972); Loraine Koga, Winnie Tse, et al., "Chinese Immigrants: A Descriptive Study" (M.S.W. thesis, University of Hawaii, 1975).

23. In the districts from which most Chinese migrated to the Islands the business class did not enjoy the prestige it gained in Hawaii's Chinese community.

24. The occupational categories were: laborers, farmers, fishermen, mariners, drivers and teamsters, mechanics, planters and ranchers, merchants and traders, clerks and salesmen, professional men and teachers, and "other occupations." For the data from the censuses of 1910, 1920, and 1930 this study follows as closely as possible the classification of "major occupational classes" adopted by the U.S. census of 1940. The occupational classes grouped under the term "preferred occupations" include those identified in the 1940 U.S. census as: professional, technical, and kindred workers; managers, officials, and proprietors; clerical and kindred workers; sales workers; craftsmen, foremen, and kindred workers.

25. *Chinese in Hawaii*, 1913, p. 33.

26. Ibid., p. 28; *Chinese of Hawaii*, 1929, p. 142.

27. Occupational index: 2.9. Unlike most Chinese migrants, those employed in these occupations were usually from the large towns and cities of Kwangtung province, although generally from the same districts as most of the Chinese in Hawaii—Chung Shan, See Yup, and Sam Yup.

28. *Honolulu Advertiser*, 20 November 1932.

29. *Chinese in Hawaii*, 1913, p. 24. One of Lee Chu's partners in this venture was Doo Wai Sing, office manager of the lumber company for eleven years and by the 1930s one of the most successful and prominent Chinese in Honolulu. See *Honolulu Advertiser*, 27 June 1932; *Chinese of Hawaii*, 1929, p. 71.

30. *Chinese in Hawaii*, 1913, p. 43.

31. The 1930 census reported 606 seamstresses and female dressmakers; 456 of these were Japanese, only 13 Chinese; the Chinese women were less than one-third of the number that would be expected according to the occupational index. Since the year 1930 Japanese women working at this occupation have become much more numerous. The 1950 census reported 1,102 women in the occupations of "dressmakers and seamstresses, except factory" but does not identify the number of Japanese and Chinese women thus employed.

32. *Chinese of Hawaii*, 1929, p. 59; *Chinese of Hawaii 2*, 1936, p. 24; *Chinese of Hawaii Who's Who*, 1957, p. 34; Lee, *Chinese in Hawaii*, 1961, p. 86.

33. Wah Chan Thom, "Chinese Business from Within," *Hawaii Chinese News*, 27 January, 28 July, 3 August 1928; 8 February 1929; 4 April, 18 July, 19 September 1930; *Pacific Herald*, 3 February 1929; Tin-Yuke Char, interview, 14 October 1931.

34. Kum Pui Lai, "The Natural History of the Chinese Language School in Hawaii" (M.A. thesis, University of Hawaii, 1935), p. 10.

35. Compiled from *Chinese of Hawaii*, 1929, pp. 81–82; *Pacific Herald*, 10 January 1929; *Honolulu Star-Bulletin*, 16 January 1929, 11 May 1931; Chung, *My Seventy-Nine Years*, pp. 92, 105. Ho Fon died in Honolulu 11 May 1931.

36. *Chinese of Hawaii*, 1929, p. 64; *Chinese of Hawaii Who's Who*, 1957, pp. 1–2; Lee, *Chinese in Hawaii*, 1961, p. 89; Chung, *My Seventy-Nine Years*, pp. 37, 43–47, 68, 83, 94, 136, 190–193, 312, 318.

37. *Chinese of Hawaii*, 1929, pp. 184, 186–187, and interviews.

38. *Chinese in Hawaii*, 1913, p. 14; *Chinese of Hawaii*, 1929, p. 51; *Honolulu Advertiser*, 18 September 1932.

39. *The Friend,* 4 January 1881, p. 4. S. P. Aheong's career as a Christian worker in Hawaii is described by Tin-Yuke Char, "S. P. Aheong, Hawaii's First Chinese Evangelist," *Hawaiian Journal of History* 11(1977):69–76, reprinted in Char, *The Bamboo Path,* pp. 232–240.

40. Char, *Sandalwood Mountains,* p. 192.

41. Ibid., p. 234. The Reverend Canon Wai On Shim, for example, son of the Reverend Shim Yin Jin of Maui, became rector of St. Elizabeth's Church in Honolulu.

42. *Chinese of Hawaii,* 1929, p. 5; *Honolulu Advertiser,* 14 February 1931. Other teachers in Hawaii's Chinese-language schools have been foreign-born students at the University of Hawaii, Hawaii-born Chinese educated in China, and in recent years post–World War II immigrants from Hong Kong and Taiwan.

43. Some of these subjects were still being taught by China-born professors in the 1970s. Since World War II refugees and the "brain drain" have added to the number of China-born scholars and scientists teaching subjects unrelated to Chinese culture. Outside the field of Chinese studies, the first faculty member at the University of Hawaii of Chinese ancestry was Ruth Lu Tet Yap, daughter of Mr. and Mrs. William Kwai Fong Yap, who became an instructor in the mathematics department in 1928 after receiving her B.A. and M.A. degrees from the University of Hawaii and two years of further graduate study at Columbia University.

44. *Chinese of Hawaii,* 1929, pp. 5, 79.

45. *Chinese in Hawaii,* 1913, p. 22; *Chinese of Hawaii 2,* 1936, p. 53; Li Ling Ai, *Life Is for a Long Time: A Chinese Hawaiian Memoir* (New York: Hastings House, 1972), p. 327. Min Hin Li, the eldest son of Dr. and Mrs. Li, was one of the first of the large number of Island-born Chinese to enter the medical profession.

CHAPTER 5

1. Bung Chong Lee, "Bucktoy Village Families in Hawaii" (unpublished manuscript, 1936), p. 1; *Honolulu Star-Bulletin,* 30 September 1933.

2. Char, *Sandalwood Mountains,* p. 127.

3. Biographies of Lee Ong and Leong Han in *Chinese of Hawaii,* 1929, pp. 112, 119.

4. Biographies of Chun Kam Chow, Doo Wai Sing, Hung Hoy, Lee Chow, and Wong But Ting in *Chinese of Hawaii,* 1929, pp. 57, 71, 86, 107, 177, and interviews.

5. *Honolulu Advertiser,* 1 December 1931.

6. C. K. Yang, *A Chinese Village in Early Communist Transition* (Cambridge: M.I.T. Press, 1959), p. 69; Hsiao Tung Fei, *Peasant Life in China* (New York: Dutton, 1939), pp. 267–274.

7. Sources for this section included *Hawaii Chinese News,* 10 August 1928; *Hawaii Hochi,* 15 October 1928; interview with Lee Kau, 8 October 1931; and student papers, Sociology Department, University of Hawaii.

8. Data on savings deposits are from *Report of the Treasurer to the Legislature, Territory of Hawaii,* 1910–1936. According to one estimate $3 to $4 million was sent by Hawaii Chinese to Hong Kong for speculative purposes in the early 1930s, re-

sulting in heavy losses. See Kum Pui Lai, "The Natural History of the Chinese Language School in Hawaii," p. 52.

9.   *Chinese in Hawaii*, 1913, p. 16.

10.   According to a tabulation made by Robert M. W. Lee from a 1950 directory, 129 of the 620 Honolulu realtors listed were Chinese. See "Vertical Mobility among the Chinese in Hawaii" (M.A. thesis, University of Hawaii, 1951), p. 52. This number was more than three times statistical parity for Chinese in this occupation in 1950.

11.   *Report of the Treasurer to the Legislature, Territory of Hawaii*, 1910–1932.

12.   Paul Kimm Chow Goo, "Chinese Economic Activities in Hawaii," *Chinese of Hawaii* 2, 1936, p. 12.

13.   High-rise apartment houses and condominiums were to come in later decades, with Island-born Chinese among those who built them and bought units for rent or speculation.

14.   Some qualification regarding particular occupations is necessary: some Hawaii-born Chinese men who, according to census tabulations, are placed in the second category of Table 3 (actually "managers, officials, and proprietors") have higher prestige than some of those in professional occupations. The migrant generation's regard for wealth as a major criterion of status is still widely shared among Island-born Chinese, as it is among other ethnic groups.

15.   Lee, *Chinese in Hawaii*, 1961, p. 34.

16.   The earliest documented reference to a Chinese woman in Hawaii concerns a servant who came with an American family from Macao in 1837 and returned to China in 1843. See Char, *Sandalwood Mountains*, pp. 42–43. The earliest archival records of Chinese wives in Hawaii appear to be those of the arrival of a woman, Nip Ashue, age twenty, in 1854 and two others, not identified by name, in 1855. The arrival of 52 Chinese women in 1865 was mentioned in Chapter 1. Census data indicate that there were 107 Chinese foreign-born women in Hawaii in 1872, 231 in 1878, 871 in 1884, and 1,419 in 1896. There were 17,068 foreign-born Chinese men in 1884; in 1896 there were 17,963. While the high sex ratio among the Chinese caused concern in Hawaii, arrivals of women in the 1890s and the first two decades of the 1900s resulted in a much more balanced sex ratio in the Islands than existed among Chinese in the continental United States.

17.   One case history in the files of a Honolulu social welfare agency in 1937 mentions a Punti woman with bound feet who was brought to Hawaii as a wife for a Chinese migrant and who found herself forced to work on her knees in the fields of her husband's peanut farm on Oahu.

18.   It was common practice for unmarried employed Chinese daughters to turn over their wages to their parents and receive an allowance in return. As late as the middle 1930s a Chinese graduate of the University of Hawaii, employed in a social welfare agency in Honolulu, was living at home and turning over her salary to her father to be combined in the family fund with the earnings of her unmarried brothers. However, this money was in a sense held in trust for her. When she went to the mainland for graduate study, her expenses were paid for from the family fund.

19.   One of these women may have been "Mother Chang" (Mrs. Chang Ki Loy),

who came to Kohala, Hawaii, in 1865 with her husband and sons. When her husband, a Hakka, died before his three-year contract on a sugar plantation ended, his widow and three sons did truck farming in Kohala for a year and then with a daughter (Miss Mary Chang) moved to Honolulu where "Mother Chang" entered domestic service with a prominent Haole family. See *Honolulu Advertiser*, 29 November 1931. In the 1890 census two women were listed under the category of "professional men and teachers." These two women may have been Miss Mary Chang and Miss Mary Kwai Shim, both Hawaii-born and Hawaii-educated Chinese who were teachers in 1890 in a school for girls started by the Reverend and Mrs. Frank W. Damon in Honolulu. See Ah Jook Ku, "The Pioneer Women," *Chinese of Hawaii Who's Who*, 1957, p. 24.

20. A few women were teaching in the Chinese-language schools.
21. See Chapter 2, "Getting Off the Plantation."
22. *Hawaii Chinese Journal*, 28 December 1939.
23. A sample survey completed in 1977 reported income data for military and civilian families in Hawaii; data here are for civilian families only. The median family income (before taxes) for Chinese was $21,183, highest for all groups for whom the median income was reported; the others, in descending order, were: Koreans, Japanese, Caucasians, part-Hawaiians, "mixed, except part-Hawaiians," Filipinos, and Hawaiians. The median income for all families was $17,000. The survey also reported that 3,824 of the 11,885 Chinese families reporting incomes received $25,000 or more. An acknowledged limitation of the survey was that income data were not obtained for 16 percent of the families surveyed and for 17 percent of the Chinese. See *Population Characteristics of Hawaii, 1977*, Department of Health and Department of Planning and Economic Development, Population Report, Issue 11 (January 1979), pp. 4–5, 25.
24. The third-generation Chinese mother of two recent university graduate sons, herself a teacher and the wife of a successful medical specialist, commented that although neither of her sons could get a job of the type for which they were qualified she was grateful they had found jobs at which "at least they were earning something." They were not, she said, like some of her friends' young Chinese sons who were "just drifting around because they can't find the kind of work they want." Interview, 2 January 1977.

CHAPTER 6

1. By the 1930s rural communities which had been centers of concentration of Chinese families had lost most of these families. In the Kohala district of the island of Hawaii the writer was told in 1935 that of the hundred or more Chinese families once living in the district, only fourteen remained, most of them broken by the departure of members for other places in the Islands, mainly Honolulu and Hilo. Chinese girls complained that no young Chinese men were left in the district.
2. *Honolulu Star-Bulletin*, 17 March 1937, and interviews.
3. Chinese Bureau, "Women Permits, 1893–1898" (AH). The numbers of Chinese women arrivals (including reentries) by decades were about as follows: 1850s, 5; 1860s, 83; 1870s, 98; 1880s, 375; 1890s, 1,588; 1900–1909,

155. It is likely that no more than 2,200 Chinese women came before Annexation and probably no more than 3,000 by 1940.

4. By 1930 some commuter suburbs had developed on Oahu which, if statistical data were available, should be included in this discussion of the concentration of Chinese in Honolulu, Oahu's central city.

5. Much of the material in this chapter is adapted from an article published by the writer in 1936: "Residential Dispersion of Urban Chinese," *Social Process in Hawaii* 2 (1936):28–34. Boundaries for wards and census enumeration districts used by the censuses did not correspond exactly with the boundaries of the Chinatown area; hence the data given in this section are only approximate. A similar residential dispersion of Chinese families occurred in the main towns on the islands of Hawaii, Maui, and Kauai, though the families were much less numerous than in Honolulu. A certain part of the main towns on these islands would be designated as Chinatown because of the location in or near the downtown section of some Chinese stores, a few clubhouses, a church, a temple. This grouping would serve as a center for Chinese activities and evidence of a Chinese presence.

6. C. C. Bennett, *Honolulu Directory and Historical Sketch of the Hawaiian or Sandwich Islands* (Honolulu, 1869).

7. Based upon records of licenses granted by the Hawaiian government.

8. *Hawaiian Annual*, 1906, p. 62.

9. "Aala Park," *The Friend*, May 1899, p. 35.

10. J. A. Cruzan, "The Chinese in Hawaii," *The Friend*, 1 November 1882, p. 115.

11. *Husted's Directory of Honolulu and of the Hawaiian Islands, 1896–1897*, p. 65.

12. By 1960 less than two thousand of the more than thirty thousand Chinese living in Honolulu resided in the Chinatown section; only about 15 percent of Chinatown's residents were Chinese.

CHAPTER 7

1. Over 2,200 of these 4,500 were married, mostly to women left with kinsmen in China; others in urban Honolulu were married to Hawaiian women.

2. A. W. Palmer, *Orientals in American Life* (New York: Friendship Press, 1934), pp. 1–2.

3. Ching-chao Wu, "Chinatowns: A Study in Symbiosis and Assimilation" (Ph.D. dissertation, University of Chicago, 1928), p. 158.

4. Interview with Young Hing Cham, 17 February 1932.

5. Bung Chong Lee, "The Chinese Store as a Social Institution," *Social Process in Hawaii* 2(1936):35–36.

6. Ibid., p. 36.

7. Sun Yun Wo, reportedly, was established in 1892; for several decades the proprietor was Hee Cho, then his son, William K. F. Hee. See *Hawaii Chinese Journal*, 15 September 1949; *Chinese of Hawaii*, 1929, p. 77.

8. Chung, *My Seventy-Nine Years*, pp. 3, 12, 17, 25, 99.

9. *Bark gup biu* is a Chinese phrase used locally for a lottery involving picking the winning combination of words from a printed list. See Chung, *My Seventy-Nine Years*, pp. 84, 96; Stewart Culin, *The Gambling Games of the Chinese in*

America, Publications of the University of Pennsylvania Series in Philology, Literature, and Archaeology, vol. 1, no. 4, 1891, pp. 1–17.

10. *Hawaiian Reports* 8(1891):206, The Queen vs. Kaka.

11. *Honolulu Advertiser,* 1 June 1930.

12. Ibid., 10, 11 March 1884; *The Friend,* June 1892, p. 42.

13. The May 1894 issue of *The Friend,* p. 37, carries a reference to gambling at this cemetery on 4 April of that year.

14. Gorham D. Gilman, "Streets of Honolulu," *Hawaiian Annual,* 1904, p. 77.

15. *PCA,* 19 February, 12 March, 22 August 1857. For supplementary details, see Lily Lim-Chong, "Opium and the Law: Hawaii, 1856–1900," Spring 1978 (paper in files of Department of Sociology, University of Hawaii).

16. *PCA,* 3 January 1887; 12, 22 September 1888; *Daily Bulletin,* 13 January 1887; *Hawaiian Gazette,* 18 January, 1, 15 February, 17 May, 28 June 1887; Chung, *My Seventy-Nine Years,* pp. 174–175.

17. Chung, *My Seventy-Nine Years,* pp. 98–99; Li, *Life Is for a Long Time,* pp. 226, 302, 305.

18. *Honolulu Star-Bulletin,* 14 November 1930; 2 February 1935; 7 February, 20 December 1936; 16 December 1938.

19. In 1933 the annual report of the Police Department, City and County of Honolulu, listed 492 arrests of noncitizen Chinese during the year; 76 of them were for drug violations, 301 for gambling. In that year there were about 2,800 foreign-born Chinese men in Honolulu.

20. Only one item concerning the possible involvement of Chinese women in prostitution in Hawaii was found in the English-language newspapers between 1880 and 1920. It referred to "the case of some Chinese women who were being landed in this country for immoral purposes," but the implication was that the attempted landing did not succeed. See *Daily Bulletin,* 17 August 1888. James Michener, in *Hawaii,* seems to imply that such a practice may have been common there as in San Francisco, but this writer found no evidence that the fictional Chinese Hakka woman character who is brought to Hawaii to be sold into prostitution has any basis in fact.

21. "Petition to the Administrators of the Government of the United States of America . . . ," 5 September 1916, p. 6.

22. Li, *Life Is for a Long Time,* pp. 297–299.

23. *PCA,* 25 January 1879.

24. Coulter and Chun, *Chinese Rice Farmers in Hawaii,* p. 45.

25. Wu, "Chinatowns," pp. 179–180. See also H. B. McDowell, "The Chinese Theatre," *Century Magazine* 8(1884):41; James D. Ball, *The Chinese at Home* (London: Religious Tract Society, 1912), p. 293.

26. Chung Pai, by Kong Leen, to Charles T. Gulick, Minister of the Interior, 28 September 1885 (AH); Hawaiian Kingdom, *Reports of Decisions Rendered by the Supreme Court of the Hawaiian Islands, in Law, Equity, Admiralty and Probate,* 8 (Honolulu: Honolulu Star-Bulletin, 1893), pp. 156–158. See *Daily Bulletin,* 23 August 1888, for a complaint about the "diabolical noise" at the Chinese Theater. In the Supreme Court decision the Minister of Interior's condition that the orchestra could not play after ten o'clock was declared to be "not reasonable."

27. Chinese movies, produced mainly in Hong Kong and Taiwan, have reappeared in recent years as part of Honolulu's cosmopolitan entertainment fare. This revival is primarily the result of the recent increase in the number of foreign-born Chinese immigrants to Hawaii. Most of the films use Kuo Yu, the Chinese national language, with English subtitles. Hence the films appeal not only to Hawaii-born Chinese who have studied Kuo Yu but to those who are interested in their ancestral culture as well.

28. Hawaiian government authorities were willing to let these men practice on the Chinese migrants, but they early saw the necessity of some regulation as shown by a law passed by the legislature in 1880 setting forth the conditions under which a person who could demonstrate his right to practice medicine in China could secure a license to do the same in Hawaii.

29. *Honolulu Star-Bulletin*, 11 May 1928. Massage, moxibustion, and acupuncture as methods of treatment are claimed to have been practiced among Chinese for some three thousand years. See K. Chimin Wong and Lien-Teh Wu, *History of Chinese Medicine* (Tientsin, China: Tientsin Press, 1932), pp. 28–30. In the 1970s Honolulu had a resurgence of the practice of acupuncture; patients and practitioners included non-Chinese as well as Chinese. Concern has arisen regarding the need for more stringent regulation of persons allowed to practice acupuncture.

30. Li, *Life Is for a Long Time*, pp. 32, 100, 105.

31. Wong and Wu, *History of Chinese Medicine*, p. 91.

32. Ah Huna Tong, "Young American Is Priest of Old Chinese Temple Here," *Honolulu Advertiser*, 20 February 1933.

33. Sau Chun Wong, "Chinese Temples in Honolulu," *Social Process in Hawaii* 3(1937):27.

34. Char, *Sandalwood Mountains*, p. 181.

35. "A Honolulu Chinese Joss House," *The Friend*, April 1880, p. 32.

36. "Idol Temples in Honolulu," *The Friend*, October 1887, p. 85.

37. C. K. Ai, who was in business in Chinatown in 1886, says that the destructive fire of that year was started by a Chinese gambler who was careless in handling candles he had bought to burn before "the altar of the Goddess of Chance." See Chung, *My Seventy-Nine Years*, p. 96.

38. Wong, "Chinese Temples in Honolulu," p. 29.

39. Ibid., pp. 32–33.

40. Char, *Sandalwood Mountains*, p. 183.

41. Chung, *My Seventy-Nine Years*, pp. 119, 313–318.

42. *St. Peter's Church, Golden Jubilee, 1886–1936* (Honolulu: W. W. Ahana Printing Co., 1936), pp. 1–4; Char, *Sandalwood Mountains*, pp. 192–196.

43. Char, *Sandalwood Mountains*, pp. 230–234.

CHAPTER 8

1. Romanzo Adams estimated that there were about 400 legal marriages of Chinese migrants to Hawaiian women during the years 1840–1870 and 400 to 500 between 1871 and 1899; he notes that the period of 1900–1916 was one of increased marriages of Chinese to Hawaiian and part-Hawaiian women. See Adams, *Interracial Marriage in Hawaii*, pp. 146–150.

2. Translated by Young Hing Cham, April 1932.
3. Adams, *Interracial Marriage in Hawaii*, pp. 90–98; Doris M. Lorden, "The Chinese-Hawaiian Family," *American Journal of Sociology* 40(1935):453–463.
4. Interview by Margaret M. Lam, in files of the Department of Sociology, University of Hawaii.
5. Ibid.
6. Chung, *My Seventy-Nine Years*, pp. 40, 43–44, 62, 75.
7. "A Chinese Family in Hawaii," *Social Process in Hawaii* 3(1937):50–55; reprinted in Char, *Sandalwood Mountains*, pp. 120–126. The writer of this account points out that one of her brothers was faced with serious conflict between the two wives in a home he established in China. The first wife was a Hawaii-born Chinese; the other, China-born, was brought into the home only eight months after his marriage to the first wife.
8. Paul C. F. Siu, "The Chinese Family in Chicago," manuscript (Department of Sociology, University of Chicago, 1933), p. 3. Samuel G. Wilder, who had been sent to Asian ports in 1870 to investigate possible sources of contract laborers, wrote to the president of the Board of Immigration from Hong Kong, 11 March 1870: "It is very seldom you can induce any Chinese high or low to take his wife No. 1 with him. . . . All the information I can get goes to prove that Chinamen never take their first wife with them." (See Interior Department, Miscellaneous: Immigration—Chinese, AH.) Wilder claimed in 1870, "You can buy, in China, all the women you want from $75 to $1,000. . . . I bought one, for which I paid 75 Mexican dollars, and she is now a servant in my household." (See *PCA*, 22 October 1870.) George N. Wilcox, in an interview on 12 November 1930, told about a Chinese rice planter at Hanalei, Kauai, who had bought a "slave girl" as a second wife after his first wife died.
9. Adams, *Interracial Marriage in Hawaii*, pp. 337–339.
10. Unless otherwise identified, materials quoted in this chapter are from papers written by Hawaii-born Chinese students.
11. Kum Pui Lai, "The Natural History of the Chinese Language School in Hawaii," p. 49.
12. Secretary, Board of Immigration to H.M.'s Consul-General in Hong Kong, 11 January 1893. (See Interior Department, Miscellaneous: Immigration—Chinese, AH.)
13. *The Friend*, 4 January 1881, Supplement, p. 1.
14. *Biennial Report of the President of the Board of Education to the Legislative Assembly of 1882*, p. 38 (AH).
15. Secretary, Board of Immigration to H.M.'s Acting Consul-General in Hong Kong, 2 June 1891. (See Interior Department, Miscellaneous: Immigration—Chinese, AH.)
16. *The Friend*, 7 July 1882, p. 80.
17. Chung, *My Seventy-Nine Years*, pp. 87, 106.
18. Lai, "Natural History," pp. 93–94.
19. Peak enrollment in one of the two large schools was 1,350; in the other it was over 1,000. By the fall of 1975 enrollment had dwindled to about 400 in one and less than 200 in the other. Only two other Chinese-language schools existed in Honolulu in 1975, both in the Kaimuki area, with less than 100 students between them. See Lehn Huff, "Chinese Language Schools in Hawaii

Today" (Honolulu: Hawaii Chinese History Center, 1975). Census data for 1970 indicate that there would have been about 9,000 Chinese from five to fourteen years old in Honolulu in 1975 and about 14,000 from five to nineteen years old.

CHAPTER 9

1. *Stephen Reynolds' Journal, 1824–1845* (Cambridge: Harvard College Library Microfilms, no. 9258, Hawaiian Mission Children's Society), 12 November 1838, 4 May 1841.

2. *Chinese of Hawaii*, 1929, Chinese section, pp. 7–8; Chock Lun, "Chinese Organizations in Hawaii," *Chinese of Hawaii* 2, 1936, p. 33. Much of Chock's description of over one hundred Chinese organizations in Hawaii is reprinted in Char, *Sandalwood Mountains*, pp. 148–159.

3. Char, *Sandalwood Mountains*, pp. 171–176. Char gives the names and locations of over thirty Chinese cemeteries. The cemetery for Hoklo people is mentioned in Tin-Yuke Char and Wai-Jane Char, "The First Chinese Contract Laborers in Hawaii, 1852," *Hawaiian Journal of History* 9(1975):133. A Chinese Chamber of Commerce of Hawaii Award of Merit states that the Lin Yee Chung Association (successor of Lin Yee Wui) was established in 1877.

4. S. Couling, "Triad Society," *Encyclopaedia Sinica* (Shanghai: Kelly and Walsh, 1917), pp. 572–573; W. A. Pickering, "Chinese Secret Societies and Their Origin," *Journal of the Straits Branch of the Royal Asiatic Society* (July 1878):67–84.

5. Hsieh T'ing-Yu [Tin-Yuke Char], "Origin and Migrations of the Hakkas," *Chinese Social and Political Science Review* 13(1929):222; G. Barth, *Bitter Strength: A History of the Chinese in the United States, 1850–1870* (Cambridge: Harvard University Press, 1964), pp. 24–25. Char's article on the Hakkas was reprinted in Char, *The Bamboo Path*, pp. 78–93.

6. Chock, "Chinese Organizations," pp. 30–31, 35; Char, *Sandalwood Mountains*, pp. 169–171. Most of the Hoong Moon societies are named in the lists by Chock and Char, but neither list is complete.

7. Lum Pui Young, "The Chinese on Windward Oahu: Waiahole, Waikane, and Hakipu," mimeographed (Honolulu: Hawaii Chinese History Center, 1975), pp. 2–3.

8. Interview with Shao Chang Lee, 13 October 1930. See also Maurice Freedman, "Immigrants and Associations: Chinese in Nineteenth-Century Singapore," in L. A. Fallers, ed., *Immigrants and Associations* (The Hague: Mouton 1967), pp. 17–48. Freedman's observations are similar to those of Professor Lee, but he found that other branches had mixed membership. A list of forty-one contributors to the reconstruction in 1917 of the Ling Hing Wui Goon building in Hilo showed that twenty were from See Yup (thirteen from Toi Shan, four from Sun Wui, three from Yen Ping); twenty were from Heung Shan (Chung Shan); and one was from Pao On. Twenty-eight surnames were on the list. Information compiled with the help of Bung Chong Lee, 28 December 1935.

9. Interviews at Halawa, Kohala, Hawaii, 25 December 1935.

10. Interviews with Tam Tinn Chong, Kahalui, Maui, and Chun Ah Lung, Hana, Maui, December 1930.

11. There is no published description of these ceremonies in the Hoong Moon societies of Hawaii. For information on Hoong Moon societies elsewhere see W. A. Pickering, "Chinese Secret Societies, II," *Journal of the Straits Branch of the Royal Asiatic Society* (July 1879):1–18; J. Dyer Ball, *Things Chinese*, 5th ed. rev. (Shanghai: Kelly and Walsh, 1925), pp. 605–614; W. P. Morgan, *Triad Societies in Hong Kong* (Hong Kong: Government Press, 1960). According to Chock Lun the last two Chinese to administer these oaths in Hawaii died in 1935.

12. Mark, *Chinese in Kula*, p. 10.

13. To disguise their real nature and activities and to make their organizations appear acceptable to the government, some Hoong Moon societies in Southeast Asia and the continental United States referred to themselves as Chinese Freemasons and even included the square and compass among their public symbols.

14. *PCA*, 5 February 1881, 29 March, 5 April 1884.

15. F. W. Damon, "Tours among the Chinese, No. 2: The Island of Kauai," *The Friend*, Chinese Supplement, 7 July 1882, p. 80.

16. *Disclosures as to Chinese Secret Societies* (Honolulu, 1884). All references to the thirty-six oaths are based on this pamphlet.

17. Leon Comber, *Chinese Secret Societies in Malaya: A Survey of the Triad Society from 1800 to 1900* (Locust Valley, N.Y.: J. J. Augustin Inc. for the Association for Asian Studies, 1959), pp. 134–136.

18. *PCA*, 9 April 1886; *Daily Bulletin*, 9 April 1886. In November 1885, three months after the act went into effect, twenty-three Chinese were arrested on the charge of maintaining an unlicensed secret society. The organization, the Tung Hing Company, was by this time located in Honolulu's Chinatown. The men were acquitted.

19. *Daily Bulletin*, 17 October 1888.

20. *Biennial Report of the Attorney-General to the Legislative Assembly of 1890*, pp. 4–16. Ling Hing Wui Goon, organized in Hilo in 1899, replaced Yee Wo Kung Si. When the writer interviewed members of the Ling Hing Wui Goon in 1935, this organization was functioning primarily as a social and benevolent society for its aging members. The Ling Hing Wui Goon clubhouse was destroyed by a tidal wave in 1960.

21. Rose Hum Lee, *The Chinese in the United States of America* (Hong Kong: Hong Kong University Press, 1960), pp. 168–169.

22. Kuykendall, *Hawaiian Kingdom* 3:425, 429; *Hawaiian Annual*, 1890, pp. 89–90.

23. Quoted in *Board of Immigration Report*, 1890, p. 80.

24. Ibid., pp. 88–89.

25. *Honolulu Star-Bulletin*, 9 November 1928.

26. Mark, *Chinese in Kula*, pp. 24–25. Additional information about the functioning of this Hoong Moon society is reported by Irma Tam Soong and Ted T. K. Gong in *A Study of the Meeting Records of the Ket Hing Society, Kula, Maui, 1913–1947* (Honolulu: Hawaii Chinese History Center, 1979).

27. Mark, *Chinese in Kula*, p. 25.

28. Char, *Sandalwood Mountains*, p. 160.

29. Interview, Halawa, Kohala, Hawaii, 25 December 1935.

30. Interview with a Caucasian-Hawaiian sugar boiler, Hana, Maui, 1930.

31. William J. Bonk, "Tong Wo Society Celebration," *Hawaii Heritage News*

(June–July 1976), pp. 1–2; working papers prepared by Tin-Yuke Char in 1972 for the Hawaii Chinese History Center include information about several Hoong Moon societies organized on the islands of Kauai, Maui, and Hawaii.

32. *Hawaiian Directory, 1880–1881*, p. 455; C. C. Bennett, *Honolulu Directory and Historical Sketch of the Hawaiian Islands,* 1869, p. 43.

33. *PCA,* 8 February 1879.

34. "Constitution and By-Laws of China Engine Company No. 5" (AH).

35. From the petition of this society in 1899 for a charter of incorporation. Unless otherwise stated, quotations from such petitions, charters granted, and constitutions and bylaws of Chinese organizations are from documents filed in the State of Hawaii Bureau of Regulatory Agencies, Honolulu.

36. *Daily Bulletin,* 4 February 1886. Another newspaper added that "the rear was brought up by a Chinese band consisting of a drum and gong."

37. The China Engine Company was said to have been ineffective in the Chinatown fire of April 1886 only a few months later.

38. Lau Cheong was also one of the organizers of a district association and a surname society. He was connected with a prominent Chinese firm located on the edge of Chinatown nearest the Haole business district and was an official interpreter for the Board of Immigration as well as a well-known recruiter of Chinese immigrants.

39. Henry A. Peirce, U.S. Minister to Hawaii, to Hawaiian Acting Consul-General F. B. Johnson, Hong Kong, 9 March 1878. (See Foreign Office Letter Book Typed Copy, No. 10, p. 17, AH.)

40. Wing-Iu Leung, University of Hawaii student from Canton, translated *shang tung* as "merchant director." "We have the *shang tung* in China. The Chamber of Commerce in Canton . . . appoints one of the big merchants as *shang tung.* He settles all commercial disputes brought before him and decides what is to be done in cases of insolvency and bankruptcy. The idea of having a *shang tung* is that people can settle their cases without taking them to the courts." Interview, March 1932.

41. The Hawaiian government recognized Afong's appointment on 18 February 1880. (See Correspondence with the Chinese Consulate, 1879–1900, AH; "The United Chinese Society," *Chinese of Hawaii,* 1929, Chinese section, pp. 65–66; Kuykendall, *Hawaiian Kingdom,* 3:138–140.) Afong was the successful bidder for the opium monopoly license in some of the years between 1860 and 1875, when the government auctioned such licenses.

42. *Bureau of Immigration Report,* 1886, pp. 163–169; letters for 12 July, 7 September, and 12 December 1881 in Correspondence with the Chinese Consulate, 1879–1900, AH; letter for 3 January 1882 in Foreign Office Letterbook No. 10, AH. A document entitled "Chinese Immigration—Forced Labor," dated July 1881, contains a copy of the translated extracts from the Afong letter to the Chinese paper regarding "Laborers of the Ship, Septima," and also a copy of a letter of Commissioner Tschen Lan-Pen (Ch'en Lan-pin) to the governor-general at Canton, translated from a German copy. (See Interior Department, Miscellaneous: Immigration—Chinese, AH.) Afong's name does not appear on the list of officers of the United Chinese Society and there is no

mention of his being present at the opening of the clubhouse in 1886. Four
years later (1890) he returned to China where he lived until his death in 1906.

43. "The United Chinese Society," *Chinese of Hawaii*, 1929, Chinese section, pp.
65–66; Kuykendall, *Hawaiian Kingdom* 3:138–139, 674–675.

44. The petition for a charter, submitted 11 February 1884, was in both English
and Hawaiian. In the English version the organization was referred to as the
Chung Wa Ui Kon (United Chinese Society); in the Hawaiian version it was
called the Chung Wa Hui Quon (Hui Pake i Hoohui ia). In the charter granted
by the government 27 August 1884 it was called Chun Wa Hui Quon (The
United Chinese Society).

45. *PCA*, 14 August 1884.

46. *The Friend*, May 1882, p. 40; August 1892, pp. 63–64; *Chinese in Hawaii*, 1913,
p. 19; *PCA*, 27 May 1892.

47. *Daily Bulletin*, 9 April 1886.

48. Sources for the account of the building of the United Chinese Society
headquarters and the opening ceremonies: *Chinese of Hawaii*, 1929, Chinese
section, pp. 65–66; "History of the Forming of the United Chinese Society,"
Tan Heong Shan Chung Wah Wui Goon Ng Sup Chow Nyin Gee Nim Duck Han
[Hawaii United Chinese Society Fiftieth Anniversary Volume] (Shanghai:
Chung Hwa Book Company, 1934), p. 9 (hereafter cited as *United Chinese Society Anniversary Volume*); *Daily Bulletin*, 3, 4 February 1886; *PCA*, 4 Februarv
1886.

CHAPTER 10

1. *Report of the Minister of Foreign Affairs, 1884*, pp. 104–105 (AH).

2. Ibid., pp. 105–106.

3. Kuykendall, *Hawaiian Kingdom* 3:273, 693.

4. Minister of Foreign Affairs to Hawaiian Consul in Hong Kong, 8 July 1885.
Foreign Office Letterbook No. 10 (AH). Almost from the beginning of restrictions on Chinese immigration, various techniques were used to gain illegal entry, including: adults claiming to be only thirteen years old in order to be admitted on a permit for children of that age or younger; merchants staying on
indefinitely after being allowed to enter for a maximum of six months; bribing ships' officers to falsely check off merchants as having boarded ship for
China; using another migrant's return permit. Several of the methods necessi-
tated continued use in Hawaii of a false identity. In the early 1900s payments
of about thirteen hundred dollars for false birth certificates gave rise to the
term *chin sam* ("thirteen hundred"), used within the Chinese community in
reference to certain migrants. For comparable reference to "slots" and "paper
sons" in the U.S. mainland see Rose Hum Lee, *Chinese in the United States*, pp.
389, 439, and Victor G. Nee and Brett de Bary Nee, *Longtime Californ': A Docu-
mentary Study of an American Chinatown* (New York: Pantheon Books, 1972), pp.
62–63.

5. Correspondence with the Chinese Consulate, 1879–1900, 1 December 1885
(AH).

6. *United Chinese Society Anniversary Volume*, 1934, p. 9.
7. Correspondence with Chinese Consulate, 9 November, 13 December 1887 (AH). It was this same "ticket" arrangement between U.S. authorities and the Chung Wah Kung Saw (Chinese Consolidated Benevolent Association) in San Francisco that more than anything else gave the Six Companies its great power. See Barth, *Bitter Strength*, pp. 51, 68, 91–99.
8. Foreign Office Letterbook No. 10, 27 June 1887, 15 October 1891 (AH).
9. *United Chinese Society Anniversary Volume*, p. 1.
10. *Report of the Minister of Foreign Affairs, 1884*, pp. 104–105 (AH).
11. Correspondence with the Chinese Consulate, 9 November 1887 (AH).
12. *Statutes*, 1887, Act Regulating Chinese Immigration.
13. *The Friend*, November 1889, p. 91; February 1895, p. 13; Chung, *My Seventy-Nine Years*, p. 173; Kuykendall, *Hawaiian Kingdom* 3:425; *Biennial Report of the Attorney-General to the Legislative Assembly of 1890*, pp. 25–26.
14. *Hawaiian Annual*, 1893, addenda, p. 8.
15. Correspondence with the Chinese Consulate, 29 January 1897 (AH).
16. *The Friend*, September 1897, p. 71; January 1899, p. 4; April 1899, p. 28.
17. "Petition to the Administrators of the Government of the United States of America . . . ," 5 September 1916, p. 7.
18. *Chinese of Hawaii*, 1929, Chinese section, pp. 6–7.
19. Ibid.
20. *Daily Bulletin*, 20, 30 August 1888; Kuykendall, *Hawaiian Kingdom* 3:180.
21. *PCA*, 19 May, 6, 12, 13 September 1888; *Daily Bulletin*, 14, 29, 30, 31 August, 3, 5, 6, 11 September 1888.
22. Hugh D. R. Baker, *A Chinese Lineage Village: Sheung Shui* (London: Frank Cass & Co., 1968), p. 13.
23. *Daily Bulletin*, 31 August 1888.
24. Char, *Sandalwood Mountains*, p. 74.
25. H.M.'s Minister in Washington to Minister of Foreign Affairs, 24 November 1890. Hawaiian Officials Abroad: Minister, Washington, July–November, 1890 (AH).
26. *The Friend*, March 1894, p. 24.
27. *Hawaiian Star*, 15 February 1894.
28. *PCA*, 1, 10 May 1897. Complaints about treatment were also made by workers on sugar plantations at Koloa, Kauai, and Honokaa, Hawaii.
29. Correspondence with the Chinese Consulate, 16 November 1897 (AH).
30. Ibid., 13 August 1897.
31. *Chinese in Hawaii*, 1913, p. 7.
32. Letter from J. A. Hassinger, Clerk, Interior Department, to R. A. Lyman, 8 August 1897. Interior Department Letterbook No. 30 (AH). See also *PCA*, 20 July 1897; Kuykendall, *Hawaiian Kingdom* 3:402, 406–407.
33. *The Friend*, June 1894, p. 45; *PCA*, 17, 18 May 1894.
34. *PCA*, 9 July 1870; Interior Department Letterbook No. 52, July 1881 (AH).
35. "Supreme Court: The Queen vs. Leong Man," *PCA*, 15 March 1892. See also *Board of Immigration Report*, 1890, p. 80.
36. *PCA*, 19 May 1888.
37. Correspondence with the Chinese Consulate, 9 April 1896, 19 September 1899 et seq. (AH).

38. *PCA*, 21 April 1892; 16, 17, 19, 30 October 1893; *The Friend*, November 1893, p. 88.

39. Li, *Life Is for a Long Time*, pp. 170–173.

40. Lana Iwamoto, "The Plague and Fire of 1899–1900 in Honolulu," *Hawaiian Historical Review* 2(1967):389. Nevertheless, *The Friend* (February 1900) notes that when a Mrs. Boardman who lived in "one of the best residence sections" (Manoa Valley) died of the plague on 16 January her home "with the whole of the furniture and Mrs. B's rare collection of curios" was burned.

41. Sixty-one persons died during the epidemic. Of the seventy-one contracting the disease nearly half (thirty-five) were Chinese; fifteen were Hawaiians, thirteen were Japanese, seven were Caucasians, and one was from the Gilbert Islands. Most of the rest of this account of the plague and fire is based upon reports in *The Friend*, February through May 1900.

42. Li, *Life Is for a Long Time*, p. 174.

43. Iwamoto, "Plague and Fire," p. 381.

44. Correspondence between the Chinese consul and the Minister of Foreign Affairs, 2, 3, 8, 15, and 22 January 1900. Foreign Office and Executive File—Consul for China (Yang Wei-pin) (AH).

45. Ibid., 16 January 1900.

46. *The Friend*, February 1900, p. 3.

47. *Honolulu Advertiser*, 22 November 1931.

48. *The Friend*, February 1900, p. 3.

49. Iwamoto, "Plague and Fire," p. 390.

50. *Chinese of Hawaii*, 1929, Chinese section, p. 8.

51. *United Chinese Society Anniversary Volume*, p. 6. According to the *Hawaiian Annual*, 1903, p. 25, some 3,728 of the 5,727 claims were filed by Chinese. The amount awarded to Chinese was nearly $850,000, slightly less than half the total claimed. About the same proportion of claims submitted was awarded to 2,574 Japanese, less than half to 278 Hawaiian and 19 Portuguese claimants. Some Chinese were dissatisfied with the settlement. According to Chung, *My Seventy-Nine Years*, p. 193, some of the dissatisfaction was caused by the delay of two or more years in settling the claims, a period during which the claimants desperately needed money in starting business again; part of the problem was that some who were dishonest had overstated the amount of their losses and honest claimants were unjustly affected.

52. George Charles Hull, "Chinese in Hawaii," *Chinese in Hawaii*, 1913, p. 1; Richard A. Greer, " 'Sweet and Clean': The Chinatown Fire of 1886," *Hawaiian Journal of History* 10(1976):33–51; *Chinese of Hawaii*, 1929, Chinese section, pp.59–60. According to Hull the aggregate insurance amounted to only $228,500.

53. *Chinese of Hawaii*, 1929, Chinese section, pp. 8, 80.

54. *PCA*, 23, 26 August 1895; *The Friend*, September 1895, p. 72.

55. *United Chinese Society Anniversary Volume*, pp. 5–6.

56. *The Friend*, October 1895, pp. 73–74, 76, 79.

57. *Chinese of Hawaii*, 1929, Chinese section, p. 65; *The Friend*, April 1897, p. 26.

58. Chung, *My Seventy-Nine Years*, pp. 269, 275, 307–310.

59. Quoted in a report of the speeches at the Chinese mass meeting, 14 February 1894, *Hawaiian Star*, 15 February 1894.

CHAPTER 11

1. The cemetery associations, Hoong Moon societies, and Chinese-language schools alone amounted to more than a hundred formal organizations. Migrants developed at least 24 organizations on the island of Hawaii, 27 on Maui, and 20 on Kauai. Well over half of the formal organizations established by migrants on these islands were of the types mentioned above.

2. Apart from the formally organized societies there were also many informal groups of migrants who shared old-world connections but did not develop formal associations. A common gathering place for an informal migrant group was a store operated by a migrant from the same district or village or with the same surname.

3. The main migration of See Yups to Hawaii was that of contract laborers in 1895–1898. Application of American immigration laws to Hawaii in 1898 meant that only a small fraction of the See Yups were able to have Chinese wives and families in Hawaii. Many of them established families in See Yup villages; it was only after World War II that some of these men, still living in the Islands, were able to bring their wives and families to Hawaii. Unlike the Chinese in Hawaii, the majority of those in the continental United States are of See Yup origin.

4. Chung Shan *hsien* ("district" or "county"), which lies in the delta region between Canton and Macao, had only about five hundred square miles; some of its subdistricts *(doo)* had less than fifty square miles; others, such as Wong Leong Doo, were larger. Under the Manchus the *doo* was the smallest administrative unit for most government purposes.

5. The petitions of several other district associations had similar opening statements: some said "merchants and taxpayers"; one had "merchants and tradesmen and taxpayers."

6. Interview with Lee Kau, March 1931. Fifty-six migrants were listed in the petition for a charter of incorporation dated 13 January 1905.

7. The formal structure and functions outlined in the constitutions and bylaws of some of the early district associations had some similarities to those of earlier district associations or "companies" on the West Coast. A translation published in 1868 of the rules of the district association formed by migrants from Chung Shan in California and of the "Sze-Yap Company" is reprinted in Rev. William Speer, *The Oldest and the Newest Empire* (Hartford, Conn.: S. S. Scranton & Co., 1870), pp. 557–567.

8. "See Yup Wei Quan Notice," *Chee Yow Sun Bo,* 25 February 1910. Chu Gem, president of this society for over twenty-five years, was the first president of the Chinese Hospital Association (1897).

9. Such beliefs had been important in the common feeling among Chinese that to become a soldier was a tragic misfortune.

10. *Chee Yow Sun Bo,* 27 September 1909. Wing Lock Ngue Hong was the fish dealers' guild; Kwock On Wui was a Hoong Moon society.

11. See Chapter 9, "Cemetery Associations."

12. Kum Pui Lai, "The Natural History of the Chinese Language School in Hawaii," pp. 37–38.

13. Interview with Lee Kau, March 1931.

14. The district associations thus repudiated some actions that members of the Hoong Moon societies swore to take on behalf of "sworn brothers" in trouble with the law. Strong social pressure by an association was likely to cause an expelled member to leave the Islands.

15. Information from records of the Lung Doo and See Dai Doo societies was tabulated for the writer by a Hawaii-born Chinese student at the University of Hawaii in 1936. The writer is indebted to the officers of these societies for making the records available for this purpose. The term "village" follows the usage of the migrants themselves. It includes market towns that might have more than five thousand inhabitants. A large collection of contiguous residences that might look to an outsider like one village might be regarded by the inhabitants as two or more villages—with separate names, separate village headmen, separate identities.

16. Interview with Bung Chong Lee, November 1935.

17. C. K. Ai, who migrated to Hawaii from Chung Shan, was inclined to restrict the term "Punti" to Chinese from Chung Shan district, particularly excluding See Yups, but he would not have considered Hakkas from Chung Shan to be Puntis. See Chung, *My Seventy-Nine Years*, pp. 14–15. But even within his home district Punti migrants from Lung Doo were somewhat set apart from other Chung Shan migrants because of the markedly different dialect they spoke—a dialect of Fukienese origin. See Tin-Yuke Char and Wai-Jane Char, "The First Chinese Contract Laborers in Hawaii, 1852," *Hawaiian Journal of History* 9(1975):132.

18. Interior Department, Miscellaneous: Immigration—Chinese, 2 March 1881 (AH). See also *Bureau of Immigration Report*, 1886, pp. 163–166. If 4,000 to 5,000 Hakkas were in Hawaii, as claimed, they would have constituted about one-third of the Chinese population at that time, which is unlikely.

19. The largest contingents of Hakkas came from two districts lying between Canton and Hong Kong: Pao On (Sun On) and Tung Kun. In the previous section it was noted that Hakkas from Pao On organized a village club in the early 1930s. There was also a lineage-village club of Hakkas from Chung Shan. Hakka migrants, as noted earlier, had established Hoong Moon societies in a few rural areas of Hawaii as well as one in Honolulu, and Honolulu Hakkas had acquired a cemetery in the 1880s.

20. Chock Lun estimated in 1936 that 7,000 of the 27,000 Chinese in Hawaii were Hakkas. *Chinese of Hawaii* 2, 1936, p. 23.

21. Lee, *Chinese in Hawaii*, 1961, p. 77.

22. A Chinese source, *Po Chia Hsing* [Hundred names], lists 408 single-character and 30 double-character surnames. Pronunciation of Chinese surnames varies among speech groups and dialects, with resulting variation in romanization, giving the Western reader the impression of a larger number of surnames— for example, Lum, Lam, Lim, Lin, Linn; Ng, Ing, Wu; Chun, Gunn, Chen, Chan, Chin. Surnames among Island-born Chinese were increased by the adoption of given names as surnames, as in the case of Chung Kun Ai who became known as C. K. Ai, with a son known as David Ai; other sons used Chung as their surname. "Hawaiianization" of Chinese names also added to

their number. See Chapter 14, "Cultural Compromises and Cultural Change."
See also Char, *Sandalwood Mountains*, p. 318; Irma Tam Soong, "East Maui
Chinese History," *Hawaii Heritage News*, November 1973.

23. Char, *The Bamboo Path*, pp. 5–6, 9; William K. Luke, "A Concise History of the
Origin of the Luke Clan of China," mimeographed (Honolulu: Hawaii Chinese History Center, n.d.); Harold C. Hill, *Ing Families Directories* (Honolulu,
1972); *Honolulu Advertiser*, 10 May 1931.

24. Lawrence W. Crissman, "The Segmentary Structure of Urban Overseas
Chinese Communities," *Man*, new series, 2(1967):185–204.

25. Societies were organized for the surnames Au, Chang, Char, Chee, Ching,
Chock, Chun, Goo, Hee, Ho, Hu, Ing, Kam, Lee, Leong, Loui, Luke, Mau,
Pang, Tom, Young, and Yuen. Twelve are discussed in Aileen O. L. Lee, "The
Surname Tongs in Hawaii," senior honors thesis under the direction of
Clarence E. Glick, University of Hawaii, 1966.

26. The historical bond between persons with these four surnames was a sworn
brotherhood between an emperor and three generals, each of one of these
surnames, in the third century A.D. According to informants, this bond has not
brought persons with these surnames together into formal societies in China
as it has in Hawaii, the continental United States, and some other immigrant
areas. Because of beliefs about this bond, migrants with these four surnames
opposed marriages among themselves.

27. During the 1890–1904 period when most of the guilds were being formed,
some craft unions in Honolulu (for example, carpenters) were exclusively
Caucasian in membership and vocally anti-Chinese and anti-Japanese.

28. *Chee Yow Sun Bo*, 19 May 1909.

29. Interview, March 1931.

30. This complex of groups involved, of course, many other organizations in
addition to those discussed in this chapter.

31. *PCA*, 4 February 1886. Much of this speech was quoted at the end of Chapter 9.

32. *Chinese of Hawaii*, 1929, Chinese section, p. 38.

33. The Chung Wah Kung Saw (Chinese Consolidated Benevolent Association)—
the "Six Companies"—in San Francisco also had this function. See William
Hoy, *The Chinese Six Companies* (San Francisco: Chinese Consolidated Benevolent Association, 1942), pp. 11, 19–20.

34. Interview, March 1931.

CHAPTER 12

1. Clarence E. Glick, "Transition from Familism to Nationalism among Chinese
in Hawaii," *American Journal of Sociology* 43(1938):734–743.

2. *Honolulu Star-Bulletin*, 14 March 1928.

3. Ibid., 25 March 1931.

4. Interview with Bung Chong Lee, June 1936.

5. *Chee Yow Sun Bo*, 17 May 1928. Amounts of money given in the text are in
U.S. dollars unless stated otherwise.

6. *Chinese of Hawaii* 2, 1936, Chinese section, pp. 31–33. Migrants from Toi Shan district also raised funds in 1927 and 1932 for the Toi Shan Middle School. Information about the hospital in Shekki was obtained by the writer in Shekki, July 1932.

7. *Honolulu Star-Bulletin*, 5, 16 June 1930; conversations with Chung Shan migrants in 1931.

8. *Chinese of Hawaii* 2, 1936, Chinese section, p. 25. Information about other fund drives for projects in Kwangtung and Hong Kong is from the same source.

9. *Honolulu Star-Bulletin*, 8 February, 3 March 1928.

10. The account that follows is based largely upon *Chinese of Hawaii*, 1929, Chinese section. The author was probably Chock Lun, one of the Chung Shan intellectuals in the Honolulu Chinese community at the time. From 1910 to 1927 he had been active in the Kuomintang as well as a translating editor for the Kuomintang newspaper, *Chee Yow Sun Bo*. Other sources include H. B. Restarick, *Sun Yat Sen: Liberator of China* (New Haven: Yale University Press, 1931); Chung, *My Seventy-Nine Years*; Phoebe Liang, "The Influence of K'ang Yu-Wei and Liang Ch'i-Ch'ao in the Making of New China" (M.A. thesis, University of Hawaii, 1933); William K. Luke, "The First Man That Shed Blood for the Chinese Republic," mimeographed (Honolulu: Hawaii Chinese History Center, n.d.); idem, "Spared by the Executioner's Sword," mimeographed, ibid.; Honolulu English-language newspapers.

11. *Chinese of Hawaii*, 1929, Chinese section, p. 16.

12. Chung, *My Seventy-Nine Years*, p. 315.

13. Char, *Sandalwood Mountains*, p. 326. Char says that another English name for the Bow Wong Wui was "Royal Protective Union of the Hawaiian Islands for the Support of Emperor Kuang-Hsu."

14. *The Friend*, April 1900, p. 28; May 1900, p. 37.

15. Li, *Life Is for a Long Time*, pp. 252–256.

16. *PCA*, 14, 21 December, 1903.

17. Mark, *Chinese in Kula*, p. 31. Some Kuomintang spokesmen have denied that Dr. Sun joined the Ket Hing Fui Kon.

18. Interview with editor, *Chee Yow Sun Bo*, 19 February 1936.

19. Information on the contested elections of the United Chinese Society in 1902 and 1912–1915 in File 77, State of Hawaii Department of Regulatory Agencies, Honolulu; also *PCA*, 11, 16, 17, 25 December 1913, 2 January 1914.

20. *Chee Yow Sun Bo*, 25 January 1909.

21. Material for this account is drawn largely from *Chinese of Hawaii* 2, 1936, Chinese section, pp. 24–36.

22. Sources for this account are: *Chinese of Hawaii*, 1929, Chinese section, pp. 79–81; Chung, *My Seventy-Nine Years*, pp. 300–306; *The Friend*, April 1900, p. 28; *PCA*, various dates, January 1900–December 1911.

23. In addition to Hawaii-born Chinese, some of the Chinese-Americans taking part in such activities were migrants who held American citizenship because of naturalization prior to Annexation.

24. The account of subsequent events is based mainly on: *PCA*, 20, 21, 30 November 1911; 4, 7, 30 December 1911; 2 January, 2 June, 18 July 1912; 27 July 1915; *Chinese of Hawaii*, 1929, Chinese section, pp. 28–30.

25. *Chinese of Hawaii,* 1929, Chinese section, p. 30.

26. *Pacific Herald,* 29 October 1928.

27. *Honolulu Advertiser,* 22, 27 May 1931; *Honolulu Star-Bulletin,* 27 May 1931; interview with Lee Kau, March 1931.

28. *Chinese of Hawaii,* 1929, Chinese section, pp. 35, 69. Along with this change in emphasis in the Chinese Constitutional Party, the party's leaders were active in 1928–1929 in developing the Hawaii Branch of the Confucian Society of China. The *Sun Chung Kwock Bo (New China News)* supported this organization, and Mun Lun School cooperated by celebrating Confucius's birthday and teaching Confucian values.

29. *PCA,* 21 May 1913; *Honolulu Star-Bulletin,* 2 December 1929.

30. This section on Chinese newspapers draws upon an article in *Chee Yow Sun Bo,* 31 August 1936; see also Char, *The Bamboo Path,* pp. 220–223.

31. *Chee Yow Sun Bo,* 27 August 1909.

32. *Chinese of Hawaii,* 1929, Chinese section, pp. 52–55.

33. Other branches of Dr. Sun's organizations established Wah Mun language schools.

34. Sources for this section include: Kum Pui Lai, "The Natural History of the Chinese Language School in Hawaii"; D. C. Chang, "The Fifty-Year History of Mun Lun School," *Mun Lun School Golden Jubilee, 1911–1961* (Honolulu, 1961), p. 36; *Chinese of Hawaii,* 1929, Chinese section, pp. 52–55.

35. *Chee Yow Sun Bo,* 23 May 1909. The United Chinese Society's fiftieth anniversary publication does not mention the conflicts within the Society during the 1901–1915 period. The editor observed that "the United Chinese Society . . . has created unity and brotherly love among the Chinese people of Hawaii."

36. *Chinese of Hawaii 2,* 1936, Chinese section, pp. 24–36.

37. *The Friend,* August 1894, p. 37.

38. Ibid., April 1899, p. 31.

39. *Chinese of Hawaii,* 1929, Chinese section, p. 39.

40. Data drawn from *Chinese of Hawaii,* 1929, Chinese section, pp. 29–30, 32; *Chee Yow Sun Bo,* 28 March 1919.

41. In 1935 Kum Pui Lai said he knew of 105 Hawaii-born Chinese holding jobs in China. Among them were 23 teachers, 17 in government service, 11 clerks and businessmen, 9 physicians, 9 engineers and mechanics, 5 YMCA and social workers. See Lai, "Natural History," p. 102. See also biography of Young Sun Yet in *Chinese of Hawaii Who's Who,* 1957, pp. 47, 176.

42. Sources for this section include: *Chinese of Hawaii 2,* 1936, Chinese section, pp. 24–32, and *Hawaii Chinese Annual,* 8 vols. (Honolulu, 1930–1937).

43. Translated by Young Hing Cham and Wing-Iu Leung, May 1932.

44. Sources for this section include: *Hawaii Chinese Journal,* 1939–1950; *Chinese of Hawaii Who's Who,* 1957, pp. 1–187; "Appendix B, List of Donations," in Chung, *My Seventy-Nine Years,* pp. 4–128.

45. Chung, *My Seventy-Nine Years,* pp. 264, 284.

46. *Honolulu Star-Bulletin,* 26 May 1930; observations by the writer of the campaigning at a Double Ten Day celebration, Mun Lun School, 10 October 1936.

47. *The Chinese of Hawaii 2,* 1936, Chinese section, p. 32.

CHAPTER 13

1. *Chinese of Hawaii Who's Who,* 1957, p. 122.
2. Interview, 25 February 1937.
3. Preamble to Registration, Lum Sai Ho Tong, 10 October 1931 (pamphlet).
4. Interview with editor, *Chee Yow Sun Bo,* 19 February 1936. In this editor's view, vitriolic attacks in the two pro-Kuomintang papers had stung backers of the *Sun Chung Kwock Bo* into keeping the paper alive.
5. "The Campaign to Raise Funds for Purchasing of Land and Erection of School Buildings in 1929," *Mun Lun High School Twenty-fifth Anniversary Edition* (Shanghai: Sincere Press, 1936), p. 6.
6. Ibid., pp. 7–10.
7. *Report on the Purchase of the Premises for the Chinese Consulate in Honolulu* (Honolulu, 1933), p. 11.
8. *PCA,* 31 March, 22 May 1896; *The Friend,* April 1896, p. 30; June 1896, p. 46.
9. Clarence E. Glick, "Residential Dispersion of Urban Chinese," *Social Process in Hawaii* 2(1936):28–34; Li, *Life Is for a Long Time,* pp. 198–201.
10. Interview with Consul King-Chau Mui, 29 September 1931.
11. *Pacific Herald,* 6 December 1928; *Chinese of Hawaii,* 1929, p. 208.
12. James Dyer Ball, *The Chinese at Home,* 1912, p. 22.
13. An earlier example is given by a notice in the *Chee Yow Sun Bo,* 25 February 1910, in which the Bark Yee Hong (Dressmakers' Guild) thanked "organizations and stores, as well as friends, for taking part in the funeral services" for the deceased president of their guild. The list included Kwock On Wui Goon, Wo On Wui Goon, Chee Kung Tong, Kwong Yee Tong, Quon On Kwock, Hoy On Tong, Yee Yi Tong, Wah Hing Tong, Chuck Sin Tong, Kwon Lock Hong, Seong Gar Hong, Hing Chung Wui, Hup Sung Co., Kum Yee Hong, Wing Lock Ngue Hong, and the Hawaii-Chinese Koong Co.

CHAPTER 14

1. *PCA,* 29 January 1892.
2. Adapted from accounts in *Polynesian,* 15 November 1856, and *PCA,* 20 November 1856. No Chinese women were mentioned as being present.
3. *PCA,* 27 June 1861.
4. Correspondence with the Chinese Consulate, 1879–1900, 12 August 1884 (AH).
5. Most of these receptions for more than twenty years after 1900 were reported in English-language newspapers at the time of Chinese New Year.
6. "Resolutions Denouncing the Boxer Uprising in China," 31 July 1900 (AH); *PCA,* 31 July 1900.
7. *PCA,* 16 January 1912; 16 May 1913.
8. Lily Lim-Chong, "Opium and the Law, Hawaii: 1856–1900" (research paper under the direction of Harry V. Ball, Department of Sociology, University of Hawaii, 1978). When the writer made his original study of the Chinese community in the 1930s, Chinese proudly pointed out the very low crime rate of their group compared with that of other groups in the Islands, a situation which continues today.

9.   Char, *Sandalwood Mountains*, p. 323; *Chinese of Hawaii*, 1929, pp. 57, 117.

10.   *Chinese of Hawaii*, 1929, Chinese section, p. 77.

11.   *Chee Yow Sun Bo*, 16 February 1910.

12.   Ibid.

13.   Li, *Life Is for a Long Time*, pp. 302–303, 305–310.

14.   *PCA*, 9 March, 14 April 1892.

15.   "Chu Gem," *Mid-Pacific Magazine*, August 1911, p. 189.

16.   *PCA*, 12 January 1912.

17.   *Board of Immigration Report*, 1890, p. 88.

18.   See, for example, Bessie C. Lai, *Ah Yā, I Still Remember* (Taipei, Taiwan: Meadea Enterprise Co., 1976), p. 15.

19.   *Honolulu Advertiser*, 28 August 1932. For an analysis of clothing changes see Douglas D. L. Chong, *Reflections of Time: A Chronology of Chinese Fashions in Hawaii* (Honolulu: Hawaii Chinese History Center, 1976); the account is accompanied by twenty-nine photos.

20.   Questions concerning wills and inheritance occasionally brought such cases to public notice. See *Reports of Decisions Rendered by the Supreme Court of the Hawaiian Islands*, vol. 3, pp. 489–498.

21.   *PCA*, 3 April 1910.

22.   Char, *Sandalwood Mountains*, p. 247. Char reprints (pp. 247–253) an account by Elizabeth Wong of the experiences of a *mui tsai* brought to Hawaii: "Leaves from the Life History of a Chinese Immigrant," *Social Process in Hawaii* 2(1936): 39–42.

23.   *The Friend*, September 1895, p. 70.

24.   *PCA*, 6 February, 30 November 1900.

25.   *Chinese of Hawaii*, 1929, p. 121; Chinese section, pp. 71–72.

26.   *The Friend*, May 1892, p. 38; *PCA*, 3 August 1912.

27.   *The Friend*, May 1895, p. 36.

28.   Ibid., October 1895, p. 85.

29.   *United Chinese Society Anniversary Volume*, 1934, p. 11.

30.   *Honolulu Star-Bulletin*, 27 March 1937. In Chinese tradition, red symbolized good luck and happiness, white death and mourning.

31.   *Chinese of Hawaii*, 1929, Chinese section, p. 2.

32.   Chock Lun, "Chinese Organizations in Hawaii," *Chinese of Hawaii* 2, 1936, pp. 31–32.

33.   *United Chinese Society Anniversary Volume*, p. 5.

34.   *Annual Report of the President of the Honolulu Chinese Chamber of Commerce for the Year 1930* (Honolulu: Honolulu Chinese Chamber of Commerce, 1931), p. 2. The president at the time was a migrant who had come to Hawaii in 1886 at the age of eighteen.

35.   Wai-Jane Char, "Three Chinese Stores in Early Honolulu," *Hawaiian Journal of History* 8(1974):34; Peggy Kai, "Chinese Settlers in the Village of Hilo before 1852," ibid., pp. 53, 62.

36.   *PCA*, 20 June 1902.

37.   Ibid., 18, 20 December 1910.

38.   "Petition to the Administrators of the Government of the United States of America . . . 5 September 1916," p. 6.

39. Sources for the following account include: *Chinese of Hawaii*, 1929, Chinese section, p. 66; *Chinese of Hawaii 2*, 1936, Chinese section, pp. 24–25; *United Chinese Society Anniversary Volume*, pp. 6–8; Kum Pui Lai, "The Chinese Home at Palolo," *Hawaii Chinese Annual* 8(1937):7–9; Chung, *My Seventy-Nine Years*, pp. 307–310; Mei-Li Lee Lo, "Palolo Chinese Home" (seminar paper under the direction of J. L. Watson, Department of Anthropology, University of Hawaii, 1973); annual reports of the Honolulu Social Service Bureau in the 1930s; *Pacific Herald*, 13 September 1928; *Honolulu Advertiser*, 7 August 1929; *Honolulu Star-Bulletin*, 4 November 1930, 19 May 1936; visits to the Home and interviews.

40. Admissions to the Palolo Chinese Home increased until a peak number of 165 were living there in 1937. During the 1930s the Home's expenses ranged between $15,000 and $20,000, and various welfare agencies were also giving outside aid to several hundred Chinese dependents. In 1935 the Social Service Bureau report showed that 1,848, over 17 percent, of the 10,706 individuals given relief were Chinese. They constituted almost 10 percent of the estimated Chinese residents of Oahu that year.

41. *Chinese of Hawaii 2*, 1936, Chinese section, p. 25; *Honolulu Star-Bulletin*, 19 May 1936.

42. *Honolulu Star-Bulletin*, 26 September 1936.

43. *Hawaii Chinese Journal*, 11 August, 1 September, 6 October, 1 December 1949.

44. During this period and later, of course, other non-Caucasian businessmen were admitted to membership in the Honolulu Chamber of Commerce.

45. *Annual Report of the Honolulu Chinese Chamber of Commerce*, p. 3.

46. *PCA*, 5 November 1881.

47. *Chee Yow Sun Bo*, 2 February 1910.

48. Ibid., 25 February 1910.

49. *PCA*, 4 June 1912.

50. *Honolulu Star-Bulletin*, 28 July 1934.

51. *PCA*, 30 January 1910; 14 October 1912; 13 October 1913; Li, *Life Is for a Long Time*, p. 239.

52. Sources for this section are mainly reports in the *Hawaii Chinese Journal* between 12 February 1948 and 16 February 1950. See also *Narcissus Festival*, issued by the Honolulu Chinese Chamber of Commerce in 1950.

Glossary

Most of the Chinese words, phrases, and names of people, places, and publications cited in this work are romanized according to their usual pronunciation in Hawaii, which is based on the speech of migrants from Heung Shan (Chung Shan) district of Kwangtung province in the nineteenth and early twentieth centuries. Because of dialectal differences among the migrants, especially between Punti and Hakka, there are local variations in romanization, some of which are included in this glossary. The Chinese characters which are given will enable those who can read Chinese to translate the terms into Kuo Yu (national speech). No effort has been made to spell Chinese words in the orthography recently adopted by the People's Republic of China; the Chinese characters will provide the necessary information for those interested in such transliteration. In the glossary surnames precede given names. Following local usage, given names of most migrants are capitalized and are not hyphenated. For persons more identified with China the given names are hyphenated with the second one in lowercase; most of these names are also in romanized Kuo Yu. Persons whose names were locally given in the Western order, with given names preceding surnames, are identified with a comma after the surname.

Achuck 程植
Achun 黃進
Afong and Achuck Co. 芳植記
Afong (Chun Fong) 陳芳
Ahana, W. W. (Wong Min Hoong)
  黃和興（黃棉鳳）
Aheong, Samuel P. 蕭雄
Ahung 陳恆
Ai, C. K. (Chung Kun Ai) 鍾工宇
American Chinese Federation 中美
  聯合會

American Security Bank 中美銀行
Amoy 廈門
Au Tin Kwai 歐天貴
Au Young (On Young) 歐讓

bark gup biu 白鴿票
Bark Yee Hong 白衣行
Bow On Guk 保安局
Bow Wong Wui 保皇會
Buck Toy Tung Heung Wui 北台
  同鄉會

but yee ga 不二價

C. Ako 程建瑞
C. Alee (Ching Lee) 程利
C. Q. Yee Hop Market 陳滾義合公司
C(hing) Winam 程蔚南
Canton (Kwangchow) 廣州
Cha Yuen Wai Bok Say 茶園惟博社
Chang Chau 鄭照
Chang, D. C. 鄭帝積
Chang, Dai Yen 鄭帝恩
Chang Nee Sun 鄭汝燊
Chang Yum Sin 鄭任先
Chaochow 潮州
Char, Tin-Yuke (Hsieh T'ing-yu)
   謝廷玉
Char, Wai-Jane 謝慧珍
chee fa 字花
Chee Kung Tong 致公堂
Chee Yow Sun Bo 自由新報
Ch'en Lan-pin 陳蘭彬
chi li 梓里
chi tong 祠堂
Chiang Kai-shek 蔣介石
chim 籤
chin sam 千三
Chinese American Bank 中美銀行
Chinese Buddhist Association of
   America 華僑佛教總會
Chinese Chamber of Commerce 中華
   總商會
Chinese Constitutionalist Party 中國
   憲政黨
Chinese Educational Association of
   Hawaii 中華教育會
Chinese-English Debating Society 中西
   擴論會
Chinese Literary Association 華僑學會
Chinese Physical Culture Association
   華人精武體育會
Chinese YMCA 華人基督教青年會
The Chinese in Hawaii, 1961 檀香山中華
   總商會金禧紀念冊
The Chinese of Hawaii, 1929 檀山華僑中
   華民國十八年
The Chinese of Hawaii 2 (1936) 檀山華僑
   第二集中華民國念五年秋

*The Chinese of Hawaii Who's Who,
   1956–1957* 檀山華僑中華民國四十
   六年
Ching Chow 程就
Ching Ming 清明
Ching Shai 程水
Cho Pu Tow (Au Clan) 左步頭（歐氏
   同宗會）
Chock Lun 卓麟
Chong Pang Yat (P. Y. Chong) 張鵬一
Chong Park Shun 張伯詢
Chong Song 張爽
Chong Sum Wing 張深榮
Choy Hung Tung Heung Wui 翠亨同
   鄉會
choy sun 財神
Chu Gem 趙錦
Chuck Hoy 卓海
Chulan Co. 朝蘭公司
Chun, Chee Kwon 陳致昆
Chun Fong (Afong) 陳芳
Chun Hoon 陳寬
Chun Kam Chow (C. K. Chow) 陳金就
Chun Kim Chow 陳錦州
Chun Kwai Hin 陳貴賢
Chun Moo Min Sun Gai Yin Wui 檀山
   振武勉愼戒煙會
Chun Quon (C. Q. Yee Hop) 陳滾
Chun Wing Chin Tong 陳穎川堂
Chung Hoon 張寬
Chung Kun Ai (C. K. Ai) 鍾工宇
Chung Kuo Hsien Cheng Tang (Hin
   Jing Dong) 中國憲政黨
Chung Shan Hsien 中山縣
Chung Shan Tung Heung Wui 中山同
   鄉會
Chung Tau Tung Heung Wui 涌頭同
   鄉會
Chung Wah Jun Chai Wui 中華賑濟會
Chung Wah Kung Bo 中華公報
Chung Wah Kung Saw (Chinese "Six
   Companies") 中華公所
Chung Wah Chung Seong Wui 中華總
   商會
Chung Wah Guck Mung Dong 中華革
   命黨
Chung Wah Wui Goon 中華會館

Confucian Society 孔教會

Dai Kwock Hin Jing Wui 帝國憲政會
dau sa bau 豆沙包
dim sum 點心
dong (tang) 黨
Doo Wai Sing 杜惠生
Dragon Boat Festival 五月龍舟節
Duck Doo Kee Loo, Duck Doo Wui
   Goon 得都寄廬, 得都會館

fan Ching *fook* Ming 反清復明
fan kwai 番鬼
fan tan 番攤
fan wa 番話
Fat Shan 佛山
Fong, Hiram Leong 鄺友良
Fong Inn (see Yuen Kwock) 芳元公司
Fook Yum Tong 福音堂
Fort Street Chinese Church 科街華人
   福音堂
Fukien 福建
fun kung 分工
fung shui 風水
Fut Mu 佛母

Goo Kim (Goo Kim Fui) 古金 (古金輝)
Goo, Paul Kimm Chow 古錦超
Gook Doo Sam Heung Tung Heung
   Wui 谷都三鄉同鄉會
Goon Yum (Kuan Yin) 觀音

Hak Seong Wui Goon 客商會館
Hakka 客家
Hawaii Chinese Buddhist Society 夏威
   夷中華佛教總會
Hawaii Chinese Civic Association 華人
   土生會
Hawaii Chinese History Center 夏威夷
   華人歷史研究中心
Hawaiian Chinese Association 夏威仁
   華人公所
Hee Cho 許初
Hee Fat 許發
Hee Jack Sun (Hee, Jackson) 許直臣
Hee, William K. F. 許桂芬
Hee Yau Kun 許有根

heung li 鄉里
Heung Shan In 香山縣
Hilo Jun Chai Wui 希爐賑濟會
Hin Tan 丈壇
Hing Chung Wui 興中會
Ho Fon 何寬
Ho Seong 何祥
Hoi Ping 開平
Hok Shan 鶴山
Hokkien 福建
Hoklo 福佬
Hon Mun Bo 漢民報
hong 行
Hoo Choo School 互助學校
Hoong Moon (Hung Men) 洪門
hop pun 合伴
hou 毫
How Wong Miu 侯王廟
Hoy On Tong 海安堂
Hsieh T'ing-yu (Tin-Yuke Char) 謝廷玉
Hsu Shih-cheng 許世昌
hui (wui) 會
Hung Hoy 洪海
Hung Sin Tong 洪善堂
Hungtai 恆泰

Inn, Henry 阮勉初

Jack Shin Tong 積善堂
jah 姐
jai 齋
Job Yee Tong 集義堂
Jup Mun Say 習文社

Kai Chee Bo 啓智報
Kai Ming Bo 啓明報
K'ang Yu-wei 康有為
Kau-Tom Post 退任軍人高譚分會
kau tse 餃子
kee lock bo 俱樂部
kee loo 寄廬
Ket Hing Fui Kon 國興會館
Ket On Fui Kon 國安會館
Kiu Tau 橋頭
Kong Chau Wei Quan 岡州會館
Kong Tai Heong 江棣香
Kong, Tet Yin 江德仁

Kong Tow Tung Heung Wui 港頭同鄉會

Kong Yet Kow Kwock Wui 抗日救國會

Kong, Yin Tet 江仁德

Koon Fah 宮花

Ku, Ah Jook Leong 顧梁祝竹

Kuan Yin (Goon Yum) 觀音

Kuang Hsu 光緒

Kum Yee Hong 錦衣行

Kung Seong Doo Wui Goon 恭常都會館

kung si 公司

Kuo Min Hsien Cheng Tang 國民憲政黨

Kuo Yu 國語

Kuomintang 國民黨

Kutt Hing Kung Soh 吉慶公所

Kwan Dai (Kuan Ti) 關帝

Kwangtung 廣東

Kwon Lok Hong 群樂行

Kwong Yee Wui Goon 廣義會館

L(au) Ahlo 劉亞羅

Lai Kee Bo 麗記報

Lai, Kum Pui 賴金佩

Lam Bin Hee 欖邊墟

Lau Cheong (Lau Chong Kong) 劉祥光

Lau Yee Chai 留餘齋

Lee, Bung Chong (B. C. Lee) 李炳昌

Lee, Charles Tim 李添

Lee Chau 李潮

Lee Chow 李秋

Lee Han 李凥

Lee Kau 李九

Lee Let 李烈

Lee Ong 李登

Lee, Robert M. [W.] 李文華

Lee, Shao Chang 李紹昌

Lee, Y. K. 李奕樞

Leong Bew 梁標

Leong Chew 梁照

Leong Doo Wui Goon 梁都會館

Leong Han 梁煊

Leong Pah On 梁百安

Li Cheung 李昌

Li Khai Fai (K. F. Li) 李啓輝

Li Ling Ai 李靈愛

li shee 利是

Li Yuan-hung 黎元洪

Liang Ch'i-ch'ao 梁啓超

Liang Kuo-ying 梁國英

Liberty Bank 自由銀行（共和銀行）

Lin Sen 林森

Lin Yee Wui (Lin Yee Chung) 聯義會（聯義塚）

Ling Hing Wui Goon 希爐聯興會館

Ling How Hing Pang Tung Heung Wui 嶺后亨彭同鄉會

Lo, Mei-Li Lee 羅李美利

Loo Ngwak 盧岳

Loo, Paul Lin 盧祺昌

Luen Hing Kee Lock Bo 聯興俱樂部

Luke Chan 陸燦

Luke, William K. 陸基

Lum Hoon 林寬

Lum, Kalfred Dip 林疊

Lum King 林文京

Lum Lop Sai 林立瑞

Lum Sai Ho Tong 林西河堂

Lum Say Yip 林社葉

Lum Yip Kee 林業舉

Lung Doo Chung Sin Tong 隆都從善堂

Lung Kee Sun Bo 隆記新報

Lung Kong Kung Shaw 龍岡公所

Lung Tau Wan Tung Heung Wui 龍頭環同鄉會

Lung Tong Tung Heung Wui 龍塘同鄉會

ma tai shu 馬蹄蘇

Manoa Chinese Cemetery 萬那聯義會

Mark, Diane Mei Lin 麥美玲

Mark, Stephen 麥廷錦

Mau Shee Tung Heung Wui 恭常都神前村毛氏同鄉會

Maui Chung Wah Jun Chai Wui 茂宜中華賑濟會

Moo Hock Kee Lock Bo 明倫務學俱樂部

Moon Festival 八月中秋節

mou 畝

Mui, King-Chau 梅景周

mui tsai 妹仔

Mun Lun School 明倫學校
Mun Sing Tong 民生堂

Nam Hoy 南海
Nam Long 南朗
nan gau chai wui 難救濟會
Ng Ung-sun 吳榮新
Ngow Yuk Hong 牛肉行
Nip Chan Poo 聶春甫
Nyin Fo Fui Kon 人和會館

On Ding (On Ting) 安定
On Kai Say 安定村安溪社
On Tong Tung Heung Wui 安堂同鄉會
Oo Sack Kee Loo 谷都烏石寄廬

pai hua 白話
pai kau 排九
pake 伯爺
Palolo Chinese Old Men's Home 華僑老人院
Pao On (Sun On) 保安（新安）
paper sons 假紙仔
Peng Larm 平嵐
Poo Get Tung Heung Wui 布吉同鄉會
Poo Shan 浦山
Pun Yu 番禺
Punti 本地

Quon On Kwock 群安閣

Sam Sui 三水
Sam Yup 三邑
Samsing & Co. 三盛公司
San Min Chu I 三民主義
sau choy 秀才
say (sheh, sha, shah) 社
See Dai Doo Wui Goon 四大都會館
See Yup Wei Quan 四邑會館
Seong Gar Hong 上架行
shang tung 商董
Shekki 石岐
Shim, Wai On 沈維安
Shim, Yin Jin 沈榮貞
Shun Tak 順德
Sing Chong Co. 昇昌公司

Sit Moon 薛滿
siu mai 燒買
Siu Yun Quon Chark Say 小隱群策社
so (soh, saw, shaw) 所
sook jut 叔姪
Soong, Ching-ling 宋慶齡
Soong, Irma Tam 宋譚秀紅
St. Peter's Church 聖彼得禮拜堂
Sun Chung Kwock Bo 新中國報
Sun Mi 孫眉
Sun Ming Ting Tung Heung Wui 申明亭同鄉會
Sun Tai-cheong 孫帝象
Sun Wan Yat Bo 希爐循環日報
Sun Wui 新會
Sun Yat-sen 孫逸仙
Sun Yun Wo 新人和
sup chai 十仔
Swatow 汕頭

tai gung 太公
Tai Ping 太平
Tam Tinn Chong 譚天祥
tan 旦
Tan Dou Wah Kiu Kau Chai Wui 檀島華僑救濟會
Tan Heung Shan 檀香山
tan heung shan hak 檀香山客
Tan, S. H. (Tan Shia Hsu) 譚學徐
Tan Shan Chung Shan School 檀山中山學校
Tan Shan Sun Bo 檀山新報
Tan Shan Wah Kiu Ju Kwock Kau Chai Tin 檀山華僑祖國救濟團
Tan Shan Wah Kiu Kwock Nan Kau Chai Wui 檀山華僑國難救濟會
Tan Sing Dramatic Club 檀聲劇社
Tan Wah Sun Bo 檀華新報
tang (dong) 黨
Thom, Wah Chan 譚華燦
Tin Hau 天后
Toi Shan (Sun Ning) 台山（新寧）
Tom Awana 譚福源
tong 堂
Tong, Ah Huna 唐亞歡
Tong Ka 唐家
Tong Phong 唐雄

tong see 糖師
Tow Yee Kwock 桃義閣
Triad Society 三點會
Tsung Li 總理
Tsung Tsin Association 崇正會
tung bau 同胞
Tung Hing Kung Si 同興公司
Tung Kun 東莞
Tung Ming Wui 同盟會
Tung Sing Tong 同善堂
Tung Wo Kung Si (Tong Wo Society)
　同和公司
Tyau Fook 刁福
Tyhune (Wong Tai Hoon) 黃帝桓

United Chinese Labor Association
　中華總工會
United Chinese Society 中華總會館
United Chinese Society Fiftieth Anni-
　versary Volume, 1934 檀香山中華
　會館五十週年特刊

wah fau 華埠
Wah Ha Bo 華夏報
Wah Hing Bo 華興報
Wah Hing Tong 華興堂
wah kiu 華僑
Wah Kiu Chung Seong Wui 華僑總
　商會
Wah Kiu Kau Kwock Wui 華僑救國會
Wah Mun School 華民學校
Wah Yun Lin Hop Wui 華人聯合會
Wai Kup Chung Chow 惠及中州
Wai Wah Yee Yuen 惠華醫院
Wang Tien Mu 王天木
Whampoa 黃浦
Wing Lock Ngue Hong 永樂魚行
Wing Sing Wo 永生和
Wing Tuck Chong 永德昌
Wing Wo Tai 永和泰
Wo Fat 和發
Wo On Wui Goon 和安會館
Wong Buck Hung 黃北洪
Wong But Ting 黃弼庭
Wong Fook Mun 黃福文
Wong Goon Sun 黃官信

Wong, Henry Awa 黃華
Wong Kong Har Tong 黃江夏堂
Wong Kwai 黃貴
Wong Leong 黃亮
Wong Leong Doo Chuck Sing Tong
　黃梁都積善堂
Wong Lum 黃林
Wong Nin 黃暖
Wong Wai Wing 黃惠永
Woo, Yee Bew 吳爾標
wui (hui) 會
wui goon (hui kuan, fui kon, wei quan) 會館

Y. Ahin (Young Ah In) 楊亞然
Y. Anin (Young Anin) 楊年
Yap See Young 葉似雲
Yap, William Kwai Fong 葉桂芳
yat poon garn sa 一盆散沙
yau ming mong 有名望
Yee Chun 余臻
Yee Hing Chung Wui 義興總會
Yee Mun Wai 余文威
Yee Wo Kung Si 義和公司
Yee Yap 余揖
Yee Yi Tong 以義堂
Yen Ping 恩平
Yim Quon 嚴崑
yin fa chee dee 淫花趣地
Yong Wei-pin 楊蔚彬
Young Ahin (Y. Ah In) 楊亞然
Young Hing Cham 楊慶簪
Young Kum Hoy 楊金海
Young Kwong Tat 楊廣達
Young, Lum Pui 容林沛
Young People's Literary Club 少年學會
Young People's Oratorical Association
　少年演說社
Young, Sun Yet 楊仙逸
Young Sung Kee (Samuel K. Young)
　楊星樞
Yuan Shih-k'ai 袁世凱
Yuen Kwock (Fong Inn) 阮鶪秋
Yuk Wong Dai Dei 玉皇大帝
Yung Mark Kee Loo (Yung Wo Tong)
　雍陌寄廬（雍和堂）

Index

Authors Cited in Notes

DATE DUE

MAR 26 1997			
DEC 0 4 2002			

Map 1. Kwangtung Province

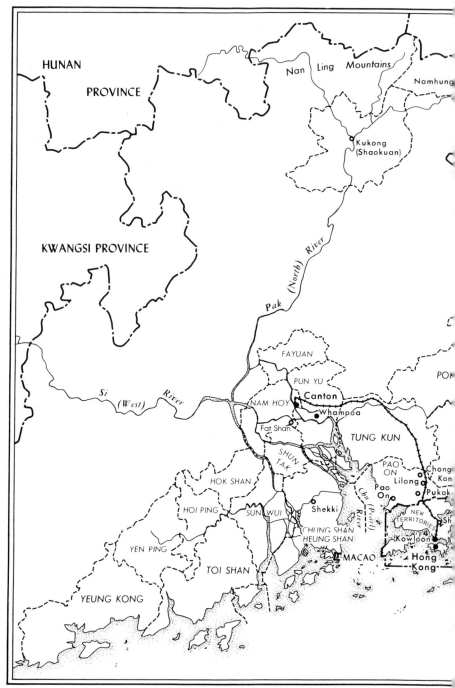

HUNAN
PROVINCE

Nan Ling Mountains

Namhung

Kukong
(Shaokuan)

KWANGSI PROVINCE

Pak (North) River

FAYUAN

PUN YU

Si (West) River

NAM HOY   Canton
Whampoa
Fat Shan
TUNG KUN

SHUN TAK

HOK SHAN

PAO ON
Lilong
Pao On
Chong Kan
Pukak

HOI PING   SUN WUI   Shekki

YEN PING

CHUNG SHAN
(HEUNG SHAN)

Chu (Pearl) River

NEW TERRITORIES
Kowloon

TOI SHAN

MACAO   Hong Kong

YEUNG KONG

Source: Tin-Yuke Char, *The Sandalwood Mountains* (Honolulu: University Press of Hawaii, 1975), pp. 18-19.